In Other Worlds

IN OTHER WORLDS

Essays in Cultural Politics

Gayatri Chakravorty Spivak

ROUTLEDGE: NEW YORK AND LONDON

First published in 1988 by
Routledge
an imprint of Routledge, Chapman & Hall, Inc.
29 West 35 Street, N.Y., N.Y. 10001

Published in Great Britain by
Routledge
11 New Fetter Lane, London, EC4P 4EE

Library of Congress Cataloging in Publication Data

Spivak, Gayatri Chakravorty.
In other worlds: essays in cultural politics / Gayatri Chakravorty Spivak.
p.   cm.
Bibliography: p.
ISBN 0-415-90002-6 (pbk)
1. Culture.   2. Feminism and literature.   3. Women
and literature.   4. Feminist criticism.   I. Title.
HM101.S773 1988   *87-37676*
306—dc19   *CIP*

Also available in Hb (ISBN 0-416-01651-0)

British Library Cataloguing in Publication Data

Spivak, Gayatri Chakravorty
In other worlds: essays in cultural
politics.
1. Culture
I. Title
306   HM101
ISBN 0-415-90002-6 (pbk.)

Also available in Hb (ISBN 0-416-01651-0)

For Michael

Contents

Foreword

Gayatri Spivak is often called a feminist Marxist deconstructivist. This might seem a rebarbative mouthful designed to fit an all purpose radical identity. To any reader of this remarkable book it will come to seem a necessarily complex description, limning not an identity, but a network of multiple contradictions, traces, inscriptions. The book does not merely state that we are formed in constitutive contradictions and that our identities are the effects of heterogenous signifying practices: its analyses start from and work towards contradiction and heterogeneity. Illumination is a necessarily transitory and conjunctural moment. Any foreword to this work is, of necessity, asked to address the three fields of feminism, Marxism, and deconstruction. However, much of the force of Spivak's work comes from its reiterated demonstration that these fields can only be understood and used in a constant attention to their interpenetration and re-articulation. Any simplifying foreword thus runs the risk of reducing the potential of this productive work. The task is, however, worth undertaking exactly because these texts are of importance to anyone concerned with our understanding of culture. Better: with the relation both of culture and its interpretation to the other practices that shape our lives.

What aid to the reader, then, is proposed by a foreword? Lurking somewhere, no doubt, is the fear that these essays are "difficult." Difficulty is, as we know, an ideological notion. What is manually difficult is just a simple job, what is easy for women is difficult for men, what is difficult for children is easy for adults. Within our ascriptions of difficulty lie subterranean and complex evaluations. So if Spivak's work is judged to be difficult, where is that difficulty held to reside? Although these texts have been published in learned journals, their effectivity to date has largely issued from their delivery as spoken addresses. Judgments of difficulty have thus tended to remain at the level of speech, of rumor. It may be of use to dispel some of those rumors, to enable the reader to engage more quickly with the pleasures and challenges of Spivak's inquiries.

Let us quickly enumerate the ways in which these texts are not difficult. They are not difficult stylistically: this is periodic English at its most pleasurable, interpolated with the occasional sharp American idiom, elegant and concise. Nor is the difficulty that all too typical obscure, omniscient, and irritating academic manner, which classes epochs and cultures with a whimsical aside and no reference to sources. Not for Spivak an analysis of Chinese culture based on a few second-hand sources, nor the empty rhetoric of "since Plato." Every analysis is carefully annotated, by someone who is, at least in this, a model product of an Indian undergraduate and an American graduate education—probably the most scholarly combination on this planet. Indeed one of the minor uses of this text is the way the footnotes offer an annotated bibliography to several of the most interesting Marxist and feminist debates of the past two decades.

There is another, more subtle way in which the whispered rumor of difficulty is often intended. What we are talking of is a "difficult woman," a "difficult native." Spivak, herself, describes so well what is at stake here in "Explanation and Culture: Marginalia" that I would find it impossible to improve on her acute account of the structures of an academic conference, and the corridors of knowledge and tables of learning where the marginal aside is made with central purpose. All that is worth stressing here is that one doesn't need the substantive, carefully erased from the academic conscious, to grasp the meaning of the adjective. What is at stake here is tone, gesture, style—a whole opera and ballet of sexist racism which continues to dominate the academic theater and which should be challenged every moment it appears—especially given the difficulty that, when challenged, it vociferously denies its own existence.

There remain, however, two real levels of difficulty in these texts, and although these two levels cannot finally be theoretically separated they can be differentiated at a practical level. The first is unavoidable—it is the difficulty which is inevitably involved in any serious attempt to reflect and analyze the world within publically available discourses. No matter how great the commitment to clarity, no matter how intense the desire to communicate, when we are trying ourselves to delineate and differentiate the practices and objects which are crucial to understanding our own functioning and for which we as yet lack an adequate vocabulary, there will be difficulty. Only those supremely confident of their own understanding—those who would deny all reality to history or the unconscious or matter—can bask in the self-satisfied certainty of an adequate language for an adequate world. This should never be taken as a *carte blanche* for a willed esotericism which figures an equally complacent certainty in the inadequacy of language: the literary countersign of technocratic stupidity. However, there will be a certain difficulty in reading *any* work which is genuinely trying to grapple with some of our most urgent problems which do not yet— and this constitutes their most problematic intellectual aspect—have the clarity of the already understood. To deny this real level of difficulty in Spivak's work would be misleading.

With much of such difficult work there are, however, immediate reference points within existing disciplines and arguments, which easily serve as an initial orientation. But this does not prove to be the case with Spivak's essays. However pleasurable the style and however detailed the references, Spivak's texts radically transgress against the disciplines, both the official divisions of anthropology, history, philosophy, literary criticism, sociology and the unofficial divisions between Marxism, feminism, deconstruction. There are few ready-made categories or reading lists into which her arguments fall. This is no accident: one of the major arguments of this book is that the academy is constituted so as to be unable to address the most serious of global questions, and that, in fact, many of the most radical critiques remain completely within terms set out by the constituted academy. Spivak's theme here is large: the micro-politics of the academy and its relation to the macro-narrative of imperialism. But this is a theme without a subject: one that lacks reading lists, introductory guides, and employment opportunities. It is not easily located in relation to the established subject divisions (what is a literary critic doing discussing economic theory?) nor vis-à-vis what are becoming the relatively well-mapped fields of Marxist, feminist, and deconstructionist criticism.

There is, therefore, some point in providing crude categorizations of these three "oppositional" positions and locating Spivak's work in terms of them. The problem is also to stress the provisionality of this categorization; to remember/ encode the fact that this homogeneity is, in each case, wrested from a heterogeneity which is forever irreducible to it but which cannot be grasped except as a limit, an excess beyond which, for a particular discourse, intelligibility fades. Such a thought is indebted to the work of Jacques Derrida, and Gayatri Spivak is still probably best known as the translator of his most famous work, *Of Grammatology*. She is, therefore, obviously a deconstructionist. She says so herself. And yet this extraordinary collection of essays, gathering together some of her most important work of this decade, lacks the defining features of deconstruction in America.

This paradox is merely an index of the poverty with which Derrida's thought has been received in the US. Norman Mailer, in one of his characteristically acute asides, remarked that Kerouac was an "Eisenhower kind of gypsy," and deconstruction-US style has been a "Reagan kind of radical theory." Its significance and importance in the United States is entirely in terms of the development of the academic discipline of literary criticism; indeed, it has become a dominant method of contemporary literary education. It subjects texts to the rigorous forms of analysis developed by Jacques Derrida, analyses which tease out the fundamental oppositions which underpin and make possible any particular discourse and which show how those oppositions are always themselves caught up in their own operations—how they become the vanishing point of a discourse's own intelligibility.

Derrida elaborated this work in the context of Heidegger's meditation on Being and in an attempt to recapture the revolutionary potential of a series of the key texts of literary modernism—Mallarmé, Artaud, Joyce, a project which found its rationale in the situation of France in the 1960s. An adequate account of that period does not exist—we even lack the most banal elements of a positivist cultural history. What can be said with some certainty, however, is that it was in large part a reaction both to the sudden advent of consumer capitalism under De Gaulle and the widely perceived exhaustion within the French Communist Party. In the decade after 1956, France went through one of those periods of accelerated and overdetermined change which were, in retrospect, to be phenomenally rich in social contradiction and cultural production. If one wanted to emblematically grasp this commitment both to radical politics and the analysis of the new and complex text of consumer capitalism, the preeminent theoretical text would be Roland Barthes's *Mythologies* (1957). Culturally one could gesture towards Jean-Luc Godard and his films of the mid-sixties such as *Deux ou trois choses que je sais d'elle* (1966). Politically one could think of the Situationists and texts such as Guy Debord's *Society of the Spectacle* and Raoul Van Eigen's *The Revolution of Everyday Life*.

These are, admittedly, very disparate figures but all, at different levels, attempted to grapple with the elaborate signifying systems of advanced capitalist society—the immense network of significations, from advertising hoarding, to magazine, to television—the circulation of signs in which the subject is constantly figured and refigured. The concept of text developed in that period— and associated concepts such as deconstruction—found a specific intellectual

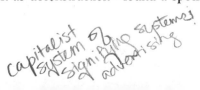

capitalist system of signifying systems: advertising

and political purpose in the attempt to both articulate the reality of the dominant culture and to escape its stereotyped identifications.

It is easy, particularly for one who lived through its boundless excitement and energy to recall this time as a simple golden age. To do so is to ignore its manifold problems. It too simply assumed the intellectual arrogance of both vanguard politics and vanguard art; and although I would argue that much of its initial emphases came from the explosion of consumer culture in France, it never actively engaged with that culture but instead postulated another radical cultural space constituted largely by a neo-surrealist canon. Its contemporary texts were theoretical rather than literary. Most importantly, it never really articulated a new politics or that thoroughgoing revision of the Marxist heritage that it promised.

By the time this project was transported to America in the 1970s—following its dubious success in France—it was transported as an individual—Derrida—and its terms were altered. The project was divorced from its attempt to refind the revolutionary force of modernism, in which the institutions of art were always in question, and relocated within a much safer and domesticated Romanticism, where art retained a clearly delineated institutional space. "Text," far from being a concept-metaphor with which to deconstruct both individual and society in order to grasp their complex of contradictory determinations, became a metonym for literature, conceived in all its exclusive and elitist forms: textuality became little more than a fig-leaf behind which one could hide all difficult questions of education and class. Deconstruction came simply to name the last privileged defense of the canon in a way brilliantly described in the second essay in this collection. It was reduced to a powerful method which would reveal the sameness and the greatness of the major literary texts.

In her long third essay on Wordsworth, Spivak dots the i's and crosses the t's on this particular development within the literary academy, reintroducing into one of the privileged texts of American deconstruction the sex and politics that Wordsworth is at such pains to erase in his attempt to construct an art which will be troubled by neither. But if Spivak is critical of the domestication of deconstruction, she is not concerned with returning to its radical origins. Independently of any deconstructionist doubt about the originality of origins, Spivak shows no enthusiasm for the project of modernism or the attempt in the sixties to revive its radical potential (she would probably want to criticize the original project and its renewal in feminist terms). The enormous contemporary interest of these essays is that they develop some of the concepts and approaches of the sixties in the context of two concrete but very different dimensions: the development of the university in the advanced world and the developing forms of exploitation in the Third World. Spivak's determination to hold both of these situations, both of her situations, in constant tension, in a perpetual deconstructive displacement, is what provides many of the astonishing insights and pleasures of *In Other Worlds*. Deconstruction, for Spivak, is neither a conservative aesthetic nor a radical politics but an intellectual ethic which enjoins a constant attention to the multiplicity of determination. At the same time, Spivak is absolutely committed to pinpointing and arresting that multiplicity at the moment in which an enabling analysis becomes possible. The difference between Spivak and Derrida is best captured in their respective attitudes toward the pathos of deconstruction: "the enterprise of deconstruction always in a certain way falls prey to its own work" writes Derrida in a comment which surfaces frequently in these essays. But what has become for Derrida, *the* abiding question, is, for Spivak, a limit which cannot obscure the value, however provisional, of the rigorous analyses that deconstruction enables.

To grasp the interest of Spivak's work necessitates going beyond the binary opposition between First World intellectual production and Third World physical exploitation. Running across both in further contradiction/production is her situation as a female academic and as one who has played a significant part in that explosion of feminist theory and practice which has marked the last twenty years.

Spivak's feminism may well seem as initially unreadable as her deconstruction. This stems from her conjunction of a rejection of any essentialism with an emphasis on the crucial importance of examining and reappropriating the experience of the female body. While Spivak avoids the sterile debates of deconstruction, or comments on them only obliquely, she is a willing participant in feminist debates, but a participant who problematically combines positions which are often held to be antithetical. Many feminists have wished to stress an essential feminine, an area repressed by male domination but within which it is possible to find the methods and values to build a different and better society. The most notable opponents of such a view have been those influenced by psychoanalysis, and specifically its Lacanian version, who stress sexuality as a construction produced through familial interaction. Neither male nor female sexuality can be understood *as such*, but only in their interdefinability as the child seeks to locate itself in the complicated exchanges within the nuclear family.

The psychoanalytic thesis thus proposes both a fundamental bisexuality, a bisexuality which finds its primary articulation in the dialectic between being and having the phallus. All questions of direct access to the body are bracketed for psychoanalysis by the need for the body to be represented or symbolised— indeed, failure of such a representation entails psychosis. Thus for Lacan the real is that to which we do not have access and whose disappearance from the field of consciousness is the condition of intersubjectivity. Feminists who accept this account do not question political struggle and the need to supersede male domination, but they argue that it must find its forms and aims in specific situations and cannot be elaborated in relation to an essential feminine nature. Spivak's opposition to essentialism is, in the first instance, deconstructive rather than psychoanalytical. Woman, like any other term can only find its meaning in a complex series of differentiations, of which the most important, or at least the most immediate, is man. It is as ludicrous, in deconstructive terms, to talk of an essential feminine as it is to talk of any other essence. It is not ludicrous, however, on this account to talk of the specificity of the female body. If deconstruction is critically sensitive to any account which bases itself on a privileged moment of experience, it is exactly to allow full force to the heterogeneity of experience. It follows that, for a woman, that heterogeneity must importantly include the experience of her body, an experience which has been subject to the most rigorous male censorship down the ages and finds a particularly shocking, but for Spivak exemplary, form in the practice of clitoridectomy.

Spivak develops the experience of the female body in two radically different directions. On the one hand she wishes to stress the clitoris as the site of a radical excess to the cycle of reproduction and production, and on the other, to emphasize that the reproductive power of the womb is crucially absent from any account of production in the classical Marxist texts. Further she argues that it is only when the excess of the clitoris has been taken into account that it will be possible to situate and assess uterine social organisation. It would be difficult to overestimate the skill with which Spivak weaves these themes together in relation to the classic Marxist theme of production.

Before moving on to Marxism, what of psychoanalysis? Only the briefest and most provisional of answers is possible. This is partially because Spivak is never interested in psychoanalytic theory as such but rather its use by literary theory as a radical fabulation with which to explicate the functioning of texts. Spivak would seem to accept an account of the child's acquisition of a sexual identity which would place that acquisition in the social interplay of desire. She would, however, explicitly, object to the phallus being made the crucial term in this relation and, implicitly, to the description of the family as the only site of significant desire. While it is clear that, for Spivak, the womb must be considered in this exchange, she does not indicate how the relation to the clitoris would figure, nor how she would displace the primacy of vision, which awards the penis pride of visible place in any psychoanalytic account. But, as I have said, psychoanalysis is not one of Spivak's most urgent concerns, and it may remain for others to develop further her extraordinarily suggestive comments in psychoanalytic terms.

Marxism is, however, an urgent concern, one that insists throughout these pages. But it is a Marxism which will be alien to at least a few Marxist critics. For this is a Marxism crucially grounded in Third World experience and is therefore a Marxism which concentrates on imperialism and exploitation, one that is both critical of, and finds no use for, the normative narrative of the modes of production. While most recent Marxist cultural criticism in the developed world has been occupying itself with revising the crude economistic models of base and superstructure, it has also been prone to a repression of economics; it has conveniently forgotten the necessity of locating those cultural analyses within the organization of production and its appropriation of surplus. Often Marxism now means nothing more than a commitment to a radical or socialist politics and the adoption of the classic mode of production narrative—the transitions from slave, to feudal, to capitalist orders. This, it must be stressed, is not meant simply as a condemnation but as a description of the difficulty of analyzing contemporary developed countries in the terms elaborated in *Capital*: the problems posed by the analysis of the enormous middle class; the decline in factory production; and, above all, the growth of computerized production in the last ten years. In this context the claim that labor power is no longer the major productive element within the developed economies becomes plausible.

From a Third World perspective, however, such a plausibility is itself seen as the management of a crisis and the classic Marxist analysis of exploitation, as expanded to account for imperialism, makes more sense—as Spivak indicates in many telling asides. In the essay "Scattered Speculations on the Theory of Value" these asides are located within a thoroughgoing argument which fully retains Marx's account of exploitation grounded in the theory of surplus value. The argument is both extraordinarily complex and interesting, and all I can hope to do here is indicate its major vectors.

Spivak clearly realizes that to retain the theory of surplus value it is necessary to retain its basis, which Marx had adopted from classical economics: the now much questioned labor theory of value. She accomplishes this by a thorough re-reading of the first section of *Capital* volume I, supplemented by the *Grundrisse*. Her most audacious move is to deny that Marx ever adopted the labor theory of value in that "continuist" reading which proceeds in relations of representation and transformation from labor to value to money to capital. Instead, Spivak argues, we have to understand Marx's account of value not as indicating the possibility of labor representing itself in value but as an analysis of the ability of capital to consume the use value of labor power. By concentrating on use-value as the indeterminate moment within the chain of value-determinations, Spivak breaks open that chain, redefining labor within a general account of value, which makes labor endlessly variable both in relation to technological change and to political struggles, particularly those around feminism. Even if I have understood it correctly, the argument is too complex to do full justice to it here. Suffice to indicate one reservation and one consequence. The reservation is that in order to explain the continuing exploitation of the third world, Spivak stresses the contradiction whereby capital has to produce more absolute and less relative surplus value. But it is not clear to me that this distinction survives her critique of the "continuist" account of value. What is clear, however, is that while Marx has perfectly grasped the constitutive crisis of capitalism, he has not provided an account of any other mode of production; for if there is no fixed relation between value and labor it is impossible to understand the appropriation of surplus outside a full understanding of the organization of value within a particular community. This consequence may be seen as endorsed by Spivak because, for her, normative accounts of mode of production have impeded third world struggles.

If she wishes to retain Marx as a theoretician of crisis she is happy to bracket him as a philosopher of history. This is not simply because the Asiatic mode of production offers a classically inadequate account of historical Asian societies but because the notion of a "transition" to capitalism has crippled liberation movements, forcing them to construe their struggles in relation to the development of a national bourgeois class. For Spivak, the attempt to understand subaltern classes only in terms of their adequation to European models has been deeply destructive. The political project becomes one of letting the subaltern speak—allowing his or her consciousness to find an expression which will then inflect and produce the forms of political liberation which might bypass completely the European form of the nation. It is this momentous project that produces a context for Spivak's final essays.

This work takes place in, and in relation to, the historical collective called *Subaltern Studies*. While Spivak endorses the group's abandonment of the modes of production narrative, she argues that such renunciation is not enough. As long as notions of discipline and subjectivity are left unexamined, the subaltern will be narrativized in theoretically alternative but politically similar ways. To avoid this dominating disablement, historians must face the contemporary critique of subjectivity both in relation to the subaltern (it cannot be a question of restoring the subaltern's consciousness but of tracing the subject effects of subalternity) and in relation to themselves (as they recognize the subject effects of their own practice). It is only when the full force of contemporary antihumanism has met the radical interrogation of method that a politically consequent historical method can be envisaged.

It is such a method that Spivak employs in the final reading of Mahasweta Devi's magnificent and terrible story "Breast Giver." Here Spivak demonstrates the importance of undoing the distinction between literary criticism and history or, which is the same undoing at another level, the distinction between imaginary and real events. This is not the aesthetic stupidity of "all history is literature." Put crudely, the thesis is no more than Marx's dictum that ideas become a material force when they grip the masses. But what Spivak argues is that to understand this process the analyst of culture must be able to sketch the real effects of the imaginary in her object of study while never forgetting the imaginary effect of the real (the impossibility of fully grasping her situation) in her own investigation. But where Lacan understands that real entirely in relation to a castration which sets the imaginary in place, Spivak understands that real as the excess of the female body which has to be placed in its cultural and economic specificity and only thus can an imaginary be figured.

The force of Mahasweta's text resides in its grounding in the gendered subaltern's body, in that female body which is never questioned and only exploited. The bodies of Jashoda and Dopdi figure forth the unutterable ugliness and cruelty which cooks in the Third World kitchen to produce the First World feasts that we daily enjoy. But these women's bodies are not yet another blank signifier for masculine signifieds. These women articulate (better construct) truths which speak of our as well as their situation. The force of Spivak's reading resides in its attention to the dialectic between real and imaginary which must be read in these texts and in its attention to how that dialectic reflects back on the imaginary and real of contemporary theory. Spivak's courage lies in confronting both sides of this dilemma—reading Mahasweta's text with the full apparatus of contemporary Western critical discourses while also, at the same time, using that text to read the presuppositions of that critical apparatus. Any other position but this would involve that simple acceptance of a subject-position which is, for Spivak, the inevitable sign of bad faith. The force of Spivak's work lies in her absolute refusal to discount any of the multiplicity of subject-positions which she has been assigned, or to fully accept any of them. In that sense Spivak is always in "another world"—always allowing herself to be pulled out of the true. This is the ever movable ground of these texts, and as one reads one is both illuminated by the thought and moved by the exhilarating and painful adventure that subtends it. But this text is not simply a personal odyssey, it is also the trace of a series of struggles: of leftist politics in Bengal, of the sixties within the American university system, of feminism worldwide. It is only insofar as these texts can be useful to such struggles that they will be effective. No guarantees for such effectivity can be given in advance. These essays on cultural politics cannot be understood simply as a set of analyses; it is only insofar as they serve as an aid to action that they could possibly complete their own undoing. That action is multiple and heterogenous. I have not the competence to speak of India or the Third World nor the scope to speak of the variety of political struggles in the advanced world. Suffice to say the full significance of this work will rest on events outside its control, and whether it will come to mean something for what comes after is not in any individual's power of choice.

It seems necessary for me, however, to end this foreword by going beyond the limits of Spivak's text, with some specific comments on the micro-politics of the university in the developed world. It immensely diminishes the potential of this book to limit it to the one world of the Western academy. But of course it is not one world—any one world is always, also, a radical heterogeneity which radiates out in a tissue of differences that undoes the initial identity. One could perhaps talk here of the dialectic between theory and politics where theory (like travel) pulls you out of the true and politics (like homecoming) is what pulls you back. One could perhaps turn to Wittgenstein here and, misquoting, argue that "differences come to an end"—in other words that particular identities, whatever their provisionality, impose themselves in specific practices.

There is one formal identity and specific practice that I share with Spivak: it is not simply that we are both university teachers, but that from this year we are teachers in the same department of English in the same university of Pittsburgh. If one limits oneself to the simple and most obvious point, one might begin by reflecting on the limitations imposed by the very notions of a discipline of "English." The construction of English as an object of study is a complex history, but it relates to the academic division of the social world enacted by capitalist imperialism in the nineteenth century and neo-colonialism in the twentieth. You can study literature, primitive societies, advanced societies, past societies, foreign societies, economic forces, political structures. You can even, if you move outside the Ivy League, study television and film. You are, however, disciplinarily constrained not to presuppose a common subject matter. The world automatically divides into these categories.

Of course, it is true that much vanguard research crosses disciplines, but this is written out of the undergraduate and graduate curricula. If, however, the humanities and social sciences are to get any serious grip on the world, if they are to enable their students to use their studies, then it is imperative that there is a general recasting of the humanities and social sciences. On the one hand students must confront the enormous problems facing the world, on the other they must understand the relation of their own situation to those problems. The degree of micro-political resistance to any such educational reform will be considerable. The individual fiefs that will fall, the networks of power and patronage that will dissolve are not negligible. But daily such fiefs disappear, daily networks dissolve.

Underlying this resistance will be a genuine problem: has not knowledge advanced to the point where the data is so vast and the specialties so complex that any possible program, which is not technically and specifically limited, will simply produce graduates who know a little about everything but have mastered nothing? This problem, however, carries with it the seeds of its own solution. It is true that knowledge is expanding exponentially, but the problem then becomes one of training students in the use and analysis of data. Within the social field it would become the task of confronting the organization of data that the child/citizen is offered in the most unified way by television, and beginning to consider the specific form of that organization. From that analysis it would then be possible to chart a way through the various disciplines in relation to the problems encountered and the questions produced. I am not proposing a media-studies for all in which pitifully thin analyses of pitifully thin programs become the privileged object of knowledge. I am, however, proposing a pedagogy which would take as its starting point the public organization of social data as the way to provide a possibility of judging and checking both the data and the organization. Such a pedagogy would be genuinely deconstructive in that the position of the analyst would never be a given but the constantly transformed ground of the inquiry. This would clearly break with many of the educational developments of the past few years in that the role of the individual teacher would become much more important as the specific starting point of inquiry would be negotiated between teacher and student. At the same time there would have to be generally agreed and assessed levels of common competence attained within these specific programs. Obviously this suggestion involves a detailed elaboration of curricula and methods. It is a project to be counted in decades rather than years, and it would be unwise to underestimate the time scale. One point must be stressed again and again. If this critique is seriously to address education then it will be crucial, as Spivak herself writes in this volume, that one qualifies students to enter society at the same time as one empowers them to criticize it.

The most important problem is, however, neither the micro-political conservatism of any institution nor the genuine problem of elaborating an educational program which emphasized both individual specificity and public competence. It is that such a project will encounter powerful macro-political resistance. The accusation of "politicization" and of "bias" will be made again and again. It is a powerful accusation and one which when it refers to the inculcation of dogma, or the specific promotion of party position, finds a justifiably large public response. What will be objected to, however, is the school and the university carrying out their historically approved and socially sanctioned function of enabling students to think and empowering them to act. There are vast interests who do not want a people educated about race or ecology or the media, about the various forms of exploitation and domination. And these interests, as Spivak constantly points out, are not forces to be located simply *outside* the university; any First World university teacher must acknowledge a certain identification with those interests.

One of the great virtues of these essays is the commitment to teaching and education that runs through them. Spivak is rare in combining an understanding of many of the most crucial problems facing the globe and the species with an interest in considering the detailed questions of specific educational situations. From the lofty heights of the development of imperialism, the study of sexuality, and the impossibility of representing Being to discussing the mundane merits of differing composition courses may seem like a fall from the sublime to the ridiculous. It is one of the delights of this book that it shrinks from neither: "I think less easily of "changing the world" than in the past. I teach a small number of the holders of the can(n)on male or female, feminist or masculist, how to read their own texts, as best I can." Any reader of these texts of Spivak will be better able to construe and construct the contradictory texts that constitute their own lives.

Colin MacCabe
University of Pittsburgh
14th February 1987

Author's Note

(Migrating?)

There would have been no "other worlds" for me if something now called deconstruction had not come to disrupt the diasporic space of a post-colonial academic. I am, then, in Jacques Derrida's debt.

Paul de Man blessed me with his encouragement at many stages of the writing of most of these essays. The often conflictual companionship of Michael Ryan during the earlier part of the decade had its own productive energy. It remains for me to thank my students for their support and their persistence.

I am grateful to the following for permission to reprint in this volume essays previously published: *Yale French Studies* for "The Letter as Cutting Edge" and "French Feminism in an International Frame"; *Social Text* for "Finding Feminist Readings: Dante–Yeats"; Praeger Publishers for "Unmaking and Making in *To the Lighthouse*," originally published in *Women and Language in Literature and Society*; *Texas Studies in Literature and Language* for "Sex and History in *The Prelude* (1805), Books Nine to Thirteen"; The University of Illinois Press for "Feminism and Critical Theory," originally published in *For Alma Mater*; *College English* for "Reading the World: Literary Studies in the 80s"; *Humanities in Society* for "Explanation and Culture: Marginalia"; *Critical Inquiry*, published by the University of Chicago Press, for "The Politics of Interpretations" and "'Draupadi' by Mahasweta Devi"; *Diacritics* for "Scattered Speculations on the Question of Value"; and *Subaltern Studies* for "Subaltern Studies: Deconstructing Historiography."

As is customary for collections such as this one, I have made hardly any changes.

one

Literature

1. The Letter as Cutting Edge

If one project of psychoanalytical criticism is to "submit to this test [of the status of speaking] a certain number of the statements of the philosophic tradition,"[1] the American common critic might well fix her glance upon Chapters Twelve and Thirteen of Samuel Taylor Coleridge's *Biographia Literaria*. These two chapters are invariably interpreted as an important paradigmatic statement of the union of the subject and object in the act of the mind, of the organic Imagination, and the autonomous self. Over the last fifty years New Criticism—the line of I. A. Richards, William Empson, and then of Brooks, Ransom, Tate, and Wimsatt has "founded [itself] on the implicit assumption that literature is an autonomous activity of the mind."[2] It is not surprising that this School, which has given America the most widely accepted ground rules of literary pedagogy, is also often a running dialogue with the Coleridge who is taken to be the prophet of the sovereign subject. I quote a passage from Richards, as he proposes to discuss Chapters Twelve and Thirteen: "In beginning now to expound Coleridge's theory of the Imagination, I propose to start where he himself in the *Biographia* . . . really started: that is, with a theory of the act of knowledge, or of consciousness, or, as he called it, 'the coincidence or coalescence of an OBJECT with a SUBJECT.'"[3]

The testing of these two chapters of the *Biographia* by the American common critic by the rules of new psychoanalysis is therefore not without a certain plausibility, not to say importance. As I describe that testing, I shall imply its ideology—an ideology of "applying" in critical practice a "theory" developed under other auspices, and of discovering an analogy to the task of the literary critic in any interpretative situation inhabiting any "science of man." At the end of this essay, I shall comment on that ideology more explicitly. For reasons that should become clear as the essay progresses, I shall make no attempt to "situate" Coleridge within an intellectual set, nor deal with the rich thematics of his so-called "plagiarisms."

The *Biographia Literaria* is Coleridge's most sustained and most important theoretical work. It is also a declared autobiography. The critic who has attended to the main texts of the new psychoanalysis has learned that any act of language is made up as much by its so-called substance as by the cuts and gaps that substance serves to frame and/or stop up: "We can conceive of the shutting [*fermeture*] of the unconscious by the action of something which plays the role of diaphragm-shutter [*obturateur*]—the object *a*, sucked and breathed in, just where the trap begins."[4] These problematics might play interestingly in a declared autobiography such as Coleridge's. Armed with this insight, the critic discovers, in Coleridge's text, logical and rhetorical slips and dodges, and what looks very much like a narrative *obturateur*. The text is so packed, and thoroughly commented upon, that here I outline the simplest blueprint of these moments.

The entire *Biographia* inhabits the narrative structure of *pre*-monition and *post*-ponement (today we might say différance—certainly avoidance *and* longing) that so many Romantic works share. "Intended in the first place as a preface to the *Sibylline Leaves* (a collection of poems), it grew into a literary autobiography, which came to demand a preface. This preface itself outgrew its purposed limits, and was incorporated in the whole work, which was finally issued in two parts— the autobiography (two vols.) and the poems."[5]

The *Biographia Literaria*, then, is not a bona fide book at all, for it was intended only as a preface, pointing to what would come after it. Only because it failed in its self-effacing task did it become a full-fledged book. Even as such it is un-well-made, for, among other reasons, it contains within it its own failed preface. One cannot situate the book in its own place. It looks forward to its promise and backward at its failure and, in a certain way, marks its own absence: autobiography by default, prefaces grown monstrous. And, even beyond this, the work as it stands is often still presented as a preface: "In the third treatise of my Logosophia," never to be written "announced at the end of this volume, I shall give (deo volente) the demonstrations and constructions of the Dynamic Philosophy scientifically arranged" (179–180). "Be assured, however," Coleridge writes to himself, "that I look forward anxiously to your great book on the CONSTRUCTIVE PHILOSOPHY, which you have promised and announced" (200).

The narrative declaration of the status of the *Biographia Literaria* is thus deliberately evasive, the writing reminder of a gap. Within such a framework, the celebrated chapter on Imagination (XIII) declares its own version of absence. Coleridge tells us that the burden of argumentation in that chapter has been suppressed at the request of a friend, (who is, as is well-known, "a figment of Coleridge's imagination," another way of saying "Coleridge himself": "Thus far had the work been transcribed for the press, when I received the following letter from a friend, whose practical judgment I have had ample reason to estimate and revere. . . . In consequence of this very judicious letter, . . . I shall content myself for the present with stating the main result of the Chapter, which I have reserved for that future publication, a detailed prospectus of which the reader will find at the close of the second volume [a fruitless promise]" (198, 201–202).

It would perhaps be more precise to say that the chapter declares its own inaccessibility rather than its proper absence. For it is supposed to exist, and Coleridge's friend, its privileged reader, has read it, but, *because the* BIOGRAPHIA *is an autobiography and a preface*, it must be suppressed: "For who, he [your reader] might truly observe," Coleridge's "friend" observes, "could from your title-page, viz. '*My* Literary Life and Opinions,' published too as introductory to a volume of miscellaneous poems, have anticipated, or even conjectured, a long treatise on ideal Realism . . ." (200–201). We are assured of the chapter's massy presence in the least refutable way; in terms of money and numbers of pages: "I do not hesitate in advising and urging you to withdraw the Chapter from the present work. . . . This chapter, which cannot, when it is printed, amount to so little as a hundred pages, will of necessity greatly increase the expense of the work" (200). Those paragraphs, beginning "The IMAGINATION then, I consider," that have been quoted so frequently as "Coleridge's theory of the Imagination," are merely "the main result of the Chapter, which I have reserved [held back] for the future publication, a detailed prospectus [which looks forward] of which the reader will find at the close of the second volume" (201–202).

The greatest instrument of narrative refraction in these chapters, the *obtura-*

teur, if you like, is, of course, the letter that stops publication of the original Chapter Thirteen. The gesture is about as far as possible from "the eternal act of creation in the infinite I AM," (202) the most abundantly quoted Coleridgean formula, descriptive of the primary Imagination. It is a written message to oneself represented as being an external interruption. And, the critic cannot forget that it is this that is presented *in the place* of the organic process and growth of the argument leading to the celebrated conclusions about the nature of the sovereign imagination. Why should a *false* disowning (since the letter is by Coleridge after all) of the name of the self as author, a *false* declaration of the power of another, inhabit the place of the greatest celebration of the self? It is a question that her psychoanalytical studies have prepared our critic to ask.

"I see clearly that you have done too much and yet not enough," Coleridge writes to Coleridge. In these chapters, in addition to the general *narrative* motif of declared and stopped-up vacancy, the reader encounters this particular sort of *rhetorical* oscillation between a thing and its opposite, sometimes displacing that opposition (as here, what is too much is presumably what is not enough, the two can never of course be *the same*), which artfully suggests the absence of the thing itself, at the same time, practically speaking and thanks to the conventions of rhetoric, suggesting its presence. The typical hiding-in-disclosure, the signifier creating "the effect of the signified" by rusing anticipation—that psychoanalysis has taught her to recognize. Here are some of these rhetorical gestures.

Consider the title of Chapter Twelve. "Requests"—looking forward to a future result—and "premonitions"—knowing the result beforehand, concerning the "perusal" *or* "omission" of "the chapter that follows." The first two pages are taken up with "understanding a philosopher's ignorance" *or* being "ignorant of his understanding." The connection between this and what follows is not immediately clear in the text. The distinction seems to be invoked simply to reinforce the rhetorical oscillation. We move next to the request that the reader "will either pass over the following chapter altogether, *or* read the whole connectedly" (162). Even if we overlook the fact that Coleridge will set up numerous obstacles to reading these chapters *connectedly*, and that this request is advanced not in its own proper place, but *"in lieu of* the various requests which the anxiety of authorship addresses to the unknown reader," (162) we might quite justifiably ask, "which following chapter?" Chapter Twelve, the chapter that has just begun and will immediately follow, or Chapter Thirteen, the chapter that comes *after* this one? I am not suggesting, of course, that common-sensically, we cannot make our choice; but that rhetorically, the request seems to blur the possibility of the presence of the matter under discussion.

Upon the rhetoric of oscillation, Coleridge now imposes the rhetoric of condition. He tells us what kind of reader he does *not* want. "If a man receives as fundamental fact, . . . the general notions of matter, spirit, soul, body, action, passiveness, time, space, cause and effect, consciousness, perception, memory and habit," et cetera, et cetera, "to such a mind I would as courteously as possible convey the hint, that for him this chapter was not written" (163). After this sentence, with its significant breakdown in parallelism once it gets to "cause and effect," Coleridge plunges into the language of "more and less" where, if we read closely, we will see that the "not more difficult is it to reduce them" and the "still less dare a favorable perusal be anticipated" do not match: "Taking [these terms] therefore in mass, and unexamined, it requires only a decent apprenticeship in logic, to draw forth their contents in all forms and colours, as the professors of legerdemain at our village fairs pull out ribbon after ribbon from their mouths. And not more difficult is it to reduce them back again to their different genera. . . . Still less dare a favorable perusal be anticipated from the proselytes of that compendious philosophy . . ." (163) The rhetoric of "more and less" is there to beguile us. In itself a device to announce the absence of a thing in its proper measure, here deflected and defective, it leads us into further dissimulative plays of presence and absence.

"But," writes Coleridge in the next paragraph, "it is time to tell the truth." A negative truth, presented in halting alternatives: "it is neither possible or necessary for all men, or for many, to be PHILOSOPHERS" (164). After this divisive move, Coleridge leaves the place of spontaneous consciousness vacant of or inaccessible to human knowledge: "we divide all the objects of human knowledge into those on this side, and those on the other side of the spontaneous consciousness" (164).

Coleridge then assumes what is recognizably the language of philosophical exposition. And here the reader repeatedly meets what must be called logical slippages.

In Chapter Twelve, simply breaking ground for the grand demonstration of Chapter Thirteen, Coleridge submits that "there are two cases equally possible. EITHER THE OBJECTIVE IS TAKEN AS THE FIRST, . . . *OR* THE SUBJECTIVE IS TAKEN AS THE FIRST." For "the conception of nature does not apparently involve the co-presence of an intelligence making an ideal duplicate of it, i.e. representing it" (175). So far so good. Yet a few pages later, Coleridge designates the ground of the first alternative as prejudice, and that of the second simply as ground. The reason being one of compulsion; otherwise thought disappears.

> THAT THERE EXIST THINGS WITHOUT US . . . remains proof against all attempts to remove it by grounds or arguments . . . the philosopher therefore *compels himself* to treat this faith as nothing more than a prejudice . . . The other position . . . is groundless indeed. . . . It is groundless; but only because it is itself the ground of all other certainty. Now the apparent contradiction . . . the transcendental philosopher *can solve only* by the supposition . . . that it is not only coherent but identical . . . with our own immediate self-consciousness (178; italics mine).

Upon this fundamental, compulsive, and necessary desire, the philosopher's desire for coherence and the possibility of knowledge—the desire for the One, Coleridge lays the cornerstone of his argument. And then suggests that to demonstrate the identity of the two positions presented in the passage above is "the office and object of philosophy!" (175–178). An office and object, as the reader sees in the next chapter, that can only be performed by deferment and dissimulation.

Indeed, in this section of Chapter Twelve, Coleridge is preparing us systematically for the analysis of Chapter Thirteen, the chapter to come, and giving us the terms for its analysis—a chapter which he warns most of us against reading, and which is not going to be there for any of us to read anyway. And all through Chapter Twelve, Coleridge grapples with the most patent contradiction in his theory: The possible priority of the object must be rejected out of hand and the identity of the subject and object, although it may be seen as no more than a compulsive project, must be presented as the theorem of philosophy. This "identity" is itself an infinite and primary property of self-*representation* and self-*signification*, both concepts that are constituted by separation from the self. Yet, despite all this, the identity must be seamless. Now this is of course not a contingency peculiar to Coleridge. If confronted at random with "mind is only what it does, and its act is to make itself the object of its own consciousness," who would assign a proper author?

In the passage I cited above Coleridge comes close to suggesting that the driving force of the philosopher's project is desire. Elsewhere Coleridge will not openly declare that the force that would bring the object and the subject, as well as the divided ground of the self, into unity, is also desire, a desire that Lacan will analyze into the desire of the other and the desire to produce the other as well as to appropriate the other, the object, the object-substitute, as well as the image of the subject or subjects—a play of all that masquerades as the "real." Yet Coleridge's desire for unitary coherence seems constantly to be betrayed by a discourse of division. First the division between a principle and its manifestation. "This principle [of identity] manifests itself . . ." (183). The manifestation of identity is itself given in *two* pieces, not one, connected by an alternative, supported by the possibility of translation, which would contradict its uniqueness, and, given the multiplicity of languages, would make it in principle open-ended. The first piece is the Latin word *sum*, suggesting on the page its English graphic equivalent: "sum." Its translated substitute breaks the unitary sum into two: "I am." "This principle, and so characterized, manifests itself in the SUM or I AM."

Soon Coleridge neatly turns the table. A few pages back, as we have noticed, he was suggesting that the objective and the subjective positions are alternatives, and "to demonstrate their identity is the office and object of . . . philosophy." Now, with the most sweeping of intermediate steps, and certainly nothing like a demonstration, Coleridge asserts: "It may be described *therefore* as a perpetual Self-duplication of *one and the same power* into object and subject" (183). The following THESIS, punctuated by "therefores" and "it follows"-es, does not in fact depend upon or look forward to proofs presented in the text, and is stated with such uncharged assurance that it has all the force of law:

for herein consists the essence of a spirit, that it is self-representative. . . .
It must follow that the spirit in all the objects which it views, views only itself. . . . It has been shown, that a spirit is that, which is its own object,

yet not originally an object, but an absolute subject for which all, itself
included, may become an object. It must therefore be an ACT. . . . Again
the spirit . . . must in some sense dissolve this identity [of subject and
object], in order to be conscious of it. . . . But this implies an act, and it
follows therefore that intelligence or self-consciousness is impossible, except by and in a will. . . . Freedom must be assumed as a *ground* of philosophy, and can never be deduced from it (184–185).

In all this barrage of compulsive argumentation, one tends to forget what is
written three pages before, where Coleridge describes the strategy of the imagination that might produce such arguments:

Equally *inconceivable* is a cycle of equal truths without a common and central principle. . . . That the absurdity does not so immediately strike us,
that it does not seem equally *unimaginable*, is owing to a surreptitious act
of the imagination, which, instinctively and without our noticing the same,
not only fills up the intervening spaces, and contemplates the *cycle* . . .
as a continuous *circle* giving to all collectively the unity of their common
orbit; but likewise supplies . . . the one central power, which renders the
movement harmonious and cyclical (181).

Does it help our critic to speculate that the instinctive, surreptitious, and unnoticed imagination, filling up the gaps in the centerless cycle of equal—infinitely substitutable—truths, each signifying the next and vice versa, might follow the graph that Lacan has plotted in "La Subversion du sujet et la dialectique
du désir?" Would Coleridge have welcomed Lacan's notion of the *points de capiton*—quilting buttons: "by means of which the signifier stops the otherwise
indefinite sliding of signification?"[6]
     The critic cannot know the answer to that question. But she can at least see
that for Coleridge, if the controlling imagination or self-consciousness is not
taken as performing its task of fixing those conditions of intelligibility, what
results is chaos, infinite way stations of sliding signification. Coleridge, in an
older language, calls this fixing or stabilizing the location of ground. "Even when
the Objective is assumed as the first, we yet can never pass beyond the principle
of self-consciousness. Should we attempt it, we must be driven back from
ground to ground, each of which would cease to be a Ground the moment we
pressed on it. We must be whirl'd down the gulf of an infinite series." But
whereas Lacan or Derrida would see the protective move against such a threat
as simply that, and perhaps as a "characteristic" of text or subject, Coleridge
speaks of it in the language of necessity and norm:

But this would make our reason baffle the end and purpose of all reason,
namely, unity and system. Or we must break off the series arbitrarily, and

affirm an absolute something that is in and of itself at once cause and effect . . . , subject and object, or rather the identity of both. *But as this is inconceivable, except in a self-consciousness, it follows . . . that . . .* we arrive at . . . a self-consciousness in which the principium essendi does not stand to the principium cognoscendi in the relation of cause to effect, but both the one and the other are co-inherent and identical (187).

Here Coleridge glosses over the possibility that if the principle of being (essence, truth) is not the cause of the principle of knowing, the two principles might very well be discontinuous rather than identical, simply on the ground that such a discontinuity would be "inconceivable." But in an argument about knowing and being, inconceivability and unreasonableness are not argument enough. One must allow the aporia to emerge. Especially since, a page earlier, Coleridge had excused himself precisely on the ground of the difference, rather than the identity, between these two principles: "We are not investigating an absolute principium essendi; for then, I admit, many valid objections might be started against our theory; but an absolute principium cognoscendi" (186). The difference—at the sensible frontier of truth and knowledge[7]—that must be covered over by an identity worries Coleridge.

And it is this gap between knowing and being that the episode of the imaginary letter occludes. At the end of Chapter Twelve, Coleridge invokes, in a sentence that seems strangely unrelated to the rest of the page, an overtly theological rather than merely logical authority for thinking unity rather than difference: "I will conclude with the words of Bishop Jeremy Taylor: he to whom all things are one, who draweth all things to one, and seeth all things in one, may enjoy true peace and rest of spirit" (194). But by the end of Thirteen, the imaginary friend, the self's fiction, takes the place of God's instrument, the good Bishop. A fallen discourse of "being as mere existence," the autobiographical anecdote, a letter from the world of others, interrupts the discourse of knowing, and prevents the movement whereby its presentation would (if it could) be identical with its proof, and halts on a promise: a promise to read and to write.

A reader of Lacan can interpret this textual gesture yet another way: the eruption of the Other onto the text of the subject. Read this way, what is otherwise seen as merely an interruption of the development of the *argument* about the imagination may not only be seen as a keeping alive, by unfulfillment, of the desire that moves the argument, but also as the ruse that makes possible the establishment of the *Law* of the imagination. The author's friend, the self split and disguised as the Other, can in this view be called the "Legislator," he who at once dictates the author's course of action and makes it possible for the law to be erected. Seeking to bring his text to the appropriate conclusion—the ex cathedra paragraphs on the Imagination—the subject in this view must ask the Other (no longer the object but what seems another subject) "What is your wish?" (My wish is that you should suppress this chapter.) "By means of which is yet more marked than revealed the true function of the Father which at bottom is to unite (and not to oppose) a desire to the Law."[8] Coleridge's text desires to be logically defective and yet be legislative. The path to such conclusions as "the IMAGINATION, then . . ." and so forth, is paved with logical dissimulation. By demanding that the path be effaced, the Lawgiver allows the unacknowledgeable desire to be united with the Law (rather than the argument, which is the text's ostensible desire) of the Imagination. The richness of the text is increased when we realize that the Law in question is not any law, but the Law of the sovereignty of the Self, and that Coleridge's text narrates this legislation in terms of an author who, rusingly, "fathers" the Legislator rather than vice versa, and that that fathering is disavowed. A labyrinth of mirrors here . . .

In Coleridge our critic seems confronted with an exemplum. Mingling the theory and the narrative of the subject, Coleridge's text seems to engage most profitably with the work of the new psychoanalysis. The double-edged play of the desire for a unitarian theory and a desire for discontinuity seems accessible to that work.

If our critic does follow the ideology I have predicted for her, she will proceed to search through the basic texts of Lacan for the meaning of her reading, and realize that she has related Coleridge's chapters to the two great psychoanalytic themes: castration and the Imaginary, the second specifically articulated by Lacan.

Although inevitably positioned and characterized by its place in the "symbolic" world of discourse, the subject nonetheless desires to touch the "real" world by constructing object-images or substitutes of that "real" world and of itself. This is the place of the Imaginary, and, according to Lacan, all philosophical texts show us its mark. "In all that is elaborated of being and even of essence, in Aristotle for example, we can see, reading it in terms of the analytic experience, that it is a question of the object a."[9] Coleridge, by declaring carefully that he will write on knowing, not being, does not seem to have escaped that mark. For all discourse, including the authors of discourses, are discourses of being in a certain way, and must therefore harbor the fascinating antagonist of discourse, the production of the Imaginary. Hence Lacan's question: "Is to have the a, to be?"[10]

The "friend" who shares in the responsibility of authorship might be a specular (thus objectified) as well as a discursive (thus subjectivized) image of the subject. "The I is not a being, it is a presupposition with respect to that which speaks."[11] "That subject which believes it can have access to [or accede to] itself by being designated in a statement [énoncé], is nothing other than such an object. Ask the person inflicted with the anguish of the white page, he will tell you who is the turd of his fantasy."[12]

The curious detail of the "friend's" letter that suddenly describes the missing chapter in terms of money and number of pages and reduces the great thought on thought to a massy thing also fits into these thematics. Lacan says again and again that the imaginary is glimpsed only through its moments of contact with the symbolic. That sentence in the letter might indeed be such a moment.

The letter as a whole is the paradigm of the "symbolic," a message conveyed in language—a collection of signifiers, a representative signifier, if such a thing can be said. As we have seen, it halts the fulfillment of the author's apparent desire to present the complete development of his theory of the Imagination, even as it encourages and promises further writing and reading. It is an instrument with a cutting edge.

The critic knows that, in psychoanalytic vocabulary, all images of a cutting that gives access to the Law is a mark of castration. It is the cut in Coleridge's discourse that allows the Law to spring forth full-fledged. The removal of the phallus allows the phallus to emerge as the signifier of desire. "Castration means that, in order to attain pleasure on the reversed scale of the Law of desire, [orgasmic] pleasure [*jouissance*] must be refused."[13] As subsequent critical reception of Coleridge has abundantly demonstrated, the letter, by denying the full elaboration of a slippery argument, has successfully articulated the grand conclusion of Chapter Thirteen with what came before. Thus is castration, as a psychoanalytic concept, both a lack and an enabling: "let us say of castration that it is the absent peg which joins the terms in order to construct a series or a set or, on the contrary, it is the hiatus, the cleavage that marks the separation of elements among themselves."[14]

As American common critics read more and more of the texts of the new psychoanalysis, and follow the ideology of application-by-analogy, exegeses like this one will proliferate.[15] And so will gestures of contempt and caution against such appropriations by critics closer to the French movement. I propose at this point to make a move toward neutralizing at once the appropriating confidence of the former and the comforting hierarchization of the latter and ask what this sort of use of a psychoanalytic vocabulary in literary criticism might indeed imply.

It is conceivable that a psychoanalytic reading of a literary text is bound to plot the narrative of a psychoanalytic scenario in the production of meaning, using a symbological lexicon and a structural diagram. Literary critics with more than the knowledge of the field normally available to the common critic, as well as the great psychoanalysts using literature as example seem to repeat this procedure. As a matter of fact, Freud on *The Sand-Man*, or Lacan on "The Purloined Letter" are more than most aware of this bind. The tropological or narratological crosshatching of a text, given a psychoanalytic description, can be located as stages in the unfolding of the psychoanalytic scenario. There are a few classic scenarios, the most important in one view being the one our critic has located in Coleridge: the access to law through the interdict of the father—the passage into the semiotic triangle of Oedipus: "The stake [setting into play—*en jeu*] of analysis is nothing else—to recognize what function the subject assumes in the order of symbolic relations which cover the entire field of human relations, and whose initial cell is the Oedipus complex, where the adoption of one's sex is decided."[16]

To plot such a narrative is to uncover the text's intelligibility (even at the extreme of showing how textuality keeps intelligibility forever at bay), with the help of psychoanalytic discourse, at least provisionally to satisfy the critic's desire for mastery through knowledge, even to suggest that the critic as critic has a special, if not privileged, knowledge of the text that the author either cannot have, or merely articulates. The problematics of transference, so important to Freud and Lacan, if rigorously followed through, would dismiss such a project as trivial, however it redefines the question of hermeneutic value. Lacan explains the transference-relationship in terms of the Hegelian master-slave dialectic, where both master and slave are defined and negated by each other. And of the desire of the master—here analyst or critic—Lacan writes: "Thus the desire of the master seems, from the moment it comes into play in history, the most off-the-mark term by its very nature."[17]

What allows the unconscious of patient and analyst to play is not the desire of the master but the production of transference, interpreted by master *and* slave as being intersubjective. Lacan cautions as much against a misunderstanding of transference as he emphasizes its importance in analysis. It is not a simple displacement or identification that the neutral analyst manipulates with care. He is as much surrendered to the process of transference as the patient. The analyst can neither know nor ignore his own desire within that process: "Transference is not the putting into action that would push us to that alienating identification which all conformization constitutes, even if it were to an ideal model, of which the analyst in any case could not be the support."[18] "As to the handling of transference, my liberty, on the other hand, finds itself alienated by the doubling that my self suffers there, and everyone knows that it is there that the secret of analysis should be looked for."[19]

I do not see how literary criticism can do more than *decide* to deny its desire as master, nor how it can not attend to the conditions of intelligibility of a text. The text of criticism is of course surrendered to the play of intelligibility and unintelligibility, but its decisions can never be more self-subversive than to question the status of intelligibility, or be more or less deliberately playful. Even when it is a question of isolating "something irreducible, *non-sensical*, that functions as the originally repressed signifier," the analyst's function is to give that irreducible signifier a "significant interpretation." "It is not because I have said that the effect of interpretation is to isolate in the subject a heart, a *Kern*, to use Freud's expression, of *non-sense*, that interpretation is itself a nonsense."[20] As Serge Leclaire stresses in *Psychanalyser*, the psychoanalyst cannot get around the problem of reference. On the other hand, it seems to me important that, in the service of intelligibility, using a text as the narrative of a scenario or even the illustration of a principle, the new psychoanalysis would allow us to doubt the status, precisely, of the intelligence, the meaning of knowledge, the knowledge of meaning. "As it [the Hegelian dialectic] is deduced, it can only be the conjunction of the symbolic with a real from which there is nothing more to be expected. . . . This eschatological excursion is there only to designate what a yawning chasm separates the two relations, Freudian and Hegelian, of the subject to knowledge."[21]

Like philosophical criticism, psychoanalytical criticism of this sort is in the famous double bind. All precautions taken, literary criticism *must* operate as if the critic is responsible for the interpretation, and, to a lesser extent, as if the writer is responsible for the text. "If then psychoanalysis and philosophy both find themselves today obliged to break with 'sense,' to 'depart' radically from the epistemology of presence and consciousness, they both find themselves equally struggling with the difficulty (impossibility?) of placing their discourse on a level with their discoveries and their programs."[22] What can criticism do?— but *name* frontier concepts (with more or less sophistication) and thus grant itself a little more elbow room to write *intelligibly*: Bloom's Scene of Instruction, de Man's Irony, Kristeva's *chora*, Lacan's *réel*. Or try frontier styles: Lacan's Socratic seminars of the seventies, Derrida's "diphallic" *Glas*, and, alas, the general air of coyness in essays like this one. At least double-bind criticism, here using a psychoanalytic vocabulary, invites us to think—even as we timidly or boister-ously question the value of such a specular invitation—that Coleridge was thus double-bound: Imagination his frontier-concept, the self-effacing/affecting lit-erary (auto)biography his frontier style.

There is yet another angle to the appropriation of the idea of transference to the relationship between text and critic: "It is fitting here then, to scrutinize the fact—which is always dodged, and which is the reason rather than the excuse for transference—that nothing can be attained *in absentia, in effigie.* . . . Quite on the contrary, the subject, in so far as it is subjected to the desire of the analyst, desires to deceive him through that subjection, by winning his affection, by himself proposing that essential duplicity [*fausseté*] which is love. The effect of transference is this effect of deceit in so far as it is repeated at present here and now."[23] Philosophically naive as it may sound, it cannot be ignored that the book cannot think it speaks for itself in the same way as the critic. Now Jacques Derrida has shown carefully that the structure of "live" speech and "dead" writing are inter-substitutable.[24] But that delicate philosophical analysis should not be employed to provide an excuse for the will to power of the literary critic. After all, the general sense in which the text and the person share a common structure would make criticism itself absolutely vulnerable. The Derridean move, when written into critical practice, would mean, not equating or making ana-logical the psychoanalytic and literary-critical situation, or the situation of the book and its reader, but a perpetual deconstruction (reversal and displacement) of the distinction between the two. The philosophical rigor of the Derridean move renders it quite useless as a passport to psychoanalytic literary criticism.

Nor will the difference between text and person be conveniently effaced by refusing to talk about the psyche, by talking about the text as part of a self-propagating mechanism. The disjunctive, discontinuous metaphor of the sub-ject, carrying and being carried by its burden of desire, does systematically mis-guide and constitute the machine of the text, carrying and being carried by its burden of "figuration." One cannot escape it by dismissing the former as the residue of a productive cut, and valorizing the latter as the only possible concern of a "philosophical" literary criticism. This opposition too, between subject "metaphor" and text "metaphor," needs to be indefinitely deconstructed rather than hierarchized.

And a psychoanalytic procedure, which supplements the category of substi-tution with the category of desire and vice versa, is a way to perform that de-construction. The transference situation will never more than lend its aura to the practice of literary criticism. We know well that all critical practice will always be defeated by the possibility that one might not know if knowledge is possible, by its own abyss-structure. But within our little day of frost before evening, a psychoanalytical vocabulary, with its charged metaphors, gives us a little more turning room to play in. If we had followed only the logical or "figurative" (as customarily understood) inconsistencies in Chapters Twelve and Thirteen of the *Biographia Literaria* we might only have seen Coleridge's prevarication. It is the thematics of castration and the Imagination that expose in it the play of the presence and absence, fulfillment and non-fulfillment of the will to Law. The psychoanalytical vocabulary illuminates Coleridge's declaration that the *Biographia* is an autobiography. The supplementation of the category of substitution by the category of desire within psychoanalytic discourse allows us to examine not only Coleridge's declaration but also our own refusal to take it seriously.

In the long run, then, the critic might have to admit that her gratitude to Dr. Lacan would be for so abject a thing as an instrument of intelligibility, a formula that describes the strategy of Coleridge's two chapters: "I ask you to refuse what I offer you because that is not it."[25]

1977

2. Finding Feminist Readings: Dante-Yeats

The fiction of mainstream literary criticism—so generally "masculist" that the adjective begins to lose all meaning (on this level of generality you could call it "capitalist," "idealist," or "humanist," as long as you show how)—is that rigorous readings come into being in a scientific field, or in the field of legalistic demonstration of validity. The other view, coming from a mind-set that has been systematically marginalized, may just as well be called "feminist": that the production of public rigor bears the strategically repressed marks of the so-called "private" at all levels. It is not enough to permit the private to play in the reservations marked out by the subdivisive energy of critical labor: the olympian or wryly self-deprecatory touch of autobiography in political polemic or high journalism. It might, on the contrary, be necessary to show the situational vulnerability of a reading as it shares its own provenance with the reader. This is especially the case with feminist alternative readings of the canon that will not find their comfort in citing the demonstrable precedents of scientific specialism. Women must tell each other's stories, not because they are simpleminded creatures, but because they must call into question the model of criticism as neutral theorem or science. This essay is an exercise in allegorizing such a situation. It is hoped that the reader will learn the point of the awkward, elaborate yet marginal "autobiography" before he gets to the straight reading.

In the spring of 1977, I participated in a feminist literary criticism symposium. One of the principal papers was an excellent scholarly presentation on Dante's *La Vita nuova*.[1] The paper took no stand on the brutal sexism of the tradition within which that text is situated. A woman in the audience asked at the end of the hour: "How can a woman learn to praise this text?" Before the speaker could answer, a distinguished woman present in the audience said, with authority: "Because the text deconstructs itself, the author is not responsible for what the text seems to say."

I was deeply troubled by that exchange. Here is male authority, I thought, being invoked by a woman to silence another woman's politics. Even at that, the most plausible way of understanding, "the text deconstructs itself" is surely that the text signals the itinerary of its desire to be "about something," and that this itinerary must ruse over the open-endedness of the field of meaning; at a certain point, it is possible to locate the moment when the rusing reveals itself as the structure of unresolvable self-cancellings. Even if one honed a critical methodology sensitive and vulnerable to this understanding, there would remain the articulated specificity of the "somethings" that the text wishes, on one level, to mean, and with which it ruses. These are the "minimal idealizations" which constitute the possibility of reading.[2] Within a shifting and abyssal frame, these idealizations are the "material" to which we as readers, with our own elusive historico-politico-economico-sexual determinations, bring the machinery of our reading and, yes, judgment. As the choice of the strategic moment of the reply from the audience amply demonstrated, to know the limits of judgment is not to be able to help judging. *"La Vita nuova* should not be judged, for it, like all poetic texts, deconstructs itself" is, after all, a judgment, even in the colloquial sense; indeed, "the text deconstructs itself" is also a judgment, if only in the philosophical sense.

I confess that I was preoccupied that evening with computing the "practical" reasons for making the judgment in the *colloquial* sense rather than the enclosure of metaphysics that made *philosophical* judgments inescapable at the limit. Both speaker and respondent were confronting tenure-decisions at the time. The institutional judgments involved in those decisions were carried out at least partially (and crucially) in terms of that very field of poetic language where judgment is supposed forever to be suspended or abandoned. As I walked out of the lecture room, I recalled the arrogance and anguish of the two women's judgments—expressed often in conversation—of the judges of their worth as judges of poetic texts.

"The poetic text should not be judged because it deconstructs itself," when used uncompromisingly to close rather than complicate discussion seemed, in that light, a wholesale exculpation of the text of one's trade, giving to the text a way of saying "I am not what I am not what I am not what I am not" and so on indefinitely or until the moment of suspended animation. When used in this way, the slogan seemed to fit only too well into the dreary scene of the mainstream pedagogy and criticism of literature in the United States—hedged in as it is by "the autonomy of the text," "the intentional fallacy," and, indeed, "the willing suspension of disbelief." In such a case, the fear of what is taken to be the vocabulary and presuppositions of deconstruction that pervades mainstream American orthodoxy at the present time might be no more than a localized historical paradox. Is this how the situation of deconstruction should be understood?

All that summer and fall the problem haunted me, and that Christmas I thought I had a formulation for it: deconstruction in the narrow sense domesticates deconstruction in the general sense. It is thus that it fits into the existing ideology of American literary criticism, which has already assimilated phenomenology's privileging of consciousness and is about to assimilate structuralism's apparent scientism. Deconstruction in the general sense, seeing in the self perhaps only a (dis)figuring effect of a radical heterogeneity, puts into question the grounds of the critic's power. Deconstruction in the narrow sense, no more than a chosen literary-critical methodology, locates this signifying or figuring effect in the "text's" performance and allows the critic authority to disclose the economy of figure and performance.

I had read Derrida's *Glas* from summer 1976 to spring 1977. I thought I saw there a different way of coping with the sabotaging of deconstruction in the general sense by deconstruction in the narrow sense. Since the two are complicit and inseparably intermingled, the critic must write the theoretically impossible historical biography of that very self that is no more than an effect of a structural resistance to irreducible heterogeneity. I read *Glas* as an autobiography, "about" Hegel, Marx, Nietzsche, Freud, Genet et al.[3] Since a faith in the autobiographical self or in the authority of historical narrative is thoroughly questioned by the deconstructive morphology, Derrida's project was there taking the necessary risk of "demonstrating" how theory is necessarily undermined—as it is operated—by practice.[4] Rather than disclaim responsibility, Derrida was, I felt, now trying to write the limits of responsibility in different ways. He put it without rancor, carefully preserving a legalistic metaphor of undisclosed hierarchies: "As always with a language, it is the *marriage* of a limitation with an opportunity."

Most of Derrida's work after *Glas* bears this mark of "historical" (auto)-biography. The essay from which I quote above begins: "I am introducing here—me (into) a translation," and ends: "not in order to decide with what intonation you will say, in the false infinity so variously declined of I—me: ME—psychoanalysis—you know."[5]

In my opening paragraph, I suggested that feminist alternative readings might well question the normative rigor of specialist mainstream scholarship through a dramatization of the autobiographical vulnerability of their provenance. It is no surprise, then, that as I pondered the exchange between my two colleagues, the "I/me" that I felt compelled to introduce in the space between deconstruction in the narrow and in the general senses (in itself not a hard distinction) was the subject of feminism. It is not one "subject" among many. It is the "object par excellence" as "subject." As such, the "gesture" of "reapply(ing) to a corpus the law with which it constitutes its object" can have for a woman a certain violence which is somewhat unlike the subtle language-displacement of the subject of psychoanalysis as critic.[6]

With the "subject" of feminism comes an "historical moment." No doubt any historical moment is a space of dispersion, an open frame of relationships that can be specified only indefinitely. Yet, as I argue above, the practice of deconstruction, like all practice and more so, undermines its theoretical rigor at every turn. Therefore, the trace of the self that struggles to define a historical moment, shoring up a space of dispersion even as that space gives the struggle the lie, must also go willy-nilly on record.[7] The answer from the audience had decided to reduce that struggle out of the ordered field of deconstructive literary criticism. My task became to articulate a reading that was irreducibly marked and defined by the subject and "historical moment" of feminism.

Thus it was that I came to teach *La Vita nuova* at a Summer Institute that year. The specified title was "Recent Theories of Interpretation." I remarked on the first day that my task was to articulate a reading that was irreducibly marked and defined by the subject and historical moment of feminism. All but two of the men sought their pleasure and instruction elsewhere and dropped the class.

Assisted by that group of enthusiastic young women and two men, I read *La Vita nuova*, Yeats's *"Ego Dominus Tuus"* (which takes its title from *La Vita nuova*), and *A Vision* (which might recall *The Divine Comedy* in its title).[8] What we most especially remarked was that, apart from any tropological or performative deconstruction launched by the language of these writings, there was also a *narrative* of self-deconstruction as their scenario; and, curiously enough, woman was often the *means* of this project of the narrative.[9]

As a group, the class agreed to produce papers that would fit together in a collection. I wrote a paper (Sections I to V of this essay) for the same deadline as the class, and it, like the rest of the papers, was subjected to class criticism.

The resolve to produce a collective volume came to nothing, of course. The papers were too uneven, the participants without self-confidence, and I couldn't take "being a leader" seriously. In a society and institution which systematically rewards individual rather than collective excellence and originality, such a private act of utopian piety is, at any rate, useless.

1.

Yeats needed ideal others. We know he knew of this need, diagnosed it often, made poetry, autobiography, and a vision out of it. "Say my glory was I had such friends" ("The Municipal Gallery Revisited"). This Yeatsian sentiment expands until it takes in select inhabitants of history and myth, even wild swans and saints in a mosaic. How and why this need was needed is a question I must leave unanswered in this short piece. All I will say here is, that Dante was perhaps the chief among these ideal others. Dante was a great nineteenth-century vogue, of course. Emerson, Rossetti, Longfellow translated him; Blake, Rossetti, and Gustave Doré illustrated him; Shelley, Matthew Arnold, and John Symonds wrote upon him; but Yeats seems to have liked him most because he loved the most exalted lady in Christendom. It was this love, thought Yeats, more than anything else, that allowed Dante as poet, but not as human being, to obtain "Unity of Being." In *A Vision*, Yeats writes: "Dante suffering injustice and the loss of Beatrice, found divine justice and the heavenly Beatrice."[10]

How is the figure of the woman used to achieve this psychotherapeutic plenitude in the practice of the poet's craft? This is the question I propose to consider. A greater question is implied within it. In Dante, as in Yeats, woman is objectified, dispersed, or occluded as a means; it is a reactionary operation that holds the texts together. If, as a woman, I deliberately refuse to be moved by such texts, what should I do with high art? As I have indicated, I am not unmindful of the deconstructive cautions against the feasibility of monolithic analyses (of "Dante," "Yeats," "myself," "art"): in Derrida the reminder that all unified concepts such as these may be no more than textual ruses to postpone the possibility of a radical heterogeneity; in Lacan that they are the symbolic masquerade of the Imaginary. (Imaginary "relationships are constructed out of images, imaginings, and fantasy, but they are constructed in such a commonly unrecognized way that we are easily induced by our society to imagine them to be real, and hence go on treating them as if they actually were.")[11] Yet, as I have also indicated, the conservatism that has developed out of these potentially radical positions—the unexamined use of the argument that great texts deconstruct themselves, and thus that the canon might be preserved after all—will also not suffice.

If, as a woman, I refuse to be moved by such texts, what should I do with high art? That greater question I put aside as well, and come back to the lesser question: How is the figure of the woman used to achieve this psychotherapeutic plenitude in the practice of the poet's craft?

2.

The title of Yeats's "*Ego Dominus Tuus*" (1917) is taken from Section Three of Dante's auto-psychological tale *La Vita nuova*. The words are spoken by Love, whose Dantean description Yeats satisfactorily translates as "Lord of terrifying aspect."

Throughout *La Vita nuova*, one of Dante's strategies is the transference of responsibility. He repeatedly reminds us of the fragmented quality of his text and its inadequacy as a transcription of what really happened. In Section Three, for example, Dante's description of his first vision of Beatrice, we read: "He [Love] spoke and said many things, of which I understood only a few; one was *Ego dominus tuus*" (p. 5; D 37).

"In dreams begins responsibility" (epigraph to *Responsibilities*) and this partially understood dream supposedly gives the first push to the previously composed collection of poems for which the prose text of *La Vita nuova* is a frame. Love and Beatrice may be dramatizations of the self-separation of auto-erotism. For the vision in question resembles a wet dream. Dante sees Beatrice on the street, becomes drunkenly ecstatic, seeks the loneliness of his room, thinks of her, falls asleep, has a vision of fear and joy, and "a short time after this"—as the romantic novels say—, though still within the dream, cannot bear the anguish, and his drowsy sleep is broken.

In the dream, Love shows the poet his own bleeding heart, and makes Beatrice, held half-naked in Love's arms, eat it against her will. If I decide to describe the events of this dream-vision through psychoanalytic structures, I can treat it as telling the story of a fantasy where the woman allows the man to acquire a "passivity" that would prohibit "activity." By devouring Dante's phallus—the bleeding heart is a thin disguise—Beatrice "incorporates" him, "identifies" with him, acts for him.[12] It is, however, not a diadic but a triangulated transaction. Love is the lord who gives Beatrice this dubious power by showing Dante his heart as an already-severed "part object."[13] Through the intermediary of Love, the scene of a fantasmatic exchange is opened.

Now that Beatrice has been unwillingly made to *intro*ject, Dante can *pro*ject, create the text as product, begin to search for significance, analyze his dream, inaugurate a war against this integrated female (she's filled with the phallus now, after all). The war is also a self-glorification since it is his own phallus. The responsibility rests elsewhere, with the Master who perpetrated the curiously enabling castration of the poet. The woman's desire is nowhere in question, she remains mute, acts against her will, and possesses the phallus by a grotesque transplant.

Transferring responsibility, Dante allows himself a passive role. This particular theme of the passive role or pre-determined victimage of the author is repeated many times over in the text, although its credibility is much complicated.

In "The Seminar on *The Purloined Letter*," Lacan, without questioning or interpreting the Freudian suggestion that women hide their pubis by weaving a pendant phallus, calls the Minister in Poe's story "feminine" when he begins to hide the letter in a certain way.[14] In that unquestioning spirit, one might say that Dante feminized himself as he chose for himself this passive role. If it is argued that tradition and convention allowed Dante to use this paradox of choosing passivity, another greater question looms: Why such traditions and conventions? A feminist-materialist analysis, menaced as it is constituted by deconstructive erasures, seems called for.

Beatrice, then, is said to *make* Dante act so. The story of Dante's extraordinary self-indulgence thus fabricates an excuse. Yet Beatrice herself does not act: she gives a greeting that is merely reported (sec. 3, p. 5; D 36). Her next gesture is the withholding of a greeting, and this withholding, too, is bypassed in Dante's narrative (sec. 10, p. 16; D 55). She is Dante's agent because she's a non-agent; by being an object who apparently regulates the subject's action, she allows the subject to deconstruct its sovereign motive and to disguise its masochism/ narcissism.

In the dream following Beatrice's withholding of a greeting, Love appears again, suggests in Latin that the Beatrice episode might be a simulacrum, and tells Dante not to write her directly, but only through Love's mediation, for it is time to do away with simulacra (sec. 12, p. 17; D 58). Before the middle of the book, and while Dante is engaged in writing a poem, Beatrice's death is reported (sec. 28, p. 60–61; D 125).

Her beatification is a reduction of her proper name to a common noun, a possible word in the language, not necessarily indicating Miss Portinari, but signifying "she who gives blessing." (I interpret thus the ambivalent statement that introduces her in *La Vita nuova*: "[She] was called Beatrice even by those who did not know what her name was" (sec. 2, p. 3), and the accompanying disclosure of the poet's "animal spirit": "*Apparuit iam beatitudo vestra*"—now your beatitude has appeared (sec. 2, p. 4; D 34).

The common signification of her name as meaning "she who gives blessing" allows her to be placed within the anagogic Christian story, to be kicked upstairs or sublated, so that she can belong to God, the absolute male who might seem to stand outside the triangulated, analytical circuit of Love-Beatrice-Dante. The deprivation of her proper-ty, to put it formulaically, is her beatification. Her "proper name," that which is most proper to her, is emptied of its proper signification as her index, and restored back to the "common" language, where, miraculously, it becomes her definitive predication in terms of a non-indexical meaning accessible to dictionaries. The work is completed by death; through a numerological fantasy that does not resemble Schreber's or Wolfson's merely by virtue of the authority of the historical Imaginary of Christian doctrine; ending thus:

> This number was she herself—I say this by the law of similitudes [*per similitudine dico*]. What I mean to say is this: the number three is the root of nine for, without any other number, multiplied by itself, it gives nine: as we see manifestly [*come vedemo manifestamente*] that three times three is nine. Therefore, if three is by itself [*per se medesimo*] factor of nine, and by itself the factor of miracles is three, that is, Father, Son, and Holy Spirit, who are Three in One, then this lady was accompanied by the number nine so that it might be understood that she was a nine, or a miracle,

whose root, namely that of the miracle, is the miraculous Trinity itself. Perhaps someone more subtle than I could find a still more subtle reason [*ragione*], but this is the one which I see and which pleases me the most (sec. 29, p. 62; D 127).

Dante cannot describe this deprivation of Beatrice's property and identity in her glorification. But he also cannot allow his passivity to remain a full mask. The masculine figure of Love permits Dante to regain control. In Section Nine, Love vanishes into him in a daydream. It is an unemphatic move, but it does reverse the reverse identification that Beatrice is made to perform in the initial dream.

It is, however, the play between Sections 24 and 25 that reflects the most resolute refusal-recuperation of control on Dante's part. In the former, Dante places the simulacra within the letter of the true and divine text and associates Beatrice with a Christ who is not named. "These ladies [Giovanna alias Primavera, and Beatrice] passed close by me, one of them following the other, and it seemed that Love spoke in my heart and said: 'The one in front is called Primavera . . . meaning she will come first on the day that Beatrice shows herself after the fantasy [*l'imaginazione*] of the faithful (one). [Here too the proper name *Primavera*—Spring—is rendered into the common language as *prima verrà*—"will come first."] And if you will also consider her first [*primo*] name, you will see that this too means *Primavera*, since the name Joan (*Giovanna*) comes from the name of that John (*Giovanni*) who preceded the True Light'" (sec. 24, p. 52; D 110–111).

This is a moment of name-changing, a reminder of similitude and the authority of origins (as in Joan from John) rather than identity. "Love seemed to speak again and say these words: 'Anyone of subtle discernment, by naming Beatrice would name Love [*quella Beatrice chiamarebbe Amore*], because she so greatly resembles me.'"

In Section 25, which immediately follows this magnificent sublation, Dante asserts his own craftsmanly control. He places the figure of Love within the poetic tradition. He has been speaking, he says, of Love as if it were a thing in itself and a bodily substance. This is, of course, patently false. He cites examples from Virgil, Lucan, Horace, and Ovid, and explains that the figure named Love is allowed to exist, here as in any text, through poetic license. There is a further twist of the screw: "The first poet to begin writing in the vernacular was moved to do so by a desire to make his words understandable to ladies who found Latin verses difficult to comprehend" (sec. 25, p. 54–55; D 115). This is an argument against those who compose in the vernacular on a subject other than love, since composition in the vernacular was from the beginning intended for the treatment of love. At one stroke, Love (Master) and women are both brought under control. Some measure of superiority is still granted to the gentlemen's Latin club, for Love speaks to Dante, though not invariably, in Latin. We remember with chagrin that Beatrice's august name had been given in the diminutive ("mona *Bice*" rather than Beatrice) in the previous exalting section.

And indeed, it is in the profession of writing that Dante comes into his own.

The story of *The New Life* is openly declared to be a frame for a collection of poems previously composed, whose priority is, of course, deconstructed by placing it within the book's frame, and so on indefinitely.[15] The truth, or the adequation to truth of the frame narrative is disclosed through the following set: Memory is called a book whose privileged *reader*, though not the writer, is the autobiographer. Yet, we are in his power, for what we read in *La Vita nuova* is merely his own decision as to what is the gist of the pages in the book of Memory. This is the deconstructor's final gesture of retrieval. As author, he almost (though not quite) abdicates his sovereignty. "It is my intention to *copy* into this little book the words *I find written* under that heading [*Incipit vita nova—* the New Life begins]" (p. 3; italics mine; D 33). But the privilege of that *collective* readership is still in effect precariously maintained when textuality is said to extend beyond the bounds of the bound book. The very first poem within Dante's tale, and many of the others, are written for the brotherhood of fellow-writers and the fellow-servants of Love. (In my opening pages, I suggest that a certain use of the slogan "the text deconstructs itself" is an example of this abdication-recuperation topos, whereby the readership is recuperated even as individual sovereignty is disclaimed.)

But even as author, rather than merely as one of many readers, Dante exercises authority. It is of course abundantly clear that he is himself written into the anagogic text, even as Beatrice is put in her place here. Yet without Dante's book in hand, that text cannot be evoked in this instance. Thus, although the business of that higher text and Beatrice remains the first cause, nearly every section of *La Vita nuova* begins with: "moved by this thought I decided to write a few words." In addition, Dante analyzes each of his poems very strictly before or after he cites it, and when he does not, is careful enough to mention that that is only because the poem is obviously clear to all readers. It is not surprising that the book ends with a promise to write further: "I hope to write of her that which has never been written of any other woman." In Dante's text, Beatrice is fully sublated into an object—to be written *of*, not *to*.

And then the woman is promoted yet further. She contemplates the One, but she does not understand him, for his predication is in Latin: *"qui est per omnia secula benedictus."* Thus, finally caught within the history of literary practice—that *entre-deux* between Latin and the vernacular—He is allowed to remain the agent. "And then it may please the One who is the Lord of graciousness that my soul ascend to behold the glory of its lady" (sec. 42, p. 86; D 164).

3.

From such a text does Yeats borrow the title of his poem. What does the title conceal? Yeats's poem breaks into two voices, each the other's accomplice. Once again the self-separation of auto-eroticism, a longing for the self expressed in two ways. I resist here the hermeneutic seduction to show how that is so. Are the two together *Ego*? Does the title describe, rather, the relationship between those two voices, each claiming lordship over the other? Or, is the title descriptive of the theme of the poem—the urge to seek either the self or its opposite. Clearly all this and more.

As a female reader, I am haunted rather by another question: Why are the names of the speakers, *Hic* and *Ille*, in Latin, not a very common thing in Yeats? Is this Yeats's version of Dante's dream? Where then, apart from those two lines in the poem:—"He found the unpersuadable justice, he found / The most exalted lady loved by a man"—is the woman?

There are, as usual, at least two ways of constructing an answer to this question, a long way and, not surprisingly, a short. A long answer would be to say: it is indeed love that is Yeats's lord, but a love as much launched into the symbolic order of literary history—coming via Dante—as God, the true Lord, is at the end of *La Vita nuova*. One could then begin to formulate a feminist-psychoanalytic genealogy of the objectification of beloved (Maud Gonne), patroness (Augusta Gregory), of the Mask and *Anima* as names for that mysterious female "thing" fallen or raised into multiplicity, of all this as a refusal of action, the broaching of an ideology of victimage, disappointment, deception, the slow forging of a defeatist hero over against the folly of collective action, until the foolish and cowardly demos is shown to triumph in the name of comfort and brute loyalty in Yeats's very last poems.

The short way, on the other hand, would be to remember that *"Ego Dominus Tuus"* is the headpiece of a longer prose text, also with a Latin title—*Per Amica Silentia Lunae* ("By the friendly silence of the moon")—its two parts titled in Latin as well—*"Anima Hominis"* (man's soul), *"Anima Mundi"* (world's soul); the whole text framed by two letters to a woman, her name disguised as a masculine name, "Maurice," within quotation marks. These letters are, indeed, "purloined or prolonged," as in Lacan's etymological fantasy in the essay to which I have already referred. I will not pursue that trajectory, for that will lead us back to the long way. I will propose rather that Yeats's technique of allusion—all that Latin is a sort of meta-narrative sign—here allows him to keep the woman out, to occlude, to neutralize, and thus to continue that entire history of the sublation and objectification of the woman.

To keep the woman out. Here the third woman in Yeats's life plays a role. She was caught on the rebound within the institution of marriage, and had a masculine nickname, "Georgie Yeats." She was the transparent medium through which the voices of Yeats's instructors, themselves at first dependent upon his own text, travelled: "On the afternoon of October 24th 1917," Yeats writes in *A Vision*, "four days after my marriage, my wife surprised me by attempting automatic writing. . . . The unknown writer took his theme at first from my just published *Per Amica Silentia Lunae*" (p. 8). We are back to *"Ego Dominus Tuus."* Is it the unknown writer who is Yeats's lord, is it Yeats who is his wife's lord? We are caught in another labyrinth of "I," "you," and mastery.

4.

The entire problematics of the objectification of woman is neutralized, encrypted, dispersed, and thus operated by the allusion in Yeats's title. In Dante, the point was not simply that the image came from outside, but that the image was of an unwilling Beatrice eating the poet's heart. Yeats's poem silently points to that image while ostensibly discoursing on the provenance of poetry.

It is not by chance that *Per Amica Silentia Lunae* is the agent, or non-agent, of *A Vision*. Even the non-Latinist female reader recognizes that the moon in the title is feminine, and remembers, of course, that the moon is Yeats's celebrated sign for subjectivity. This, then, is a subjective text, and the poet is of the moon/ woman's party! I seem almost to lose my argument. I recover it, in part, by pointing out that it is when the moon is silent that the poet speaks. And then I remind myself that Milton's shadow is all over Yeats's work. Milton's blind Samson, absorbed with Delilah as Homer with Helen or Raftery with Mary Hines—all those eyeball-less poets singing of women—sings:

> The Sun to me is dark
> And silent as the Moon,
> When she deserts the night
> Hid in her vacant interlunar cave.
>
> (*Samson Agonistes*, 11. 86–89)

"Vacant" (meaning "vacationing") is almost Latin here, and the silence of the moon, within the outlines of Yeatsian allegory, is anything but friendly, for it is the dark of the moon, close to pure objectivity, when what is not the self takes over.[16] Indeed, the objective sun is inaccessible, "the sun to me is dark." The Miltonic allusion carries a charge which complicates Yeats's "system." It is as if the poet wishes to force a personal "meaning" out of the impersonal truth of "allegory," to operate forcibly in spite of allegorical calculation. In these well-known lines from "The Tower," he repeats the gesture more openly:

> But I have found an answer in those eyes
> That are impatient to be gone;
> Go therefore; but leave Hanrahan,
> For I need all his mighty memories.
>
> ("The Tower," 11. 101–104)

Why should we believe this declaration of "finding," when all that the poet shows himself as manipulating is his own past creation Hanrahan? He must coax the fictive memory of his own creation to produce the desirable answer— not a dismissal but a resignation (that was the point about the benighted in-surrectionists at "Easter 1916" as well— "they resigned their part in the casual comedy"), not a rejection but a conscientious renunciation, not a fulfillment but loss:

> Does the imagination dwell the most
> Upon a woman won or woman lost?
> If on the lost, admit you turned aside
> From a great labyrinth out of pride,
> Cowardice, some silly over-subtle thought
> Or anything called conscience once.

("The Tower," 11. 113–118)

In *Per Amica* as well, it is literary history rather than allegoric system that declares the silence of the moon to be friendly. The phrase is Virgilian, comes from Dante's guide. The Virgilian line is given in full within Yeats's text, in the opening sentence of "Anima Mundi," after an invocation of ruins, broken architraves: "*A Tenedo tacitae per amica silentia lunae*" (*The Aeneid*, II, 255–256).

To read and undo that long problematic sentence in Yeats is another temptation I resist. I ask instead, who came from Tenedos by the friendly silence of the quiet moon? It is a moment of great cunning. The Argives arrive and free the Greeks from the wooden horse. Troy is destroyed. It is this scene of carnage in the name of the transgressing woman as sexual agent that is hidden behind that line. Yet, Helen is mentioned only twice, and incidentally, in the second book of the *Aeneid*. The hero recounts a dream of the mutilated Hector passing the relay to himself, Aeneas. The audience of one is Dido, a "lady in love," dressed in Helen's clothes brought from Aeneas's ship, caught in the in-fighting (moderated by a benign Zeus) between spiteful Juno and Venus; part of the story is a justification (provided by Aeneas's dead wife in yet another dream) for Aeneas's desertion of his wife in the face of the advancing Greek army. Whatever one makes of this *mise-en-scène*, the matter is a transaction between men, on the occasion here of a fallen woman, the harlot queen, as much a stereotype as the virgin mother. It is a transaction from Homer to Virgil to Dante to Milton to Yeats. Fill in the interstices and you have the Great Tradition of European poetry.[17] It is not for nothing that Yeats, allowing textuality though not ostensibly the sovereign author, to triumph, looks for a reader at the end of "*Ego Dominus Tuus*." What had been mere "magical shapes" has become, through the poem, "characters" to be deciphered. The figure of writing passes the relay to a mysterious future reader. And now,

> I call to the mysterious one who yet
> . . . standing by these characters, disclose[s]
> All that I seek; and whisper it as though
> He were afraid the birds, who cry aloud
> Their momentary cries before it is dawn,
> Would carry it away to blasphemous men.

Like Dante or Poe's Minister, Yeats makes himself passive, "feminizes" himself. It is clearer at the end of *Per Amica* where Yeats writes, "I wonder will I take to them [my 'barbarous words'] once more, for I am baffled by those voices . . . or now that I shall in a little be growing old, to some kind of simple piety like that of an old woman" (p. 366).

5.

What have I performed here? Tried to read two versions of the in-built exploitation of the figure of the woman in two autobiographical and self-deconstructive texts. What, then, must a woman do with the reactionary sexual ideology of high art? It is not enough to substitute "low" for "high," and perpetrate an ideology of complacent rejectionism, or an academic populist reverse sexism. On the other hand, it is also not enough to search mightily for a way of conserving and excusing the canon at all costs.

Is this dilemma itself symptomatic of the fear of the risks that all great changes might involve? Must one simply honor the breach between "the field of action" and "the field of art" and function by means of an ever-abreactive historical analysis, and try to undo deliberately structures of fear, desire, and pleasure that, even if metaleptic, are beyond one's control? Whatever the program might be, it involves at least a decision to re-read, "as a feminist." I am helpless before the fact that all my essays these days seem to end with projects for future work.[18] I seem to be surrendered to the Great Tradition in closing my piece with a promise.

6.

Here ends the paper written in haste for a class deadline with a collective purpose out of a feminist anguish with academic deconstructive practice. Since then I have read it four times for money, once for an interview, once at a conference, once at a women's lunch. This is not to make a romantic disclaimer against what minimal effectiveness the essay might have. This is simply to echo wearily that old pedantic sentiment: "to make changes would have been too drastic; I have let it stand as it was."

I *would* like to touch, however, in a formal if not a substantive way, a few of the unanswered questions left in the earlier paper. For example: Why are the traditions and conventions of art so brutally sexist? Here an immense work of genealogical investigation awaits us. Unfortunately, traditional positivistic historical (or herstorical) work of documentation and restoration remains caught in an ideology of cause and effect which catches us on the rebound into self-congratulation and cannot touch those metaleptic ruses of psycho-social structuring that represent themselves as the rigorous infallibility of that very historical method. [The dictionary meaning of "metalepsis" is "the substitution by metonymy of one figurative sense for another." Following Marx (the argument from fetishization, the money-form, and ideology), Nietzsche (the argument from genealogy and the true-false fiction), Freud (the argument from the unconscious and irreducible distortion [*Enstellung*]), and Heidegger (the argument from secondary dissembling and the double withdrawal), the post-structuralist tendency (Lacan, the later Barthes, Foucault, Deleuze and Guattari, Derrida) would present "cause" and "effect" as two such "figures." Thus the substitution of "effect" for "cause" which is one of the chief abuses of history would become a special case of metalepsis.] The present essay is a brief analysis of the discursive practice of two "literary" texts, an analysis permitted at least formally by the definition of the field of "literary criticism." The task is to analyze the discursive practice of "documentary" texts, and not merely from the point of view of the dominant "trope" or "rhetorical figure." (That would be to privilege the permissive discipline of "literary criticism" and thus neutralize genealogical analysis.) The task is to mark, rather, how "discursive practices are characterized by the delimitation of a field of objects, the definition of a legitimate perspective for the agent of knowledge, and the fixing of norms for the elaboration of concepts and theories."[19] And to avoid the quick citing of slogans (as in the comment from the audience at the feminist symposium) that will cut off such "nonliterary" analyses, the following might be remembered: "The movements of deconstruction [or genealogical analysis] do not destroy structures from the outside. They are not possible and effective, nor can they take accurate aim, except by inhabiting those structures. . . . Operating necessarily from the inside, borrowing them structurally, that is to say without being able to isolate their elements and atoms, the enterprise of deconstruction always in a certain way falls prey to its own work."[20] (In *Glas* Derrida undertakes such a *complicit* genealogical analysis of the history of philosophy.) If all analysis is a shoring up of a self in the midst of the irreducible and originary ruins of being, it seems necessary to acknowledge that analyzing, we borrow structures from that which we analyze, that the limits of judging can only be given in a judgment.

I had also not shown how *Hic* and *Ille*, the two choices of Yeats's poem, are each other's accomplice. Ezra Pound caught it in a jest when he called them *Hic* and *Willie*.[21] Here is a brief blueprint: *Hic* has arrived at *Ille's* "summons"—he is what *Ille* wants (11. 7–10). Looking for the real face rather than a mask-image, *Hic* describes Dante as if Dante had made a mask: "he has made that hollow face of his / More plain to the mind's eye" (11. 21–22). *Ille* grants that original face as the place of the hunger that motivates the making of the stone image that *Ille* then presents as Dante's face:

> And did he find himself
> Or was the hunger that had made it hollow
> A hunger for the apple on the bough . . .

> (11. 23–25)

What then, one might ask, is the difference between the psychological status— this being a poem about the artist's psychology—of Dante's stone image and Keats's luxurious song? *Ille* does not deny *Hic* that Keats looked for happiness, but only that he found it. But *Hic* had already taken care of it in his adjective "deliberate" (1. 54). All these slidings and blurrings of the two positions are kept at bay by the authority of the sententious binary opposition:

> The rhetorician would deceive his neighbours,
> The sentimentalist himself; while art
> Is but a vision of reality.
>
> (11. 47–49)

The final lines of the poem, like lines 7–10, can in principle be a description of *Hic*, in which case the aura of mystery is dramatic irony against the pompous *Ille*, as the aura of oppositions in the poem might be dramatic irony against the reader. Pound's mistake, if that is what it was, had been to take this duplicitous complexity for a mere failure of logic. Ours would be to take this labyrinth of self-deconstruction to be free of the charge that "communicates" the topos of the artist's negative capability at the expense of the repression or occlusion of the woman.

I shall end with the exquisitely orchestrated sentence in *Per Amica* that delivers *A Tenedo tacitae per amica silentia lunae*:

> I have always sought to bring my mind close to the mind of Indian and Japanese poets, old women in Connacht, mediums in Soho, lay brothers whom I imagine dreaming in some mediaeval monastery the dreams of their village, learned authors who refer all to antiquity; to immerse it in the general mind where that mind is scarce separable from what we have begun to call "the subconscious"; to liberate it from all that comes of councils and committees, from the world as it is seen from universities or from populous towns; and that I might so believe I have murmured evocations and frequented mediums, delighted in all that displayed great problems through sensuous images or exciting phrases, accepted from abstract schools but a few technical words that are so old they seem but broken architraves fallen amid bramble and grass, and have put myself to school where all things are seen: *A Tenedo tacitae per amica silentia lunae*. (p. 343)

This attempt at reading will bring me back to some working hypotheses submitted at the opening of this essay: there remains the articulated specificity of the "somethings" that the text might mean, and with which it ruses. These are the "minimal idealizations" which constitute the possibility of reading. Within a shifting and abyssal frame, these idealizations and things are the "material" to which we as readers, with our own elusive historico-politico-economico-sexual determinations, bring the machinery of our reading and our judgment. The machinery is to look for identities and differences—to make connections. To choose not to read is to legitimate reading, and to read no more than allegories of unreadability is to ignore the heterogeneity of the "material."

Yeats's sentence states a program, but obstacles are placed, in a mood of self-deconstruction, between the subject and his action. The program is, through making oneself passive, to pass from a limited *anima* to a general. The allusive metaphor chosen to describe the program is that stealthy entry into Troy.

One might say that, by this passively enhanced activity fabricated to get in touch with *Anima Mundi*—"the most exalted lady in creation"—, Yeats hopes to undo the harm that the language of abstraction and technique have done to the mind. He will, however, use that language, even if minimally and guarded with the "[nothing] but" construction—a little abstraction, "a few technical words . . . so old" (although "the subconscious" will hardly fill this bill)—"naturalize" it through an invocation of time's tyranny and a metaphor of ruins among brambles. Yet those old words only "seem" broken architraves, just as the wooden horse *seemed* innocent. We are free to imagine that Yeats dreams of making them the chief beam (arch + trave) of an edifice associated with the goal of all abstraction and technique: writing, "where all things are *seen*," *A Vision* between covers.

It must be emphasized that Yeats's sentence is a deliberate search for the areas of the mind thought to be almost beyond deliberation. "I have sought to bring my mind close to [certain kinds of mind], to immerse it [my mind] in the general mind where that mind [we know the antecedent, but in this masterfully clumsy prose the 'it' and the 'that' begin a subtextual exchange, 'my mind' usurping 'general mind' and vice versa] *is scarce separable* from what we have begun to call 'the subconscious'" (italics mine). Indeed, the sentence moves toward *increased* deliberation. From an image of ideal others (within the larger movement, the predication of these others rises in rank from racial, sex-class-based, heterodox-professional qualities of mind; to trained and truant dreaming; to learned reference) to delight in chosen kinds of art to a judicious choice of language culminating, precisely, in a learned reference. What interests me specifically is that in Yeats's language, chosen from what is millenially available, the *anima*, end and means of the program, is elaborated into figures of woman; and that the historical signal, in Latin, and indirectly commanded by Dante, is that particular Virgilian-Homeric line.

1980

3. Unmaking and Making in *To The Lighthouse*

This essay is not necessarily an attempt to illuminate *To the Lighthouse* and lead us to a correct reading. It is rather an attempt to use the book by the deliberate superimposition of two allegories—grammatical and sexual—and by reading it, at moments, as autobiography. This modest attempt at understanding criticism not merely as a theoretical approach to the "truth" of a text, but at the same time as a practical enterprise that produces a reading is part of a much larger polemic.* I introduce *To the Lighthouse* into this polemic by reading it as the story of Mr. Ramsay (philosopher-theorist) and Lily (artist-practitioner) around Mrs. Ramsay (text).

Virginia Woolf's *To the Lighthouse* can be read as a project to catch the essence of Mrs. Ramsay. A certain reading of the book would show how the project is undermined; another, how it is articulated. I will suggest that the undermining, although more philosophically adventurous, is set aside by Woolf's book; that the articulation is found to be a more absorbing pursuit.

On a certain level of generality the project to catch the essence of Mrs. Ramsay is articulated in terms of finding an adequate language. The first part of the book ("The Window") looks at the language of marriage: is Mrs. Ramsay's "reality" to be found there? The third part of the book ("The Lighthouse") uncovers the language of art: Lily catches Mrs. Ramsay in her painting. Or at least, a gesture on the canvas is implicitly given as a representation of a possible vision (implicitly of Mrs. Ramsay or the picture itself):

> With a sudden intensity, as if she saw it clear for a second, she drew a line there, in the centre. It was done; it was finished. Yes, she thought, laying down her brush in extreme fatigue, I have had my vision.[1]

The second part of the book couples or hinges I and III. In Part I, Mrs. Ramsay is, in the grammatical sense, the subject. In Part III, the painting predicates her.* I could make a grammatical allegory of the structure of the book: Subject (Mrs. Ramsay)—copula—Predicate (painting). That would be the structure of the

---

* The simplest articulation of the polemic, which "starts" with Martin Heidegger's approach to the tradition of philosophy, is still Jacques Derrida's Of Grammatology (Baltimore: Johns Hopkins University Press, 1976), pp. 157–64. I have tried to follow Derrida's suggestion regarding productive or "forced" readings in my piece (in preparation) "Marx after Derrida."
* This sort of allegorical fancy should of course not be confused with the "narrative typology" outlined in Tzvetan Todorov, "Narrative Transformations," The Poetics of Prose, trans. Richard Howard (Ithaca: Cornell University Press, 1977), pp. 218–33. Todorov indicates in that essay the precursors of his own approach.

proposition, the irreducible form of the logic of non-contradiction, the simplest and most powerful sentence. Within this allegory, the second part of the book is the place of the copula. That too yields a suggestive metaphor. For the copula is not only the pivot of grammar and logic, the axle of ideal language, the third person singular indicative of "to be"; it also carries a sexual charge. "Copulation" happens not only in language and logic, but also between persons. The metaphor of the copula embraces Mr. Ramsay both ways. As the custodian of the logical proposition ("If Q is Q, then R . . ."), he traffics in the copula; and, as father and husband, he is the custodian of copulation. Lily seeks to catch Mrs. Ramsay with a different kind of copula, a different bridge to predication, a different language of "Being," the language not of philosophy, but of art. Mr. Ramsay has seemingly caught her in the copula of marriage.

A certain rivalry and partnership develop between Lily and Mr. Ramsay in Part III. But this rivalry and partnership do not account for Part II, where the search for a language seems strangely unattached to a character or characters. One is tempted to say, this is the novel's voice, or, here is Woolf. I will suggest that, in this strange section, the customary division between work and life is itself vague, that the language sought here is the language of madness.

Within the grammatical allegory of the structure of the book, it would run thus: the strongest bond, the copula in the proposition, the bastion of language, the place of the "is," is almost uncoupled in the coupling part of *To the Lighthouse*. How does that disarticulation and undermining take its place within the articulation of the project to catch the essence of Mrs. Ramsay in an adequate language?

1. The Window

The language of marriage seems a refusal of "good" language, if a good language is that which brings about communication. When she speaks, Mrs. Ramsay speaks the "fallen" language of a civility that covers over the harshness of interpersonal relations. (The most successful—silent—communication between herself and her husband is to deflect his fury at Mr. Carmichael's request for a second helping of soup!) When she and Mr. Ramsay speak to each other or read together, their paths do not cross. She knows marriage brings trouble, yet, when she speaks of marriage, it is with complete and prophetic optimism. Her own privileged moments are when words break down, when silence encroaches, or when the inanimate world reflects her. In the end she turns her refusal of discourse into an exclamation of triumph, the epitome, in this book, of a successful con-jugal (copulative) relationship.

All of section twelve presents conjugal non-communication with a light touch. I quote two moments: "All this phrase-making was a game, she thought, for if she had said half what he said, she would have blown her brains out by now" (106). "And,"

> looking up, she saw above the thin trees the first pulse of the full-throbbing star, and wanted to make her husband look at it; for the sight gave her

such keen pleasure. But she stopped herself. He never looked at things. If he did, all he would say would be, Poor little world, with one of his sighs. At that moment, he said, "Very fine," to please her, and pretended to admire the flowers. But she knew quite well that he did not admire them, or even realize that they were there (108).

If I were reading the relationship between her knowledge and her power, I would remark here on her matchmaking, or her manipulation of men through deliberate self-suppression. But I am interested only in establishing that she relies little on language, especially language in marriage. Her privileged moments (a privilege that is often nothing but terror), are when words disappear, or when the inanimate world reflects her. One such terrifying moment of privilege is when the men cease talking and the sea's soothing song stops:

> The gruff murmur, . . . which had kept on assuring her, though she could not hear what was said . . . that the men were happily talking; this sound, which had . . . taken its place soothingly in the scale of sounds pressing on top of her . . . had ceased; so that the monotonous fall of the waves on the beach, which for the most part . . . seemed consolingly to repeat over and over again as she sat with the children the words of some old cradle song . . . but at other times . . . had no such kindly meaning, but like a ghostly roll of drums remorselessly beat the measure of life. . . .— this sound which had been obscured and concealed under the other sounds suddenly thundered hollow in her ears and made her look up with an impulse of terror.
> They had ceased to talk: that was the explanation (27–28).

Why should language be an ally for her, or promise any adequation to her selfhood? Her discourse with "life," her "old antagonist"—her "parleying" (92)—though not shared with anyone, is "for the most part" a bitterly hostile exchange. Her sexuality the stage for action between son and husband, does not allow her more than the most marginal instrument and energy of self-signification: "There was scarcely a shell of herself left for her to know herself by; all was so lavished and spent; and James, as he stood stiff between her knees, felt her rise in a rosy-flowered fruit tree laid with leaves and dancing boughs into which the beak of brass, the arid scimitar of his father, the egotistical man, plunged and smote, demanding sympathy" (60). It is not surprising that, when she feels free (both to "go" and "rest"), "life sank down for a moment," and not only language, but personality and selfhood were lost: "This core of darkness could go anywhere. . . . Not as oneself did one find rest ever . . . but as a wedge of darkness losing personality . . ." (96).

Any dream-dictionary would tell us that knitting stands for masturbation. A text-dictionary would alert us that one knits a *web*, which is a text. Woolf uses the image of Mrs. Ramsay's knitting (an auto-erotic textuality) strategically. It may represent a reflexive act, a discursivity. It emphasizes the second kind of privileged moment that is Mrs. Ramsay's secret: when she leans toward inanimate things, which reflect her. The structure of that reflection is indeed that of sexual intercourse (copulation) and of self-mirroring in the other. Within that structure, however, she is, in this last move, the object not the subject, the other not the self. The moment of self-privilege is now its own preservative yielding to the world of things.

Imagining herself as a wedge of darkness, she "looked out to meet that stroke of the *Lighthouse*, the long steady stroke, the last of the three, which was her stroke" (96). I must think of "stroke" as the predicate, the last stroke in the three-stroke sentence (S is P) of the house of light, which, as any dictionary of symbols will tell us, is the house of knowledge or philosophy. If Mrs. Ramsay recognizes her own mark in being predicated rather than in subjectivity, she is still caught within copulation. As Woolf knits into her text the image of a suspended knitting she moves us, through the near-identification ("like," "in a sense") of mirroring, to deliver a satisfying image of the threshold of copulation ("a bride to meet her lover"):

> She looked up over her knitting and met the third stroke and it seemed to her like her own eyes meeting her own eyes. . . . It was odd, she thought, how if one was alone, one leant to inanimate things; trees, streams, flowers; felt they expressed one; felt they became one; felt they knew one, in a sense were one. . . . There rose, and she looked and looked with her needles suspended, there curled up off the floor of the mind, rose from the lake of one's being, a mist, a bride to meet her lover (97–98).

"One" can be both "identity" (the word for the unit), and "difference" (an impersonal agent, not she herself); "in a sense" might be understood both "idiomatically" and "literally" (meaning "within a meaning").

But these are not the last words on Mrs. Ramsay in "The Window." Mostly she remains the protector (13), the manager (14), the imperialist governor of men's sterility (126). At the end of her section she mingles charmingly, as women will, the notions of love, beauty in the eye of the male beholder, and power. By refusing to *say* "I love you," she has taken away his power to deny it; by saying "you were right," she has triumphed:

> She never could say what she felt. . . . He was watching her. She knew what he was thinking. You are more beautiful than ever. And she felt herself very beautiful. . . . She began to smile, for though she had not said a word, he knew, of course he knew, that she loved him. . . .
> "Yes, you were right." . . . And she looked at him smiling. For she had triumphed again. She had not said it: Yet he knew (186).

And what of the language of academic philosophy, Mr. Ramsay's tool for making a connection between subject and predicate? Words come easily to him. Woolf shows him to us as he plans a lecture (67). He assimilates the leaves of the trees into leaves of paper: "Seeing again the . . . geraniums which had so often decorated processes of thought, and bore, written up among their leaves, as if they were scraps of paper on which one scribbles notes in the rush of reading . . ." (66). And he finds them dispensable: "He picked a leaf sharply. . . . He threw away the leaf" (67).

The most celebrated formulation of Mr. Ramsay is through the image of the keyboard-alphabet. Here is the traditional copular proposition in the service of the logic of identity and geometrical proof: If Q is Q, then R is. . . .*

"For if thought is like the keyboard of a piano, "—is it? never mind, this is the exclusivist move, taking for granted a prior proposition, that lets the copula play—" divided into so many notes, or like the alphabet is ranged in twenty-six letters all in order, then his splendid mind had no sort of difficulty in running over those letters one by one . . . until it had reached, say, the letter A." Q is an interesting letter, starting "questions," "quid," "quod," "quantity," "quality," and of course, "q.e.d." "Q he could demonstrate. If Q then is Q—R—. . . 'Then R . . .'" (54).

"But after Q? What comes next?" After the discourse of demonstration, the language of "q," comes the discourse of desire. If only he could reach R! Could identify the place in thought with the initial letter of his own name, his father's name, and his son's! If Mrs. Ramsay repeatedly endorses the copulation of marriage—as in the case of the Rayleys—for the sake of a materialist genealogy, Mr. Ramsay would exploit the copulation of philosophy for the sake of paternalistic appropriation.* But the Rayleys' marriage comes to nothing, and Mr. Ramsay is convinced "he would never reach R" (55).

2. Time Passes

I do not know how to read a roman à clef, especially an autobiographical one. I do not know how to insert Woolf's life into the text of her book. Yet there is a case to be made here. I will present the material of a possible biographical

---

* It is not insignificant that he draws strength for his splendid burst of thinking from a glance at that safe symbol, his wife-and-child as a functioning unit: "Without his distinguishing either his son or his wife, the sight of them fortified him and satisfied him and consecrated his effort to arrive at a perfectly clear understanding of the problem which now engaged the energies of his splendid mind" (53).

* Here are bits of Mrs. Ramsay's maternalistic endorsement of marriage. "Divining, through her own past, some deep, some buried, some quite speechless feeling that one had for one's mother at Rose's age" (123). "All this would be revived again in the lives of Paul and Minta; 'the Rayleys'— she tried the new name over. . . . It was all one stream. . . . Paul and Minta would carry it on when she was dead" (170–71). As for Mr. Ramsay's enterprise, the irony is sharpened if we remind ourselves that Virginia Stephen's father was engaged in compiling The Dictionary of National Biography.

speculation, adumbrate a relationship between life and book that I cannot theoretically present, consider the case made, and give a certain reading.

Since the printing date inside the cover of *To the Lighthouse* is 1927, it seems clear that the war in "Time Passes" is the Great War of 1914–1918. The somewhat enigmatic sentence that begins its last section is, "then indeed peace had come" (213). Lily, the time-keeper of the book, tells us that the events of "The Window" were "ten years ago [in 1908]." Shortly thereafter, Mrs. Ramsay "died rather suddenly" (194).

The Stephen family (the "real" Ramsays) had visited Talland House in St. Ives (the "real" location of *To the Lighthouse*) for the last time in 1894. Julia Stephen (the "real" Mrs. Ramsay, Virginia Woolf's mother) died in 1895. In a certain sense, "Time Passes" compresses 1894–1918—from Mrs. Stephen's death to the end of the war.

For Woolf those years were marked by madness. She broke down after her mother's death in 1895, after her father's death in 1904, once again in 1910, briefly in 1912, lingeringly in 1913, most violently in 1915 (as "Time Passes" ostensibly begins). From 1917 on, there was a period of continued lucidity. In 1919 (as "Time Passes" ostensibly ends) *Night and Day* was published. In the next section, I will argue that it is significant that *Night and Day* is "about" her painter-sister Vanessa Bell.

I should like to propose that, whatever her writing intent, "Time Passes" narrates the production of a discourse of madness within this autobiographical roman à clef. In the place of the copula or the hinge in the book a story of unhinging is told.

Perhaps this unhinging or "desecrating" was not unsuspected by Woolf herself. One is invited to interpret the curious surface of writing of Virginia Stephen's 1899 diary as a desecration of the right use of reason. It was written in "a minute, spidery, often virtually illegible hand, which she made more difficult to read by gluing her pages on to or between Dr. Isaac Watt's *Logick/or/the right use of Reason/with a variety of rules to guard against error in the affairs of religion and human life as well as in the sciences*. . . . Virginia bought this in St. Ives for its binding and its format: "'Any other book, almost, would have been too sacred to undergo the desecration that I planned.'"[2]

At the beginning of "Time Passes," the sense of a house as the dwelling-place of reason and of light as the sign of reason are firmly implied. It is within this framework that "certain airs" and an "immense darkness" begin to descend (189, 190). Human agency is attenuated as the house is denuded of human occupancy. "There was scarcely anything left of body or mind by which one could say, 'This is he' or 'This is she.' Sometimes a hand was raised as if to clutch something or ward off something, or somebody laughed aloud as if sharing a joke with nothingness. . . . Almost one might imagine them" (190). The soothing power of Mrs. Ramsay's civilized language is wearing away into indifference. The disintegration of the house is given through the loosening of the shawl she had wrapped around the death's head: "With a roar, with a rupture, as after centuries of quiescence, a rock rends itself from the mountain and hurtles crashing into the valley, one fold of the shawl loosened and swung to and fro" (195–96).

(The covering of the death's head by the shawl in "The Window" is a marvelous deceptive deployment of undecidability. Cam, the girl-child, must be reminded of the animal skull; James, the male child, not; Mrs. Ramsay covers it, draws Cam's attention to what is under, and James's to what is over, and puts them to sleep by weaving a fabulous tale.)

There are glimpses of the possibility of an accession to truth in this curiously dismembered scene; but at the same time, a *personal* access is denied:

> It seemed now as if, touched by human penitence and all its toil, divine goodness had parted the curtain and displayed behind it, single, distinct, the hare erect; the wave falling; the boat rocking, which, did we deserve them, should be ours always. But alas, divine goodness twitching the cord, draws the curtain; it does not please him; he covers his treasures in a drench of hail, and so breaks them, so confuses them that it seems impossible that their calm should ever return, or that we should ever compose from their fragments a perfect whole or read in the littered pieces the clear words of truth (192–93).

I cannot account for, but merely record that strange twinge of guilt: "it does not please him." The guardian of the truth behind the veil is no longer the beautiful but lying mother; it is rather the good God-father, for "divine goodness" is a "he" and he "covers his treasures," hides his genitals, in what would customarily be a "feminine" gesture. This sexual shift—for the author of *To the Lighthouse* is a woman—also indicates a denial of access. The next bit of writing about a vision of truth is given as "imaginations of the strangest kind—of flesh turned to atoms." Man and woman are rendered to "gull, flower, tree, . . . and the white earth itself" (199). "Cliff, sea, cloud, and sky" must "assemble outwardly the scattered parts of the vision within" (198). Human agency is now dispensable. And access to truth is still denied. For "if questioned," the universe seemed "at once to withdraw."

In another move within the same paragraph, "the absolute good" is seen as "something alien to the processes of domestic life," processes that would, in the manner of Mrs. Ramsay, keep the house of reason in order. Through a silent gap between two sentences, Woolf brings us back to those domestic processes, as if to ward off the menace of madness at any price. By way of a logically unacceptable "moreover," "the spring," one of the agents in the outer world, constitutes a domestic and feminine image recalling not only Mrs. Ramsay but pointing genealogically, in the next sentence, to her daughter Prue. Yet here too, only the dark side of domesticity may be seen: "Prue died that summer in some illness connected with childbirth" (199).

Earlier in that paragraph "the minds of men" are called "those mirrors . . . those pools of uneasy water." And indeed, as human agency is turned down, light begins a narcissistic troping that produces an extra-human text: "Now, day after day, light turned, like a flower reflected in water, its sharp image on the wall opposite" (194). Mrs. Ramsay's shawl is changed into a silent writing that envelops sound: "The swaying mantle of silence which, week after week in the empty room, wove into the falling cries of birds, ships hooting, the drone and hum of the fields, a dog's bark, a man's shout, and folded them round the house in silence" (195). "The empty rooms seemed to murmur with the echoes of the fields and the hum of the flies . . . the sun so striped and barred the rooms" (200).

The last image brings us back to the vague imagery of guilt and torture, a humanity-excluding tone that is also heard when the narcissism of light and nature turns to masturbation: "The nights now are full of wind and destruction. . . . Also the sea tosses itself ['tossing off' is English slang for masturbation], and should any sleeper fancying that he might find on the beach an answer to his doubts, a sharer of his solitude, throw off his bed-clothes and go down by himself to walk on the sand, no image with semblance of serving and divine promptitude comes readily to hand bringing the night to order and making the world reflect the compass of his soul" (193). Nature is occupied with itself and cannot provide a mirror or a companion for the human seeker of the copula, the word that binds.

It is the War that brings this narrative of estrangement to its full destructive potential: "Did Nature supplement what man advanced? . . . With equal complacence she saw his misery, his meanness, and his torture. That dream, of sharing, completing, of finding in solitude on the beach an answer, was then but a reflection in a mirror, and the mirror itself was but the surface glassiness which forms in quiescence when the nobler powers sleep beneath? . . . to pace the beach was impossible; contemplation was unendurable" (201–2).

Before this large-scale estrangement, there was some possibility of truth in the never-fulfilled always troping and uncoupling narcissism of the light, and in the bodiless hand clasp of loveliness and stillness with their "*scarcely disturbed . . . indifference*" and their "*air of pure integrity*" (195). There was comfort in the vouchsafing of an answer (however witless) to the questions of subject and object: "The mystic, the visionary, walking the beach on a fine night . . . asking themselves 'What am I,' 'What is this?' had suddenly an answer vouchsafed them, (*they could not say what it was*) so that they were warm in the frost and had comfort in the desert" (197–98; italics are mine).

Indeed, "Time Passes" as a whole does not narrate a full encroachment of the discourse of madness. Even in the passage that describes what I call a large-scale estrangement, there is a minute trace of comfort, hardly endorsed by the author. It is perhaps marked in the double-edged fact that in this woman's book, complacent and uncooperating nature is feminine, and she shares with the human mind the image of the mirroring surface. In the following passage, however, the absence of a copula between "nature" and "mind," leading to a lustful wantonness of blind copulation cum auto-eroticism, seems the very picture of madness rampant:

Listening (had there been any one to listen) from the upper rooms of the empty house only gigantic chaos streaked with lightning could have been heard tumbling and tossing, as the winds and waves disported themselves like amorphous bulks of leviathans whose brows are pierced by no light of reason, and mounted one on top of another, and lunged and plunged in the darkness of daylight (for night and day, month and year ran shapelessly together) in idiot games, until it seemed as if the universe were battling and tumbling, in brute confusion and wanton lust aimlessly by itself. . . . The stillness and the brightness of the day were as strange as the chaos and the tumult of night, with the trees standing there, looking up, yet beholding nothing. The mirror was broken (202–3).

The disappearance of reason and the confusion of sexuality are consistently linked: "Let the poppy seed itself and the carnation mate with the cabbage" (208). Now all seems lost. "For now had come that moment, that hesitation when the dawn trembles and night passes, when if a feather alight in the scale it will be weighed down . . . the whole house . . . to the depths to lie upon the sands of oblivion" (208–9).

But the feather does not fall. For in the long "wanton lust" passage it is a coupling that only *seems* onanistic. The differentiation of night and day, if almost obliterated (itself a possible copulation—night is day is night is day), is restored in the last image of the eyeless trees. Further, the *possibility* of a perspective from "the *upper rooms* of the empty house" of reason is broached. And Mrs. McNab the charwoman is allowed the hint of a power to recuperate the mirror. She stands in front of the looking glass, but we are not sure she contemplates her image. The copula is uncertain. Does she say "I *am* I [my image]," as Narcissus said *iste ego sum*? All we have is a parenthesis: "(she stood arms akimbo in front of the looking glass)" [203].

Thus Mrs. McNab halts disaster in the allegory of a reason menaced by madness, an ontology on the brink of disaster by the near-uncoupling of the copula. She is related to "a force working; something not highly conscious" (209). Once again, the copula between her and this description is not given. They simply inhabit contiguous sentences.

The house is rehabilitated and peace comes as "Time Passes" comes to an end. But the coupling between "Window" and "Lighthouse" (or the predication of Mrs. Ramsay's "is-ness") remains open to doubt. When "the voice of the beauty of the world" now entreats the sleepers to come down to the beach, we know that there are times of violence when a sleeper may entreat and be brutally refused. And indeed the voice murmurs "too softly to hear what it said—but what mattered if the meaning were plain?" (213). Is it? Woolf does not make clear what the "this" is in that further entreaty the voice "might resume": "why not accept this, be content with this, acquiesce and resign?" (214). We are free to say that "this" is the limits of language.

3. The Lighthouse

In the third section Woolf presents the elaborate story of the acquisition of a vision of art. We must compare this to the affectionately contemptuous and brief description of Mr. Ramsay preparing his lecture. Lily would create the copula through art, predicate Mrs. Ramsay in a painting rather than a sentence. Before reading that story, I must once again present certain halting conclusions that would link life and book.

It seems clear to every reader that "Virginia Woolf" is both Cam and Lily Briscoe. In Cam at seven, as in "The Window," she might see, very loosely speaking, a kind of pre-Oedipal girlhood: "I think a good deal about . . . how I was a nice little girl here [at St. Ives]. . . . Do you like yourself as a child? I like myself, before the age of 10, that is—before consciousness sets in."[3] Cam is tied up with James (as Shakespeare with Shakespeare's sister in *A Room of One's Own*), a shadow-portrait of Virginia's brothers Thoby and Adrian. *Together* Cam-James go through an Oedipal scene that involves both father *and* mother as givers of law and language, and thus they allow Virginia Woolf to question the orthodox masculinist psychoanalytic position.* But that is not my subject here. I must fix my glance on Lily.

Lily is the same age (43) as Woolf when she began *To the Lighthouse*. Lily has just gone through the gestatory ten years taken over by "Time Passes," and Woolf has a special feeling for decades:

> Every 10 years, at 20, again at 30, such agony of different sorts possessed me that not content with rambling and reading I did most emphatically attempt to end it all. . . . Every ten years brings, I suppose, one of those private orientations which match the vast one which is, to my mind, general now in the race. I mean life has to be faced: to be rejected; then accepted on new terms with rapture. And so on, and so on; till you are 40, when the only problem is to grasp it tighter and tighter to you, so quick it seems to slip, and so infinitely desirable is it. (L II.598–99)

But Lily is a painter. She "is" also Virginia's artist-sister Vanessa Bell. There is that curious incident between Lily and Mr. Ramsay, where, "in complete silence she stood there, grasping her paintbrush" (228). It is a situation often repeated between Vanessa and Leslie Stephen.[4] There is also the fact that this book is the laying of a mother's ghost, and it is to Vanessa that Virginia directs the question: "Why did you bring me into the world to go through these ordeals?" (L II.458).

Lily begins or finishes her painting just after "peace had come." At the "actual" time of the Armistice, Virginia was finishing a book about Vanessa: "The guns have been going off for half an hour, and the sirens whistling; so I suppose we are at peace. . . . How am I to write my last chapter in all this shindy? . . . I don't suppose I've ever enjoyed any writing so much as I did the last half of *Night and Day* . . . Try thinking of Katharine [the heroine] as Vanessa, not me"

---

* *The references to Freud are elaborated in my discussion of Luce Irigaray's reading of Freud's "Femininity" later in this essay.*

(L II.290, 295, 400). Lily, as she is conceived, could thus be both artist (Virginia) and material (Vanessa), an attempted copula ("the artist *is* her work") that must forever be broken in order that the artist survive.

If I knew how to manipulate erotic textuality, I should read the incredible charge of passion in the long letters to Vanessa, addressed to "Dearest," "Beloved," "Dolphin." Is it too crude to say that the sane, many-lovered, fecund Vanessa was a kind of ideal other for Virginia? She wrote that she wanted to confuse the maternity of Vanessa's daughter. And there are innumerable letters where she asks Vanessa's husband, Clive Bell, or her lover Duncan Grant, to caress the beloved vicariously for her. I quote one of those many entreaties: "Kiss her, most passionately, in all my private places—neck—, and arm, and eyeball, and tell her—what new thing is there to tell her? How fond I am of her husband?" (L I. 325). If indeed Lily, Mr. Ramsay's contender and Mrs. Ramsay's scribe, is the name of Vanessa-Virginia, only the simplest genitalist view of sexuality would call her conception androgynous. But, as I must continue to repeat, I cannot develop that argument.

Let us talk instead of Lily's medium: it is writing and painting. Always with reference to Vanessa, Virginia wonders at the relationship between the two: "How strange it is to be a painter! They scarcely think; feelings come only every other minute. But then they are profound and inexpressible, tell Nessa" (L H. 541). And in the book: "If only she could . . . write them out in some sentence, then she would have got at the truth of things. . . . She had never finished that picture. She would finish that picture now" (219–20). "Her mind kept throwing up from its depths, scenes, and names, and sayings . . . over that glaring, hideously difficult white space, while she modelled it with greens and blues" (238). "How could one express in words these emotions of the body? . . . Suddenly, . . . the white wave and whisper of the garden become like curves and arabesques flourishing round a centre of complete emptiness" (266). A script, half design, half word, combining words and picturing, getting at the truth of things, expressing the body's feelings, this is Lily's desired "discourse." "But what she wished to get hold of was that very jar on the nerves, the thing itself before it had been made anything" (287). Woolf's language, or Lily's, like all language, cannot keep these goals seamless and unified. It is the truth *of* things, the feelings *of* the body, and, as we can easily say since Derrida, "any" is always already inscribed in "the thing" for it to be open to being "made anything."* So she too, like the philosopher, must search for a copula, for her goal, however conceived, also splits into two. In a most enigmatic wish, perhaps she wishes beauty to be self-identical, as Q *is* Q: "Beauty would *roll itself up*; the space would fill" (268; italics are mine). She wants to bridge a gap and make a sphere, not merely by a love of learning (philosophy) but a love of play, or a play of love: "There might be lovers whose gift it was to choose out the elements of things and place them together and so, giving them a wholeness not theirs in life, make of some

---

* *I am referring to the idea of supplementarity. Derrida has suggested that, if a hierarchical opposition is set up between two concepts, the less favored or logically posterior concept can be shown to be implicit in the other, supply a lack in the other that was always already there. See "The Supplement of the Copula," Tr. James Creech and Josué Harari,* Georgia Review 30 *(Fall 1976):527–64.*

scene, or meeting of people (all now gone and separate), one of those globed compacted things over which thought lingers, and love plays" (286). Perhaps she wants to erase "perhaps" and make first and last coincide: "Everything this morning was happening for the first time, perhaps for the last time" (288).

She grasps at two "visions" that ostensibly provide a copula, a bridge between and beyond things. The first: "One glided, one shook one's sails (there was a good deal of movement in the bay, boats were starting off) between things, beyond things. Empty it was not, but full to the brim. She seemed to be standing up to the lips in some substance, to move and float and sink in it, yes, for these waters were unfathomably deep" (285–86). Alas, since this is language, one can of course find traces of division here if one looks, if one wants to find them. But even beyond that, this sense of plenitude is betrayed by a broad stroke, the incursion of "temporality," and the rhetoric of measure, of the "almost." For "it was *some such* feeling of completeness *perhaps* which, *ten years ago*, standing *almost* where she stood now, had made her say that she must be in love with the place" (286; italics are mine).

The other vision is of Mrs. Ramsay. It is introduced gently, parenthetically, on page 290. "A noise drew her attention to the drawing-room window—the squeak of a hinge. The light breeze [we are reminded of the empty house of 'Time Passes'] was toying with the window . . . (Yes; she realized that the drawing-room step was empty, but it had no effect on her whatever. She did not want Mrs. Ramsay now.)" By means of a delicate workwomanlike indirection, Lily makes the vision mature through eight-and-a-half pages. She is then rewarded:

> Suddenly the window at which she was looking was whitened by some light stuff behind it. At last then somebody had come into the drawing-room; somebody was sitting in the chair. For Heaven's sake, she prayed, let them sit still there and not come floundering out to talk to her. Mercifully, whoever it was stayed still inside; had settled by some stroke of luck so as to throw an odd-shaped triangular shadow over the step. It altered the composition of the picture a little. (299)

How is this indefiniteness ("somebody," "whoever," "by a stroke of luck") transformed into the certitude and properness of a vision? Through *declaring* this indefiniteness (a kind of absence) as a definiteness (a kind of presence), not through the fullness of presence itself. It is, in other words, turned into a *sign* of presence. The "origin of the shadow" remains "inside the room." It is only the shadow that is on the steps. Lily *declares* that the origin of the shadow is not "somebody" but Mrs. Ramsay. And, paradoxically, having forced the issue, she "wants" *Mr.* Ramsay, now, for he too reaches R only through a sign or symbol. He gets to the Lighthouse, although he "would never reach R." The "metaphorical" language of art falls as short of the "true" copula as the "propositional" language of philosophy. As Woolf writes, "One wanted" the present tense of "that's a chair, that's a table, and yet at the same time, It's a miracle, it's an ecstasy." But all one got was the past tense of "there she sat," the in-substantiated present perfect of "I have had my vision," the negative subjunctive of "he would never reach R," the adverbial similetic clauses of "as if he were saying 'there is no God,' . . . as if he were leaping into space" (308). The provisional copula, always a linear enterprise, a risky bridge, can only be broached by deleting or denying the vacillation of "Time Passes," by drawing a line through the central section of *To the Lighthouse*. "With a sudden intensity, as if she saw it clear for a second, she drew a line there, in the centre" (310).

It would be satisfying to be able to end here. But in order to add a postscript to this allegorical reading of *To the Lighthouse*, I must dwell a moment on Lily's sexuality. Is she in fact androgynous, self-sufficient?

I would like to remind everyone who cites *A Room of One's Own* that "one must be woman-manly or man-womanly" is said there in the voice of Mary Beton, a persona.[5] Woolf must break her off in mid-chapter and resume in her authorial voice. Who can disclaim that there is in her a longing for androgyny, that artificially fulfilled copula? But to reduce her great texts to *successful* articulations of that copula is, I believe, to make a mistake in reading.

In an uncharacteristically lurid and unprepared for passage Lily holds the fear of sex at bay:

> Suddenly . . . a reddish light seemed to burn in her mind, covering Paul Rayley, issuing from him. . . . She heard the roar and the crackle. The whole sea for miles round ran red and gold. Some winey smell mixed with it and intoxicated her. . . . And the roar and the crackle repelled her with fear and disgust, as if while she saw its splendour and power she saw too how it fed on the treasure of the house, greedily, disgustingly, and she loathed it. But for a sight, for a glory it surpassed everything in her experience, and burnt year after year like a signal fire on a desert island at the edge of the sea, and one had only to say "in love" and instantly, as happened now, up rose Paul's fire again (261).

The erotic charge that I would like to see between Virginia and Lily-Vanessa does not preclude the fact that Woolf makes Lily Briscoe repress, exclude, rather than accommodate or transcend, this vision of Rayley as phallus in order to get on with her painting. And the relationship she chooses—as Mr. Ramsay chooses to say "If Q is Q . . . ,"—is gently derided for its prim sensitive exclusivism: "She loved William Bankes. They went to Hampton Court and he always left her, like the perfect gentleman he was, plenty of time to wash her hands" (263).

Has she no use for men then? My point is precisely that she makes use of them. They are her instruments. She uses Tansley's goad—"They can't write, they can't paint"—to keep herself going. And she uses Mrs. Ramsay's imagining of Charles Tansley to change her own. "If she wanted to be serious about him she had to help herself to Mrs. Ramsay's sayings, to look at him through her eyes" (293). "Through William's eyes" (264) she gets Mrs. Ramsay in grey. But her most indispensable instrument is Mr. Ramsay.

(Leslie Stephen died nine years after his wife, without ever returning to St. Ives. One could almost say that he is brought back to life in _To the Lighthouse_ so that the unfinished business of life can be settled, so that he can deliver Vanessa-Virginia's vision.)

I am thinking, of course, of the double structuring of the end of the book. As Lily paints on the shore, Mr. Ramsay must sail to the lighthouse. "She felt curiously divided, as if one part of her were drawn out there— . . . the lighthouse looked this morning at an immense distance; the other had fixed itself doggedly, solidly, here on the lawn" (233–34). Mr. Ramsay on his boat is the tool for the actualization of her self-separation: a sort of shuttling instrumental copula. It is always a preserved division, never an androgynous synthesis. "So much depends, Lily thought, upon distance" (284). With the same sort of modal uneasiness as in "I have had my vision," she can only say "he must have reached it" (308) rather than "he has," when Mr. Ramsay springs upon the rock.

Let me say at once that I must read the alternating rhythm of Lighthouse-canvas in the last part of the book as a copulation. To sleep with father in order to make a baby (a painting, a book) is supposed to be woman's fondest wish. But, here as well, Woolf gives that brutal verdict a twist. For the baby _is_ mother—it is a sublimated version of Mrs. Ramsay that Lily would produce—whereas Freud's point is that the emergence of this wish is to learn to hate the mother. Woolf's emphasis falls not on the phallus that reappears every other section, but on the workshop of the womb that delivers the work. In fact, in terms of the text, Mr. Ramsay's trip can begin because Lily "decides" it must. "She decided that there in that very distant and entirely silent little boat Mr. Ramsay was sitting with Cam and James. Now they had got the sail up; now after a little flagging and hesitation the sails filled and, shrouded in profound silence, she watched the boat take its way with deliberation past the other boats out to sea" (242).

4. Postscript

Knowledge as noncontradiction (identity) is put into question in "The Window"; it is shown to be based on nothing more immutable than "_if_ Q is then Q," and Mr. Ramsay's "Character" is shown to be weak and petulant. Marriage as copulation is also devalorized in "The Window"; it is shown to be a debilitating and self-deceived combat, and Mrs. Ramsay's "character" is shown to be at once manipulative and deceitful, and untrusting of language. "Time Passes" allegorically narrates the terror of a (non-human or natural) operation without a copula. "The Lighthouse" puts into question the possibility of knowledge (of Mrs. Ramsay) as trope; for a metaphor of art is also a copula (the copula is, after all, a metaphor) that joins two things.

Lily does not question this impasse, she merely fights it. She makes a copula by drawing a line in the center, which can be both an invitation to fill in a blank or a deliberate erasure. If the latter, then she erases (while keeping legible) that very part of the book that most energetically desires to recuperate the impasse, to achieve the undecidable, to write the narrative of madness,—"Time Passes"—for that section is "in the centre."

But Lily's "line in the centre" is also part of a picture, the picture is part of a book, there is a product of some kind in the story as well as in our hands. I can read this more fully as an allegory of sexual rather than grammatical production: it is not only that Lily decides to copulate, she also shows us her wombing. A great deal of the most adventurous criticism in philosophy and literature for the last 15 years has been involved with putting the authority of the proposition (and, therefore, of the copula) into question.* This questioning has been often misunderstood as an invitation to play with the copula. I reserve the occasion for arguing that this "new criticism" in fact asks for what might be called the "feminine mode of critical production."* Here I am reading *To the Lighthouse* as if it corrects that possible misunderstanding. As if it suggests that, for anyone (and the generic human examplar is a woman) to play with the copula is to go toward the grim narrative of the discourse of madness and war. One must use the copula as a necessarily limited instrument and create as best one can.

(This is not as far-fetched as it might sound. In a recent essay in *Screen*, Stephen Heath collects once again the evidence to show how close the questioning of the copula comes to the psychoanalytic description of hysteria, "the female ailment," where the patient is not sure if she has or has not a penis.[6] And Derrida, trying to catch Jean Genet's mother Mme. Genet in his book *Glas*, as Lily tries to "catch" Mrs. Ramsay, stops at the fetish, of which no one may be sure if it signifies the possession or lack of a penis.[7] In this part of my essay I am suggesting that *To the Lighthouse*, in its emphasis not merely on copulation but on gestation, rewrites the argument from hysteria or fetishism.)

In her reading of Freud's late essay "Femininity" the French feminist Luce Irigaray suggests that Freud gives the girl-child a growth (warped) by penis-envy (pre-Oedipally she is a boy!) because the Father (a certain Freud) needs to seduce through pronouncing the Law (42, 44), because once "grown," she must console and hide man's anguish at the possibility of castration (6, 74) and because she is made to pay the price for keeping the Oedipus complex going (98). And then Irigaray asks, why did Freud not articulate vulvar, vaginal, uterine stages (29, 59), why did he ignore the work of the production of the child in the womb? (89).[8]

---

* *Once again I am thinking of the deconstructive criticism of Jacques Derrida. The proposition is dismantled most clearly in* Speech and Phenomena and Other Essays on Husserl's Theory of Signs, *trans. David Allison (Evanston: Northwestern University Press, 1973). Among other texts in the field are Jacques Lacan, "La Science et la vérité," Ecrits (Paris: Seuil, 1966), pp. 855–77 and Gilles Deleuze, Logique du sens (Paris: Minuit, 1969).*

* *It is from this point of view that the many helpful readers' reports on this study troubled me as well. They reflected the desire for theoretical and propositional explicitness that, via Woolf and the "new criticism," I am combating here: "There is something coy about this paper and all its 'copulas,' but at the same time, the reading of Wolf [sic] is genuinely suggestive and I found myself ever convinced by the power of what seemed a pun [it is in response to this that I wrote my first paragraph]. It is difficult to understand just what the author's interest in language (as a formal system, with copulae, etc.) is concerned with, where it comes from and why she thinks it should lead to the sorts of insights she discovers. Some sort of theoretical explicitness would help here!"*

I know, of course, that the text of Freud has to be banalized in order to be presented as a sexist text. I know also that, in that very text that Irigaray reads, Freud hints at his own fallibility in a sentence that is no mere rhetorical gesture: "If you reject this idea as fantastic and regard my belief in the influence of lack of penis on the configuration of femininity as an *idée fixe*, I am of course defenceless."[9] But I do not write to dispraise Freud, simply to take a hint from Irigaray's reading of Freud.

I am proposing, then, that it is possible to think that texts such as Woolf's can allow us to develop a thematics of womb-envy. I hasten to add that I do not advance womb-envy as a "new" or "original" idea. From Socrates through Nietzsche, philosophers have often wished to be midwives or mothers. I am only placing it beside the definition of the physical womb as a lack. I speculate that the womb has always been defined as a lack *by* man in order to cover over a lack *in* man, the lack, precisely, of a tangible place of production. Why does man say he "gives" a child to a woman? Since we are in the realm of fanciful sex-vocabularies, it is not absurd to suggest that the question of "giving" might be re-formulated if one thought of the large ovum "selecting" among millions of microscopic spermatozoa, dependent for effectiveness upon the physiological cycles of the woman. Freud finds the ovum "passive."[10] It is just as appropriate to point out that, if one must allegorize, one must notice that the uterus "releases," "activates" the ovum. It is simply that the grave periodic rhythm of the womb is not the same as the ad hoc frenzy of the adjudicating phallus. And so forth. I hope the allegoric parallels with *To the Lighthouse* are clear. I am of course not discounting penis-envy, but simply matching it with a possible envy of the womb. As Michel Foucault has written, "it's not a question of emancipating truth from every system of power . . . but of detaching the power of truth from the forms of hegemony (social, economic, and cultural) within which it operates at the present time."[11] This might be the secret of "the rivalry and partnership" between Lily Briscoe and Mr. Ramsay that I mention on the opening page of the essay.

To conclude, then, *To the Lighthouse* reminds me that the womb is not an emptiness or a mystery, it is a place of production. What the hysteron produces is not simply the contemptible text of hysteria, an experimental madness that deconstructs the copula. As a tangible place of production, it can try to construct the copula, however precarious, of art. I am not sure if this ennobling of art as an alternative is a view of things I can fully accept. I can at least honor it as an attempt to articulate, by using a man as an instrument, a woman's vision of a woman;* rather than to disarticulate because no human hand can catch a vision, because, perhaps, no vision obtains.

1980

---

* *This aspect of the book allows me to justify our use of theories generated, surely in part by historical accident, by men.*

4. Sex and History in *The Prelude* (1805): Books Nine to Thirteen

Whatever the "truth" of Wordsworth's long life (1770–1850), Books Nine through Thirteen of the 1805 version of his autobiographical poem *The Prelude* present the French Revolution as the major crisis of the poet's poetic formation. As one critic has put it, "his allegiance to revolutionary enthusiasm was so strong that, when, as he saw it, the revolutionary government resorted to nationalistic war (and after he had set up residence with his sister, as they had so long desired), Wordsworth was thrown into a catastrophic depression that has led many modern critics to treat the Revolution (or having a child by and 'deserting' Annette Vallon, one is never quite sure) as the trauma of his life."[1] As this analysis reminds us, the "revolution" in Wordsworth's life also involved two women. As in the critic's sentence, so also in *The Prelude*, the story of Annette is in parenthesis, the desertion in quotation marks. "His sister"—and indeed Wordsworth does not name her—is also in parenthesis.

The consecutive parts of *The Prelude* were not consecutively composed. The account in the text is not chronological. I have taken the textual or narrative consecutivity imposed by an authorial decision as given. Such a decision is, after all, itself part of the effort to cope with crisis.

As I read these books of *The Prelude*, I submit the following theses:

1. Wordsworth not only needed to exorcise his illegitimate paternity but also to reestablish himself sexually in order to declare his imagination restored.
2. He coped with the experience of the French Revolution by transforming it into an iconic text that he could write and read.
3. He suggested that poetry was a better cure for the oppression of mankind than political economy or revolution and that his own life had the preordained purpose of teaching mankind this lesson.

My critique calls for a much more thorough reading of the history and politics of the French Revolution and the English reaction than I am able to provide here.

I sometimes use the Derridian words "trace" and "trace-structure" in the following way. In our effort to define things, we look for origins. Every origin that we seem to locate refers us back to something anterior and contains the possibility of something posterior. There is, in other words, a trace of something else in seemingly self-contained origins. This, for the purposes of my argument, "is" the trace-structure.

The trace, since it breaks up every first cause or origin, cannot be a transcendental principle. It would thus be difficult to distinguish clearly between the trace as a principle and cases of the trace, such as writing or a stream. The trace-structure does not simply undermine origins; it also disrupts the unified and self-contained description of things. By isolating three theses in Wordsworth's work, I am inconsistent with the notion of the trace-structure. No discourse is possible, however, without the unity of *something* being taken for granted. It is not possible to attend to the trace *fully*. One's own self-contained critical position as attendant of the trace also leads back and forward. It is possible to read them as references, to consolidate them as one's "history" and "politics." Since the trace cannot be fully attended to, one possible alibi is to pay attention to the texts of history and politics as the trace-structuring of positions, knowing that those two texts are themselves interminable.

Wordsworth's Exorcism of Illegitimate Paternity; Sexual Self-Establishment to Restore Imagination

It is commonly acknowledged that the story of Vaudracour and Julia, as told in Book Nine of *The Prelude* (1805), is a disguised version of the affair between Wordsworth and Annette Vallon. The real story is much more banal: Annette did not have a chance to begin with. She was romantic and undemanding. Plans for marriage were tacitly dropped over the years. No money was forthcoming even after Wordsworth received his modest legacy. Annette got deeply involved in the Royalist resistance and died poor at seventy-five. The story is told in detail in Emile Legouis's *William Wordsworth and Annette Vallon*.[2] "It is only fair to add that Wordsworth made some provision for his daughter from the time of her marriage in February, 1816. This took the form of an annuity for £30, which continued until 1835 when the annuity was commuted for a final settlement of £400."[3] In "Vaudracour and Julia" the woman is in a convent, the child dead in infancy, and the man insane.

It is not my concern in this section to decide whether Wordsworth can be excused or if Annette was worth his attentions. It is rather to remark that, in these books of *The Prelude*, one may find textual signs of a rejection of paternity, of a reinstatement of the subject as son (rather than father) within Oedipal law, and then, through the imagination, a claim to androgyny.

The acknowledgment of paternity is a patriarchal social acknowledgment of the trace, of membership in what Yeats has called "those dying generations." Through this acknowledgment, the man admits that his end is not in himself. This very man has earlier accepted sonship and admitted that his *origin* is not in himself either. This makes it possible for the man to declare a history. Wordsworth the autobiographer seems more interested at this point in transcending or coping with rather than declaring history—in producing a poem rather than a child. He deconstructs the opposition and cooperation between fathers and sons. The possibility of his being a father is handled in the Vaudracour and Julia episode. The rememoration—the symbolic reworking of the structures—of his being a son is constructed in the famous "spots of time" passages. Then, since mothers are not carriers of names, by means of Nature as mother, Wordsworth projects the possibility of being son *and* lover, father *and* mother of poems, male *and* female at once.

I will try to show this projection through the reading of a few passages. But first I should insist that I am not interested in a personal psychoanalysis of William Wordsworth, even if I were capable of undertaking such a task. The thematics of psychoanalysis as a regional science should be considered as part of the ideology of male universalism, and my point here would be that Wordsworth is working with and out of that very ideology. If indeed one wished to make a rigorous structural psychoanalytic study, one would have to take into account "the death of Wordsworth's mother when Wordsworth was eight." One would have to plot not only "the repressions, fixations, denials, and distortions that attend such traumatic events in a child's life and the hysteria and unconscious obsessions that affect the life of the grown man, and more than likely his poetic practice"[4] but also the search for "the lost object" and the recourse to fetishism in the text as signature of the subject.

The story of Vaudracour and Julia begins as a moment of dissonance in the story of the French Revolution, marking a deliberate postponement or substitution:

> *I shall not, as my purpose was, take note*
> Of other matters which detain'd us oft
> In thought or conversation, *public* acts,
> And *public* persons, and the emotions wrought
> Within our minds by the ever-varying wind
> Of *Record* or *Report* which day by day
> Swept over us; but I will here *instead*
> Draw from obscurity a tragic Tale
> *Not in its spirit singular indeed*
> But haply worth memorial . . .
>
> (IX, 541–50; italics mine)

Not only does the story not have its proper place or singularity, but its narrative beginning is given as two random and not sufficiently differentiated choices out of plural possibilities: "Oh/Happy time of youthful Lovers! thus/My story may begin, Oh! balmy time . . ." (IX, 554–55). In the final version of *The Prelude* (1850), its revisions dating probably from 1828, the beginning is even less emphatic: "(thus/The story might begin)" is said in parenthesis, and the story itself is suppressed and relegated to the status of nothing but a trace of a record that exists elsewhere: "So might—and with that prelude did begin/The record" (IX, 557–58 [1850]). If in the serious public business of *The Prelude* such a nonserious theme as love and desertion were to be introduced, the 1850 text asks, "Fellow voyager! / Woulds't thou not chide?" (IX, 563–64).

The end of Book Nine in both versions gives us an unredeemed Vaudracour, who, situated in an indefinite temporality, remains active as an unchanging pretext at the same time as the prospective and retrospective temporality of Books Ten to Thirteen puts together a story with an end. The mad Vaudracour is "always there":

> Thus liv'd the Youth
> Cut off from all intelligence with Man,

> And shunning even the light of common day;
> Nor could the voice of Freedom, which through France
> Soon afterwards resounded, public hope,
> Or personal memory of his own deep wrongs,
> Rouse him: but in those solitary shades
> His days he wasted, an imbecile mind.
>
> (IX, 926–33)

In this autobiography of origins and ends, Vaudracour simply lives on, wasting his days; the open-ended temporality does not bring his life to a close. In this story of the judgment of France, he remains unmoved by the voice of Freedom. In this account of the growth of a poet's mind, his mind remains imbecile. This is the counterplot of the origin of the prelude, the author's alias. The author stands in contrast to, yet in complicity with, the testamentary figures of the endings of the later books, who are in fact sublated versions of Vaudracour.

At the end of Book Ten an acceptable alter ego is found. He is quite unlike the Vaudracour who marks the story of guilt. This is of course Coleridge, the Friend to whom *The Prelude* is addressed. Rather than remain suspended in an indefinite temporality, this sublated alter ego looks toward a future shaped by the author:

> Thou wilt stand
> Not as an Exile but a Visitant
> On Etna's top.
>
> (X, 1032–34)

Unlike the fictive Vaudracour in his uncomfortable suspension, Coleridge, now in degraded Sicily, *is* the parallel of Wordsworth, then in unruly France. Wordsworth had not been able to find a clue to the text of the September Massacres in Paris:

> upon these
> And other sights looking as doth a man
> Upon a volume whose contents he knows
> Are memorable, but from him lock'd up,
> Being written in a tongue he cannot read,
> So that he questions the mute leaves with pain
> And half upbraids their silence.
>
> (X, 48–54)

That failure seems recuperated in all the textual examples—Empedocles, Archimedes, Theocritus, Comates—brought to bear upon contemporary Sicily, precisely to transform it to a pleasant sojourn for Coleridge. Imagination, a faculty of course denied to Vaudracour's imbecile mind, is even further empowered:

> by pastoral Arethuse
> Or, if that fountain be in truth no more,
> Then near some other Spring, *which by the name*
> *Though gratulatest, willingly deceived,*
> Shalt linger as a gladsome Votary,
> And not a Captive.
>
> (X, 1034–38; italics mine)

As I will show later, the end of Book Eleven welcomes Coleridge as a companion in an Oedipal scene, and the end of Book Twelve cites Coleridge as guarantor that in Wordsworth's early poetry glimpses of a future world superior to the revolutionary alternative are to be found.

The end of Book Thirteen, the end of *The Prelude* as a whole, is a fully negating sublation of Vaudracour. If *his* life was a waste of days, by trick of grammar indefinitely prolonged, the poet's double is here assured

> yet a few short years of useful life,
> And all will be complete, thy race be run,
> Thy monument of glory will be raised.
>
> (XIII, 428–30)

If Vaudracour had remained unchanged by revolution as an imbecilic mind, here the poet expresses a hope, for himself and his friend, that they may

> Instruct . . . how the mind of man becomes
> A thousand times more beautiful than
> . . . this Frame of things
> (Which, 'mid all revolutions in the hopes
> And fears of men, doth still remain unchanged)
>
> (XIII, 446–50)

Julia is obliterated rather quickly from the story. By recounting these successive testamentary endings and comparing them to Vaudracour's fate, which ends Book Nine, I have tried to suggest that Vaudracour, the unacknowledged self as father, helps, through his disavowal and sublation, to secure the record of the progress and growth of the poet's mind. Let us now consider Wordsworth's use of Oedipal signals.

There is something like the use of a father figure by a son—as contrasted to acknowledging oneself as father—early in the next book (X, 467–515). Wordsworth recounts that he had felt great joy at the news of Robespierre's death. Is there a sense of guilt associated with ecstatic joy at *anyone's* death? We are free to imagine so, for, after recounting this excess of joy, Wordsworth suddenly recalls the faith in his own professional future felt by a father figure, his old teacher at Hawkshead. (As is often the case in *The Prelude*, there is no causal connection between the two episodes; however, a relationship is strongly suggested.) The memory had come to him by way of a thought of the teacher's epitaph, dealing with judgments on Merits and Frailties, written by Thomas Gray, a senior and meritorious member of the profession of poetry. This invocation of the tablets of the law of the Fathers finds a much fuller expression in later passages.

In a passage toward the beginning of Book Eleven, there is once again a scene of disciplinary judgment. Of the trivium of Poetry, History, Logic, the last has, at this point in Wordsworth's life, seemingly got the upper hand. As for the other two—"their sentence was, I thought, pronounc'd" (XI, 94). The realization of this inauspicious triumph of logic over poetry is given in a latent image of self-division and castration:

> Thus strangely did I war against myself
> . . . Did like a Monk who hath forsworn the world
> Zealously labour to cut off my heart
> From all the sources of her former strength.
>
> (XI, 74, 76–77)

Memories of the "spots of time" bring enablement out of this predicament. The details are explicit and iconic.[5] The poet has not yet reached man's estate: "When scarcely (I was then not six years old)/My hand could hold a bridle" (XI, 280–81). As he stumbles lost and alone, he accidentally discovers the anonymous *natural* inscription, *socially* preserved, of an undisclosed proper name, which is all that remains of the phallic instrument of the law:

> The Gibbet-mast was moulder'd down, the bones
> And iron case were gone; but on the turf,
> Hard by, soon after that fell deed was wrought
> Some unknown hand had carved the Murderer's name.
> The monumental writing was engraven
> In times long past, and still, from year to year,

By superstition of the neighbourhood
The grass is clear'd away; *and to this hour*
The letters are all fresh and visible.

(XI, 291–99; italics mine)

At the time he left the spot forthwith. Now the memory of the lugubrious discovery of the monument of the law provides

A virtue by which pleasure is enhanced
That penetrates, enables us to mount
When high, more high, and lifts us up when fallen.

(XI, 266–68)

Many passages in these later books bring the French Revolution under control by declaring it to be a *felix culpa*, a necessary means toward Wordsworth's growth as a poet: this is such a suggestion. Nothing but the chain of events set off by the Revolution could have caused acts of rememoration that would abreactively fulfill memories of Oedipal events that childhood could not grasp.

As in the case of the memory of the teacher's grave, a metonymic though not logical or metaphoric connection between the second spot of time and the actual father is suggested through contiguity. Here Wordsworth and his brothers perch on a parting of the ways that reminds us of the setting of Oedipus' crime: "One of two roads from Delphi,/another comes from Daulia."[6] Ten days after they arrive at their father's house, the latter dies. There is no logical connection between the two events, and yet the spiritual gift of this spot of time is, precisely, that "the event/With all the sorrow which is brought appear'd / A chastisement" (XI, 368–70).

One might produce a textual chain here: joy at Robespierre's *judgment* (averted by a father figure); the self-castrating despair at Poetry's *judgment* at the hand of Logic (averted by a historical reminder of the *judgment* of the Law); final acceptance of one's own gratuitous, metonymic (simply by virtue of temporal proximity) guilt. Now, according to the canonical Oedipal explanation, "Wordsworth" is a man as son. And just as the murderer's name cut in the grass can be seen *to this day*, so also this rememorated accession to manhood retains a continuous power: "in this later time . . . unknown to me" (XI, 386, 388). It is not to be forgotten that the false father Vaudracour, not established within the Oedipal law of legitimate fathers, also inhabits this temporality by fiat of grammar.

Near the end of Book Eleven, Coleridge, the benign alter ego—akin to the brothers at the recalled "original" event—is once again called forth as witness to the Oedipal accession. Earlier, Wordsworth had written:

> . . . I shook the habit off
> Entirely and for ever, and again
> In Nature's presence stood, *as I stand now*,
> A sensitive, and a creative soul.
>
> (XI, 254–57; italics mine)

Although the "habit" has a complicated conceptual antecedent dispersed in the argument of the thirty-odd previous lines, the force of the metaphor strongly suggests a sexual confrontation, a physical nakedness. One hundred fifty lines later, Wordsworth welcomes Coleridge into the brotherhood in language that, purging the image of all sexuality, still reminds us of the earlier passage:

> Behold me then
> Once more in Nature's presence, thus restored
> *Or otherwise*, and strengthened once again
> *(With memory left of what had been escaped)*
> To habits of devoutest sympathy.
>
> (XI, 393–97; italics mine)

History and paternity are here fully disclosed as mere traces, a leftover memory in parenthesis (1.396), or one among alternate methods of restoration (11.394–95). All that is certain is that a man, stripped and newly clothed, stands in front of Nature.

It is interesting to note that Wordsworth's sister provides a passage into the rememoration of these Oedipal events, and finally into the accession to androgyny. Unlike the male mediators who punish, or demonstrate and justify the law—the teacher, the murderer, the father, Coleridge—Dorothy Wordsworth restores her brother's imagination as a living agent. And, indeed, William, interlarding his compliments with the patronage typical of his time, and perhaps of ours, does call her "wholly free" (XI, 203).[7] It is curious, then, that the predication of *her* relationship with Nature, strongly reminiscent of "Tintern Abbey," should be entirely in the conditional:

> Her the birds
> And every flower she met with, could they but
> Have known her, would have lov'd. Methought such charm
> Of sweetness did her presence breathe around
> That all the trees, and all the silent hills
> And every thing she look'd on, should have had

An intimation how she bore herself
Towards them and to all creatures.

(XI, 214–21)

The only indicative description in this passage is introduced by a controlling "methought."

Although Wordsworth's delight in his sister makes him more like God than like her—"God delights / In such a being" (XI, 221–22)—she provides a possibility of transference for him. The next verse paragraph begins—"Even like this Maid" (XI, 224). Julia as object of desire had disappeared into a convent, leaving the child in Vaudracour's hands. Vaudracour as the substitute of the poet as father can only perform his service for the text as an awkward image caught in an indefinitely prolonged imbecility. Dorothy as sister is arranged as a figure that would allow the poet the possibility of a replaying of the Oedipal scene, the scene of sonship after the rejection of premature fatherhood. If the historical, though not transcendental, authority of the Oedipal explanation, especially for male protagonists, is given credence, then, by invoking a time when he was like her, William is invoking the pre-Oedipal stage when girl and boy are alike, leading to the passage through Oedipalization itself, when the object of the son's desire is legally, though paradoxically, defined as his mother.[8] Nature sustains this paradox: for Nature is that which is not Culture, a place or stage where kinships are not yet articulated. "One cannot confound incest as it would be in this intensive nonpersonal régime that would institute it, with incest as represented in extension in the state that prohibits it, and that defines it as a transgression against persons. . . . Incest as it is prohibited (the form of discernible persons) is employed to repress incest as it is desired (the substance of the intense earth)."[9]

Wordsworth would here clear a space beyond prohibitions for himself. Dorothy carries the kinship inscription "sister" and provides the passage to Nature as object choice; Wordsworth, not acknowledging paternity, has not granted Annette access to a kinship inscription (she was either Madame or the Widow Williams). The text of Book Eleven proceeds to inscribe Nature as mother and lover. The predicament out of which, in the narrative, Dorothy rescues him, can also be read as a transgression against both such inscriptions of Nature:

I push'd without remorse
My speculations forward; yea, set foot
On Nature's holiest places.

(X, 877–79)

The last link in this chain is the poet's accession to an androgynous self-inscription which would include mother and lover. Through the supplementary presence of Nature, such an inscription seems to embrace places historically "outside" and existentially "inside" the poet. We locate a passage between the account of the discovery of the name of the murderer and the account of the death of the father:

> Oh! mystery of Man, *from what a depth*
> *Proceed* thy honours! I am lost, but see
> In simple childhood something of the base
> On which thy greatness stands, but this I feel,
> That from thyself it is that thou must give,
> Else never canst receive. The days gone by
> Come back upon me from the dawn almost
> Of life: *the hiding-places of my power*
> *Seem open; I approach,* and *then they close;*
> I see by glimpses now; when age comes on,
> May scarcely see at all, and I would give,
> While yet we may, as far as words can give,
> A substance and a life to what I feel:
> I would enshrine the spirit of the past
> For future restoration.
>
> (XI, 329–43; italics mine)

We notice here the indeterminacy of inside and outside: "from thyself" probably means "from myself," but if addressed to "mystery of man," that meaning is, strictly speaking, rendered problematic; there are the "I feel"'s that are both subjective and the subject matter of poetry; and, of course, the pervasive uncertainty as to whether memory is ever inside or outside. We also notice the double inscription: womb or depths that produce the subject and vagina where the subject's power finds a hiding place. Consummation is as yet impossible. The hiding places of power seem open but, upon approach, close. It is a situation of seduction, not without promise. It is a palimpsest of sex, biographic memorialization, and psychohistoriography.

Dorothy is in fact invoked as chaperon when Nature is his handmaiden (XIII, 236–46). And when, in the same penultimate passage of the entire *Prelude*, she is apostrophized, William claims for the full-grown poet an androgynous plenitude which would include within the self an indeterminate role of mother as well as lover:

> And he whose soul hath risen
> Up to the height of feeling intellect
> Shall want no humbler tenderness, his heart
> Be tender as a nursing Mother's heart;
> Of female softness shall his life be full,

> Of little loves and delicate desires,
> Mild interests and gentlest sympathies

> (XIII, 204–10)

This intimation of androgynous plenitude finds its narrative opening in the last book of *The Prelude* through the thematics of self-separation and autoeroticism, harbingers of the trace. The theme is set up as at least twofold, and grammatically plural. One item is Imagination, itself "another name" for three other qualities of mind, and the other is "that intellectual love" (XIII, 186), with no grammatical fulfillment of the "that" other than another double construction, twenty lines above, where indeed Imagination is declared to be *another* name for something else. Of Imagination and intellectual love it is said that "they are each in each, and cannot stand / Dividually" (XIII, 187–88). It is a picture of indeterminate coexistence with a strong aura of identity ("each in each," not "each in the other"; "dividually," not "individually"). In this declaration of theme, as he sees the progress of the representative poet's life in his own, Wordsworth seems curiously self-separated. "This faculty," he writes, and we have already seen how pluralized it is, "hath been the moving soul / Of our long labour." Yet so intrinsic a cause as a moving soul is also described as an extrinsic object of pursuit, the trace as stream:

> We have traced the stream
> From darkness, and the very place of birth
> In its blind cavern, whence is faintly heard
> The sound of waters.

> (XIII, 172–75)

The place of birth, or womb, carries a trace of sound, testifying to some previous origin. The explicit description of the origin as place of birth clarifies the autoerotic masculinity of "then given it greeting, as it rose once more / With strength" (XIII, 179–80). For a time the poet had "lost sight of it bewilder'd and engulph'd" (XIII, 178). The openness of the two adjective/adverbs keeps the distinction between the poet as subject (inside) and Imagination as object (outside) indeterminate. The autoerotic image of the subject greeting the strongly erect phallus that is his moving soul slides quickly into a logical contradiction. No *rising* stream can "reflect" anything in its "solemn breast," let alone "the works of man and face of human life" (XIII, 180–81). It is after this pluralized and autoerotic story of Imagination as trace that Wordsworth assures "Man" that this "prime and vital principal is thine / In the recesses of thy nature" and follows through to the openly androgynous claims of lines 204–10, cited above.

The itinerary of Wordsworth's securing of the Imagination is worth recapitulating. Suppression of Julia, unemphatic retention of Vaudracour as sustained and negative condition of possibility of disavowal, his sublation into Coleridge, rememorating through the mediation of the figure of Dorothy his own Oedipal accession to the Law, Imagination as the androgyny of Nature and Man— Woman shut out. I cannot but see in it the sexual-political program of the Great Tradition. If, in disclosing such a programmatic itinerary, I have left aside the irreducible heterogeneity of Wordsworth's text, it is also in the interest of a certain politics. It is in the interest of suggesting that, when a man (here Wordsworth) addresses another man (Coleridge) in a sustained conversation on a seemingly universal topic, we must *learn* to read the microstructural burden of the woman's part.

Transforming Revolution into Iconic Text

To help introduce this section, let us reconsider those lines from Book Ten:

> upon these
> And other sights looking as doth a man
> Upon a volume whose contents he knows
> Are memorable, but from him lock'd up,
> Being written in a tongue he cannot read,
> So that he questions the mute leaves with pain
> And half upbraids their silence.

> (X, 48–54)

The contents of the book of revolution must be transformed into a personal memory. The autobiographer assures us that, at twenty-two, he knew them to be "memorable." He uses strong language to describe the task of learning to read them. It would be to transgress an interdiction, for the book is "lock'd up" from him.

In Book Nine help in reading the text of the landscape and, then, of the landscape of revolution, comes from Tasso, Spenser, and the Milton of *Paradise Lost*. As his despair thickens, Wordsworth begins to *identify* with Milton's personal position, as described, say, in *Samson Agonistes*. The sleepless city articulates its guilt through Macbeth. His own guilt by transference (including perhaps the unacknowledged guilt of paternity) makes him echo Macbeth's nightmares. He admires and sympathizes with the Girondists because they identified with the ancient Greeks and Romans.

A little over halfway through Book Ten, Wordsworth does a double take which seems to purge the experience of the revolution of most of what one would commonly call its substance. In line 658, he "reverts from describing the conduct of the English government in 1793–4, to recount his own relation to public events from the time of his arrival in France (Nov. 1791) till his return to England. He is therefore traversing again the ground covered by Books IX and X, 1–227" (de Selincourt, p. 583).

This gesture of distancing seems to mark an important advance in the chain I am now describing. Instead of leaning on the great masters of art and poetry for *models* by means of which to organize the discontinuous and alien landscape and events, in the latter half of Book Ten Wordsworth begins to compose *icons* out of English and natural material. The vision of the sacrifice on Sarum Plain can be seen as the last link in this chain. (The great icon of the ascent of Mount Snowdon in Book Thirteen triumphantly takes us back to a time *before* Wordsworth's experience in France.) Since we have looked at the occluded chain of the thematics of paternity, sonship, and androgyny, this overt and indeed often ostensive effort should not occupy us long. This section will involve little more than fleshing out, through a reading of a few passages, of what I have summarized in the last two paragraphs. It remains merely to add that this is of course rather different from a consideration of Wordsworth's own declared political allegiance at the time of the composition of these Books.[10]

The sensible or visible is not simply the given of immediate experience. It carries the trace of history. One must learn to read it. Wordsworth records this impulse in a reasonable way when he judges his initial response to French events as follows:

> I was unprepared
> With needful knowledge, had abruptly pass'd
> Into a theatre, of which the stage
> Was busy with an action far advanced.
> Like others I had read, and eagerly
> Sometimes, the master Pamphlets of the day;
> Nor wanted such half-insight as grew wild
> Upon that meagre soil, help'd out by Talk
> And public News; but having never chanced
> To see a regular Chronicle which might shew,
> (If any such indeed existed then)
> Whence the main Organs of the public Power
> Had sprung, their transmigrations when and how
> Accomplish'd, giving thus unto events
> A form and body . . .

> (IX, 91–106)

As far as the record in *The Prelude* is concerned, Wordsworth never did go in search of an originary, formalizing as well as substantializing chronicle of the power structure of the French Revolution. Instead he sought alternate literary-historical cases within which he could insert the historical and geographical landscape. If I quote Marx in his middle twenties here, it is only because we should then witness two textualist solutions to similar problems, going in opposed directions. Ludwig Feuerbach also seems not to have known how to read a social text, and Marx proposes the following:

> the sensuous world around [us] is not a thing given direct from all eternity, remaining ever the same, but the product of industry and of the state of society; and, indeed, in the sense that it is an historical product, the result of the activity of a whole succession of generations, each standing on the shoulders of the preceding one, developing its industry and its inter-course, and modifying its social system according to the changed needs. Even the objects of the simplest "sensuous certainty" are only given [us] through social development, industry and commercial intercourse. [Because he lacks this approach] Feuerbach sees [in Manchester] only factories and machines, where a hundred years ago only spinning-wheels and weaving-looms were to be seen, or in the Campagna of Rome he finds only pasture lands and swamps, where in the time of Augustus he would have found nothing but the vineyards and villas of Roman capitalists.[11]

Confronted with a little-known historical text, Wordsworth's solution is to disavow historical or genealogical production and attempt to gain control through a private allusive positing of resemblance for which he himself remains the authority and source; at least so he writes almost a decade later. Most of these "resemblances," being fully implicit, are accessible, of course, only to a reader who is sufficiently versed in English literary culture. For example, Words-worth makes his task of describing the French experience "resemble" the open-ing of *Paradise Lost*, Book IX, where Milton turns from the delineation of sinless Paradise to describe

> foul distrust, and breach
> Disloyal on the part of Man, revolt,
> And disobedience; on the part of Heav'n
> Now alienated, distance and distaste,
> Anger and just rebuke, and judgment giv'n.

> (de Selincourt, p. 566)

It must be pointed out that the "sin" is not just France's against Paradise, which Wordsworth will judge. It could more "literally" be Wordsworth's own carnal knowledge, which this text must subliminally obliterate.

Michel Beaupuy makes an attempt to fill Wordsworth in on the sources of the present trouble, and on the hope for the future. As Wordsworth commemorates these conversations, which for him came closest to a "regular Chronicle" of the times, he gives them apologetic sanction, for Coleridge's benefit, in the name of Dion, Plato, Eudemus, and Timonides, who waged a "philosophic war / Led by Philosophers" (II, 421–22). Indeed, Wordsworth's sympathies were with the Girondists because they "were idealists whose speeches were full of references to ancient Greece and Rome" (de Selincourt, p. 576). Here too it is interesting to compare notes with Marx:

> Luther put on the mask of the apostle Paul; the Revolution of 1789–1814 draped itself alternately as the Roman republic and the Roman empire; and the revolution of 1848 knew no better than to parody at some points 1789 and at others the revolutionary traditions of 1793–5. In the same way, the beginner who has learned a new language always retranslates it into his mother tongue: he can only be said to have appropriated the spirit of the new language and so be able to express himself in it freely when he can manipulate it without reference to the old, and when he forgets his original language while using the new one.[12]

A new and unknown language has been thrust upon William Wordsworth. Even as its elements are being explained to him, he engages in a bizarre "re-translation" into the old. What he describes much more carefully than the substance of the conversation is when "from earnest dialogues I slipp'd in thought / And let remembrance steal to other times" (IX, 444–45). In these interstitial moments, the proferred chronicle is sidestepped through the invocation of "straying" hermit and "devious" travelers (IX, 446, 448). Next the poet reports covering over the then present discourse with remembered stories of fugitive maidens or of "Satyrs . . . / Rejoicing o'er a Female" (IX, 460–61). Geography, instead of being textualized as "the result of the activity of a whole succession of generations, each standing on the shoulders of the preceding one," is "re-translated" into great literary accounts of the violation or flight of women. The sight of a convent "not by reverential touch of Time / Dismantled, but by violence abrupt" (IX, 469–70) takes its place upon this list and prepares us for Julia's tale. The verse paragraph that intervenes between the two does give us something like an insight into Beaupuy's discourse. Let us consider the strategy of that paragraph briefly.

First, invocation of an unrememorated castle (third on the list after Romorentin and Blois)—"name now slipp'd / From my remembrance" (IX, 483–84)—inhabited by a nameless mistress of Francis I. This visual object, as Wordsworth remembers, gives Imagination occasion to inflame two kinds of emotions: one was, of course, "virtuous wrath and noble scorn" though less so than in the case of "the peaceful House / Religious" (IX, 496, 492–93); the other was a

> mitigat[ion of] the force
> Of civic prejudice, the bigotry,
> So call it, of a youthful Patriot's mind

and, Wordsworth goes on, "on these spots with many gleams I look'd / Of chivalrous delight!" (IX, 500–01). Beaupuy in the written text is able to produce a summary of his argument only by metaphorizing the object of the French Revolution as "a hunger-bitten Girl" . . . "'Tis against *that* / Which we are fighting'" (IX, 510, 517–18). Here is the summary:

> All institutes for ever blotted out
> That legalised exclusion, empty pomp
> Abolish'd, sensual state and cruel power
> Whether by the edict of the one or few,
> And finally, as sum and crown of all,
> Should see the People having a strong hand
> In making their own Laws, whence better days
> To all mankind.
>
> (IX, 525–32)

This admirable summary is followed by a proleptic rhetorical question that reminds us that due process was suspended under the Reign of Terror. As a deviation from this theme, the story of Vaudracour and Julia is broached. One is reminded that Beaupuy, the only good angel on the Revolutionary side, is himself a deviation, "of other mold," and that his own retranslation of the events into art and sexual courtesy (in an unwitting display of class and sex prejudice) serves, as it were, to excuse his Revolutionary sentiments:

> He thro' the events
> Of that great change wander'd in perfect faith,
> As through a Book, an old Romance or Tale
> Of Fairy, or some dream of actions . . .
>   . . . Man he lov'd
> As Man; and to the mean and the obscure . . .
> Transferr'd a courtesy which had no air
> Of condescension, but did rather seem
> A passion and a gallantry, like that
> Which he, a Soldier, *in his idler day*
> Had pay'd to Woman[!]
>
> (IX, 303–06, 311–12, 313–18; italics mine)

It is the passage through the long Book Ten that allows the poet of *The Prelude* to represent himself as generative subject. The literary-historical allusions and retranslations of Book Nine change to icons of the poet's own making. In an intermediate move, Wordsworth tells the tale of lost control by *interiorizing* literary analogues. We have seen how, in the final passages about the androgynous Imagination, the distinction between inside and outside is allowed to waver. As Wordsworth tries to transform revolution into iconic text, again the binary opposition between the inside of literary memory and the outside of the external scene is no longer sufficient. The distinction begins to waver in a use of Shakespeare that has puzzled many readers.

Book Ten, lines 70–77, is worth considering in all its versions.

> "The horse is taught his manage, and the wind
> Of heaven wheels round and treads in his own steps,
> Year follows year, the tide returns again,
> Day follows day, all things have second birth;
> The earthquake is not satisfied at once."
> And in such a way I wrought upon myself,
> Until I seem'd to hear a voice that cried,
> To the whole City, "Sleep no more."

Most of it is within quotation marks, the poet "wrighting" upon himself. About two years after the completion of the 1805 *Prelude*, the quotation marks were lifted, and thus the sense of a unique sleepless night was removed. As the passage stands in 1805, the exigency seems to be more to invoke Shakespeare than to achieve coherence. The lines begin with a peculiarly inapt quotation from the lighthearted opening of *As You Like It*, where Orlando complains that his brother's horses are treated better than he. Wordsworth wrests the line from its context and fits it into a number of sentences, all either quotations or self-quotations (thus confounding the inside of the self with the outside), which seem to echo two different kinds of sentiments: that wild things are tamed and that things repeat themselves. The sentences do not seem to provide much solace against the massacres, guaranteeing at once their taming and their return, though perhaps the idea of a wild thing obeying the law of its own return is itself a sort of taming.

In the allusion to *Macbeth* that follows, however, the result of becoming so agitated seems to be an acknowledgment of the guilt of the murder of a father/king. The voice in Shakespeare had seemingly cried, "Sleep no more!" to all the house because Macbeth had murdered Duncan. Although in Wordsworth's eyes it is Paris who is guilty of killing the king, the Shakespearean reference where the guilty Macbeth is himself the speaker implicates Wordsworth in the killing of his own paternity through the rejection of his firstborn. A peculiar line in the collection of sayings stands out: "All things have second birth." When in an extension of the *Macbeth* passage nearly two hundred lines later, he confides to Coleridge that although the infant republic was doing well, all the injustices involved in its inception gave him sleepless nights, an overprotesting parenthesis stands out in the same unsettling way:

Most melancholy at that time, O Friend!
Were my day-thoughts, my dreams were miserable;
Through months, through years, long after the last beat
Of these atrocities (*I speak bare truth,*
As if to thee alone in private talk)
I scarcely had one night of quiet sleep
Such ghastly visions had I of despair
And tyranny, and implements of death,
And long orations which in dreams I pleaded
Before unjust Tribunals, with a voice
Labouring, a brain confounded, and a sense,
of *treachery and desertion* in the place
The holiest that I knew of, my own soul.

(X, 369–81; italics mine)

The image of the victorious republic is that of a Herculean female infant (Annette bore a daughter, Caroline) who had throttled the snakes about her cradle. I am suggesting, of course, that even as Wordsworth seeks to control the heterogeneity of the revolution through literary-historical and then iconic textuality, the occlusion of the personal guilt of the unacknowledged paternity is still at work.

Shakespearean echoes are scattered through the pages of *The Prelude*. Most of the time, however, Milton helps Wordsworth get a grip on the Revolution. I have already mentioned that Book Nine opens with a Miltonic echo. Wordsworth describes the beginning of the Reign of Terror in words recalling the Miltonic lines, "So spake the Fiend, and with necessitie, / The Tyrant's plea, excus'd his devilish deeds" (*Paradise Lost*, IV, 394–95; de Selincourt, p. 579).

Lines 117–202 of Book Ten are limpid in their conscious sanctity. These are the lines that end in recounting that Wordsworth left France merely because he was short of funds and that this was by far the best thing that could have happened because this way his future contributions as a poet were spared. Here Wordsworth speaks of himself as comparable to an angel and of his courageous hopes for France, not in the voice of Shakespeare's guilty Macbeth, but as Milton's saintly Samson, undone by a woman:

But patience is more oft the exercise
Of saints, the trial of their fortitude,
Making them each his own Deliverer
And Victor over all
That tyrannie or fortune can inflict.

(*Samson Agonistes*, 1287–91; de
Selincourt, p. 577)

Indeed, it is the language of *Paradise Lost* that helps give the joy at Robespierre's death the authority of just condemnation: "That this foul Tribe of Moloch was o'erthrown, / And their chief Regent levell'd with the dust" (X, 469–70).

We have so far considered some examples of allusive textualization and also of the interiorization of literary allusion. Let us now turn to the composition of icons.

The point is often made that it was not so much the experience of the French Revolution, but the fact of England's warring with France, that finally brought Wordsworth to despair. Wordsworth's initial reaction to the Revolution matched a good English model: "There was a general disposition among the middle and upper classes to welcome the first events of the Revolution—even traditionalists argued that France was coming belatedly into line with British notions of the 'mixed constitution.'"[13] In addition, Wordsworth claims three personal reasons for sympathy: "born in a poor district," he had never, in his childhood, seen

> The face of one, who, whether Boy or Man,
> Was vested with attention or respect
> Through claims of wealth or blood
>
> (IX, 223–25)

At Cambridge he had seen that "wealth and titles were in less esteem / Than talents and successful industry" (IX, 234–35). (A superficial but understandable analysis.) And all along, "fellowship with venerable books . . . and mountain liberty" prepared him to

>   hail
> As best the government of equal rights
> And individual worth.
>
> (IX, 246–48)

Support for idealistic revolutionary principles based on such intuitive-patriotic grounds would be ill prepared for England's French policy. Fortunately for Wordsworth's long-term sanity, the martial conduct of the French, the "radicalization of The Revolution," and the fear of French invasion provided him with a reason to withdraw into the ideology-reproductive "passive" politics that is apolitical and individualistic, as it allowed Pitt to become "the diplomatic architect of European counter-revolution."[14] If the reverence due to a poet is laid aside for a moment and Wordsworth is seen as a human being with a superb poetic gift as defined by a certain tradition, then his ideological victimization can be appreciated:

The invasion scare resulted in a torrent of broadsheets and ballads . . .
which form a fitting background for Wordsworth's smug and sonorous
patriotic sonnets:

> It is not to be thought of that the Flood
> Of British freedom, which, to the open sea
> Of the world's praise from dark antiquity
> Hath flowed, "with pomp of waters, unwithstood," . . .

"Not to be thought of"; and yet, at this very time, freedom of the press,
of public meeting, of trade union organisation, of political organisation
and of election, were either severely limited or in abeyance. What, then,
did the common Englishman's "birth-right" consist in? "Security of property!" answered Mary Wollstonecraft: "Behold . . . the definition of English liberty."[15]

It might be remembered that the elation of first composition at the inception of
The Prelude is not unmixed with the security of a legacy and a place of one's
own.

This "revolutionary" nationalism articulates itself in one of the first full-
fledged icons that will situate politics and history for Wordsworth, his select
readership, and students of the Romantic period. The components of the icon
are scattered through lines 254 to 290 of Book Ten: a tree, a steeple, a congregation, plucked flowers. The overt argument begins by setting up a strong binary
opposition of nature and antinature. Wordsworth uses the honorable but confused appellation of patriotism as a "natural" sentiment, based on the assumption of a "natural" tie between man and the soil (as if indeed he were a tree),
rather than an "ideological" connection needed to support a political and economic conjuncture bearing its own history.[16] Thus the initial feeling against
England's French policy is already dubbed "unnatural strife / In my own heart"
as the icon is set up. And since the so-called conceptual justification for the icon
is based on what may as well be called the "metaphoric" axiomatics of a man
as a tree, or an organism "literally" rooted in the soil, the metaphor which is
the first component of the icon has more than a sanction by analogy:

>   I, who with the breeze
> Had play'd, a green leaf on the blessed tree
> Of my beloved country; nor had wish'd
> For happier fortune than to wither there,
> Now from my pleasant station was cut off,
> And toss'd about in whirlwinds.

A limited and controlling play is changed by the war into an untimely death which, in an induced motion, imitates life. Just as the subjectivistic element of the anti-Vietnam War movement was not for communist principles but a cleaner America, so also Wordsworth's icon casts a vote here not for revolutionary principles but an England worthy of her name.

The tree is a natural image. The next bit of the icon secures the social and legal dimension. Although the situation is a church, the iconic elements are steeple, congregation, Father worship. Wordsworth's practice is different when he wants to invoke transcendental principles. Here the preparation slides us into a situation where Wordsworth feels alienated because, unlike the "simple worshippers" (sharing in "mountain liberty") who gave him his taste for revolution, he cannot say, "God for my country, right or wrong." The power of the icon, with the status of conceptual-literal-metaphoric lines made indeterminate, wrests our support for Wordsworth's predicament without questioning its strategic structure; indeed indeterminacy is part of both the rhetorical and the thematic burden of the passage, as the opening lines show:

> It was a grief,
> *Grief call it not, 'twas anything but that,*
> *A conflict of sensations without name,*
> Of which he only who may love the sight
> Of a Village Steeple as I do can judge
> When in the Congregation, bending all
> To their great Father, prayers were offer'd up,
> Or praises for our Country's Victories,
> And 'mid the simple worshippers, perchance,
> I only, like an uninvited Guest
> Whom no one own'd sate silent, shall I add,
> Fed on the day of vengeance yet to come?
>
> (X, 264–75; italics mine)

It is not by chance that the responsibility for such a mishap is thrown on an unspecified "they":

> Oh much have they to account for, who could tear
> By violence at one decisive rent
> From the best Youth in England, their dear pride,
> Their joy, in England.
>
> (X, 276–79)

We are no longer sure whether the warmongers of England or revolution itself is to blame. The condemned gesture is still the act of cutting or rending. But the icon ends with an ambiguous image. At first it is alleged that, at the time, the French Revolution was considered a higher advent than nationalism—just as Christ was greater than John the Baptist. Then this very thought is "judged" in the following lines:

> A time in which Experience would have pluck'd
> Flowers out of any hedge to make thereof
> A Chaplet, in contempt of his grey locks.

> (X, 289–90)

This is indeed a contemptuous picture of a revolution that goes against any established institution. The image of age pretending to youthful self-adornment is unmistakable in tone. The force of the whirlwind has been reduced to weaving a chaplet, cutting off a leaf to plucking flowers. The coherence of a historical or revolutionary argument is on its way to being successfully rejected as mere folly.

I now turn to what in my reading is the place where the chain stops and the mind triumphs over the French Revolution: Book Twelve, lines 298–353, the reverie on Sarum Plain.

The lines are addressed to that certain Coleridge who, as "Friend," is witness, interlocutor, and alter ego of *The Prelude*. They are an apology for a hubristic professional concept of self: poets like prophets can see something unseen before. This is not a unique and self-generative gift, for poets are connected in "a mighty scheme of truth"—a "poetic history" that is presumably other and better than "history as such," which by implication here, and by demonstration elsewhere in *The Prelude*, has failed in the task of prediction and prophecy. The gift is also a "dower" from an undisclosed origin, but the Friend is encouraged to establish something like a relationship between that gift or "influx" and *a* work of Wordsworth's (not necessarily *The Prelude*?), whose origin is caught in a negative which necessarily carries the trace of that which it negates. The thing negated (logically "prior") would, in this case, seem paradoxically to imply a chronological posteriority: "the depth of untaught things." This vertiginous deployment of indeterminacy and traces culminates in the hope that this work will deconstruct the opposition between Nature and Art—"might become / A power like one of Nature's." Yet to be like *one* of Nature's powers, bringing in the entire part-whole/identity problem, makes even that possible deconstruction indeterminate. Such a collocation of indeterminacy, where nothing can be fixed, is the antecedent of the deceptively simple and unified word "mood" to which Wordsworth was "raised" and which is, presumably, both the origin and the subject matter of what I am calling an iconic recuperation of the events of 1791–93. (The date of the "actual" walk is July–August, 1793.)

It is by now no longer surprising that the immediate setting of the reverie is also marked by tracings and alternations. The ranging walks took place either *without* a track or *along* the dreary line of roads. The trace-structure here is not

the obstreperous heterogeneous material or opening of political history; a vaster
time scale seems to make the experience safe for poetry: "through those vestiges
of ancient times I ranged." The disingenuous line "I had a reverie and saw the
past" carries this overwhelming and conditioning frame.

In his vision of Sarum Plain, the poet sees multitudes *and* "a single Briton."
This Briton is a *subject*-representative or alter ego of great subtlety. He is also
the *object* of Wordsworth's attentive reverie. There is the same sort of self-deconstructive ego splitting as in the autoerotic passage on the Imagination as
object of attention that I discussed earlier. He is not necessarily singular though
"single," as the following words make clear: "Saw . . . here and there, / A single
Briton. . . ." The relationship between him and the prophetic voice is one of
metonymic contiguity, not of agency or production. The voice itself, though "of
spears" and thus war-making, is "heard" like that prophetic "voice of the turtle,"
announcing peace and safety from God's wrath: a revolution controlled and
soothed into the proper stuff of poetry. The consciousness that produced the
voice is itself undermined and dispersed into a compound image and common
nouns that hold encrypted the proper name of the leader of Wordsworth's calling, Shakespeare:

> The voice of spears was heard, the rattling spear
> Shaken by arms of mighty bone, in strength
> Long moulder'd of barbaric majesty.
>
> (XII, 324–26)

I have already remarked upon Wordsworth's use of a metonymic or sequen-
tial, rather than a metaphoric or consequential, rhetoric. Here that habit seems
specifically to blur the relationship between selves and voices. Imagination, or
Poetry, is presented as an august trace, other and greater than what can be
uttered by a mere individual. Since the poet carefully orchestrates this presentation, the intolerable trace-structure of history as catastrophe can now be tamed.

The relationship between Shakespeare's encrypted name and the poet's successful invocation of a darkness that took or seemed to take (the rhetoric of
alternation yet again) all objects from his sight to produce a highly precarious
"center" where the icon is finally visible is thus predictably metonymic: "It is
the sacrificial Altar." At last the carnage of the French Revolution is recon-
structed into a mere image of a generalized "history" on the occasion of a highly
deconstructive and self-deconstructed Imagination. Wordsworth can now
"read" the September Massacres:

> It is the sacrificial Altar, fed
> With living men, how deep the groans, the voice
> Of those in the gigantic wicker thrills

> Throughout the region far and near, pervades
> The monumental hillocks.
>
> (XII, 331–35)

"History" has at last come alive and animated the native landscape. And indeed the next few images are of a collective possibility of reading; no longer a reverie but actual geometric shapes which figure over a precultural soil—the very image of the originary institution of a trace, what Heidegger would call "the worlding of a world."[17] The precultural space of writing is as carefully placed within a *mise-en-abîme* as the origin of Wordsworth's unspecified work a few lines earlier: "untill'd ground" matching "untaught things." This particular inscription is not a reminder of Oedipal law but a charming and pleasant access to science. The principle of figuration is multiple: "imitative form," "covert expression," "imaging forth" of the constellations. This principle, the relationship between representation and represented, is finally itself figured forth as that connection among poets (the Druids and Wordsworth) with which the argument began:

> I saw the bearded Teachers, with white wands
> Uplifted, pointing to the starry sky
> Alternately, and Plain below.
>
> (XII, 349–51)

The icon is sealed at the beginning of the next verse paragraph: "This for the past" (XII, 356).

The intolerable trace-structure of history is thus brought under control by the authorial positing of the elaborate trace-structure of the Imagination and the brotherhood of poets. The control is emphasized all through the next verse paragraph, the closing lines of Book Twelve. Coleridge is called forth to testify that at this time Wordsworth began to produce good poetry. But even Coleridge is superseded, for "the mind is to herself / Witness and judge." Out of the self-evidence of such supreme self-possession, and by way of an elaborate iconic self-deconstruction, Wordsworth competes successfully with the revolution and records the articulation of a new world; the double privilege matches the accession to androgyny:

> I seem'd about this period to have sight
> Of a new world, a world, too, that was fit
> To be transmitted and made visible
> To other eyes, as having for its base
> That whence our dignity originates
>
> (XII, 370–74)

and so on. Reading Romantic poetry will bring about what the French Revolution could not accomplish. What we need to learn from is "'An unpublished Poem on the Growth and *Revolutions* of an Individual Mind,'" as Coleridge's description of *The Prelude* has it "as late as February 1804" (de Selincourt, p. xxvi; italics mine).

Yet a postscript must be added. These books of *The Prelude* have curious moments when what is suppressed projects into the scene. Vaudracour and the murderer's name operate unceasingly as textual time passes. And elsewhere the poet apologizes most unemphatically for having neglected details of time and place, and for not having given his sister her rightful place in his poem. If these two items are seen as hardly displaced representatives of the matter of France and the matter of woman, the poet is here excusing the very constitutive burden of these Books:

> Since I withdrew unwillingly from France,
> The Story hath demanded less regard
> To time and place; and where I lived, and how
> Hath been no longer scrupulously mark'd.
> Three years, until a permanent abode
> Receiv'd me with that Sister of my heart
> Who ought by rights the dearest to have been
> Conspicuous through this biographic Verse,
> Star seldom utterly conceal'd from view,
> I led an undomestic Wanderer's life
>
> (XIII, 334–43)

(The sister, incidentally, disappears completely from the 1850 version.) I comment on a comparable narrative intrusion at the end of this next section.

Poetry as Cure for Oppression: A Life Preordained to Teach This Lesson

Wordsworth offers his own poetry as a cure for human oppression and suffering because it teaches one where to look for human value.

In lines 69–158 of Book Twelve the ostensible grounds for such a suggestion are researched and presented. The narrative has just passed through the Oedipal encounters. Now Wordsworth is ready to undertake his own critique of political economy. His conclusion is that the true wealth of nations is in

> The dignity of individual Man,
> Of Man, no composition of the thought,
> Abstraction, shadow, image, but the man

> Of whom we read [a curious distinction!], the man whom we behold
> With our own eyes.
>   (XII, 84–87)

Man as a category is of course always an abstraction, whether we see him, read of him, or make him a part of "public welfare," which last, according to Wordsworth in this passage, is "plans without thought, or bottom'd on false thought / And false philosophy" (XII 74–76). Without pursuing that point, however, let us insist that although, following his rhetorical bent, Wordsworth does not equate the true wealth of nations with individual male dignity, but leaves them suggestively contiguous on a list, there can be no doubt that he here recounts the history of someone who *seriously* and with experience, knowledge, and wisdom confronts the problems of social justice and political economy. He refers to "the Books / Of modern Statists" (XII, 77–78), most specifically, of course, to Adam Smith's *The Wealth of Nations*, first published in 1776.[18] (In the 1850 version of *The Prelude*, the phrase—"The Wealth of Nations"—is put within quotation marks, as the title of a book.)

Quite appropriately, though always by implication, Wordsworth finds the increasing of the *wealth* of nations, as understood by classical economists, to be a hollow goal. Adam Smith was a proponent of the labor-command theory of value: "The value of any commodity, therefore, to the person who possesses it, and who means not to use or consume it himself, but to exchange it for other commodities, is equal to the quantity of labour which it enables him to purchase or command. Labour, therefore, is the real measure of the exchangeable value of all commodities."[19] His method of increasing the wealth of a nation is therefore greater division of labor, greater specialization, deregulation of trade, economic interaction between town and country, the establishment of colonies—all based on a view of human nature reflected in the following famous passage:

> Man has almost constant occasion for the help of his brethren, and it is
> in vain for him to expect it from their benevolence only. He will be more
> likely to prevail if he can interest their self-love in his favour, and shew
> them that it is for their own advantage to do for him what he requires of
> them . . . It is not from the benevolence of the butcher, the brewer, or
> the baker, that we expect our dinner, but from their regard to their own
> interest. We address ourselves, not to their humanity but to their self-
> love, and never talk to them of our own necessities but of their
> advantages.[20]

Wordsworth predictably does not concern himself with the practical possibilities of laissez-faire capitalism. He implicitly questions its presuppositions regarding human nature—which he considers an aberration. He does not, however, suggest that the production of commodities requires and produces this aberrant version of human nature. He posits, rather, a subjective theory of human value, where the work of salvation would consist of disclosing that man's essential wealth lay inside him.

He therefore asks: Why is the essential individual who is the standard of measurement of this subjective theory of value (yet, curiously enough, not an abstraction) so rarely to be found? Wordsworth poses a rhetorical question: "Our animal wants and the necessities / Which they impose, are these the obstacles?" (XII, 94–95). If this question were answered in the affirmative, then the entire occluded chain of the nonacknowledgment of paternity might, even in so seemingly self-assured a passage, be making itself felt; in other words, Wordsworth would then be in the most uncharacteristic position of "taking himself as an example," making of his animal nature the inevitable reason for the failure of perfectibility. If in the negative, then Wordsworth's case against political justice, against Godwin, Adam Smith, and the French Revolution is won. As in all rhetorical questions, the questioner obliquely declares for one alternative: "If not, then others vanish into air" (XII, 96). And the asymmetry of the rhetorical question constitutes *The Prelude*'s politics as well as the condition of its possibility.

The position, then, is that social relations of production cannot touch the inner resources of man. The corollary: Revolutionary politics, seeking to change those social relations, are therefore superfluous; poetry, disclosing man's inner resources, is the only way. Although Wordsworth cannot ask how there will come to pass a set of social relations in which everyone will have the opportunity and education to value poetry for its use, he does ask a preliminary question that seems appropriate if the poet is to disclose the wealth of man:

> how much of real worth
> And genuine knowledge, and true power of mind
> Did at this day exist in those who liv'd
> By *bodily labour, labour far exceeding*
> *Their due proportion,* under all the weight
> Of that injustice which upon ourselves
> *By composition of society*
> Ourselves entail
>
> (XII, 98–105; italics mine)

If this question is asked rigorously, we arrive at the problem of human alienation in the interest of the production of surplus-value:

The fact that half a day's labour is necessary to keep the worker alive during twenty-four hours does not in any way prevent him from working a whole day. Therefore the value of labour-power and the value which that labour-power valorizes [*verwertet*] in the labour-process, are two entirely different magnitudes; and this difference was what the capitalist had in mind when he was purchasing the labour-power.[21]

Whether he has stumbled upon the crucial question of social injustice or not, Wordsworth's ideological preparation and predilection lead him to a less than useful answer. The ground rules of the academic subdivision of labor would make most of us at this point piously exclaim, "One does not judge poets in this way! This is only Wordsworth's personal story, and since this is poetry, it is not even that—the 'I' of *The Prelude* is to be designated 'the speaker,' not 'Wordsworth.'" Suffice it to say that I am deliberately wondering seeing if indeed poetry can get away *a posteriori* with a narrative of political investigation when it never in fact "irreducibly intends" anything but its own "constitution."
Although

> an intermixture of distinct regards
> And truths of individual sympathy . . . often might be glean'd
> From that great City,
>
> (XII, 119–20)

Wordsworth "to frame such estimate [of human worth],"

> . . . chiefly look'd (what need to look beyond?)
> Among the natural abodes of men,
> Fields with their rural works.
>
> (XII, 105–08)

"What need," indeed! Wordsworth is tracing out a recognizable ideological circuit here, deciding that the peculiarities of one's own locale give the *universal* norm. (In fact, even in terms of *rural* England, the situation in Cumberland and Westmorland was not representative.)[22] "Feuerbach's 'conception' of the sensuous world [in the *Principles of A Philosophy of the Future*] is confined on the one hand to mere contemplation of it, and on the other to mere feeling; he posits 'Man' instead of 'real historical man.' *'Man' is really 'the German.'*"[23]
There is something to admire in Wordsworth's impulse. Not only does he ask the question of disproportionate labor, he also emphasizes that the excluded margins of the human norm are where the norm can be properly encountered; his own thematics are of depth and surface:

> There [I] saw into the depth of human souls,
> Souls that appear to have no depth at all
> To vulgar eyes.
>
> (XII, 166–68)

This is all the more laudable because of the deplorable consequences of the vagrancy laws, some of them of Tudor origin, that began to be sharply felt as a result of the rise of industrial capitalism. It is noteworthy, however, that at the crucial moment of decision in *The Prelude* Wordsworth does not speak of the dispossessed "small proprietors" of the Lake Country, of whose plight he had considerable knowledge, nor of "an ancient rural society falling into decay."[24]

The ideologically benevolent perspective Wordsworth had on these vagrants would not allow him to argue here for a fairer distribution of labor or wealth, but would confine him to the declaration that virtue and intellectual strength are not necessarily the property of the so-called educated classes—and hedge even that declaration by an "if" and a personal preference:[25]

> If man's estate, by doom of Nature yoked
> With toil, is therefore yoked with ignorance,
> If virtue be indeed so hard to rear,
> And intellectual strength so rare a boon
> I prized such walks still more.
>
> (XII, 174–78)

It is of course worth noticing that the conditions for prizing the walk are askew. In terms of the overt argument of this part of *The Prelude*, we are not sure whether Wordsworth thinks the first "if" is correct; this uncertainty makes the "therefore" rhetorically undecidable, since the declared charge of the argument suggests that the last two "if's" are false suppositions. But I prefer to ask simpler questions: Why is the doom of Nature not equally exigent upon everyone, and why should a man who does not want to reduce Man (*sic*) to a homogenizing abstraction be unable to entertain the question of heterogeneity?

If, indeed, one continues the analogy, it looks like this: Wordsworth will work on the human wealth represented by the solitaries and produce poetry which will teach others to be as wealthy as the originals. It should be repeated that such an analogy ignores such questions as "Who reads poetry?" "Who makes Laws?" "Who makes money?" as well as "What is the relationship between the interest on Wordsworth's capital and the production of this theory?" The greatness of Marx was to have realized that, within capitalism, that interest is part of a surplus the production of which is the sole prerogative of wage labor and that production is based on exploitation. "Productive labor" and "free labor" in this context are not positive concepts; they are the bitter names of human degradation and alienation: the "'productive' worker cares as much about the crappy shit he has to make as does the capitalist himself who employs him, and who also couldn't give a damn for the junk."[26] Within the historical situation of the late eighteenth century, to offer only poetry as the means of changing this definition of "productive" is class-bound and narrow. Since it denies the reality of exploitation, it need conceive of no struggle. An example of this attitude can still be found in the official philosophy of current Departments of English:

"The goal of ethical criticism is transvaluation, the ability to look at contemporary social values with the detachment of one who is able to compare them in some degree with the infinite vision of possibilities presented by culture."[27]

Wordsworth's choice of the rural solitary as theme, then, is an ideologically symptomatic move in answer to a critical question about political economy. It is neither to lack sympathy for Wordsworth's predicament nor to underestimate "the verbal grandeur" of the poetry to be able to recognize this program.

We have so far considered Wordsworth's suggestion that poetry is a better cure for human oppression or suffering than revolution. His second suggestion is that his own life is preordained to teach this lesson. In making my previous arguments, I have amply presented the elements of this well-known suggestion. So much so, that I will not reformulate it here. Suffice it to mention that this particular chain of thought in *The Prelude* is rounded off most appropriately, in a verse paragraph of exquisite beauty, where Wordsworth expresses an unconvincing uncertainty about that very telos of his life; even as he finds, in the "private" memory of the "public" poetic records of his "private" exchange with Coleridge, a sufficient dialogic justification for *The Prelude*:

> To thee, in memory of that happiness
> It will be known, by thee at least, my Friend,
> Felt, that the history of a Poet's mind
> Is labour not unworthy of regard:
> To thee the work shall justify itself.
>
> (XIII, 406–10)

Yet, just as there is a moment when France and Dorothy jut into the text as apology when all seemed to have been appeased (p. 350), so also is there a moment when, in this final book, something apparently suppressed juts into the scene. Life is seen to have a telos or at least a place that is distinct from the poet's self. And such a life is seen as capable of launching an unanswerable or at least unanswered reproach. There is even a hint that *The Prelude* might be but an excuse. If the passage I quote above narrates a poetic career, this passage narrates the career of *The Prelude* not just as text but as discourse:

> O Friend! the termination of my course
> Is nearer now, much nearer; yet even then
> In that distraction and intense desire
> I said unto the life which I had lived,
> Where art thou? Hear I not a voice from thee
> Which 'tis reproach to hear? Anon I rose
> As if on wings, and saw beneath me stretch'd
> Vast prospect of the world which I had been

And was; and hence this Song, which like a lark
I have protracted . . .

(XIII, 372–81)

No answer to Wordsworth's question of the first six lines is articulated in the next four; only a strategy is described. If one pulled at a passage like this, the text could be made to perform a self-deconstruction, the adequacy of *The Prelude* as autobiography called into question. But then the politics of the puller would insert itself into the proceeding. I have stopped short of the impossibly duped position that such a person with pull is politics free, oscillating freely in "the difficult double bind" of an aporia, like the Cumaean sybil in a perpetual motion machine.

In these pages I have read a poetic text attempting to cope with a revolution and paternity. I have not asked the critic to be hostile to poetry or to doubt the poet's good faith; although I have asked her to examine the unquestioning reverence or—on the part of the poets themselves—the credulous vanity that seems to be our disciplinary requirement. As a feminist reader of men on women, I thought it useful to point out that, in the texts of the Great Tradition, the most remotely occluded and transparently mediating figure is woman.

1981

5. Feminism and Critical Theory

What has been the itinerary of my thinking during the past few years about the relationships among feminism, Marxism, psychoanalysis, and deconstruction? The issues have been of interest to many people, and the configurations of these fields continue to change. I will not engage here with the various lines of thought that have constituted this change, but will try instead to mark and reflect upon the way these developments have been inscribed in my own work. The first section of the essay is a version of a talk I gave several years ago. The second section represents a reflection on that earlier work. The third section is an intermediate moment. The fourth section inhabits something like the present.

1.

I cannot speak of feminism in general. I speak of what I do as a woman within literary criticism. My own definition of a woman is very simple: it rests on the word "man" as used in the texts that provide the foundation for the corner of the literary criticism establishment that I inhabit. You might say at this point, defining the word "woman" as resting on the word "man" is a reactionary position. Should I not carve out an independent definition for myself as a woman? Here I must repeat some deconstructive lessons learned over the past decade that I often repeat. One, no rigorous definition of anything is ultimately possible, so that if one wants to, one could go on deconstructing the opposition between man and woman, and finally show that it is a binary opposition that displaces itself.[1] Therefore, "as a deconstructivist," I cannot recommend that kind of dichotomy at all, yet, I feel that definitions are necessary in order to keep us going, to allow us to take a stand. The only way that I can see myself making definitions is in a provisional and polemical one: I construct my definition as a woman not in terms of a woman's putative essence but in terms of words currently in use. "Man" is such a word in common usage. Not *a* word, but *the* word. I therefore fix my glance upon this word even as I question the enterprise of redefining the premises of any theory.

In the broadest possible sense, most critical theory in my part of the academic establishment (Lacan, Derrida, Foucault, the last Barthes) sees the text as that area of the discourse of the human sciences—in the United States called the humanities—in which the *problem* of the discourse of the human sciences is made available. Whereas in other kinds of discourses there is a move toward the final truth of a situation, literature, even within this argument, displays that the truth of a human situation *is* the itinerary of not being able to find it. In the general discourse of the humanities, there is a sort of search for solutions, whereas in literary discourse there is a playing out of the problem as the solution, if you like.

The problem of human discourse is generally seen as articulating itself in the play of, in terms of, three shifting "concepts": language, world, and consciousness. We know no world that is not organized as a language, we operate with no other consciousness but one structured as a language—languages that we cannot possess, for we are operated by those languages as well. The category of language, then, embraces the categories of world and consciousness even as it is determined by them. Strictly speaking, since we are questioning the human being's control over the production of language, the figure that will serve us better is writing, for there the absence of the producer and receiver is taken for granted. A safe figure, seemingly outside of the language-(speech)-writing opposition, is the text—a weave of knowing and not-knowing which is what knowing is. (This organizing principle—language, writing, or text—might itself be a way of holding at bay a randomness incongruent with consciousness.)

The theoreticians of textuality read Marx as a theorist of the world (history and society), as a text of the forces of labor and production-circulation-distribution, and Freud as a theorist of the self, as a text of consciousness and the unconscious. This human textuality can be seen not only *as* world and self, *as* the representation of a world in terms of a self at play with other selves and generating this representation, but also *in* the world and self, all implicated in an "intertextuality." It should be clear from this that such a concept of textuality does not mean a reduction of the world to linguistic texts, books, or a tradition composed of books, criticism in the narrow sense, and teaching.

I am not, then, speaking about Marxist or psychoanalytic criticism as a reductive enterprise which diagnoses the scenario in every book in terms of where it would fit into a Marxist or a psychoanalytical canon. To my way of thinking, the discourse of the literary text is part of a general configuration of textuality, a placing forth of the solution as the unavailability of a unified solution to a unified or homogeneous, generating or receiving, consciousness. This unavailability is often not confronted. It is dodged and the problem apparently solved, in terms perhaps of unifying concepts like "man," the universal contours of a sex-, race-, class-transcendent consciousness as the generating, generated, and receiving consciousness of the text.

I could have broached Marx and Freud more easily. I wanted to say all of the above because, in general, in the literary critical establishment here, those two are seen as reductive models. Now, although nonreductive methods are implicit in both of them, Marx and Freud do also seem to argue in terms of a mode of evidence and demonstration. They seem to bring forth evidence from the world of man or man's self, and thus prove certain kinds of truths about world and self. I would risk saying that their descriptions of world and self are based on inadequate evidence. In terms of this conviction, I would like to fix upon the idea of alienation in Marx, and the idea of normality and health in Freud.

One way of moving into Marx is in terms of use-value, exchange-value, and surplus-value. Marx's notion of use-value is that which pertains to a thing as it is directly consumed by an agent. Its exchange-value (after the emergence of the money form) does not relate to its direct fulfillment of a specific need, but is rather assessed in terms of what it can be exchanged for in either labor-power or money. In this process of abstracting through exchange, by making the worker work longer than necessary for subsistence wages or by means of labor-saving machinery, the buyer of the laborer's work gets more (in exchange) than the worker needs for his subsistence while he makes the thing.[2] This "more-worth" (in German, literally, *Mehrwert*) is surplus-value.

One could indefinitely allegorize the relationship of woman within this particular triad—use, exchange, and surplus—by suggesting that woman in the traditional social situation produces more than she is getting in terms of her subsistence, and therefore is a continual source of the production of surpluses, *for* the man who owns her, or *by* the man for the capitalist who owns *his* labor-power. Apart from the fact that the mode of production of housework is not, strictly speaking, capitalist, such an analysis is paradoxical. The contemporary woman, when she seeks financial compensation for housework, seeks the abstraction of use-value into exchange-value. The situation of the domestic workplace is not one of "pure exchange." The Marxian exigency would make us ask at least two questions: What is the use-value of unremunerated woman's work for husband or family? Is the willing insertion into the wage structure a curse or a blessing? How should we fight the idea, universally accepted by men, that wages are the only mark of value-producing work? (Not, I think, through the slogan "Housework is beautiful.") What would be the implications of denying women entry into the capitalist economy? Radical feminism can here learn a cautionary lesson from Lenin's capitulation to capitalism.

These are important questions, but they do not necessarily broaden Marxist theory from a feminist point of view. For our purpose, the idea of externalization (*Entäußerung/Veräußerung*) or alienation (*Entfremdung*) is of greater interest. Within the capitalist system, the labor process externalizes itself and the worker as commodities. Upon this idea of the fracturing of the human being's relationship to himself and his work as commodities rests the ethical charge of Marx's argument.[3]

I would argue that, in terms of the physical, emotional, legal, custodial, and sentimental situation of the woman's product, the child, this picture of the human relationship to production, labor, and property is incomplete. The possession of a tangible place of production in the womb situates the woman as an agent in any theory of production. Marx's dialectics of externalization-alienation followed by fetish formation is inadequate because one fundamental human relationship to a product and labor is not taken into account.[4]

This does not mean that, if the Marxian account of externalization-alienation were rewritten from a feminist perspective, the special interest of childbirth, childbearing, and childrearing would be inserted. It seems that the entire problematic of sexuality, rather than remaining caught within arguments about overt sociosexual politics, would be fully broached.

Having said this, I would reemphasize the need to interpret reproduction within a Marxian problematic.[5]

In both so-called matrilineal and patrilineal societies the legal possession of the child is an inalienable fact of the property right of the man who "produces" the child.[6] In terms of this legal possession, the common custodial definition, that women are much more nurturing of children, might be seen as a dissimulated reactionary gesture. The man retains legal property rights over the product of a woman's body. On each separate occasion, the custodial decision is a sentimental questioning of man's right. The current struggle over abortion rights has foregrounded this unacknowledged agenda.

In order not simply to make an exception to man's legal right, or to add a footnote from a feminist perspective to the Marxist text, we must engage and correct the theory of production and alienation upon which the Marxist text is based and with which it functions. As I suggested above, much Marxist feminism works on an analogy with use-value, exchange-value, and surplus-value relationships. Marx's own writings on women and children seek to alleviate their condition in terms of a desexualized labor force.[7] If there were the kind of rewriting that I am proposing, it would be harder to sketch out the rules of economy and social ethics; in fact, to an extent, deconstruction as the questioning of essential definitions would operate if one were to see that in Marx there is a moment of major transgression where rules for humanity and criticism of societies are based on inadequate evidence. Marx's texts, including *Capital*, presuppose an ethical theory: alienation of labor must be undone because it undermines the agency of the subject in his work and his property. I would like to suggest that if the nature and history of alienation, labor, and the production of property are reexamined in terms of women's work and childbirth, it can lead us to a reading of Marx beyond Marx.

One way of moving into Freud is in terms of his notion of the nature of pain as the deferment of pleasure, especially the later Freud who wrote *Beyond the Pleasure Principle*.[8] Freud's spectacular mechanics of imagined, anticipated, and avoided pain write the subject's history and theory, and constantly broach the never-quite-defined concept of normality: anxiety, inhibition, paranoia, schizophrenia, melancholy, mourning. I would like to suggest that in the womb, a tangible place of production, there is the possibility that pain exists *within* the concepts of normality and productivity. (This is not to sentimentalize the pain of childbirth.) The problematizing of the phenomenal identity of pleasure and unpleasure should not be operated only through the logic of repression. The opposition pleasure-pain is questioned in the physiological "normality" of woman.

If one were to look at the never-quite-defined concepts of normality and health that run through and are submerged in Freud's texts, one would have to redefine the nature of pain. Pain does not operate in the same way in men and in women. Once again, this deconstructive move will make it much harder to devise the rules.

Freud's best-known determinant of femininity is penis-envy. The most crucial text of this argument is the essay on femininity in the *New Introductory Lectures*.[9] There, Freud begins to argue that the little girl is a little boy before she discovers sex. As Luce Irigaray and others have shown, Freud does not take the womb into account.[10] Our mood, since we carry the womb as well as being carried by it, should be corrective.[11] We might chart the itinerary of womb-envy in the production of a theory of consciousness: the idea of the womb as a place of production is avoided both in Marx and in Freud. (There are exceptions to such a generalization, especially among American neo-Freudians such as Erich Fromm. I am speaking here about invariable presuppositions, even among such exceptions.) In Freud, the genital stage is preeminently phallic, not clitoral or vaginal. This particular gap in Freud is significant. The hysteron remains the place which constitutes only the text of hysteria. Everywhere there is a non-confrontation of the idea of the womb as a workshop, except to produce a surrogate penis. Our task in rewriting the text of Freud is not so much to declare the idea of penis-envy rejectable, but to make available the idea of a womb-envy as something that interacts with the idea of penis-envy to determine human sexuality and the production of society.[12]

These are some questions that may be asked of the Freudian and Marxist "grounds" or theoretical "bases" that operate our ideas of world and self. We might want to ignore them altogether and say that the business of literary criticism is neither your gender (such a suggestion seems hopelessly dated) nor the theories of revolution or psychoanalysis. Criticism must remain resolutely neuter and practical. One should not mistake the grounds out of which the ideas of world and self are produced with the business of the appreciation of the literary text. If one looks closely, one will see that, whether one diagnoses the names or not, certain kinds of thoughts are presupposed by the notions of world and consciousness of the most "practical" critic. Part of the feminist enterprise might well be to provide "evidence" so that these great male texts do not become great adversaries, or models from whom we take our ideas and then revise or reassess them. These texts must be rewritten so that there is new material for the grasping of the production and determination of literature within the general production and determination of consciousness and society. After all, the people who produce literature, male and female, are also moved by general ideas of world and consciousness to which they cannot give a name.

If we continue to work in this way, the common currency of the understanding of society will change. I think that kind of change, the coining of new money, is necessary. I certainly believe that such work is supplemented by research into women's writing and research into the conditions of women in the past. The kind of work I have outlined would infiltrate the male academy and redo the terms of our understanding of the context and substance of literature as part of the human enterprise.

2.

What seems missing in these earlier remarks is the dimension of race. Today I would see my work as the developing of a reading method that is sensitive to gender, race, and class. The earlier remarks would apply indirectly to the development of class-sensitive and directly to the development of gender-sensitive readings.

In the matter of race-sensitive analyses, the chief problem of American feminist criticism is its identification of racism as such with the constitution of racism in America. Thus, today I see the object of investigation to be not only the history of "Third World Women" or their testimony but also the production, through the great European theories, often by way of literature, of the colonial object. As long as American feminists understand "history" as a positivistic empiricism that scorns "theory" and therefore remains ignorant of its own, the "Third

World" as its object of study will remain constituted by those hegemonic First World intellectual practices.[13]

My attitude toward Freud today involves a broader critique of his entire project. It is a critique not only of Freud's masculism but of nuclear-familial psychoanalytical theories of the constitution of the sexed subject. Such a critique extends to alternative scenarios to Freud that keep to the nuclear parent-child model, as it does to the offer of Greek mythical alternatives to Oedipus as the regulative type-case of the model itself, as it does to the romantic notion that an extended family, especially a community of women, would necessarily cure the ills of the nuclear family. My concern with the production of colonial discourse thus touches my critique of Freud as well as most Western feminist challenges to Freud. The extended or corporate family is a socioeconomic (indeed, on occasion political) organization which makes sexual constitution irreducibly complicit with historical and political economy.[14] To learn to read that way is to understand that the literature of the world, itself accessible only to a few, is not tied by the concrete universals of a network of archetypes—a theory that was entailed by the consolidation of a political excuse—but by a textuality of material-ideological-psycho-sexual production. This articulation sharpens a general presupposition of my earlier remarks.

Pursuing these considerations, I proposed recently an analysis of "the discourse of the clitoris."[15] The reactions to that proposal have been interesting in the context I discuss above. A certain response from American lesbian feminists can be represented by the following quotation: "In this open-ended definition of phallus/semination as organically *omnipotent* the only recourse is to name the clitoris as orgasmically phallic and to call the uterus the reproductive extension of the phallus. . . . You must stop thinking of yourself privileged as a heterosexual woman."[16] Because of its physiologistic orientation, the first part of this objection sees my naming of the clitoris as a repetition of Freud's situating of it as a "little penis." To the second part of the objection I customarily respond: "You're right, and one cannot know how far one succeeds. Yet, the effort to put First World lesbianism in its place is not necessarily reducible to pride in female heterosexuality." Other uses of my suggestion, both supportive and adverse, have also reduced the discourse of the clitoris to a physiological fantasy. In the interest of the broadening scope of my critique, I should like to reemphasize that the clitoris, even as I acknowledge and honor its irreducible physiological effect, is, in this reading, also a short-hand for women's excess in all areas of production and practice, an excess which must be brought under control to keep business going as usual.[17]

My attitude toward Marxism now recognizes the historical antagonism between Marxism and feminism, *on both sides*. Hardcore Marxism at best dismisses and at worst patronizes the importance of women's struggle. On the other hand, not only the history of European feminism in its opposition to Bolshevik and Social Democrat women, but the conflict between the suffrage movement and the union movement in this country must be taken into account. This historical problem will not be solved by saying that we need more than an analysis of capitalism to understand male dominance, or that the sexual division of labor as the primary determinant is already given in the texts of Marx. I prefer the work that sees that the "essential truth" of Marxism or feminism cannot be separated from its history. My present work relates this to the ideological development of the theory of the imagination in the eighteenth, nineteenth, and twentieth centuries. I am interested in class analysis of families as it is being practiced by, among others, Elizabeth Fox-Genovese, Heidi Hartman, Nancy Hartsock, and Annette Kuhn. I am myself bent upon reading the text of international feminism as operated by the production and realization of surplus-value. My own earlier concern with the specific theme of reproductive (non) alienation seems to me today to be heavily enough touched by a nuclear-familial hysterocentrism to be open to the critique of psychoanalytic feminism that I suggest above.

On the other hand, if sexual reproduction is seen as the production of a product by an irreducibly determinate means (conjunction of semination-ovulation), in an irreducibly determinate mode (heterogeneous combination of domestic and politico-civil economy), entailing a minimal variation of social relations, then two original Marxist categories would be put into question: use-value as the measure of communist production and absolute surplus-value as the motor of primitive (capitalist) accumulation. For the first: the child, although not a commodity, is also not produced for immediate and adequate consumption or direct exchange. For the second: the premise that the difference between subsistence-wage and labor-power's potential of production is the origin of original accumulation can only be advanced if reproduction is seen as identical with subsistence; in fact, the reproduction and maintenance of children would make heterogeneous the original calculation in terms of something like the slow displacement of value from fixed capital to commodity.[18] These insights take the critique of wage-labor in unexpected directions.

When I earlier touched upon the relationship between wage-theory and "women's work," I had not yet read the autonomist arguments about wage and work as best developed in the work of Antonio Negri.[19] Exigencies of work and limitations of scholarship and experience permitting, I would like next to study the relationship between domestic and political economies in order to establish the subversive power of "women's work" in models in the construction of a "revolutionary subject." Negri sees this possibility in the inevitable consumerism that socialized capitalism must nurture. Commodity consumption, even as it realizes surplus-value as profit, does not itself produce the value and therefore persistently exacerbates crisis.[20] It is through reversing and displacing this tendency within consumerism, Negri suggests, that the "revolutionary subject" can be released. Mainstream English Marxists sometimes think that such an upheaval can be brought about by political interventionist teaching of literature. Some French intellectuals think this tendency is inherent in the "pagan tradition," which pluralizes the now-defunct narratives of social justice still endorsed by traditional Marxists in a post-industrial world. In contrast, I now argue as follows:

It is women's work that has continuously survived within not only the varieties of capitalism but other historical and geographical modes of pro-

duction. The economic, political, ideological, and legal heterogeneity of
the relationship between the definitive mode of production and race- and
class-differentiated women's and wives' work is abundantly recorded. . . .
Rather than the refusal to work of the freed Jamaican slaves in 1834, which
is cited by Marx as the only example of zero-work, quickly recuperated
by imperialist maneuvers, it is the long history of women's work which
is a sustained example of zero-work: work not only outside of wage-work,
but, *in one way or another*, "outside" of the definitive modes of production.
The displacement required here is a transvaluation, an uncatastrophic *im-
plosion* of the search for validation via the circuit of productivity. Rather
than a miniaturized and thus controlled metaphor for civil society and the
state, the power of the *oikos*, domestic economy, can be used as the model
of the foreign body unwittingly nurtured by the *polis*.[21]

With psychoanalytic feminism, then, an invocation of history and politics
leads us back to the place of psychoanalysis in colonialism. With Marxist feminism, an invocation of the economic text foregrounds the operations of the New
Imperialism. The discourse of race has come to claim its importance in this way
in my work.

I am still moved by the reversal-displacement morphology of deconstruction,
crediting the asymmetry of the "interest" of the historical moment. Investigating
the hidden ethico-political agenda of differentiations constitutive of knowledge
and judgment interests me even more. It is also the deconstructive view that
keeps me resisting an essentialist freezing of the concepts of gender, race, and
class. I look rather at the repeated agenda of the situational production of those
concepts and our complicity in such a production. This aspect of deconstruction
will not allow the establishment of a hegemonic "global theory" of feminism.

Over the last few years, however, I have also begun to see that, rather than
deconstruction simply opening a way for feminists, the figure and discourse of
women opened the way for Derrida as well. His incipient discourse of woman
surfaced in *Spurs* (first published as "La Question du Style" in 1975), which also
articulates the thematics of "interest" crucial to political deconstruction.[22] This
study marks his move from the critical deconstruction of phallocentrism to "affirmative" deconstruction (Derrida's phrase). It is at this point that Derrida's
work seems to become less interesting for Marxism.[23] The early Derrida can
certainly be shown to be useful for feminist practice, but why is it that, when
he writes under the sign of woman, as it were, that his work becomes solipsistic
and marginal? What is it in the history of that sign that allows this to happen?
I will hold this question until the end of this essay.

3.

In 1979–80, concerns of race and class were beginning to invade my mind.
What follows is in some sense a check list of quotations from Margaret Drabble's
The Waterfall that shows the uneasy presence of those concerns.[24] Reading lit-

erature "well" is in itself a questionable good and can indeed be sometimes productive of harm and "aesthetic" apathy within its ideological framing. My suggestion is to use literature, with a feminist perspective, as a "nonexpository" theory of practice.

Drabble has a version of "the best education" in the Western world: a First Class in English from Oxbridge. The tradition of academic radicalism in England is strong. Drabble was at Oxford when the prestigious journal *New Left Review* was being organized. I am not adverse to a bit of simple biographical detail: I began to re-read *The Waterfall* with these things in mind as well as the worrying thoughts about sex, race, and class.

Like many woman writers, Drabble creates an extreme situation, to answer, presumably, the question "Why does love happen?" In place of the mainstream objectification and idolization of the loved person, she situates her protagonist, Jane, in the most inaccessible privacy—at the moment of birthing, alone by choice. Lucy, her cousin, and James, Lucy's husband, take turns watching over her in the empty house as she regains her strength. *The Waterfall* is the story of Jane's love affair with James. In place of a legalized or merely possessive ardor toward the product of his own body, Drabble gives to James the problem of relating to the birthing woman through the birth of "another man's child." Jane looks and smells dreadful. There is blood and sweat on the crumpled sheets. And yet "love" happens. Drabble slows language down excruciatingly as Jane records how, wonders why. It is possible that Drabble is taking up the challenge of feminine "passivity" and making it the tool of analytic strength. Many answers emerge. I will quote two, to show how provisional and self-suspending Jane can be:

> I loved him inevitably, of necessity. Anyone could have foreseen it, given those facts: a lonely woman, in an empty world. Surely I would have loved anyone who might have shown me kindness. . . . But of course it's not true, it could not have been anyone else. . . . I know that it was not inevitable: it was a miracle. . . . What I deserved was what I had made: solitude, or a repetition of pain. What I received was grace. Grace and miracles. I don't much care for my terminology. Though at least it lacks that most disastrous concept, the concept of free will. Perhaps I could make a religion that denied free will, that placed God in his true place, arbitrary, carelessly kind, idly malicious, intermittently attentive, and himself subject, as Zeus was, to necessity. Necessity is my God. Necessity lay with me when James did [pp. 49–50].

And, in another place, the "opposite" answer—random contingencies:

> I loved James because he was what I had never had: because he belonged to my cousin: because he was kind to his own child: because he looked unkind: because I saw his naked wrists against a striped tea towel once,

seven years ago. Because he addressed me an intimate question upon a
beach on Christmas day. Because he helped himself to a drink when I did
not dare to accept the offer of one. Because he was not serious, because
his parents lived in South Kensington and were mysteriously depraved.
Ah, perfect love. For these reasons, was it, that I lay there, drowned was
it, drowned or stranded, waiting for him, waiting to die and drown there,
in the oceans of our flowing bodies, in the white sea of that strange familiar
bed [p. 67].

If the argument for necessity is arrived at by slippery happenstance from thought
to thought, each item on this list of contingencies has a plausibility far from
random.

She considers the problem of making women rivals in terms of the man who
possesses them. There is a peculiar agreement between Lucy and herself before
the affair begins:

I wonder why people marry? Lucy continued, in a tone of such academic
flatness that the topic seemed robbed of any danger. I don't know, said
Jane, with equal calm. . . . So arbitrary, really, said Lucy, spreading butter
on the toast. It would be nice, said Jane, to think there were reasons. . . .
Do you think so? said Lucy. Sometimes I prefer to think we are victims. . . . If there were a reason, said Jane, one would be all the more a
victim. She paused, thought, ate a mouthful of the toast. I am wounded,
therefore I bleed. I am human, therefore I suffer. Those aren't reasons
you're describing, said Lucy. . . . And from upstairs the baby's cry reached
them—thin, wailing, desperate. Hearing it, the two women looked at each
other, and for some reason smiled [pp. 26–27].

This, of course, is no overt agreement, but simply a hint that the "reason" for
female bonding has something to do with a baby's cry. For example, Jane records
her own deliberate part in deceiving Lucy this way: "I forgot Lucy. I did not
think of her—or only occasionally, lying awake at night *as the baby cried*, I would
think of her, with pangs of irrelevant inquiry, pangs endured not by me and in
me, but at a distance, pangs as sorrowful and irrelevant as another person's
pain" [p. 48; italics mine].

Jane records inconclusively her gut reaction to the supposed natural connection between parent and child: "Blood is blood, and it is not good enough to
say that children are for the motherly, as Brecht said, for there are many ways
of unmothering a woman, or unfathering a man. . . . And yet, how can I deny
that it gave me pleasure to see James hold her in his arms for me? The man I
loved and the child to whom I had given birth" [p. 48].

The loose ending of the book also makes Jane's story an extreme case. Is this
love going to last, prove itself to be "true," and bring Jane security and Jane
and James happiness? Or is it resolutely "liberated," overprotesting its own

impermanence, and thus falling in with the times? Neither. The melodramatic and satisfactory ending, the accident which might have killed James, does not in fact do so. It merely reveals all to Lucy, does not end the book, and reduces all to a humdrum kind of double life.

These are not bad answers: necessity if all fails, or perhaps random contingency; an attempt not to rivalize women; blood bonds between mothers and daughters; love free of social security. The problem for a reader like me is that the entire questioning is carried on in what I can only see as a privileged atmosphere. I am not saying, of course, that Jane is Drabble (although that, too, is true in a complicated way). I am saying that Drabble considers the story of so privileged a woman the most worth telling. Not the well-bred lady of pulp fiction, but an impossible princess who mentions in one passing sentence toward the beginning of the book that her poems are read on the BBC.

It is not that Drabble does not want to rest her probing and sensitive fingers on the problem of class, if not race. The account of Jane's family's class prejudice is incisively told. Her father is headmaster of a public school.

> There was one child I shall always remember, a small thin child . . . whose father, he proudly told us, was standing as Labour Candidate for a hopeless seat in an imminent General Election. My father teased him unmercifully, asking questions that the poor child could not begin to answer, making elaborate and hideous semantic jokes about the fruits of labour, throwing in familiar references to prominent Tories that were quite wasted on such . . . tender ears; and the poor child sat there, staring at his roast beef . . . turning redder and redder, and trying, pathetically, sycophantically, to smile. I hated my father at that instant [pp. 56–57].

Yet Drabble's Jane is made to share the lightest touch of her parents' prejudice. The part I have elided is a mocking reference to the child's large red ears. For her the most important issue remains sexual deprivation, sexual choice. *The Waterfall*, the name of a card trick, is also the name of Jane's orgasms, James's gift to her.

But perhaps Drabble is ironic when she creates so class-bound and yet so analytic a Jane? It is a possibility, of course, but Jane's identification with the author of the narrative makes this doubtful. If there is irony to be generated here, it must come, as they say, from "outside the book."

Rather than imposing my irony, I attempt to find the figure of Jane as narrator helpful. Drabble manipulates her to examine the conditions of production and determination of microstructural heterosexual attitudes within her chosen enclosure. This enclosure is important because it is from here that rules come. Jane is made to realize that there are no fixed new rules in the book, not as yet. First World feminists are up against that fact, every day. This should not become an excuse but should remain a delicate responsibility: "If I need a morality, I will create one: a new ladder, a new virtue. If I need to understand what I am doing, if I cannot act without my own approbation—and I must act, I have changed,

I am no longer capable of inaction—then I will invent a morality that condones
me. Though by doing so, I risk condemning all that I have been" [pp. 52–53].

If the cautions of deconstruction are heeded—the contingency that the desire
to "understand" and "change" are as much symptomatic as they are revolutionary—merely to fill in the void with rules will spoil the case again, for women
as for human beings. We must strive moment by moment to practice a taxonomy
of different forms of understanding, different forms of change, dependent perhaps upon resemblance and seeming substitutability—figuration—rather than
on the self-identical category of truth:

> Because it's obvious that I haven't told the truth, about myself and James.
> How could I? Why, more significantly, should I? . . . Of the truth, I haven't
> told enough. I flinched at the conclusion and can even see in my hesitance
> a virtue: it is dishonest, it is inartistic, but it is a virtue, such discretion,
> in the moral world of love. . . . The names of qualities are interchangeable:
> vice, virtue: redemption, corruption: courage, weakness: and hence the
> confusion of abstraction, the proliferation of aphorism and paradox. In
> the human world, perhaps there are merely likenesses. . . . The qualities,
> they depended on the supposed true end of life. . . . Salvation, damna-
> tion. . . . I do not know which of these two James represented. Hysterical
> terms, maybe: religious terms, yet again. But then life is a serious matter,
> and it is not merely hysteria that acknowledges this fact: for men as well
> as women have been known to acknowledge it. I must make an effort to
> comprehend it. I will take it all to pieces. I will resolve it to parts, and
> then I will put it together again, I will reconstitute it in a form that I can
> accept, a fictitious form [pp. 46, 51, 52].

The categories by which one understands, the qualities of plus and minus, are
revealing themselves as arbitrary, situational. Drabble's Jane's way out—to resolve and reconstitute life into an acceptable fictional *form* that need not, perhaps, worry too much about the categorical problems—seems, by itself, a classical privileging of the aesthetic, for Drabble hints at the limits of self-
interpretation through a gesture that is accessible to the humanist academic.
Within a fictional form, she confides that the exigencies of a narrative's unity
had not allowed her to report the whole truth. She then changes from the third
person to first.

What can a literary critic do with this? Notice that the move is absurdity twice
compounded, since the discourse reflecting the constraints of fiction-making
goes on then to fabricate another fictive text. Notice further that the narrator
who tells us about the impossibility of truth-in-fiction—the classic privilege of
metaphor—is a metaphor as well.[25]

I should choose a simpler course. I should acknowledge this global dismissal
of any narrative speculation about the nature of truth and then dismiss it in
turn, since it might unwittingly suggest that there is somewhere a way of speaking about truth in "truthful" language, that a speaker can somewhere get rid

of the structural unconscious and speak without role playing. Having taken note of the frame, I will thus explain the point Jane is making here and relate it to what, I suppose, the critical view above would call "the anthropomorphic world": when one takes a rational or aesthetic distance from oneself one gives oneself up to the conveniently classifying macrostructures, a move dramatized by Drabble's third-person narrator. By contrast, when one involves oneself in the microstructural moments of practice that make possible and undermine every macrostructural theory, one falls, as it were, into the deep waters of a first person who recognizes the limits of understanding and change, indeed the precarious necessity of the micro-macro opposition, yet is bound not to give up.

The risks of first-person narrative prove too much for Drabble's fictive Jane. She wants to plot her narrative in terms of the paradoxical category—"pure corrupted love"—that allows her to *make* a fiction rather than try, *in* fiction, to report on the unreliability of categories: "I want to get back to that schizoid third-person dialogue. I've one or two more sordid conditions to describe, and then I can get back there to that isolated world of pure corrupted love" [p. 130]. To return us to the detached and macrostructural third person narrative after exposing its limits could be an aesthetic allegory of deconstructive practice.

Thus Drabble fills the void of the female consciousness with meticulous and helpful articulation, though she seems thwarted in any serious presentation of the problems of race and class, and of the marginality of sex. She engages in that microstructural dystopia, the sexual situation in extremis, that begins to seem more and more a part of women's fiction. Even within those limitations, our motto cannot be Jane's "I prefer to suffer, I think"—the privatist cry of heroic liberal women; it might rather be the lesson of the scene of writing of *The Waterfall*: to return to the third person with its grounds mined under.

4.

It is no doubt useful to decipher women's fiction in this way for feminist students and colleagues in American academia. I am less patient with literary texts today, even those produced by women. We must of course remind ourselves, our positivist feminist colleagues in charge of creating the discipline of women's studies, and our anxious students, that essentialism is a trap. It seems more important to learn to understand that the world's women do not all relate to the privileging of essence, especially through "fiction," or "literature," in quite the same way.

In Seoul, South Korea, in March 1982, 237 woman workers in a factory owned by Control Data, a Minnesota-based multinational corporation, struck over a demand for a wage raise. Six union leaders were dismissed and imprisoned. In July, the women took hostage two visiting U.S. vice-presidents, demanding reinstatement of the union leaders. Control Data's main office was willing to release the women; the Korean government was reluctant. On July 16, the Korean male workers at the factory beat up the female workers and ended the dispute. Many of the women were injured and two suffered miscarriages.

To grasp this narrative's overdeterminations (the many telescoped lines—

sometimes noncoherent, often contradictory, perhaps discontinuous—that allow us to determine the reference point of a single "event" or cluster of "events") would require a complicated analysis.[26] Here, too, I will give no more than a checklist of the overdeterminants. In the earlier stages of industrial capitalism, the colonies provided the raw materials so that the colonizing countries could develop their manufacturing industrial base. Indigenous production was thus crippled or destroyed. To minimize circulation time, industrial capitalism needed to establish due process, and such civilizing instruments as railways, postal services, and a uniformly graded system of education. This, together with the labor movements in the First World and the mechanisms of the welfare state, slowly made it imperative that manufacturing itself be carried out on the soil of the Third World, where labor can make many fewer demands, and the governments are mortgaged. In the case of the telecommunications industry, making old machinery obsolete at a more rapid pace than it takes to absorb its value in the commodity, this is particularly practical.

The incident that I recounted above, not at all uncommon in the multinational arena, complicates our assumptions about women's entry into the age of computers and the modernization of "women in development," especially in terms of our daily theorizing and practice. It should make us confront the discontinuities and contradictions in our assumptions about women's freedom to work outside the house, and the sustaining virtues of the working-class family. The fact that these workers were women was not merely because, like those Belgian lacemakers, oriental women have small and supple fingers. It is also because they are the true army of surplus labor. No one, including their men, will agitate for an adequate wage. In a two-job family, the man saves face if the woman makes less, even for a comparable job.

Does this make Third World men more sexist than David Rockefeller? The nativist argument that says "do not question Third World mores" is of course unexamined imperialism. There *is* something like an answer, which makes problematic the grounds upon which we base our own intellectual and political activities. No one can deny the dynamism and civilizing power of socialized capital. The irreducible search for greater production of surplus-value (dissimulated as, simply, "productivity") through technological advancement; the corresponding necessity to train a consumer who will need what is produced and thus help realize surplus-value as profit; the tax breaks associated with supporting humanist ideology through "corporate philanthropy"; all conspire to "civilize." These motives do not exist on a large scale in a comprador economy like that of South Korea, which is neither the necessary recipient nor the agent of socialized capital. The surplus-value is realized elsewhere. The nuclear family does not have a transcendent ennobling power. The fact that ideology and the ideology of marriage have developed in the West since the English revolution of the seventeenth century has something like a relationship to the rise of meritocratic individualism.[27]

These possibilities overdetermine any generalization about universal parenting based on American, Western European, or laundered anthropological speculation.

Socialized capital kills by remote control. In this case, too, the American managers watched while the South Korean men decimated their women. The managers denied charges. One remark made by a member of Control Data management, as reported in *Multinational Monitor*, seemed symptomatic in its self-protective cruelty: "Although 'it's true' Chae lost her baby, 'this is not the first miscarriage she's had. She's had two before this'"[28] However active in the production of civilization as a by-product, socialized capital has not moved far from the presuppositions of a slave mode of production. "In Roman theory, the agricultural slave was designated an *instrumentum vocale*, the speaking tool, one grade away from the livestock that constituted an *instrumentum semi-vocale*, and two from the implement which was an *instrumentum mutum*."[29]

One of Control Data's radio commercials speaks of how its computers open the door to knowledge, at home or in the workplace, for men and women alike. The acronym of this computer system is PLATO. One might speculate that this noble name helps to dissimulate a quantitative and formula-permutational vision of knowledge as an instrument of efficiency and exploitation with an aura of the unique and subject-expressive wisdom at the very root of "democracy." The undoubted historical-symbolic value of the acronym PLATO shares in the effacement of class-history that is the project of "civilization" as such: "The slave mode of production which underlay Athenian civilization necessarily found its most pristine ideological expression in the privileged social stratum of the city, whose intellectual heights its surplus labour in the silent depths below the *polis* made possible."[30]

"Why is it," I asked above, "that when Derrida writes under the sign of woman his work becomes solipsistic and marginal?"

His discovery of the figure of woman is in terms of a critique of propriation—proper-ing, as in the proper name (patronymic) or property.[31] Suffice it to say here that, by thus differentiating himself from the phallocentric tradition under the aegis of a(n idealized) woman who is the "sign" of the indeterminate, of that which has im-propriety as its property, Derrida cannot think that the sign "woman" is indeterminate by virtue of its access to the tyranny of the text of the proper. It is this tyranny of the "proper"—in the sense of that which produces both property and the proper name of the patronymic—that I have called the suppression of the clitoris, and that the news item about Control Data illustrates.[32]

Derrida has written a magically orchestrated book—*La carte postale*—on philosophy as telecommunication (Control Data's business) using an absent, unnamed, and sexually indeterminate woman (Control Data's victim) as a vehicle, to reinterpret the relationship between Socrates and Plato (Control Data's acronym) taking it through Freud and beyond. The determination of that book is a parable of my argument. Here deconstruction becomes complicit with an essentialist bourgeois feminism. The following paragraph appeared recently in *Ms*: "Control Data is among those enlightened corporations that offer social-service leaves. . . . Kit Ketchum, former treasurer of Minnesota NOW, applied for and got a full year with pay to work at NOW's national office in Washington, D.C. She writes: 'I commend Control Data for their commitment to employing and promoting women. . . .' Why not suggest this to your employer?"[33] Bourgeois feminism, because of a blindness to the *multi*national theater, dissimulated by "clean" national practice and fostered by the dominant ideology, can participate in the tyranny of the proper and see in Control Data an extender of the Platonic mandate to women in general.

The dissimulation of political economy is in and by ideology. What is at work and can be used in that operation is at least the ideology of nation-states, nationalism, national liberation, ethnicity, and religion. Feminism lives in the master-text as well as in the pores. It is not the determinant of the last instance. I think less easily of "changing the world" than in the past. I teach a small number of the holders of the can(n)on, male or female, feminist or masculist, how to read their own texts, as best I can.

1986

two

Into the World

6. Reading the World: Literary Studies in the Eighties

After my public lecture on "Literature and Life" in March 1980 at Riyadh University Center for Girls (*sic*), a student asked me with some asperity: "It's all very well to try to live like a book; but what if no one else is prepared to read? What if you are dismissed as an irresponsible dreamer?" I found an answer to her question at the tail end of a metaphor: "Everyone reads life and the world like a book. Even the so-called 'illiterate.' But especially the 'leaders' of our society, the most 'responsible' nondreamers: the politicians, the businessmen, the ones who make plans. Without the reading of the world as a book, there is no prediction, no planning, no taxes, no laws, no welfare, no war. Yet these leaders read the world in terms of rationality and averages, as if it were a textbook. The world actually writes itself with the many-leveled, unfixable intricacy and openness of a work of literature. If, through our study of literature, we can ourselves learn and teach others to read the world in the 'proper' risky way, and to act upon that lesson, perhaps we literary people would not forever be such helpless victims." It is difficult to say that very last bit to a woman in Saudi Arabia. So I added, half to myself, and with a sense of failure: "Mere literary studies cannot accomplish this. One must fill the vision of literary form with its connections to what is being read: history, political economy—the world. And it is not merely a question of disciplinary formation. It is a question also of questioning the separation between the world of action and the world of the disciplines. There is a great deal in the way."

In that exchange I was obliged to stress the distinction between my position and the position that, in a world of massive brutality, exploitation, and sexual oppression, advocates an aesthetization of life. Here I must stress that I am also not interested in answers to questions like "What is the nature of the aesthetic?" or "How indeed are we to understand 'life'?" My concern rather is that: 1) The formulation of such questions is itself a determined and determining gesture. 2) Very generally speaking, literary people are still caught within a position where they must say: Life is brute fact and outside art; the aesthetic is free and transcends life. 3) This declaration is the condition and effect of "ideology." 4) If "literary studies" is to have any meaning in the coming decade, its ideology might have to be questioned.

If the student and critic of literature is made to believe in and to perpetuate the received dogma of my second point, then the work of the "world" can go on without the interference suggested in my fourth point. But the disciplinary situation of the teacher of literature is inscribed in that very text of the "world" that the received dogma refuses to allow us to read. As a result, even as in classroom and article we mouth the freedom of the aesthetic, in bulletin and caucus and newspaper and meeting we deplore our attenuation and betrayal by society. The effort to invite a persistent displacement of the bewildering contradiction between life and art relates to the displacement of the bewildering contradiction between the conditions of life and the professions of our profession.

I have recently described our unwitting complicity with a world that efficiently marginalizes us in the following way:

> We are the disc jockeys of an advanced technocracy. The discs are not "records" of the old-fashioned kind, but productions of the most recent technology. The trends in taste and the economic factors that govern them are also products of the most complex interrelations among a myriad of factors such as foreign relations, the world market, the conduct of advertisement supported by and supporting the first two items, and so on. To speak of the mode of production and constitution of the radio station complicates matters further. Within this intricately determined and multiform situation, the disc jockey and his audience think, indeed are made to think, that they are free to play. This illusion of freedom allows us to protect the brutal ironies of technocracy by suggesting either that the system nourishes the humanist's freedom of spirit, or that "technology," that vague evil, is something the humanist must transform by inculcating humanistic "values," or by drawing generalized philosophical analogies from the latest spatio-temporal discoveries of the magical realms of "pure science." ("Explanation and Culture: Marginalia," Humanities in Society, 2, No. 3 (1979), p. 209; modified)

In the context of this marginalization our in-house disputes seem not only trivial but harmful. I refer, of course, to the disputes between composition and literature, and between practical criticism/literary history and "theory."

In the case of the dispute between composition and literature, the bewildering contradiction I speak of above is clearly to be seen. Teaching composition is recognized inside and outside the academy to be socially useful. If indeed the pages of the *ADE Bulletin* are to be believed, since 1976 the number of jobs in composition has doubled, and the area has held steady as the largest provider of jobs in the profession. Yet in terms of the politics and economics of the university, the college, the department, and the profession, it is the composition teacher whose position—with some significant exceptions—is less privileged and more precarious. The culprit is not far to see. It is the received dogma of the freedom of the aesthetic and literature's refusal to soil itself by rendering service to the state—when that very refusal is the greatest service that it can render to a polity that must disguise the extraction of surplus value as cultural dynamism.

Although my general argument and my metaphor of the humanist as disc jockey directly question this illusion of freedom from the "world" and the state, it is in the matter of the dispute between theory and practical criticism/literary history that I find myself most directly touched. I should of course admit that my concern reflects my own increasing speculation in "theory." (By "theory" is meant un-American activities that employ a vocabulary and sometimes methods belonging to the history of ideas rather than strictly to the domain of literary criticism, such as those of phenomenology, structuralism, deconstruction, semiotics. "Psychological" and "Marxist" criticism, long accused of reductivism and determinism, have entered "theory" through Jacques Lacan, Louis Althusser, and the Frankfurt School. The preferred and "American" side of the dispute endorses "pluralism," according to which some points of view are clearly delineated as more equal and more fundamental than others. The terms can be seen outlined in such exchanges as "The Limits of Pluralism," M. H. Abrams, Wayne Booth, J. Hillis Miller, _Critical Inquiry_, 3 (1977), 407–447; such works as Gerald Graff's _Literature Against Itself: Literary Ideas in Modern Society_ (Chicago: University of Chicago Press, 1979); and such forums as most of the "theoretical" sessions at annual conventions of national or regional literary organizations.)

Unfortunately enough, what I call the received dogma of the discipline of literary study affects the so-called theoretical field and the so-called practical-historical field equally. The two sides of the dispute in fact leave our general marginalization intact. When "theory" brings up questions of ideological "interest," or the limitations of the merely aesthetic norm, the terminology becomes fearfully abstract. On the other hand, when "theory" seeks to undo this situation by attempting a reading of a hidden ethical or ideological agenda in a literary text, a curious topos rises up to resist: the critic is accused, if only by implication, of being a charlatan, of playing Pied Piper to the young, while mature wisdom consists in leaving Business as Usual.

I was troubled by this at our own conference when, after an excellent talk on the resources and techniques for getting grants in our profession, Professor Steven Weiland remarked about Robert Scholes' performance the previous night: "I confess that the paragraph I am about to quote could perhaps be read to mean quite another thing by a semiotician. I suppose I am just not young enough to be able to learn that sort of reading." (I cannot quote his exact words, of course. It was an unrehearsed aside. Scholes had attempted a delicate reading of the theme of the inexhaustible volubility of nonintellectual women as a topos of masculist ideology as it operates in the discourse of Hemingway's "A Very Short Story.")

The same veiled accusation appears at the end of Denis Donaghue's ill-considered review of the most notorious "theory" stalking the halls of American literary criticism today—"deconstruction": "I think Deconstruction appeals to the clerisy of graduate students, who like to feel themselves superior to the laity of common readers" ("Deconstructing Deconstruction," _The New York Review of Books_, 27, No. 10 (1980), p. 41).

The fear of a critical reading that would question the writer's direct access to his or her meaning is related to the received dogma of the illusion of freedom. Strictly speaking, received dogma is another name for ideology. Ideology in the critical sense does not signify an avowed doctrine. It is rather the loosely articulated sets of historically determined and determining notions, presuppositions, and practices, each implying the other by real (but where does one stop to get a grip on reality?) or forced logic, which goes by the name of common sense or self-evident truth or natural behavior in a certain situation. What I have been talking about so far has been the displacing of the ideology of our discipline of literature.

Such an effort need not involve questioning the individual good will of author

or critic. The fear of critical reading ill-concealed in the following words is what
an ideology-critical pedagogy would constantly question: "The wretched side
of this is that Deconstruction encourages (graduate students) to feel superior
not only to undergraduates but to the authors they are reading" (Donaghue, p.
41). Wasn't it the "intentional fallacy" that did that? "Wordsworth's Preface to
the *Lyrical Ballads* is a remarkable document, but as a piece of Wordsworthian
criticism nobody would give it more than about a B plus" (Northrop Frye, *Anatomy of Criticism: Four Essays* [Princeton: Princeton University Press, 1957], p. 5).

A pedagogy that would constantly seek to undo the opposition between the
verbal and the social text at the same time that it knows its own inability to
know its own ideological provenance fully is perhaps better understood in the
American context as a de-archaeologized and de-teleologized version of the Baconian project to discover the idols of the mind, which would constitute rather
than lead to, in a fragmented rather than a continuous way, a New Philosophy
or Active Science.[1] It is an experiment in using an expertise in reading literature
to read the text of a world that has an interest in preserving that expertise merely
to propagate, to use the Baconian word, an idolatry of literature, perhaps even
a species of self-idolatry as the privileged reader.

Rather than continue in this abstract vein, let me beguile you with some
examples.

I taught a seminar for first-year Plan II students at the University of Texas
last fall. Plan II is an interdisciplinary, four-year honors program for exceptionally gifted liberal arts undergraduates; everything else in the college is Plan I.

At the first class meeting, the young men and women sat, as did I, in movable
chairs around a hollow square of four oblong tables. I was a little late for the
second class meeting. The students had left the same chair empty, and thus
given me a chance to introduce to them the theme that is my subject tonight.
Here is a gist of my homily: "You are amazingly intelligent young people of
unquestionable personal good will. The university has rightly rewarded your
outstanding merit by adjudicating some extra freedoms for you. You have, for
example, been granted a serious degree of freedom by the arrangement of furniture. You sit with your teacher in a small group in movable chairs around a
center; your less gifted peers are in large, well-monitored classes in fixed seats
gazing upon authority on a dais. But history and the institutions of power and
authority are stronger than the limits of personal good will. If you deny them,
they will get in through the back door. Because I warmed that particular chair
with my bottom the last time, I seem to have baptized it as the seat of authority
and you have left it empty for me. Your historical-institutional imperatives are
proving stronger than your personal good will. Since our topic this semester is
going to be 'Images of Woman and Man in the Texts of Men and Women,' what
I am saying now might be useful for us. We will read some great texts of the
past—such as *The Eumenides*, the *Vita nuova*, and *Émile*—and see in them the
blueprints for rather questionable sexual attitudes. Now you must remember,
every day in class, and as you write your papers, that this is not to belittle
Aeschylus, Dante, or Rousseau as individuals, but to see in and through them

something like their 'age,' to take into account how we are ourselves caught in a time and a place, and then to imagine acting within such an awareness."

I made some good friends in that class—although I could not always be sure of a chair if I was late—partly because they saw repeatedly that the readings advanced by their teacher, that figure of authority, were not authoritatively backed up by the traditional readings of, say, Aeschylus, or Dante, or yet Rousseau. There was, however, a certain problem the class could not get over.

Since our theme was so clearly socio-historical, I would often ask these students to write their papers from a point of view that was not only that of private but also of public individuals. After a variety of valiant efforts, nearly every paper faced with that specific charge ended in variations of the following argument: In the final analysis, no public generalization of this question is possible or even desirable, because we are all unique individuals.

I think I had made it clear to my students that, although I was often critical of European or American ideology, I was in no way at all offering them, as a native of India, a so-called "Indian spiritual" solution. I was able to talk to them about the problem in their papers, therefore, in a dialogue resembling what follows:

"Do you know what indoctrination is?"

"Yes."

"Do you know where it is to be found?"

"The Soviet Union and the Islamic world."

"Suppose an outsider, observing the uniformity of the moves you have all sketched in your papers, were to say that you had been indoctrinated? That you could no longer conceive of public decision-making except in the quantified areas of your economics and business classes, where you learn all about rational expectations theories? You *know* that decisions in the public sphere, such as tax decisions, legal decisions, foreign policy decisions, fiscal decisions, affect your *private* lives deeply. Yet in a speculative field such as the interpretation of texts, you feel that there is something foolish and wrong and regimented about a public voice. Suppose someone were to say that this was a result of your indoctrination to keep moral speculation and decision-making apart, to render you incapable of thinking collectively in any but the most inhuman way?"

For my second example I will go back to Saudi Arabia, this time to the male faculty of the Riyadh University Faculty of Arts. I met a group of faculty members twice—I think it was the first time a woman had run what amounted to a faculty development seminar there. The impression I carried away strengthened my conviction about not only literature, but the humanities in general in the service of the state.

Since 1973, Saudi Arabia has been one of America's strongest allies among OPEC countries. As a result of the incredible boom following the surprise defeat of Israel that year, Saudi Arabia is "modernizing" itself at an extremely rapid pace. Part of the "modernizing" package is, quite properly, education; most of it, for reasons much larger than individual enthusiasm for American education, from the United States. As far as I could tell, the methodologies of the humanities that were being imported through visiting or U.S. trained faculty sustain and are sustained by the ideology or received dogma of disinterestedness and freedom that I have been describing in the case of literature. I compiled this checklist while I was there: analytical and speech act theory in philosophy; quantitative analysis, structural functionalism, and objective structuralism in history and anthropology; mathematization on a precritical psychological model in linguistics; descriptive and biologistic clinical approaches, behaviorism, and delibidinized ego-psychology in psychology; objective structuralism, New Criticism, history- and ideology-transcendent aestheticism in literature—and so on. (I received such lavish hospitality from my hosts that it seems churlish to add that I had probably been invited to add to this package the message of Deconstruction American Style.)

Following my general viewpoint, I would not for a moment suggest that one or more evil geniuses here or in Saudi Arabia are necessarily planning this export-import business in methodologies. My entire pedagogic approach would then come to nothing. The point is, first, that the ideological/material concatenation that produces this can be read and acted upon, although not once and for all, but rather constantly, persistently, like all repeated gestures of life-sustenance. Saudi Arabia, with American help, is in fact slowly fabricating for itself a "humanist" intellectual elite that will be unable to read the relationship between its own production and the flow of oil, money, and arms. A diversified technocratic elite whose allegiance to humanism, if at all in evidence, will be sentimental, will take care of those dirtier flows. The apparent lack of contact between rational expectations in the business world and freedom and disinterest in the humanist academy will support each other, as here, and to America's advantage. To call it "cultural imperialism" is to pass the buck, in every sense. I am attempting to suggest our pedagogic responsibility in this situation: to ask not merely how literary studies, more correctly the universitarian discipline of English studies, can adjust to changing social demands, but also how we could, by changing some of our assumptions, contribute toward changing those demands in the very long run.

An Arab-American linguist trained on the American West Coast asked me at one of the meetings in Riyadh, "How do you propose to fit, say, Shakespeare, into this pedagogic program?" I did give him an answer, in some detail, referring to my experience as a student in India and a teacher in the American Middle West and Texas. That reply will have to wait till next time. Let me, however, indicate that I have outlined an answer with reference to Wordsworth's *The Prelude* in an essay—"Sex and History in Wordsworth's *The Prelude* (1805): Books Nine to Thirteen"—forthcoming in *Texas Studies in Language and Literature*.[2]

The point of these far-flung digressions has been, then, that a literary study that can graduate into the 80s might teach itself to attend to the dialectical and continuous crosshatching of ideology and literary language. Further, that such an activity, learned in the classroom, should slide without a sense of rupture into an active and involved reading of the social text within which the student and teacher of literature are caught.

The after-dinner speech as genre allows me to add another story. Toward the beginning of May this year, Sir James Cavenham, the English financier, was looking to buy out "35 percent of Diamond (International)'s stock." He already owned "nearly 6 percent." This was in opposition to Diamond's "proposed acquisition of Brooks-Scanlon Inc., a forest products company" (*New York Times*, 13 May 1980, Sec. 4, p. 4), because it would reduce Cavenham's share to a much smaller percentage. Diamond is a paper company.

"As the battle intensified," the *Times* reported next week, "Wall Street professionals eagerly watched the in-fighting on both sides. The highly respected Merrill Lynch Whiteweld Capital Market Group had assured Diamond a month ago that the merger terms were fair to Diamond's stockholders. The equally prestigious house of Warburg Paribas Becker gave the same assurance to Brooks-Scanlon investors." In the same issue of the *Times*, an advertisement covering an entire page exhorted Diamond's stockholders to vote "no" on the merger, assuring them that it would be to their benefit and advantage.

We have here what the latest literary theory would call—borrowing a word from the Greek—an aporia, an unresolvable doubt. We show our ideological acceptance of error-as-truth when we say, no, one is a paid ad, the other is news, the first therefore is more liable to be false. Is it? If the exchange of money allows for lie-as-truth, what are Diamond, Brooks-Scanlon, Merrill Lynch, and Warburg Paribas Becker working in the interest of? Where is there a decidable truth free of the circuit of exchange to be found? What about the fact that most people would rather read the full-page ad and believe it than read the details of printed news and understand it? Has that fact anything to do with the self-marginalizing dogma of the teaching of literature? Is there an active-philosophical (to remind you of the Baconian term) analysis of that? On May 14, Diamond's annual meeting took place in Bangor, Maine, where Cavenham's French Company Générale Occidentale, S.A., planned to oppose the Brooks-Scanlon-Diamond merger. In nearby Orono, the International Association for Philosophy and Literature met from May 8 to 11. Considerable amounts of paper—Diamond's direct and Brooks-Scanlon's indirect product—were consumed. A considerable amount of intellectual energy and acrimony were spent on the work of a French philosopher who had suggested that "truth" is indeterminate and always "interested"; it was advanced that he and his followers were undermining the seriousness of the American academy. Would the assembled philosophers and literary critics have been capable of drawing a lesson from the accepted indeterminacy, conventionally and by tacit agreement presented as factual truth, that operates and informs the "serious" business that determines the "materiality" of their existence?

The after-dinner speech demands by definition a certain vague euphoria. If you think I have fulfilled that demand only too well, let me hasten to assure you that I am well aware of the complicated organizational assumptions underlying my suggestions. To mention only a few of the heavies: faculty development, fundamental curricular revision, overhauling of disciplinary lines until the term "English literary studies" changes drastically in meaning. I am indeed foolhardy enough to look forward to a struggle for such painstaking and painful transformations. But I do not suggest that the struggle should begin at the expense of our students' immediate futures. I think rather that our efforts should be on at least two fronts at once. We should work to implement the changes even as we prepare our students to fit into the job market as it currently exists. It is merely that we should not mistake the requirements of the job market for the ineffable determinants of the nature of literary studies.

To explain what I mean, I will offer you a final example, a diffident and humble one, the description of a course that I found myself designing on my feet— largely because of the predilections I have elaborated so lengthily above. It is a required course for incoming graduate students: Practical Criticism.

You will have gathered that I am deeply doubtful of the isolationist ideology of practical criticism—to explicate the text as such, with all "outside knowledge" put out of play,[3] even as I think its strategies are extremely useful in interpreting and changing the social text. How can one launch a persistent critique of the ideology without letting go of the strategy? I put together a working answer to the question *while* I taught the course for the first time.

We begin with a situational definition of "practical criticism": a criticism that allows for departmental qualification for the PhD. (My department no longer has the qualifying examination, but the standards for qualification remain implicitly the same.) A little over the first half of the course is a criticism workshop, where we read each other's work and learn to write in the approved institutional way, trying to cope with its difficulties and to reveal its subtleties. The rest of the course is given to readings and discussions of texts that offer fundamental critiques of the ideology that would present this technique as *the* description of the preferred practice of the critic—the list can be wide enough to accommodate Percy Shelley, Walter Benjamin, and Michel Foucault. What I hope to achieve through such a bicameral approach is to prepare the student for the existing situation even as I provide her with a mind-set to change it. A very minor individual effort that looks forward to the major collective efforts that are on my mind.[4]

I have so far tried to follow the notes of the talk I gave at the ADE Seminar in Iowa City. I would like to end by recalling a moment after the talk. Lawrence Mitchell, chairman of the English department at the University of Minnesota, and a friend of long standing from his graduate student days at the University of Iowa, asked if perhaps my critical attitude did not reflect the fact that I, like him—he was born in England—was an outsider? I have thought about that question. Even after nineteen years in this country, fifteen of them spent in full-time teaching, I believe the answer is yes. But then, where is the inside? To define an inside is a decision, I believe I said that night, and the critical method I am describing would question the ethico-political strategic exclusions that would define a certain set of characteristics as an "inside" at a certain time. "The text itself," "the poem as such," "intrinsic criticism," are such strategic definitions. I have spoken in support of a way of reading that would continue to break down these distinctions, never once and for all, and *actively* interpret "inside" and "outside" as texts for involvement as well as for change.[5]

1985

7. Explanation and Culture: Marginalia

I tried writing a first version of this piece in the usual disinterested academic style. I gave up after a few pages and after some thought decided to disclose a little of the undisclosed margins of that first essay. This decision was based on a certain program at least implicit in all feminist activity: the deconstruction of the opposition between the private and the public.

According to the explanations that constitute (as they are the effects of) our culture, the political, social, professional, economic, intellectual arenas belong to the public sector. The emotional, sexual, and domestic are the private sector. Certain practices of religion, psychotherapy, and art in the broadest sense are said to inhabit the private sector as well. But the institutions of religion, psychotherapy, and art, as well as the criticism of art, belong to the public. Feminist practice, at least since the European eighteenth century, suggests that each compartment of the public sector also operates emotionally and sexually, that the domestic sphere is not the emotions' only legitimate workplace.[1]

In the interest of the effectiveness of the women's movement, emphasis is often placed upon a reversal of the public-private hierarchy. This is because in ordinary sexist households, educational institutions, or workplaces, the sustaining explanation still remains that the public sector is more important, at once more rational and mysterious, and, generally, more masculine, than the private. The feminist, reversing this hierarchy, must insist that sexuality and the emotions are, in fact, so much more important and threatening that a masculinist sexual politics is obliged, repressively, to sustain all public activity. The most "material" sedimentation of this repressive politics is the institutionalized sex discrimination that seems the hardest stone to push.

The shifting limit that prevents this feminist reversal of the public-private hierarchy from freezing into a dogma or, indeed, from succeeding fully is the displacement of the opposition itself. For if the fabric of the so-called public sector is woven of the so-called private, the definition of the private is marked by a public potential, since it *is* the weave, or texture, of public activity. The opposition is thus not merely reversed; it is displaced. It is according to this practical structure of deconstruction as reversal-displacement then that I write: the deconstruction of the opposition between the private and the public is implicit in all, and explicit in some, feminist activity. The peculiarity of deconstructive practice must be reiterated here. Displacing the opposition that it initially apparently questions, it is always different from itself, always defers itself. It is neither a constitutive nor, of course, a regulative norm. If it were either, then feminist activity would articulate or strive toward that fulfilled displacement of public (male) and private (female): an *ideal* society and a sex-*transcendent* humanity. But deconstruction teaches one to question all transcendental idealisms. It is in terms of this peculiarity of deconstruction then that the displacement of male-female, public-private marks a shifting limit rather than the desire for a complete reversal.

At any rate, this is the explanation that I offer for my role at the Explanation and Culture Symposium and for the production of this expanded version of my essay. The explanatory labels are "feminist," "deconstructivist."

We take the explanations we produce to be the grounds of our action; they are endowed with coherence in terms of our explanation of a self. Thus willy-nilly, the choice of these two labels to give myself a shape produces between them a common cause. (Alternatively, the common cause between feminism and deconstruction might have made me choose them as labels for myself.) This common cause is an espousal of, and an attention to, marginality—a suspicion that what is at the center often hides a repression.

All this may be merely a preamble to admitting that at the actual symposium I sensed, and sensing cultivated, a certain marginality. Our intelligent and conscientious moderator seemed constantly to summarize me out of the group. After hearing us make our preliminary statements, he said that we were all interested in culture as process rather than object of study. No, I would not privilege process. After the next batch of short speeches, he said that it was evident that we wanted to formulate a coherent notion of explanation and culture that would accommodate all of us. No, I would not find unity in diversity; sometimes confrontation rather than integration seemed preferable. Leroy Searle, an old friend, spoke of the model of explanation having yielded to interpretation and threw me a conspirator's look. George Rousseau spoke of distrusting the text, and I wondered if he had thought to declare solidarity with a deconstructor by publicly aligning himself with what Paul Ricoeur has called "the hermeneutics of suspicion."[2] But I was not satisfied with hermeneutics—the theory of "interpretation rather than explanation"—"suspicious" or not, as long as it did not confront the problem of the critic's practice in any radical way. I thought the desire to explain might be a symptom of the desire to have a self that can control knowledge and a world that can be known; I thought to give oneself the right to a correct self-analysis and thus to avoid all thought of symptomaticity was foolish; I thought therefore that, willy-nilly, there was no way out but to develop a provisional theory of the practical politics of cultural explanations.

The group repeatedly expressed interest in my point of view because it appeared singular. But the direct question of what this point of view was was never posed or was posed at the end of a three-hour session given over to the correct definition of the role, say, of cognition in aesthetics. Is a poem cognitive? A picture? And so on. But I had no use for these phantasmic subdivisions (cognition, volition, perception, and the like) of the labor of consciousness except as an object of interpretation of which I was a part. A deconstructive point of view would reverse and displace such hierarchies as cognitive-aesthetic. I would bleat out sentences such as these in the interstices of the discussion. Kindly participants would turn to me, at best, and explain what I meant or didn't mean. At worst, the discussion of cognition and aesthetics would simply resume. On one occasion I had captured the floor with a rather cunning, if misguided series of illustrations from Nietzsche. The response was a remark that Nietzsche was a worthless philosopher, although rather fun. I countered hotly that cheap derision was out of place in a scholarly discussion. I was assured that fun was an essential element in all proper philosophers, and no harm had been meant.

This exchange illustrates yet another way I had solidly put myself in the margin. I questioned the structure of our proceedings whenever I felt it to be necessary—for the structure or means of production of explanations is, of course, a very important part of the ideology of cultural explanations that cannot be clearly distinguished, in fact, from the explanations themselves. It seemed an unrecognizable principle to this group of pleasant and gifted scholars. It didn't help that my manner in such situations is high-handed, and my sentences hopelessly periodic and Anglo-Indian. Every intervention was read as an expression of personal pique or fear. "Don't worry, no one will bother you on the big public day." I kept myself from gnashing my teeth, because that would only show that I still legitimated the male right to aggression. In fact, I was quite tough in public, having been trained before the hard-won triumphs of the latest wave of the women's movement, indeed, initially in a place out of comparison more sexist than academic America; my arguments had not been in the interest of *my* personal safety but rather against *their* masculist practice, mistaken as the neutral and universal practice of intellectuals. In fact, I was assured at one point that male animals fought, even in play. I believe I did say that I knew it only too well; it was just that I thought some of it was curable.

Following the precarious and unrigorous rule of the deconstruction of the public and the private, I spoke of my marginality at the public session. I did not reserve my thrusts for the privacy of the bedroom or the kitchen table (in this case, the collegial dinner, lunch, or corridor chat), where decent men reprimanded their wives. (It would take me too far afield to develop and present the idea, based on a good deal of observation, that the academic male model for behavior toward their so-called female equals was that of the bourgeois husband.) I received no personal criticism "in public," of course. Taken aside, I was told I had used my power unfairly by posing as marginal; that I could criticize the establishment only because I spoke its language too well (English, masculinese, power play?). Both of these kinds of remark would have produced lively and profitable discussion about explanation and cultural persuasion if, in fact, they had been put to me in public. But in this case, one kind of situational explanation was culturally prohibited, except as the exceptional, but more "real" matter of marginal communication.

About the worst of these asides even I feel obliged to remain silent.

Now when a Jacques Derrida deconstructs the opposition between private and public, margin and center, he touches the texture of language and tells how the old words would not resemble themselves any more if a trick of rereading were learned. The trick is to recognize that in every textual production, in the production of every explanation, there is the itinerary of a constantly thwarted desire to make the text explain. The question then becomes: What is this explanation as it is constituted by and as it effects a desire to conserve the explanation itself; what are the "means devised in the interest of the problem of a possible objective knowledge"?[3]

I wrote above that the will to explain was a symptom of the desire to have a self and a world. In other words, on the general level, the possibility of explanation carries the presupposition of an explainable (even if not fully) universe and an explaining (even if imperfectly) subject. These presuppositions assure our being. Explaining, we exclude the possibility of the *radically* heterogeneous.

On a more specific level, every explanation must secure and assure a certain *kind* of being-in-the world, which might as well be called our politics. The general and specific levels are not clearly distinguishable, since the guarantee of sovereignty in the subject toward the object is the condition of the possibility of politics. Speaking for the specific politics of sexuality, I hoped to draw our attention to the productive and political margins of our discourse in general. I hoped to reiterate that, although the prohibition of marginality that is crucial in the production of any explanation is politics as such, what inhabits the prohibited margin of a particular explanation specifies its particular politics. To learn this without self-exculpation but without excusing the other side either is in my view so important that I will cite here a benign example from Derrida before he became playful in a way disturbing for the discipline.[4]

In *Speech and Phenomena* (1967), Derrida analyzes Edmund Husserl's *Logical Investigations* I. In the last chapter of the book, he produces this explanation: "The history of metaphysics therefore can be expressed as the unfolding of the structure or schema of an absolute will to hear-oneself-speak."[5]

Now this is indeed the product of the careful explication of Husserl through the entire book. This is also, as we know, one of the architraves of Derrida's thought. Yet if *Speech and Phenomena* is read carefully, by the time we arrive at this sentence we know that the role of "expression" as the adequate language of theory or concept is precisely what has been deconstructed in the book. Therefore, when Derrida says, "can be expressed as," he does not mean "is." He proffers us his analytical explanation in the language that he has deconstructed. Yet he does not imply that the explanation is therefore worthless, that there is a "true" explanation where the genuine copula ("is") can be used. He reminds us rather that all explanations, including his own, claim their centrality in terms of an excluded margin that makes possible the "can" of the "can be expressed" and allows "is" to be quietly substituted for it.

The implications of this philosophical position cannot remain confined to academic discourse. When all my colleagues were reacting adversely to my invocations of marginality, they were in fact performing another move within the center (public truth)-margin (private emotions) set. They were inviting me into the center at the price of exacting from me the language of centrality.

"Several of our excellent women colleagues in analysis," Freud wrote, explaining femininity, "have begun to work at the question [of femininity]. . . . For the ladies, whenever some comparison seemed to turn out unfavourable to their sex, were able to utter a suspicion that we, the male analysts, had been unable to overcome certain deeply rooted prejudices against what was feminine, and that this was being paid for in the partiality of our researches. We, on the other hand, standing on the ground of bisexuality, had no difficulty in avoiding impoliteness. We had only to say: 'This doesn't apply to you. You're an exception, on this point you're more masculine than feminine.'"[6]

That passage was written in 1932. Adrienne Rich, speaking to the students of Smith College in 1979, said:

> There's a false power which masculine society offers to a few women who "think like men" on condition that they use it to maintain things as they

are. This is the meaning of female tokenism: that power withheld from the vast majority of women is offered to few, so that it may appear that any truly qualified woman can gain access to leadership, recognition, and reward; hence that justice based on merits actually prevails. The token woman is encouraged to see herself as different from most other women, as exceptionally talented and deserving; and to separate herself from the wider female condition; and she is perceived by "ordinary" women as separate also: perhaps even as stronger than themselves.[7]

In offering me their perplexity and chagrin, my colleagues on the panel were acting out the scenario of tokenism: you are as good as we are (I was less learned than most of them, but never mind), why do you insist on emphasizing your difference? The putative center welcomes selective inhabitants of the margin in order better to exclude the margin. And it is the center that offers the official explanation; or, the center is defined and reproduced by the explanation that it can express.

I have so far been explaining our symposium in terms of what had better be called a masculist centralism. By pointing attention to a feminist marginality, I have been attempting, not to win the center for ourselves, but to point at the irreducibility of the margin in all explanations. That would not merely reverse but displace the distinction between margin and center. But in effect such pure innocence (pushing all guilt to the margins) is not possible, and, paradoxically, would put the very law of displacement and the irreducibility of the margin into question. The only way I can hope to suggest how the center itself is marginal is by not remaining outside in the margin and pointing my accusing finger at the center. I might do it rather by implicating myself in that center and sensing what politics make it marginal. Since one's vote is at the limit for oneself, the deconstructivist can use herself (assuming one is at one's own disposal) as a shuttle between the center (inside) and the margin (outside) and thus narrate a displacement.

The politics in terms of which all of us at the symposium as humanists are marginalized is the politics of an advanced capitalist technocracy.[8] I should insist here that the practice of capitalism is intimately linked with the practice of masculism.[9] As I speak of how humanists on the margin of such a society are tokenized, I hope these opening pages will remind the reader repeatedly how feminism, rather than being a special interest, might prove a model for the ever-vigilant integration of the humanities. Here, however, in the interest of speaking from inside our group at the symposium, I will speak of this marginalization as a separate argument.

Although there are a mathematician and a physicist in our midst, we represent the humanist enclave in the academy. The mathematician is a philosopher, and the physicist, a philosopher of science. As such they represent acts of private good sense and intellectual foresight, which does not reproduce itself as a collective ideological change. These colleagues bring a flavor of pure science into our old-fashioned chambers and become practicing humanists much more easily than we could become practicing theoreticians of science. Together we represent the humanist enclave in the academy.

Our assigned role is, seemingly, the custodianship of culture. If as I have argued the concept and self-concept of culture as systems of habit are constituted by the production of explanations even as they make these explanations possible, our role is to produce and be produced by the *official* explanations in terms of the powers that police the entire society, emphasizing a continuity or a discontinuity with past explanations, depending on a seemingly judicious choice permitted by the play of this power. As we produce the official explanations, we reproduce the official ideology, the structure of possibility of a knowledge whose effect is that very structure. Our circumscribed productivity cannot be dismissed as a mere keeping of records. We are a part of the records we keep.

It is to belabor the obvious to say that we are written into the text of technology. It is no less obvious, though sometimes deliberately less well recognized (as perhaps in our symposium), that as collaborators in that text we also write it, constitutively if not regulatively. As with every text in existence, no sovereign individual writes it with full control. The most powerful technocrat is in that sense also a victim, although in brute suffering his victimhood cannot be compared to that of the poor and oppressed classes of the world. Our own victimhood is also not to be compared to this last, yet, in the name of the disinterested pursuit and perpetration of humanism, it is the only ground whose marginality I can share with the other participants, and therefore I will write about it, broadly and briefly.

Technology in this brief and broad sense is the discoveries of science applied to life uses. The advent of technology into society cannot be located as an "event." It is, however, perfectly "legitimate" to find in the so-called industrial revolution, whose own definitions are uncertain, a moment of sociological rupture when these applications began to be competitors and substitutes rather than supplements of human labor. This distinction cannot be strictly totalized or mastered by the logic of parasitism, by calling the new mode merely an unwelcome and unnatural parasite upon the previous. But for purposes of a positivistic computation of our marginalization, we can locate the moments spread out unevenly over the map of the industrial revolution, when what had seemed a benign enhancement of exchange value inserted itself into circulation in such a way as to actualize the always immanent condition of possibility of capital. In terms of any of these crudely located moments, it is impossible to claim that the priority of technological systems has been anything but profit maximization disguised as cost effectiveness. It is indeed almost impossible not to recognize everywhere technological systems where "sheer technological effectiveness"—whatever that might be, since questions of labor intensification introduce a peculiar normative factor—is gainsaid by considerations of the enhancement of the flow and accumulation of capital. No absolute priority can be declared, but technology takes its place with politics and economics as one of those "determinants" that we must grapple with if we wish to relate ourselves to any critique of social determinacy.[10] The production of the universities, the subdivision of their curricula, the hierarchy of the management-labor sandwich with the peculiarly flavored filling of the faculty, the specialization emphases, the grants and in-house financial distributions that affect choice of research and specialty, faculty life- and class-style: these "items of evidence" are often brushed aside as we perform our appointed task of producing explanations from our seemingly isolated scholarly study with its well-worn track to the library.[11]

It is a well-documented fact that technological capitalism must be dynamic in order to survive and must find newer methods of extracting surplus value from labor. Its "civilizing" efforts are felt everywhere and are not to be dismissed and ignored. In every humanistic discipline and every variety of fine art, the exigencies of the production and reproduction of capital produce impressive and exquisite by-products. In our own bailiwick, one of them would be such a group as ourselves, helping to hold money in the institutional humanistic budget, producing explanations in terms of pure categories such as cognition, epistemology, the aesthetic, interpretation, and the like; at the other end might be the tremendous exploitable energy of the freshman English machine as a panacea for social justice. Between the two poles (one might find other pairs) the humanities are being trashed.[12]

(I have not the expertise to speak of the hard sciences. But it would seem that the gap between the dazzling sophistication of the technique and the brutal precritical positivism of the principle of its application in the practice of technology indicates the opposite predicament. For, as we hear from our friends and colleagues in the so-called "pure sciences" and as we heard from the "pure scientists" on the panel, the sophistication there extends to ontology, epistemology, and theories of space and time. Here the marginalization is thus produced by excess rather than lack [a distinction that is not tenable at the limit]. While the main text of technocracy makes a ferocious use of the substantive findings of a certain kind of "science," what is excluded and marginalized is precisely the workings of the area where the division of labor between "the sciences" and "the humanities"—excellent for the purposes of controlling and utilizing the academy for ideological reproduction—begins to come undone.)

In the case of the humanities in general as in the case of feminism, the relationship between margin and center is intricate and interanimating. Just as the woman chosen for special treatment by men (why she in particular was chosen can only be determined and expressed in terms of an indefinitely prolonged genealogy) can only be tolerated if she behaves "like men," so individuals in the chosen profession of humanists can only be tolerated if they behave in a specific way. Three particular modes of behavior are relevant to my discussion: (1) to reproduce explanations and models of explanation that will take so little notice of the politico-economico-technological determinant that the latter can continue to present itself as nothing but a support system for the propagation of civilization (itself a species of cultural explanation), instrumental rather than constitutive; (2) to proliferate scientific analogies in so-called humanistic explanations: learned explanation of high art in terms of relativity or catastrophe theory, presentations of the mass seduction of the populace as the organic being-in-art of the people; and (3) at the abject extreme, the open capitulation at the universities by the humanities as agents of the minimization of their own expense of production.

It is in terms of this intricate interanimating relationship between margin and center that we cannot be called mere keepers of records. I would welcome a metaphor offered by a member of the audience at the symposium.

We are, rather, the disc jockeys of an advanced capitalist ethnocracy. The discs are not "records" of the old-fashioned kind, but productions of the most recent technology. The trends in taste and the economic factors that govern them are also products of the most complex interrelations among a myriad factors such as international diplomacy, the world market, the conduct of advertisement supported by and supporting the first two items, and so on. To speak of the mode of production and constitution of the radio station complicates matters further. Now within this intricately determined and multiform situation, the disc jockey and his audience think, indeed are made to think, that they are free to play. This illusion of freedom allows us to protect the brutal ironies of technocracy by suggesting either that the system protects the humanist's freedom of spirit, or that "technology," that vague evil, is something the humanist must confront by inculcating humanistic "values," or by drawing generalized philosophical analogues from the latest spatio-temporal discoveries of the magical realms of "pure science," or yet by welcoming it as a benign and helpful friend.[13]

This has been a seemingly contextual explanation of our symposium. It should be noted, however, that the explanation might also be an analysis of the production of contexts and contextual explanations through marginalization centralization. My explanation cannot remain outside the structure of production of what I criticize. Yet, simply to reject my explanation on the grounds of this theoretical inadequacy that is in fact its theme would be to concede to the two specific political stances (masculist and technocratic) that I criticize. Further, the line between the politics of explanation and the specific politics that my text explains is ever wavering. If I now call this a heterogeneous predicament constituted by discontinuities, I hope I will be understood as using vocabulary rather than jargon.[14] This is the predicament as well as the condition of possibility of all practice.

———————

The accounts of each other's work that we had read before the symposium can also be examined through the thematics of marginalization-centralization. Writing today in Austin, Texas (typing the first draft on the way to Ann Arbor, in fact), I cannot know what relationship those hastily written pre-symposium summaries will have with the finished essays for *Humanities in Society* nor if the participants will have taken into account the public session whose indescribable context I describe above. The blueprint of an interminable analysis that I include in this section might therefore be of special interest to our readers. It might give them a glimpse of the itinerary telescoped into the text they hold in their hands.

A specific sense of the importance of politics was not altogether lacking in these preliminary accounts. Norton Wise's project description concerned an especially interesting period in modern political and intellectual history. "In my present research I am attempting to draw connections between scientific and social concerns for a particularly revealing historical case: the reception of thermodynamics in Germany between about 1850 and 1910, including both the period of political unification and consolidation under Bismarck and the increasingly tension-ridden Wilhelmian period prior to the First World War."[15] The focus at work in the symposium did not allow him to develop his ideas in detail; I look forward to the finished project, to be completed through study of "internal published sources," "public discussions," and "general biographical information on approximately fifty people." Although the only limits to speculation that Wise can envisage are "empirical" rather than irreducibly structural, the idea that the reception of scientific "truths" can be historically vulnerable I find appealing.

It is more interesting, however, that Wise did not notice that it was not merely "Ernst Haeckel [who] employed his notion of a 'mechanical cell soul' to bridge the gap between mechanical reduction in biology and organic purposive action in the individual and the state." Here is a passage from the preface to the first edition of the first volume of *Capital*:

> The value-form, whose fully developed shape is the money-form, is very simple and slight in content. Nevertheless, the human mind has sought in vain for more than 2,000 years to get to the bottom of it, while on the other hand there has been at least an approximation of a successful analysis of forms which are much richer in content and more complex. Why? Because the complete body is easier to study than its cells. Moreover, in the analysis of economic forms neither microscopes nor chemical reagents are of assistance. The power of abstraction must replace both. But for bourgeois society, the commodity form of the product of labour, or the value-form of the commodity, is the economic cell-form. To the superficial observer, the analysis of these forms seems to turn upon minutiae. It does in fact deal with minutiae, but so similarly does microscopic anatomy.[16]

Such a metaphor does indeed "reveal," as it is produced by, or as it conditions, "connections between social and scientific values and beliefs." Wise has put his finger upon the great nineteenth-century theme of ideology (an unquestioningly accepted system of ideas that takes material shape in social action) and extended it to the production of scientific values. This is interesting because many contemporary critics of ideology maintain that a scientific politico-economic and socio-cultural explanation *can* be produced through a rigorous ideological critique, and that a series of structural explanations can indeed be ideology-free. Another group of thinkers, generally of a different political persuasion(s), suggest that the production of the discourse and even the methods of science must remain ideological and interpretable and need not be reasonable to be successful.[17] Wise's study would therefore be enriched if it were situated within this debate about cultural (in the broadest sense) explanation.

The study of "organic purposive action in the individual and the state" through the efficient method of scientific reduction is the issue here. Even the critics of a value-free scientific *discourse* and method would not question the plausibility of such a project, allowing for a system of compensations when the object of study is human reality.[18] The opening section of my essay should have made clear that I would be most pleased if a powerful project such as Wise's questioned even this last assumption: that "the sign" (in this case the various documentary and other evidence of the reception of thermodynamics at a certain period in Germany) is a "representation of the idea" (the basic assumptions of sociopolitical reality) "which itself represented the object perceived" (both the *real truth* of that sociopolitical reality *and* thermodynamics as such).[19] Not to be open to such questioning is, in the long run, not merely to privilege a transcendent truth behind words but also to privilege a language that can capture (versions of) such a truth and to privilege one's trade as the place where such a language can be learned.[20] I shall come back to this point.

I have a suspicion that the same sort of disciplinary vision that makes Wise overlook the Marxian passage makes Hooker and Rousseau limit their political concern in specific ways.

Rousseau speaks of the "politics of the academy": "yet ironically, only for a brief moment during the late sixties was it apparent to most American academics that the 'politics of the academy' count." It seems to me, all structural analyses aside, that it could just as easily be argued that a political activity often operating out of an academic base had an apparent effect upon American foreign policy in the sixties precisely because the academy began to see itself as the active margin of a brutal political centralism. The politics of the academy ceased to be merely academic. There are, of course, a good many problems with even this convenient cultural explanation. Many of the workers in the political arena of the sixties chose to step out of the academy. And even those workers have increasingly come to express, if one could risk such a generalization, the structure and thematics of the technocracy they inhabit.[21]

These pages are obviously not the appropriate place for disputing such specific issues. Yet, even as I applaud Rousseau's introduction of the political into our agenda, I feel this particular myopia appears also in his definition of *pluralism*: "Pluralism, originally an economic and agricultural concept, is the notion of the one over the many, as in pluralistic societies." Nearly every survivor of the sixties would rather identify pluralism with "repressive tolerance." "Tolerance is turned from an active into a passive state, from practice to non-practice: laissez-faire the constituted authorities."[22]

Clifford Hooker, too, is concerned with the effect of social reality upon the production of knowledge. His project is particularly impressive to me because he is a "hard scientist," a theoretical physicist. I am moved by his enquiry into science "as a collective (species) institutionalized activity." I am disappointed though when the emphasis falls in the very next sentence upon science as an "*epistemic* institution." The explanation of the production of scientific knowledge is then to be explained, we surmise, in terms of abstract theories of how an abstractly defined human being *knows*. We are to be concerned, not with a cultural, but a phenomenological explanation. No mention will be made of the complicity of science and technology except by way of the kind of comment to which I have already pointed: that the technocrats know nothing about the vast changes in the concepts of space and time and knowledge that have taken place in the "pure" sciences. The confident centrality of the "purity" of science with hapless technology in the margins has a certain old-world wistfulness about it. Ignoring the immensely integrative effect of the world market, such a denial of history can only hope to establish an integrated view of all human activity through the supremacy and self-presence of the cognizing supra-historical self. The arts will be legitimated as a possible special form of cognition. This further centralism of the all-knowing mind, which can also know itself and thus the universe, is, once again, something I will mention in my last section.

In my opening pages I call "politics as such" the prohibition of marginality that is implicit in the production of any explanation. From that point of view, the choice of particular binary oppositions by our participants is no mere intellectual strategy. It is, in each case, the condition of the possibility for centralization (with appropriate apologies) and, correspondingly, marginalization.

Humanities/Culture—Are the humanities culture-bound?

Philosophy/Science—In the eighteenth century social philosophy was transformed into social science.

Scientific/Social—What is the connection between the scientific and the social?

Internal/External—Internal criticism is to examine the coherence of a system with its premises; external criticism is to examine how those premises and the principles of coherence are produced and what they, in turn, lead to.

Speculative/Empirical—Speculative possibilities are limited only by empirical observations.

Theory/Cultural ideology—Many objections adduced as "theoretical" are instead objections to a cultural ideology.

Biological activity/Abstract structure—Is science most fruitfully viewed as one or the other (I am curious about the first possibility: "science as a biological activity")?

Description-prediction/Prescription-control—Is science aimed at one or the other?

Human artifacts/Nature—Does the study of one or the other constitute an important difference among the sciences?

(In fact, a compendious diagram accompanying Hooker's statement offers, like most diagrams, a superb collection of binaries and shows us, yet once again, how we think we conquer an unknown field by dividing it repeatedly into twos, when in fact we might be acting out the scenario of class [marginalization-centralization] and trade [knowledge is power].)

These shored-up pairs, a checklist that might have led to an exhaustive description of the field that was to have been covered by the symposium cannot, I think, allow that "theory" itself is a "cultural ideology" of a specific class and trade which must seek to reproduce itself; and upon whose reproduction a part of the stability of a technocracy depends. They cannot allow that the exclusivist ruses of theory reflect a symptom and have a history. The production of theoretical explanations and descriptions must, in this view, be taken to be the worthiest task to be performed towards any "phenomenon"; it must be seen as the best aid to enlightened practice and taken to be a universal and unquestioned good. Only then can the operation of the binaries begin. It is this unspoken premise that leads us to yet another "intellectual strategy," not necessarily articulated with the splitting into binaries: the declaration of a project to integrate things into adequate and encompassing explanations. The integration is sometimes explicitly, and always implicitly, in the name of the sovereign mind. Thus one project will work through "a conflation of social, philosophical, and scientific ideas," refusing to recognize the heterogeneity of the nonsocial, the nonphilosophical, the nonspecific that is not merely the other of society, philosophy, science. Another will attempt an "integrated view of human activity" and place the chart of this activity within a firmly drawn outline called a "consistency loop," banishing the risk of inconsistency at every step into the outer darkness.

It is thus not only the structure of marginalization centralization that assures the stability of cultural explanations in general. The fence of the consistency loop, as I argue, also helps. To go back to my initial example, in order to make my behavior as a female consistent with the rest of the symposium, I would have to be defined as a sexless (in effect, male) humanist—and the rest of me would be fenced out of the consistency loop. The strongest brand of centralization is to allow in only the terms that would be consistent anyway, or could be accommodated within an argument based on consistency. The consistency loop also keeps out all the varieties of inconsistencies to which any diagram plotted in language owes its existence. Every word, not to mention combinations or parts of words, in a language, is capable of producing inexhaustible significations linked to contextual possibilities, possibilities that include citation or fictionalization "out of context." The strictly univocal or limited multivocal status of the words in a diagram operates by virtue of their difference from all the rest of this inexhaustible field. The field is kept out by reinterpreting the difference as the unique and most viable identity of the word.

In a more specific way, the plan for sweeping integrations also assures the stability of *one specific kind* of explanation, whose idealism would exclude all inconsistencies of what had best be called class, race, sex; although, if the analyses were taken far enough, even these names would begin to show the ragged edges of their own limits as unitary determinations. Thus in the theoretical establishment of the establishment of theory, mind is allowed to reign over matter, explanation, in a certain sense, over culture as the possibility of history, or as the space of dispersion of the politics of class, race, and sex. All human activity is seen as specifically integrative *cognitive* activity and the end becomes a "theory of theories." "[Literary] critical theorizing" is, in one case, seen as the "central *discipline* [the italics are presumably there to emphasize the sense of law and ordering rather than that of academic division of labor] in what we loosely call the 'humanities' or the 'human sciences' . . . the central form of self-conscious reflective thought." Such a frame of mind must disavow the *possibility* that the dream of the centralization of one's trade and one's class, and the dream of a self-present self-consciousness, intimately linked as they are, might be symptomatic and class-protective. Here the will to power through knowledge is so blind to itself that it takes the ontological question as necessarily answerable *before* theory: "the *self-evident fact* that no discipline can possibly pretend to have an adequate theory until it is possible to say *what* such a theory would have to explain."

> Oh! Blessed rage for order, pale Ramon
> The maker's rage to order words of the sea,
> Words of the fragrant portals, dimly-starred,
> And of ourselves and of our origins,
> In ghostlier demarcations, keener sounds.[23]

Within the disciplinary mapping of the humanities, which permits them to remain preoccupied with hubris, poetry, especially modern poetry, is the thing that is allowed to make the kinds of suggestions that I have been making above. And this neutralizing permissiveness, resembling the permissiveness enjoyed by the humanities in general, would allow literary critics of even the most "theoretical" or "Marxist" bent to put the language of poetry (as well as "the *avant-garde* text and the discourse of the unconscious") out of play by claiming for them the status of special "uses of language which exceed communication."[24] That is not very far from the entrenched privatism of "spontaneous overflow of powerful feeling," the controlled detachment of "willing suspension of disbelief" or "escape from personality," the olympian (and oblivious) transhistoricity of "criticism of life."[25] Given such ferocious apartheid, the binary opposition of the literalist language of the conceptualism of pure theory and the metaphorical language of the figurative "cognition" of art becomes fully plausible. Your political allegiance can be pretty well plotted out in terms of which one you want to centralize—the concept or the metaphor.

If we could deconstruct (as far as possible) this marginalization between metaphor and concept, we would realize not only that no pure theory of metaphor is possible, because any premetaphoric base of discussion must already assume the distinction between theory and metaphor; but also that no priority, by the same token, can be given to metaphor, since every metaphor is contaminated and constituted by its conceptual justification. If neither metaphor nor concept is given priority (or both are), the passage of poetry above could be taught as a *serious* objection to the privileging of theory that takes place when humanists gather to discuss "cultural explanations." Yes, I know "blessed" is an ambiguous and overdetermined expression, that "pale Ramón" aesthetically neutralizes the "real" Ramón Fernández, that "to order" and "for order" are not synonymous, that "of" (meaning perhaps "out of" or "belonging to" or both) is undecidable and that lacking a predication, the lines carry no apparent judgment. But, questioning the prejudice that a "serious objection" must look like a literalist proposition, these very poetic and figurative gestures can be read as the conditions of the possibility of a stand against a "rage for order." Indeed, "to order" and "for order" can then be seen as at least the field of measure and coherence as well as unquestioning command and obedience, even the mass production of consumer goods for no one's particular use; and not merely for the sake of an exercise in polysemic interpretation.

At a time when the rage for order defeminates the humanities from every side, I can "make use" of such lines.[26] I have little interest in vindicating Wallace Stevens or in disclosing a plethora of "valid" readings, where *valid* is a word to dodge around the harsher and more legalistic *correct*. The line I am suggesting I have called, in a feminist context, "scrupulous and plausible misreadings." Since all readings, including the original text, are constituted by, or effects of, the necessary possibility of misreadings, in my argument the question becomes one of interpretations for use, built on the old grounds of coherence, without the cant of theoretical adequacy. And the emphasis falls on alert pedagogy.

It is not only poetry that can be taught in this way, of course. The eighteenth-century historian Giambattista Vico had a theory of language that put metaphor at the origin and suggested, I think, that first was best. It so happens that Vico took this theory seriously and at crucial moments in his argument put the burden of proof upon metaphorical production. In his speculation upon the principles of the history of human nature, Vico suggested that the sons of Noah, terrified by the first thunderclap, overcome by guilt and shame, hid in caves, dragging with them the indocile women they had been pursuing. In those caves, "gentile humanity" was founded. Although the place of guilt and shame in this story is very important, the reason for those two emotions, unlike in the Adam and Eve story, is not made clear. (Pursuing indocile women is clearly no grounds for either.) "Thus it was fear which created gods in the world . . . not fear awakened in men by other men, but fear awakened in men by themselves." It is because Vico was working his origin through metaphoric practice that this curious lack of clarity is encountered. It cannot be caught within the discourse of literalist explanations, where the adequation of cause and effect is the criterion of success. According to the literalist view, the fear of the thunderclap is itself produced through a metaphorical "mistake." Thinking of nature as "a great animated body," our fathers (Noah's sons) interpret the thunder as a threatening growl, the *response* to an act that should bring guilt and shame. The figure is metalepsis or prolepsis. The threat of the thunder, *result* of a transgression, is seen as the *cause* of the flight into the caves; or, variously, the threatening thunder *anticipates* the guilt and shame that should have produced it. Whichever is the case, the explanation hinges on a metaphor.

Again, speaking of legal marriage, or "solemn matrimony," which imposes civil status upon the patrician, Vico uses the metaphor of light. "[Juno] is also known as Lucina, who brings the offspring into the light; not natural light, for that is shared by the offspring of slaves, but the civil light by reason of which the nobles are called illustrious." Now there is a previous invocation of light at the beginning of Book I, Section III ("Principles") which seems to anticipate the light that can only come with marriage and render the one I quoted first (but which comes later in the book) logically suspect. "But in the night of thick darkness enveloping the earliest antiquity, so remote from ourselves, there shines the eternal and never-failing light of a truth beyond all question: that the world of civil society has certainly been made by men, and that its principles are therefore to be found within the modification of our human mind." For the first figure of light seems to anticipate the effect and origin of the civil light that can shine only with the establishment of domestic society in the distant future. In other words, once again it is prolepsis at work. Vico used the same mechanism, the structure of figuration, to produce his theoretical discourse, which, he argued, produced the first and best language.[27]

If the discipline of literary criticism is merely permitted to indulge in the praise of metaphor, the discipline of history is expected to eschew metaphor as anything but the incidental ornamentation of the reportage of fact. The sort of reading I am describing would be dismissed by most self-respecting academic historians as reading "Vico as literature." The contribution of a critical humanist pedagogy in this case would be to take the metaphors in Vico as yet another example of the questioning of the supremacy of adequate theory, and not to relegate it to (or exalt it as) the semipoetic free-style social *philosophy* that preceded social *science*. Thus my two examples would emphasize the conceptuality of poetic language and the metaphoricity of historical language *to similar pedagogical ends*.

These examples are not audacious and revolutionary. It is not possible for a lone individual to question her disciplinary boundaries without collective effort. That is why I had hoped to hear some news of pedagogy at our symposium, not merely theory exchange. In the humanities classroom the ingredients for the methods of (the official) cultural explanation that fixes and constitutes "culture" are assembled. As a feminist, Marxist deconstructivist, I am interested in the theory-practice of pedagogic practice-theory that would allow us constructively to question privileged explanations even as explanations are generated.

It should be clear by now that I could not be embarked upon a mere reversal— a mere centralizing of teaching-as-practice at the same time as research-as-theory is marginalized. That slogan has led to the idea of teaching as the creation of human rapport or the relieving of anxiety and tension in the classroom that I have heard described as "pop psych" teaching and that I myself call "babysitting."[28] What I look for rather is a confrontational teaching of the humanities that would question the students' received disciplinary ideology (model of legitimate cultural explanations) even as it pushed into indefiniteness the most powerful ideology of the teaching of the humanities: the unquestioned explicating power of the theorizing mind and class, the need for intelligibility and the rule of law. If we meet again, as I hope we will, that is the question I will put on the agenda: the pedagogy of the humanities as the arena of cultural explanations that question the explanations of culture.

1979

8. The Politics of Interpretations

It is difficult to speak of a politics of interpretation without a working notion of ideology as larger than the concepts of individual consciousness and will. At its broadest implications this notion of ideology would undo the oppositions between determinism and free will and between conscious choice and unconscious reflex. Ideology in action is what a group takes to be natural and self-evident, that of which the group, as a group, must deny any historical sedimentation. It is both the condition and the effect of the constitution of the subject (of ideology) as freely willing and consciously choosing in a world that is seen as background. In turn, the subject(s) of ideology are the conditions and effects of the self-identity of the group as a group. It is impossible, of course, to mark off a group as an entity without sharing complicity with its ideological definition. A persistent critique of ideology is thus forever incomplete. In the shifting spectrum between subject-constitution and group-constitution are the ideological apparatuses that share the condition/effect oscillation.

I am always obliged to quote Stuart Hall's excellent historical study of ideology whenever I refer to the notion in the U.S. context: "two radically different styles of thought—the European (where the concept [of ideology] has played a significant role) and the American (where it had up to [1949] been largely absent). . . . An interesting essay could be written on what concepts did duty, in American social theory, for the absent concept of 'ideology': for example, the notion of norms in structural functionalism, and of 'values' and the 'central value system' in [Talcott] Parsons."[1] I would add to this list a concept of the "unconscious" as a continuous and homogeneous part of the mind that is simply "not conscious."

I will here suggest the usefulness of a broader concept of ideology and note some marks of ideology at work: conserving the sovereign subject; excluding a monolithic Marx(ism); and excluding or appropriating a homogeneous woman. The text of the symposium does not contain a hidden ideological truth but is operated by as it operates an imperfectly hidden ideological agenda; that is one of its structural alterities.

It is in Stephen Toulmin's "The Construal of Reality" that the absence of a theory of ideology is felt the most; for Toulmin's project is to undo the disciplinary-ideological opposition between the human sciences and the natural sciences, between logic and rhetoric.[2] Toulmin writes: "What P. F. Strawson calls a 'conceptual framework,' and Bakhtin—*a little misleadingly*—an 'ideology,' the theoretical physicist thus calls a 'treatment'" (p. 107; italics mine). A broader notion of ideology would of course situate the merely conceptual framework within a more extended and heterogeneous field. The physicist's treatment, a decision where "the interpretive element is quite explicit," would occupy a different place within a field similarly heterogeneous and extended.

In the absence of a heterogeneous concept of ideology, Toulmin's text produces definitions that keep the ideology-constitutive distinctions between center and periphery, explanation and interpretation, cause and effect intact:

In dealing with [peripheral factors that may influence the work of professionals], we are centrally concerned with a larger and more turbulent world of *causes*, for example, the interactions between the professionals and their human contexts, as well as with any consequential influences that contextual factors may exert on the professional argument itself. [Pp. 104–5]

Accordingly, in both today's postmodern natural and human sciences and the critical disciplines of the humanities, we are concerned with a mix, or blend, of explanation and interpretation. [P. 109]

A critical view of the subject of ideology would call the clarity of these distinctions into question and thus ask the critic to address a less simplified view of the world. It would deconstitute and situate (*not* reject) the "we" who experiences the productivity of alternative investigative postures, the "legitima[cy]" and "power" of the "acceptable standpoints." Such a view does not allow for a personal-subjective category to be set up over against an intellectual-interpretive category either, since it would see complicity between the constitution of subjectivity and the desire for objective identity.

These problematic distinctions are necessary for Toulmin's argument because it cannot accommodate the concept of ideology. The never fortuitous choice of normative metaphors sometimes seems to suggest this necessity: "There is more *temptation* to present *all* [author's italics] interpretations in the human sciences as being essentially political in character than there is in the physical sciences. Still, it is a *temptation* that we *ought to resist*" (p. 102; italics mine). This resistance wins a space for us where it is possible to overlook the tremendous ideological over-determination of the relationship between the "pure" and "applied" sciences, as well as their relationship with private- and public-sector technology and the inscription of the whole into the social and material relations of production. All is reduced to the classical split between subject and object—"two-way interactions between the observer and the system being observed" (p. 106). If the clarity of the theory is dependent upon so stringent a reduction, it loses persuasive value when applied to the sociopolitical scene. A statement like the following, concluded from the subject-object premises I quote above, remains *merely* theoretical, *normed* into ethical decoration: "That being so, there is, a fortiori, no longer any reason to assume that studying human beings from a scientific point of view necessarily involves dehumanizing them" (p. 106).

Ronald Dworkin attempts to cut loose from the task of recovering the legislator's intention in the interpretation of the law. He takes literary interpretation as a model, however self-divided, and offers us two interesting and related versions of the subject of lawmaking: a pluralized subject that is one link in a chain of supplementations and a double subject who is at once writer and reader. I shall give a brief example of how a general theory of ideology would enhance his argument.

Following through the notion of the pluralized subject in the interpretation of the law, Dworkin is obliged to call a halt at a point which is worth remarking:

Perhaps [putting together a collective novel sequentially] is an impossible assignment . . . because the best theory of art requires a single creator or, if more than one, that each have some control over the whole. But what about legends and jokes? I need not push that question further because I am interested only in the fact that the assignment makes sense, that each of the novelists in the chain can have some idea of what he or she is asked to do, whatever misgivings each might have about the value or character of what will then be produced. [P. 193]

That Dworkin has made fiction and the law each other's tenor and vehicle is in itself significant. In this passage yet another possibility is implicit. Legends and jokes are phenomena where the condition-effect relationship with ideology (in the U.S. the preferred word in this case is "culture") is readily granted. The point might be to see that the difference between these phenomena and the novel is, in the ideological view, one of degree rather than of kind. The single author also has only "*some* idea" of what he is asked to do, for the *entire* idea is spread like a map across the text of ideology. The nonexhaustive constitution of the subject *in* ideology (which is in turn constitutive *of* ideology) would include, in this revised version of Dworkin's argument, the so-called ideology-free language of Western European and U.S. law. It is only a homogeneous, isomorphic, and adequate cause-and-effect view of social production that would advance the doubtful claim that "liberalism can . . . be traced [to] . . . a discrete epistemological base . . . [which] could be carried forward into aesthetic theory and there yield a distinctive interpretive style" (p. 200). The view I am describing would suggest that such items are related as the interanimating complicity of the shifting components of an ideological system. The productive undecidability of the borderlines of politics, art, law, and philosophy, as they sustain and are sustained by the identity of a composite entity such as the state, is operated by the heterogeneous and discontinuous concept of ideology. Lacking such a concept, Dworkin is obliged to indicate it in the name of a unifying philosophy. It is the strength of his essay that the unification is not seen as a necessarily sublating synthesis: "I end simply by acknowledging my sense that politics, art, and law are united, somehow, in philosophy" (p. 200).

If Dworkin, without pronouncing the word, seems to make room for a broader concept of ideology, Donald Davie would choose to "bypass" its workings: "Doubtless such interrelations exist, and doubtless they can be exploited to sinister purpose. Rather than inveighing against this, or (with [Stanley] Fish) more or less blithely acquiescing in it, we can best spend our time bypassing the network altogether, as the truly independent and illuminating interpreters always have" (p. 43).

One cannot of course "choose" to step out of ideology. The most responsible "choice" seems to be to know it as best one can, recognize it as best one can, and, through one's necessarily inadequate interpretation, to work to change it, to acknowledge the challenge of: "*Men* make their own history, but they do not choose the script" (italics mine).[3] In fact, I would agree with Edward Said that the ideological system that one might loosely name as contemporary U.S.A.

expects its poets to *seem* to choose to ignore it and thus allows its businessmen to declare: "Solid business practices transcend ideology if you are willing to work for it."[4]

Both Hayden White and Said concentrate upon ideological formations—the former with respect to a group identity called "a discipline," the latter with respect to the discipline in the service of the group identity called "the state." I shall not linger on their arguments here. It is my feeling, however, that in the absence of an articulated notion of ideology as larger than and yet dependent upon the individual subject, their essays sometimes seem a tirade against the folly or knavery of the practitioners of the discipline. The relationship between art and ideology—in this case, bourgeois ideology in the *broader* sense—is T. J. Clark's explicit subject matter. In his comments on Terry Eagleton, Clark suggests that, "in the years around 1910, . . . it was possible for Marxist intellectuals . . . to see themselves as bourgeois . . . [and oppose] the ideologies of a bourgeois élite" (pp. 148–49, n. 6). The critical practice Clark describes is close to what I suggest as an alternative to Davie's conviction of "bypassing" the ideological network or Said and White's ideology-free accusations.

It is Wayne Booth who pronounces the word "ideology" most often; and in his essay, it is the word "language" that performs the curious function of covering over the absence of a broader concept of ideology. In Mikhail Bakhtin's text, language is not immediately understood as verbal discourse. Ideology as language is an effect that assumes a subject for its cause, defining it within a certain convention of signification. For Booth, language as ideology is the expression of a (group) subject who must constantly assure us, and himself, that he is not merely of the group but also unique. There is a moment in the essay when Booth is almost within reach of Bakhtin's position, a position that today would call itself the politics of textuality, seeing that the network of politics-history-society-sexuality, and the like, defines itself in ideology by acknowledging a textual or weblike structure. Booth's language, however, like Toulmin's, articulates Bakhtin's position within a vocabulary of free choice: "Each language we take in is a *language,* something already blessed or cursed with symbolic richness, with built-in effects of past choices, invitations to new choices, and a knowledge that some choices are in fact better than the others" (I quote from an earlier version of the essay). Bakhtin's implicit dialectical hinging of subject and language in/of ideology seems to elude Booth here.

When Booth thinks of ideology as beliefs and practices rather than, strictly speaking, language or voice, it is possible for him to hint at this dialectical structure: "Ideology springs from and in turn influences systems of belief and human practice" (p. 50).* Yet he constantly reduces the situation of art and ideology to the conscious-unconscious opposition that I invoked at the outset as one of the substitutes for ideology upon the Anglograph scene. Bakhtin is laudable because he "plac[es] as high a value as he does on the deliberate introduction of counter-ideologies," whereas "conventional Marxists [hold that] . . . selves and societies

---

* *Booth has since changed the word "ideology" to "art" in this sentence.—Editor's note, Critical Inquiry*

are radically dependent on the ideologies of art" (earlier version). Here consciousness and the unconscious are understood with reference to a pre-psychoanalytic model, as if they belonged to a continuous system where the mark of good practice was to raise the unconscious into consciousness. The strongest diagnosis of ideological victimization in this view is: "I confess, with considerable diffidence, that I think the revelation [of Rabelais' double standard] quite unconscious" (p. 65). The sense of ideology as free choice is the goal: "The question we now face, then, as believers in feminist (or any other) ideology, is this: Am I free, in interpreting and criticizing a work of art, to employ that ideology as one element in my appraisal of the artistic value of that work?" (p. 56).

It is not too far from the truth to suggest that this freedom of choice by a freely choosing subject, which operates the essays of Toulmin, Davie, Dworkin, and Booth, is the ideology of free enterprise at work—recognizably a politics of interpretation. That is why we accepted as common sense that the best theory of art required a single author. Within a broad concept of ideology, the subject does not lose its power to act or resist but is seen as *irretrievably* plural. In that perspective, all novels are seen to be composed as serials by various hands. Dworkin's analogy between literature and the law can, in that perspective, be read differently as a *case* of this politics of interpretation, just as the novelist and his reader, requiring a single creator and therefore overlooking the novel's being an effect within a larger text, are another case. In a serial novel by various hands of the kind Dworkin presupposes, the narrative is supposed to advance while preserving some presumed *unity*, whereas in a series of interpretations of the *same* law, we have not progress but repetition—each repetition presumably claiming to be most adequate to the ipseity of the law in question. Lawyers, even when they, like Dworkin, grant the actual plurality of interpretations, are bent on the search for the "real" law, the "proper" law, the "best" interpretation, its single true intention. As cases of ideology formation, Dworkin's analogy and its attendant definition of authorship seem to betray their "politics"—free enterprise and the rule of law.

"Betray their 'politics.'" A better formulation of this is to be found in Pierre Macherey: "We always eventually find, *at the edge of the text*, the language of ideology, momentarily hidden, but eloquent by its very absence."[5] Let us consider moments on the edges or borders of some of these essays, the ideological traces that allow them to define their interiors. Such a gesture will yield a hint of their politics as well, a politics of the freely choosing subject who, divining his own plurality, breaks his theory as he takes a stand.

Such a definitive moment comes at the end of Stanley Cavell's piece: "If deconstruction, as in de Man's recommendation of it, is to disillusion us, it is a noble promise and to be given welcome. Disillusion is what fits us for reality, whether in Plato's terms or in D. W. Winnicott's. But then we must be assured that this promise is based on a true knowledge of what our illusions are" (p. 178). I am not altogether convinced by Cavell's reading of deconstruction in this essay, especially when he associates de Man and Derrida without much differentiation.[6] I will merely remark that the assurance to the subject of true knowledge, a self-evident ideological requirement for self-evidence, is the one thing deconstruction cannot promise. A number of arguments that Cavell undoubtedly can anticipate might be advanced here: there is no disillusion without illusion; a true knowledge of illusions can lead to a knowledge of reality only as that which is not illusion; to predicate reality as the death of illusion is to ignore the syntax or practice that passes from illusion to reality via dis-illusion; not to acknowledge that deconstruction distinguishes itself from dialectics precisely by this attention to the syntax that is otherwise ignored in the interest of the semantics of reality is not to speak of deconstruction at all.[7] I shall not dwell upon these arguments here but suggest that Cavell's interpretation of voice and writing is also in the interest of this ideological requirement.

Cavell writes: "For me it is evident that the reign of repressive philosophical systematizing—sometimes called metaphysics, sometimes called logical analysis—has depended upon the suppression of the human voice. It is as the recovery of this voice (as from an illness) that ordinary language philosophy is . . . to be understood" (p. 173). Derrida admires this project and relates it to Nietzsche's attention to the force of language rather than its signification alone. What Derrida critiques is what Cavell seems to be showing here: the tendency common to most radical philosophies, including speech-act theory, to perceive their task as the restoration of voice. The systematic philosophies, on the other hand, although their aura seems to be altogether mediated and therefore akin to the common understanding (here Cavell's) of writing, develop systems which depend upon *phono*centrism as their final reference. Thus the commonsense perception—that systematic philosophies suppress and radical philosophies restore voice—depends upon varieties of phonocentric assumptions. "Writing" in this view becomes the name for that which must be excluded so that the interiority of a system can be defined and guarded. "The essential predicate of [the] *specific difference*" between writing and the field of voice is seen in such a reading as "the absence of the sender [and] of the receiver (*destinateur*), from the mark that he abandons."[8] The place of such an understanding of writing within a self-professed project of the restoration of speech should be clear.

Writing as the name of that which must be excluded as the other in order to conserve the identity of the same can be related to Macherey's other formulation: "What is important in the work is what it does not say. This is not the same as the careless notation 'what it refuses to say,' although that would in itself be interesting. . . . But rather than this, what the work cannot say is important because there the elaboration of the journey is acted out, in a sort of journey to silence."[9] It is not surprising that, within a definition of writing as a *deliberate* withholding of voice, the one sense of "turn"—in Thoreau's "You only need sit still long enough in some attractive spot in the woods that all its inhabitants may exhibit themselves to you by turns"—that Cavell does not (cannot?) mention is "trope," the irreducible turn of figuration that is the condition of (im)-possibility of any redemption of voice.

It is in terms of saving the freely choosing subject whose concept insinuates itself into the most radical commun(al)ist politics of collectivity that Said uses *écriture* as a code word suggesting (I cannot be sure, since the word hangs unexplained on the borders of his essay) linguistic reductionism at a second remove. The thumbnail explanation of *écriture* as the excluded other that I have given above would have helped his general argument: "A principle of silent exclusion operates within and at the boundaries of discourse; this has now become so internalized that fields, disciplines, and their discourses have taken on the status of immutable durability" (p. 16).

Since I find myself more than usually sympathetic with Said's position, I must point out another mark of ideology at work in his essay. The essay is written by a subject who is not only freely choosing but is also a star within a star system. There is no recognition or support here for the thousands of teachers and students across the country who are attempting to keep alive a critical cultural practice. Their track is to be picked up not only in journals such as *Radical Teacher* or *Radical America* but in course syllabi, in newsletters, and increasingly on the rolls of young teachers denied tenure. In order to recognize these workers, pedagogy as political interpretation must be seriously considered. A phenomenon cannot be nonexistent when a political spectrum extending from Michael Harrington to *U.S. News and World Report* accounts for its workings.[10] Said's statement that "the Left [is] in a state of intellectual disarray" is indeed true with respect to political sectarianism (p. 3). But if our own field of work is seen as outside of generalizations such as "high culture here is assumed to be above politics as a matter of unanimous convention" and also outside of the perspective of self-described Marxist "celebrities" (the third item in the title of Regis Debray's *Teachers, Writers, Celebrities*, which Said cites) who seem obliged to hear themselves as lonely personalities proselytizing in the wilderness, then the extent of our predicament, that *all this effort* goes awry, is seen as a much more menacing problem.

An awareness of solidarity with the ongoing pedagogic effort would have allowed Said to step out of the chalk circle of the three thousand critics and recognize that the task—"to use the visual faculty (which also happens to be dominated by visual media such as television, news photography, and commercial film, all of them fundamentally immediate, 'objective,' and ahistorical) to restore the nonsequential energy of lived historical memory and subjectivity as fundamental components of meaning in representation"—is attempted every day by popular-culture teachers on the Left (p. 25). I quote *Tabloid* as a metonym: "Many of our articles over the past months have given examples of this daily subversion—women in the home mutating the 'planned' effect of TV soap operas, political activists creating pirate radio stations, the customization of cars, clothing, etc."[11]

One of the most productive moments at the "Politics of Interpretation" symposium as an exchange between Davie and Said. Davie singled out Said's work for Palestine (Lebanon in Davie's script) as an example of patriotism. Said appropriately amended that praise by suggesting that he was working for the Palestinian state to establish itself so that he could then become its critic. Consciousness of national identity is marked by the use to which it is put. The thin line between national liberation and maintenance of the ideology of the state must be kept clean by the critic's vigilance. Otherwise, Davie's endorsement of patriotism becomes the condition and effect of a political ideology that denies the workings of an economic multinationalism. The production of archaic politico-nationalist explanations, irreducibly asymmetrical with the economico-multinationalist network, shows itself most brutally as war and most divisively as the indoctrination of the labor force. The mechanics of that denial are implicit in Davie's lament:

> By thus loftily declaring ourselves "citizens of the world" [which is of course not what I suggest above] we cut ourselves off not just from the majority of our fellow-citizens at the present day but from the far more numerous multitude of the dead. For there can be no doubt that to Virgil and Dante and Machiavelli, to Milton and Wordsworth, to Washington and Jefferson and Walt Whitman, the patria was meaningful, and its claims upon us were real and must be honoured, in just the ways that this sort of modern enlightenment refuses to countenance. [P. 29]

The march of capital has cut Davie off from the network that sustains and is sustained by a full-fledged patriotic ideology. He undoubtedly has no objection to the mode of sociomaterial production (since his deliberate stance is to bypass it) that shores him up in Tennessee or in front of a high-toned audience in Chicago. Nearly all the candidates on his list had intervened in rather than bypassed social relations of production in their time. At any rate, it was within that entire network that the "patriotism" of earlier generations could find its function and place. Davie as expatriate, consumer, taxpayer, voter, and investor has (been) moved into so different a network that merely to hang on to the one item on the list that seems sentimentally satisfying will produce, at best, a self-congratulatory simulacrum of community with the illustrious dead.

By force of the ideology appropriate to his place in the world, Davie unwittingly inhabits a country different from merely England. Let us look for a moment at the way he outlines that country, reminding ourselves that it is at those borders of discourse where metaphor and example seem arbitrarily *chosen* that ideology breaks through.

> For when a poet or a literary scholar, *British or American or Australian*, addresses not his fellow-Britons or his fellow-Americans or fellow-Australians but the international community of literary scholars, that intention shows up at once in the sort of English that he uses. [P. 29, italics mine]
>
> Must we assume that British English, American English, and New Zealand English are on the way to becoming distinct languages, as Romanian and Portuguese once became distinct languages by diverging differently from the parent stock of Roman Latin? [P. 35]

The point is not that the case would be altered (as indeed it would, in interesting ways) if the Caribbean, the Indian subcontinent, and Kenya-Uganda-Tanganyika (the colonial name for Tanzania)—also English speaking—were introduced into the company. The point is that a discourse such as Davie's, ignoring the difference between the linguistic self-concept of national liberation and patriotism, "naturally" or "only by chance" excludes them from the English-speaking Union. Indeed, to alter one of Davie's sentences a little: "[my] suggestion will seem bizarre except to those . . . who [are involved with admission into and granting degrees from U.S. English departments]" (p. 35). Davie's entire argument would have to be recast if the candidate were not "Georges [from] Bucharest" or "Lucille in Vincennes" but Echeruo from Nigeria or Towheed in Pakistan. Of course "all the languages are precious, every one is unique, and so no one is replaceable by any other" (p. 29). But if one examines the figures of foreign-language enrollment in the *Chronicle of Higher Education* or comparable journals, one knows instantly that they are not in fact equally precious, and the demand depends on the politico-economic text. One need only think of the case of Japanese, Arabic, and Persian in recent years. From a somewhat different point of view, one might think of the status of a Shakespeare scholar who has read all of his Shakespeare in Bengali and a scholar of Bengali culture who has had a semester's Bengali in a U.S. graduate school. (This is not an imaginary example, although it "will seem bizarre except to those of us who [are involved in judging fellowship applications on the national level].")

There is disciplinary ideology in Davie's certainty of the secure role of the poet in contemporary society; in Said's conviction that the literary critic rather than the other human scientists are the custodians of sociopolitical interpretation; and, *malgré tout*, in White's admonition that "to appeal to sociology, anthropology, or psychology for some basis for determining an appropriate perspective on history is rather like basing one's notion of the soundness of a building's foundations on the structural properties of its second or third story" (p. 130).

But the most interesting sign of disciplinary privileging is found in Julia Kristeva's "Psychoanalysis and the Polis." At the end or center of delirium, according to Kristeva, is that which is desired, a hollow where meaning empties out in not only the presymbolic but the preobjective, "the ab-ject." (A deconstructive critique of thus "naming" an undifferentiated telos of desire before the beginning of difference can be launched but is not to my purpose here.) The desire for knowledge involved in mainstream interpretation (which Kristeva calls "Stoic" by one of those undocumented sweeping generalizations common to a certain kind of "French" criticism) shares such a hollow center and is thus linked with delirium. Certain kinds of fiction writers and, one presumes, analysands and social engineers try to dominate, transform, and exterminate improper "objects" awakened in the place of the abject. The psychoanalyst, however, wins out over both mad writer and man of politics. "*Knowing* that he is constantly in abjection [none of the problems of this position is discussed in Kristeva's text][12] and in neutrality, in desire and in indifference, the analyst builds a strong ethics, not normative but directed, which no transcendence guarantees" (p. 92; italics mine). This is the privileged position of synthesis within a restrained dialectic: the psychoanalyst persistently and symmetrically sublates the contradiction between interpretation and delirium. To privilege delirium (interpretation *as* delirium) in the *description* of this symmetrical synthesis is to misrepresent the dialectic presented by the essay, precisely in the interest of a politics that can represent its excluded other as an analysis that privileges interpretation. It should also be mentioned, of course, that the indivisibility and inevitability of the archaic (Christian) mother comes close to a transcendental guarantee. To know her *for what she is*, rather than to seek to transform her, is the psychoanalyst's professional enterprise.

I cannot pretend that the born-again recovery of Christianity and particularly Mariolatry in the latest *Tel Quels* is not disturbing to me. Not only does Kristeva fail to question the sociohistorical symptomaticity of psychoanalysis as a disciplinary practice but she has this to say about the abject mother of psychoanalysis and the messianic role of psychoanalysis as sublation of Christianity:

> *Our* cultural orb is *centered* around the axiom that "the Word became flesh."
> Two thousand years after a tireless exploration of the comings and goings
> between discourse and the object [traditional interpretation] to be named
> or interpreted, an object which is the solicitor of interrogation, we have
> finally achieved a discourse on discourse, an interpretation of interpre-
> tation. For the psychoanalyst, this vertigo in abstraction is, nevertheless,
> a means of protecting us from a masochistic and jubilatory fall into nature,
> into the full and *pagan* mother. [P. 87, italics mine]

Who is the excluded other that privileges interpretation? Not the writer, in this case Louis Ferdinand Céline, whose abject-transcending paranoia, otherwise known as anti-Semitism, the analyst-critic interprets for us through a somewhat positivistic analysis of sentence structure. The ideological scapegoat, hanging out on the borders, is that old favorite, Karl Marx. Kristeva makes an unproblematic analogy between the single-person situation of analysis and the vastly multitudinous, multi-racial, and multinational (including "pagan" cultures) political arena and gives us a species of Reichian diagnosis of the revolutionary leader's promise of a utopia in the place of abjection. The psychoanalyst by contrast is *poly*topian (not merely the Second Coming of the Hebraic Christ but perhaps also the fulfillment of the Hellenic Homer, who asked the full pagan mother-Muse to sing *in* him the poly-*tropic*—much tricking, in many tropes—Odysseus, at the beginning of his epic). It would be interesting to follow this homogenizing analogy and ask: Who in politics takes the place of the analyst who, knowingly, sometimes participates in the patient's delirium and draws back just enough to offer the healing interpretation which, "removing obvious, immediate, realistic meaning from discourse . . . [reveals] every phantasm . . . as an attempt to return to the unnameable" (pp. 85–86)? White argues that the interpretation of history as sublimely meaningless is "conventionally associated with the ideologies of fascist regimes" (p. 130). "Such a mobilizing interpretation can be called revolution or demagogy," Kristeva writes (p. 86). How can one take such an alternative seriously?

At any rate, to prove that political interpretations cannot be true, Kristeva argues as follows: "Unlike the analytic dynamic, however, the dynamic of political interpretation does not lead its subjects to an elucidation of their own (and its own) truth. . . . Of course, no political discourse can pass into nonmeaning. Its goal, Marx stated explicitly, is to reach the goal of interpretation: interpreting the world in order to transform it according to our needs and desires" (pp. 86–87). One might of course wonder if leading a subject to truth is not a species of transformation of the subject or, yet, if what Marx says about politics is necessarily the truth of all political discourse.

Let us rather investigate Marx's "explicit statement." Is it the eleventh of Marx's *Theses on Feuerbach* that Kristeva quotes in the epigraph? "Up until now philosophers have only *interpreted* the world. The point now is to change it [Die Philosophen haben die Welt nur verschieden *interpretiert*, es kommt drauf an, sie zu *verändern*]" (italics mine). As close a reader as Kristeva should note that the relationship between interpretation and change in that statement is exceedingly problematic. *Ankommen auf* in this context probably means "what matters" (within philosophic effort). Even in the most farfetched reading, such as "advent" (*ankommen*, or arrival), a contrastive juxtaposition can hardly be avoided. "To interpret . . . *in order to* transform" (italics mine) seems wishful thinking. The point can also be made that these theses, aphoristic statements parodying and imitating Luther, were written in 1845. Marx had not yet seen a "revolution," not even 1848. It would be like taking an epigraph from *Studies in Hysteria*, basing an entirely unfavorable comparison upon it, and clinching the case with "Freud has explicitly stated. . . ."

I have suggested that in Kristeva's essay psychoanalysis is shown to sublate the contradiction between interpretation and delirium. When Kristeva claims that political discourse cannot pass into nonmeaning, it remains to be asked how it can be posited that the Hegelian dialectic—Marx's morphology—does not accommodate a negative moment, a passing into nonmeaning, in order to accede to truth. I have suggested elsewhere that Marx's theory of practice goes beyond this restrained dialectic.[13] But I have tried to show here that even if Marx is not given the benefit of that doubt and even on Kristeva's own terms, it would be inadvisable to attempt to critique Marx with so little textual evidence. If one wishes to support a major component of one's argument on Marx, he demands at least as much attention as Céline.

I am not altogether comfortable with Louis Althusser's theory of the epistemological cut in Marx's work, although I am moved by his explanations in *Essays in Self-Criticism*. It is, however, well known that the generation influenced by Althusser's teaching, dissatisfied with the failure of 1968 and the subsequent move on the French Left toward a nonrevolutionary Eurocommunism, turned away from the *Capital* and Marx's later writings as endorsed by Althusser and toward, especially, the 1844 manuscripts, as had Jean-Paul Sartre an intellectual half-generation before Althusser; unlike Sartre, this younger generation sought to find in these manuscripts negative proof of an irreducible will to power. When Kristeva writes "this abject awakens in the one who speaks archaic conflicts with his own improper objects, his ab-jects, at the edge of meaning, at the limits of the interpretable [and] it arouses the paranoid rage to dominate those objects, to transform them," she is writing not only of Céline's anti-Semitism but also of the revolutionary impulse (p. 91). What is at stake here is a politics of interpretation.

The ideological exclusion of a "Marx" as other operates also in White's essay. Although no textual analysis is forthcoming, the assertion that Marx was interested in making sense out of history seems to be indisputable. But I am troubled when White submits that this urge to explain history arose in the nineteenth century, that Marx was caught up in that specific moment of historiography's practice, and that the Jews regarded history as a meaningless sublime spectacle until the establishment of Israel. Surely the grand plans of Judeo-Christian psychobiography and historiography should not be thus dismissed! I am not suggesting, as Kristeva does for psychoanalysis, that the discipline of history in Europe is a fulfillment of these earlier plans. I am merely indicating that the discipline of history did not suddenly fall upon previously virgin ground.

Whatever the truth of the assertion that the pursuit of meaning links Marx with the bourgeois historian (as it links him with the anti-Semitic writer in "Psychoanalysis and the Polis"), it seems bizarre to place him within the change from the sublime to the beautiful without *some* textual consideration. On the other hand, if one sees White's and Kristeva's moves as part of a contemporary academic-ideological network of explaining Marx away by the most general possible means as a foreclosure of exclusion, it becomes less odd. Some questions remain. Does the sublime historian's promise of a perception of meaning*less*ness not assume a preliminary understanding of what meaning in/of history might be? According to White, "the theorists of the sublime had correctly divined that whatever dignity and freedom human beings could lay claim to could come only by way of what Freud called a 'reaction-formation' to an apperception of history's meaninglessness" (p. 128). I will not bring up once again the vexed question of the passage from individual to group psychology here. I will sum up this part of my reading with the following suggestion: If, for political reasons touched upon by Clark and Said in their different ways, it is expedient to valorize the savant who can apperceive meaninglessness, then both Kristeva and White, in *their* different ways, claim "meaninglessness" too easily. I have tried to indicate this in my discussion of Kristeva. In White, "confusion," "uncertainty," and "moral anarchy" are equated with meaninglessness. Such a loose colloquial use deprives the word of any theoretical value.

By way of conclusion I will consider woman as the ideologically excluded other. Although I have some problems with Booth's essay, let me at the outset express my solidarity with his effort to correct this situation.

Almost all the personal pronouns in all the essays are "he." I am not asking for the quick fix of a mandatory "he or she." Just as, if the West Indian were introduced into Davie's script or the Arab academic style into Cavell's hilarious list of (English, French, and U.S.) academic styles, the argument itself would have to accommodate an otherwise unwitting race privileging—I think in twenty years the Japanese will come to inhabit these lists "naturally"—so also, if the "she" is seriously introduced into these essays, the general argument might need to change its shape. I believe it is with this sense of things that I find myself violated by the impregnable agent of an apparently benign statement such as the following by White: "But imagination is dangerous for the historian, because *he* cannot know that what *he* has imagined was actually the case, that it is not a product of *his* 'imagination' in the sense in which that term is used to characterize the activity of the poet or writer of fiction" (p. 123; italics mine). The masculist critic might well say, What am I going to do if an objection is brought against the very grain of my prose? Indeed, the feminist critic would urge, if he became aware that the indefinite personal pronoun is "produced-producing" rather than "natural," then he would also realize that, in this specific case, for example, since woman's place within the discipline and as subject of history is *different* from man's all along the race-class spectrum, and since a woman's right to "imagine" history is fraught with perils of a different *kind*, the validity of the critic's entire argument is put into question by that objection. As long as feminism is considered a special-interest glamorization of mainstream discourse (and I am grateful again to Booth for revealing the way feminist appproaches are discussed in "academic locker rooms"), this problem will go unrecognized. And *within the tacitly acknowledged and bonded* enclosure of masculist knowledge-production, a partial (masculist) account of intellectual history will, even as it critiques the narrative mode of "doing history," persistently imply that it is larger than the "whole"—the latter being an account that will confront the fundamental problem of sexual difference in material and ideological production. No history of consciousness can any longer be broached without this confrontation.

The problem cannot be solved by noticing celebrated female practitioners of the discipline, such as Hannah Arendt. The collective situation of the ideologically constituted-constituting sexed subject in the production of and as the situational object of historical discourse is a structural problem that obviously goes beyond the recognition of worthy exceptions. This critique should not be understood as merely an accusation of personal guilt; for the shifting limits of ideology, as I have suggested earlier, are larger than the "individual consciousness." Understood as such, my desperation at the smooth universality of Dworkin's discussion of law as interpretation will not seem merely tendentious. For it is not a questioning of the power of Dworkin's thesis; it is an acknowledgment that, if woman as the subject in law, or the subject of legal interpretation, is allowed into the argument in terms of the differential ethico-political dimension of these relationships, then the clarity might have to be seen as narrow and gender-specific rather than universal. (I am of course not mentioning the possibility that the eruption of Judeo-Christian sanctions within the recent debate on abortion shows how questions of sexual difference challenge the secular foundation of Western law.[14]

Let us consider Davie's two quick stabs at feminists before turning to woman in the essays by Kristeva, Said, and Booth. By way of introduction, let us insist that the word "patria" is not merely masculine in gender but names the father as the source of legitimate identity. (The appropriation of mother figures into this naming is similarly related to the place of Arendt in White's essay.) One way of explaining this would be to look again at Vico's fable of the origin of civil society—the *patricians*—in *The New Science*.[15] Here I shall point at the accompanying "hieroglyph or fable of Juno hanging in the air with a rope around her neck and her hands tied by another rope and with two heavy stones tied to her feet. . . . (Juno was in the air to signify the auspices essential to solemn nuptials. . . . She had a rope about her neck to recall the violence used by the giants on the first wives. Her hands were bound in token of the subjection of wives to their husbands. . . . The heavy stones tied to her feet denoted the stability of marriage.)"[16]

Davie's first stab comes when he reproaches feminists for not differentiating among women of different countries:

> Where is it acknowledged, for instance, in the vocabulary of feminism that "woman," as conceived by an American writing about Italians, cannot help but be significantly different from "woman" as conceived by an Italian looking at Americans? Or again, an Italian woman may well, we must suppose, be an Italian patriot; but where, in the current vocabulary of feminists, is that dimension of her "woman-ness" allowed for? Let it be acknowledged only so as to be deplored; but let it in any event be acknowledged. At the moment, it isn't. [P. 34]

This is of course a ridiculous mistake. The heterogeneity of international feminisms and women's situations across race and class lines is one of the chief concerns of feminist practice and theory today. To document this claim would be to compile a volume of bibliographical data.[17] And no feminist denies that women's as well as men's consciousness can be raised with reference to such notions as patriotism or total womanhood.

The second stab is with respect to Said's mother:

> When his Palestinian parents married, they had to register the marriage with the authorities of what was at that time a British mandate. The British officer, having registered the marriage, then and there tore up Mrs. Said's Palestinian passport, explaining that by doing so he made one more vacancy in the quota of permitted immigrants to Palestine from among the dispossessed of war-devastated Europe. The feminist response to this— "Aha, it was *the wife's* passport that was destroyed, not the husband's"— wholly fails to recognize the outrage that Mrs. Said felt, which her son now feels on her behalf. For if the law had been such that the husband took his bride's name, so that it was the man's passport that was destroyed, the outrage would have been just the same. [P. 34]

If I may descend into unseemly levity for a moment, I will quote my long-deceased father: "If Grandmother had a beard, she would be Grandfather." For the point is precisely that in a patriarchal society there are no such laws.[18]

Said calls for a criticism that would account for "quotidian politics and the struggle for power" (p. 14). At its best, feminist hermeneutics attempts precisely this. Part of the attempt has been to articulate the relationship between phallocracy and capital, as well as that between phallocracy and the organized Left.

I refer Said to two representative titles: Zillah R. Eisenstein's *Capitalist Patriarchy and the Case for Socialist Feminism* and the collection *Beyond the Fragments: Feminism and the Making of Socialism.*

I have been commenting on the politics of exclusion. The deliberate politics of inclusion can also turn into an appropriative gesture. We see it happen in Terry Eagleton's *Walter Benjamin; or, Towards a Revolutionary Criticism.* "Let us briefly imagine," Eagleton writes,

> what shape a "revolutionary literary criticism" would assume. It would dismantle the ruling concepts of "literature," reinserting "literary" texts into the whole field of cultural practices. It would strive to relate such "cultural" practices to other forms of social activity, and to transform the cultural apparatuses themselves. It would articulate its "cultural" analyses with a consistent political intervention. It would deconstruct the received hierarchies of "literature" and transvaluate received judgments and assumptions; engage with the language and "unconscious" of literary texts, to reveal their role in the ideological construction of the subject; and mobilize such texts, if necessary by hermeneutic "violence," in a struggle to transform those subjects within a wider political context. If one wanted a paradigm for such criticism, already established within the present, there is a name for it: feminist criticism.[19]

Just as Eagleton earlier accommodates deconstruction as a property of the dialectic, so does he accommodate feminism as a movement within the evolution of Marxist criticism.[20] The vexed question of how to operate race-, class-, and gender-analyses together is not even considered, for the safe space of feminist critique within "cultural practice" is assured even as that critique is neutralized by such a situating gesture. In a moment, however, the motives for this accommodation may themselves be situated within an ideological ground. Having praised feminist criticism (carrying his own name on the list by proxy; see n. 20) for its revolutionary-Marxist potential, Eagleton proceeds to trash it in three paragraphs: his main contention, feminism is theoretically thin, or separatist. Girls, shape up!

If I were writing specifically on Eagleton on feminism, I should question this unexamined vanguardism of theory. In the present context, other questions seem pertinent. First, where does this undifferentiated, undocumented, monolithic feminist criticism hang out? The gesture of constituting such an object in order that it may be appropriated and then devalued has something like a relationship with the constitution of a monolithic Marx, Marxism, Marxist critics that we have encountered in most of these essays. Davie's reprimand that *we* do not distinguish among women becomes all the more risible in this context. Even to Booth's benevolent impulse one must add the cautionary word, lest it share a niche with Eagleton's strategy here: woman's voice is not one voice to be added to the orchestra; *every* voice is inhabited by the sexual differential.

Why is it that male critics in search of a cause find in feminist criticism their best hope? Perhaps because, unlike the race and class situations, where academic people are not likely to get much of a hearing, the women's struggle is one they can support "from the inside." Feminism in its academic inceptions is accessible and subject to correction by authoritative men; whereas, as Clark has rightly pointed out, for the bourgeois intellectual to look to join other politico-economic struggles is to toe the line between hubris and bathos.

Perhaps a certain caution can be recommended to Kristeva as well. I have suggested that she lacks a political, historical, or cultural perspective on psychoanalysis as a movement. I would also suggest that the notion that the ultimate object-before-objectity is invariably the Mother is fraught with the monolithic figure of Woman rather than women heterogeneously operating outside of masculist kinship inscriptions. No neologism is merely etymological. No nomenclature is ideologically pure. It is therefore necessary to question, paleonymically, why the archaic mother is called, precisely, ab-ject. (The argument that it can mean "thrown away from"—as "object" means "thrown toward"—by its Latin derivation is not enough.)

I have tried to read some aspects of the interpretive politics that seemed to produce and was produced by the symposium on "The Politics of Interpretation." I have pointed first at the usefulness of a broader notion of ideology and then proceeded to notice some of the marks of ideology at work: conserving the sovereign subject; excluding a monolithic Marx(ism); and excluding or appropriating a homogeneous woman. But perhaps the strongest indicator of another item on the ideological agenda—the implicit race idiom of our politics—is the explicit charge I failed to fulfill.

In a report on our symposium in the *Chicago Grey City Journal*, Ken Wissoker said about my inclusion in the panel: "She was there, I assume, because she translated Derrida's *Of Grammatology*."[21] Reading those words, Elizabeth Abel's long and gracious letter of invitation to me came to mind. It was my point of view as a Third World feminist that she had hoped would enhance the proceedings. Apart from a pious remark that the maids upstairs in the guest quarters were women of color and a show of sentiment, involving Thomas Macaulay, when Said and I held the stage for a moment, the Third World seemed exorbitant to our concerns. As I reflect upon the cumulative politics of our gathering, that seems to strike the harshest note.

1982

9. French Feminism in an International Frame

A young Sudanese woman in the Faculty of Sociology at a Saudi Arabian University said to me, surprisingly: "I have written a structural functionalist dissertation on female circumcision in the Sudan." I was ready to forgive the sexist term "female circumcision." We have learned to say "clitoridectomy" because others more acute than we have pointed out our mistake.

But Structural Functionalism? Where "integration" is "social control [which] defines and *enforces . . . a degree of solidarity*"? Where "interaction, seen from the side of the economy," is defined as "consist[ing] of the supply of income and wealth applied to purposes strengthening the persistence of cultural patterns?"[1] Structural functionalism takes a "disinterested" stance on society as functioning structure. Its implicit interest is to applaud a system—in this case sexual—because it functions. A description such as the one below makes it difficult to credit that this young Sudanese woman had taken such an approach to clitoridectomy:

> In Egypt it is only the clitoris which is amputated, and usually not completely. But in the Sudan, the operation consists in the complete removal of all the external genital organs. They cut off the clitoris, the two major outer lips (*labia majora*) and the two minor inner lips (*labia minora*). Then the wound is repaired. The outer opening of the vagina is the only portion left intact, not however without having ensured that, during the process of repairing, some narrowing of the opening is carried out with a few extra stitches. The result is that on the marriage night it is necessary to widen the external opening by slitting one or both ends with a sharp scalpel or razor so that the male organ can be introduced.[2]

In my Sudanese colleague's research I found an allegory of my own ideological victimage:

The "choice" of English Honors by an upper-class young woman in the Calcutta of the fifties was itself highly overdetermined. Becoming a professor of English in the U.S. fitted in with the "brain drain." In due course, a commitment to feminism was the best of a collection of accessible scenarios. The morphology of a feminist theoretical practice came clear through Jacques Derrida's critique of phallocentrism and Luce Irigaray's reading of Freud. (The stumbling "choice" of French avant-garde criticism by an undistinguished Ivy League Ph.D. working in the Midwest is itself not without ideology-critical interest.) Predictably, I began by identifying the "female academic" and feminism as such. Gradually I found that there was indeed an area of feminist scholarship in the U.S. that was called "International Feminism": the arena usually defined as feminism in England, France, West Germany, Italy, and that part of the Third World most easily accessible to American interests: Latin America. When one attempted to think of so-called Third World women in a broader scope, one found oneself caught, as my Sudanese colleague was caught and held by Structural Functionalism, in a web of information retrieval inspired at best by: "what can I do *for* them?"

I sensed obscurely that this articulation was part of the problem. I re-articulated the question: What is the constituency of an international feminism? The following fragmentary and anecdotal pages approach the question. The complicity of a few French texts in that attempt could be part both of the problem—the "West" out to "know" the "East" determining a "westernized Easterner's" symptomatic attempt to "know her own world"; or of something like a solution,—reversing and displacing (if only by juxtaposing "some French texts" and a "certain Calcutta") the ironclad opposition of West and East. As soon as I write this, it seems a hopelessly idealistic restatement of the problem. I am not in a position of choice in this dilemma.

To begin with, an obstinate childhood memory.

I am walking alone in my grandfather's estate on the Bihar-Bengal border one winter afternoon in 1949. Two ancient washerwomen are washing clothes in the river, beating the clothes on the stones. One accuses the other of poaching on her part of the river. I can still hear the cracked derisive voice of the one accused: "You fool! Is this your river? The river belongs to the Company!"—the East India Company, from whom India passed to England by the Act for the Better Government of India (1858); England had transferred its charge to an Indian Governor-General in 1947. India would become an independent republic in 1950. For these withered women, the land as soil and water to be used rather than a map to be learned still belonged, as it did one hundred and nineteen years before that date, to the East India Company.

I was precocious enough to know that the remark was incorrect. It has taken me thirty-one years and the experience of confronting a nearly inarticulable question to apprehend that their facts were wrong but the fact was right. The Company does still own the land.

I should not consequently patronize and romanticize these women, nor yet entertain a nostalgia for being as they are. The academic feminist must learn to learn from them, to speak to them, to suspect that their access to the political and sexual scene is not merely to be *corrected* by our superior theory and enlightened compassion. Is our insistence upon the especial beauty of the old necessarily to be preferred to a careless acknowledgment of the mutability of sexuality? What of the fact that my distance from those two was, however micrologically you defined class, class-determined and determining?

How, then, can one learn from and speak to the millions of illiterate rural and urban Indian women who live "in the pores of" capitalism, inaccessible to the capitalist dynamics that allow us our shared channels of communication, the definition of common enemies? The pioneering books that bring First World feminists news from the Third World are written by privileged informants and can only be deciphered by a trained readership. The distance between "the informant's world," her "own sense of the world she writes about," and that of the non-specialist feminist is so great that, paradoxically, *pace* the subtleties of reader-response theories, here the distinctions might easily be missed.

This is not the tired nationalist claim that only a native can know the scene. The point that I am trying to make is that, in order to learn enough about Third World women and to develop a different readership, the immense heterogeneity of the field must be appreciated, and the First World feminist must learn to stop feeling privileged *as a woman*.

These concerns were well articulated in my approach to feminism when I came across Julia Kristeva's *About Chinese Women*.[3] Here again I found a link with my own ideological victimage, "naturalization" transformed into privilege.

French theorists such as Derrida, Lyotard, Deleuze, and the like, have at one time or another been interested in reaching out to all that is not the West, because they have, in one way or another, questioned the millennially cherished excellences of Western metaphysics: the sovereignty of the subject's intention, the power of predication and so on. There is a more or less vaguely articulated conviction that these characteristics had something like a relationship with the morphology of capital. The French feminist theory that makes its way to us comes to a readership more or less familiar with this enclave.

During the 1970s, the prestigious journal *Tel Quel*—Kristeva is on the editorial committee—pursued an assiduous if somewhat eclectic interest in the matter of China.[4] Before I consider that interest as it is deployed in *About Chinese Women*, let us look briefly at the solution Kristeva offers Frenchwomen in the first part of her book:

> We cannot gain access to the temporal scene, i.e., to political affairs, except by identifying with the values considered to be masculine (dominance, superego, the *endorsed communicative word* that institutes stable social exchange) . . . [We must] achieve this identification in order to escape a smug polymorphism where it is so easy and comfortable for a woman here to remain; and by this identification [we must] gain entry to social experience. [We must] be wary from the first of the premium on narcissism that such an integration may carry with it: to reject the validity of homologous woman, finally virile: and to act, on the socio-politico-historical stage, as her negative: that is, to act first with all those who "swim against the tide," all those who refuse . . . But neither to take the role of revolutionary (male or female): to refuse all roles . . . to summon this timeless "truth"— formless, neither true nor false, echo of our pleasure, of our madness, of our pregnancies—*into the order of speech* and *social symbolism*. But how? By listening; by recognizing the unspoken in speech, even revolutionary speech; by calling attention at all times to whatever remains unsatisfied, repressed, new, eccentric, incomprehensible, disturbing to the *status quo* (p. 38; italics mine).

This is a set of directives for class- and race-privileged literary women who can ignore the seductive effects of identifying with the values of the other side while rejecting their validity;[5] and, by identifying the political with the temporal and linguistic, ignore as well the micrology of political economy. To act with individualistic rather than systematic subverters in order to summon timeless "truths" resembles the task of the literary critic who explicates the secrets of the avant-garde artist of western Europe; the program of "symptomatic and semiotic reading"—here called "listening"—adds more detail to that literary-critical task.[6] The end of this chapter reveals another line of thought active in the group I mention above: to bring together Marx and Freud: ("An analyst conscious of history and politics? A politician tuned into the unconscious? A woman perhaps .)." (p. 38).

Kristeva is certainly aware that such a solution cannot be offered to the nameless women of the Third World. Here is her opening description of some women in Huxian Square: "An enormous crowd is sitting in the sun: they wait for us wordlessly, perfectly still. Calm eyes, not even curious, but slightly amused or anxious: in any case, piercing, and certain of belonging to a community with which we will never have anything to do" (p. 11). Her question, in the face of those silent women, is about her *own* identity rather than theirs: "Who is speaking, then, before the stare of the peasants at Huxian?" (p. 15). This too might be a characteristic of the group of thinkers to whom I have, most generally, attached her. In spite of their occasional interest in touching the *other* of the West, of metaphysics, of capitalism, their repeated question is obsessively self-centered: if we are not what official history and philosophy say we are, who then are we (not), how are we (not)?

It is therefore not surprising that, even as she leaves the incredibly detailed terrain of the problem of knowing who she herself is exactly—the speaking, reading, listening "I" at this particular *moment*—she begins to compute the reality of who "they" are in terms of *millennia*: "One thing is certain: a revolution in the rules of kinship took place in China, and can be traced to sometime around B.C. 1000" (p. 46).

The sweeping historiographical scope is not internally consistent. Speaking of modern China, Kristeva asserts drastic socio-sexual structural changes through legislation in a brisk reportorial tone that does not allow for irony (p. 118; p. 128). Yet, speaking of ancient China, she finds traces of an older matrilineal and matrilocal society (evidence for which is gleaned from two books by Marcel Granet, dating from the twenties and thirties, and based on "folk dance and legend" [p. 47]—and Lévi-Strauss's general book on elementary structures of kinship) lingering through the fierce Confucian tradition to this very day because, at first, it seems to be speculatively the more elegant argument (p. 68). In ten pages this speculative assumption has taken on psychological causality (p. 78).

In another seventy-odd pages, and always with no encroachment of archival evidence, speculation has become historical fact: "The influence of the powerful system of matrilinear descent, and the Confucianism that is so strongly affected by it, can hardly be discounted" (p. 151). Should such a vigorous conclusion not call into question the authority of the following remark, used, it seems, because at that point the author needs a way of valorizing the women of the countryside today over the women of the cities: "An intense life-experience has thrust them from *a patriarchal world which hadn't moved for millennia* into a modern universe where they are called upon to command" (p. 193; italics mine)? Where then are those matrilocal vestiges that kept up women's strength all through those centuries?[7]

It is this wishful use of history that brings Kristeva close to the eighteenth-century Sinophiles whom she criticizes because "they deformed those systems in order to assimilate them into their own" (p. 53). In the very next page, "the essential problem" of the interpretation of Chinese thought, defined (under cover of the self-deprecatory question) as a species of differential semiotics: "The heterogeneity of this Li [form and content at once] defies symbolism, and is actualized only by derivation, through a combination of opposing signs (+ and −, earth and sky, etc.), all of which are of equal value. In other words, there is no single isolatable symbolic principle to oppose itself and assert itself as transcendent law." Even as the Western-trained Third World feminist deplores the absence of the usual kind of textual analysis and demonstration, she is treated to the most stupendous generalizations about Chinese writing, a topos of that very eighteenth century that Kristeva scorns: "Not only has Chinese writing maintained the memory of matrilinear pre-history (collective and individual) in its architectonic of image, gesture, and sound; it has been able as well to integrate it into a logico-symbolic code capable of ensuring the most direct, 'reasonable,' legislating—even the most bureaucratic—communication: all the qualities that the West believes itself unique in honouring and that it attributes to the Father" (p. 57). Kristeva's text seems to authorize, here and elsewhere, the definition of the essentially feminine and the essentially masculine as non-logical and logical. At any rate, this particular movement ends with the conclusion that "the Chinese give us a 'structuralist' or 'warring' (contradictory) portrait" (p. 57).

Kristeva prefers this misty past to the present. Most of her account of the latter is dates, legislations, important people, important places. There is no transition between the two accounts. Reflecting a broader Western cultural practice, the "classical" East is studied with primitivistic reverence, even as the "contemporary" East is treated with realpolitikal contempt.

On the basis of evidence gleaned from lives of great women included in translated anthologies and theses of the *troisième cycle* (I take it that is what "third form thesis" p. 91] indicates) and no primary research; and an unquestioning acceptance of Freud's conclusions about the "pre-oedipal" stage, and no *analytic* experience of Chinese women, Kristeva makes this prediction: "If the question [of finding a channel for sexual energy in a socialist society through various forms of sublimation outside the family] should be asked one day, and if the analysis of Chinese tradition that the *Pi Lin Pi Kong* [against Lin and Kong] Campaign seems to have undertaken is not interrupted, it's not altogether impossible that China may approach it with much less prudishness and fetishistic neurosis than the Christian West has managed while clamouring for 'sexual freedom'" (p. 90). Whether or not the "Christian West" as a whole has been clamoring for sexual freedom, the prediction about China is of course a benevolent one; my point is that its provenance is symptomatic of a colonialist-benevolence.

The most troubling feature of *About Chinese Women* is that, in the context of China, Kristeva seems to blunt the fine edge of her approach to literature. She draws many conclusions about "the mother at the centre" in ancient China from "all the manuals of the 'Art of the Bedchamber'—which date back to the first century A.D." and "a novel of the Qing Dynasty . . . *The Dream of the Red Pavilion*" (p. 61, 79). Let us forget that there is no attempt at textual analysis, not even in translation. We must still ask, are these manuals representative or marginal, "normal" or "perverse," have they a class fix? Further, is the relationship between "literature and life" so unproblematic as to permit *The Dream* to be described as "an accurate portrait of noble families" because it "is currently studied in China as evidence of the insoluble link between class struggle and intra/inter-familial attitudes?" (pp. 78–79). How may it differ when a Chinese person with a "Chinese experience" studies it in Chinese, apparently in this way? Is it only the West that can afford its protracted debate over the representationality of realism? Similar questions haunt the reader as Kristeva launches into a running summary of the female literati of China since 150 A.D., in terms of dominant themes. She offers this impressionistic comment on a poet who, we are told, is "among the greatest, not only in China, but in the literature of the entire world" (p. 50): "Li Qingzhao breathes into these universal traits of Chinese poetry a musicality rarely attained by other poets: the brilliantly intertwined rhythms and alliterations, the shape of the characters themselves, create a language where the least aural or visual element becomes the bearer of this symbiosis between body, world, and sense, a language that one cannot label 'music' or 'meaning' because it is both at once." The poem is then "quoted". twice—first in English transcription and literal translation, and next in "a translation (from a French version by Philippe Sollers)." What would happen to Louise Labé in such a quick Chinese treatment for a Chinese audience with a vestigial sense of European culture as a whole? What is one to make of the gap between the last lines of the two translations: "This time / how a single word / sadness is enough" and "this time one / word death won't be enough?" What would happen to "Absent thee from felicity awhile" in a correspondingly "free" Chinese version?

As we come to the literatures of modern China, all the careful apologies of the opening of the book seem forgotten: "Let us examine the findings of a few researchers on family psychology or its representation in modern fiction, as a means of understanding the forms these feudal / Confucian mores take in Chinese culture today" (p. 95). As far as I can tell, the author's source of literary information—a few simple statistics—is a single article by Ai-Li S. Chin, "Family Relations in Modern Chinese Fiction," in M. Freedman, ed., *Family and Kinship in Chinese Society*.[8] It seems startling, then, that it can be said with apparent ease: "Are these [mother-daughter] problems intensified by those passionate and archaic rivalries between women which, in the West, produce our Electras, who usurp their mothers' roles by murdering them in the names of their fathers? *Chinese literature is not explicit here*" (p. 146; italics mine).

This brings us to a certain principled "anti-feminism" in Kristeva's book which may be related to what has been called "the New Philosophy" in France.[9] "The Electras—deprived forever of their hymens—militants in the cause of their fathers, frigid with exaltation—are dramatic figures where the social consensus corners any woman who wants to escape her condition: nuns, 'revolutionaries,' 'feminists'" (p. 32). I think such a sentiment rests upon certain unexamined questions: What is the relationship between myth (the story of Electra), the socio-literary formulation of myths (Aeschylus's *Oresteia*, written for a civic competition with choruses, owned by rich citizens, playing with freelance troupes) and "the immutable structures" of human behavior? What hidden agenda does Freud's use of Greek myth to fix the father-daughter relationship—specially at the end of "Analysis Terminable and Interminable"—contain? Although Kristeva sometimes speaks in a tone reminiscent of *Anti-Oedipus*, she does not broach these questions, which are the basis of that book.[10]

This principled "anti-feminism," which puts its trust in the individualistic critical avant-grade rather than anything that might call itself a revolutionary collectivity is part of a general intellectual backlash—represented, for instance, by *Tel Quel's* espousal of the Chinese past after the disappointment with the Communist Party of France during the events of May 1968 and the movement toward a Left Coalition through the early 1970s.

The question of how to speak *to* the "faceless" women of China cannot be asked within such a partisan conflict. The question, even, of who speaks in front of the mute and uncomprehending women in Huxian Square must now be articulated in sweeping macrological terms. The real differences between "our Indo-European, monotheistic world . . . still obviously in the lead" (p. 195) and the Chinese situation must be presented as the fact that the "Chinese women whose ancestresses knew the secrets of the bedchamber better than anyone . . . are similar to the men" (p. 198). Thus when Chinese Communism attacks the tendencies—"pragmatic, materialistic, psychological"—that "are considered 'feminine' by patriarchal society," it does not really do so; because in China the pre-patriarchal society has always lingered on, giving women access to real rather than representative power. I have indicated above my reasons for thinking that the evidence for this lingering maternal power, at least as offered in this book, is extremely dubious. Yet that is, indeed, Kristeva's "reason" for suggesting that in China the Party's suppression of the feminine is not really a suppression of the "feminine": "By addressing itself thus to women, [the Party] appeals to their capacity to assume the symbolic function (the structural constraint, the law of the society): a capacity which itself has a basis in tradition, since it includes the *world prior to and behind the scenes of Confucianism*" (p. 199; italics mine).

My final question about this macrological nostalgia for the pre-history of the East is plaintive and predictable: what about us? The "Indo-European" world whose "monotheism" supports the argument of the difference between China and the West is not altogether monotheistic. The splendid, decadent, multiple, oppressive, and more than millennial polytheistic tradition of India has to be written out of the *Indo*-European picture in order that this difference may stand.

The fact that Kristeva thus speaks for a generalized West is the "naturalization transformed into privilege" that I compared to my own ideological victimage. As she investigates the pre-Confucian text of the modern Chinese woman, her own pre-history in Bulgaria is not even a shadow under the harsh light of the Parisian voice. I hold on to a solitary passage:

For me—having been educated in a "popular democracy," having benefited from its advantages and been subjected to its censorship, having left it inasmuch as it is possible to leave the world of one's childhood, and probably not without bearing its "birthmarks"—for me what seems to be "missing" in the system is, indeed, the stubborn refusal to admit anything is missing (p. 156).

Who is speaking here? An effort to answer that question might have revealed more about the mute women of Huxian Square, looking with qualified envy at "the incursion of the West."

I am suggesting, then, that a *deliberate* application of the doctrines of French High "Feminism" to a different situation of political specificity might misfire. If, however, International Feminism is defined within a Western European context, the heterogeneity becomes manageable. In our own situation as academic feminists, we can begin thinking of planning a class. What one does not know can be worked up. There are experts in the field. We can work by the practical assumption that there is no serious communication barrier between them and us. No anguish over uncharted continents, no superstitious dread of making false starts, no questions to which answers may not at least be entertained.

Within such a context, after initial weeks attempting to define and name an "American" and an "English" feminism, one would get down to the question of what is specific about French feminism. We shall consider the fact that the most accessible strand of French feminism is governed by a philosophy that argues the impossibility of answering such a question.

We now have the indispensable textbook for this segment of the course: *New French Feminisms: An Anthology*, edited by Elaine Marks and Isabelle de Courtivron. [11] In the United States, French feminism or, more specifically, French feminist theory, has so far been of interest to a "radical" fringe in French and Comparative Literature departments rather than to the feminists in the field. A book such as this has an interdisciplinary accessibility. This is somewhat unlike the case in England, where Marxist feminism has used mainstream (or masculist) French "theory"— at least Althusser and Lacan—to explain the constitution of the subject (of ideology or sexuality)—to produce a more specifically "feminist" critique of Marx's theories of ideology and reproduction. [12]

Because of a predominantly "literary" interest, the question in French feminist texts that seems most relevant and urgent is that of a specifically feminine discourse. At the crossroads of sexuality and ideology, woman stands constituted (if that is the word) as object. As subject, woman must learn to "speak 'otherwise,'" or *"make audible* [what] . . . suffers silently in *the holes of* discourse" (Xavière Gauthier, p. 163).

The relationship between this project of "speaking" (writing) and Kristeva's project of "listening" (reading) is clear. Such a writing is generally though not invariably attempted in feminist fiction or familiar-essay-cum-prose-poem such as Cixous's *Préparatifs de noces au delà de l'abîme* or Monique Witting's *Lesbian Body*. [13] As such it has strong ties to the "evocative magic" of the prose poem endorsed by Baudelaire—the power of indeterminate suggestion rather than determinate reference that could overwhelm and sabotage the signifying conventions. Baudelaire is not often invoked by the French theorists of feminist or revolutionary discourse. Is it because his practice remains caught within the gestures of an embarrassingly masculist decadence (linked to "high capitalism" by Walter Benjamin, *A Lyric Poet in the Era of High Capitalism*?)[14]

The important figures for these theorists remain Mallarmé and Joyce. Julia Kristeva and Hélène Cixous, the two feminist discourse-theorists who are most heard in the U.S., do not disavow this. Kristeva seems to suggest that if women can accede to the avant-garde in general, they will fulfill the possibilities of their discourse (p. 166). Cixous privileges poetry (for "the novelists [are] allies of representation" [p. 250]) and suggests that a Kleist or a Rimbaud can speak as women do. Older feminist writers like Duras ("the rhetoric of women, one that is anchored in the organism, in the body" [p. 238]—rather than the mind, the place of the subject) or Sarraute are therefore related to the mainstream avant-garde phenomenon of the *nouveau roman*.

In a certain sense the definitive characteristic of the French feminist project of founding a woman's discourse reflects a coalition with the continuing tradition of the French avant-garde. It can be referred to the debate about the political potential of the avant-garde, between Expressionism and Realism.[15]

It is also an activity that is more politically significant for the producer/writer than the consumer/reader. It is for the writer rather than the reader that Herbert Marcuse's words may have some validity: "There is the inner link between dialectical thought and the effort of avant-garde literature: the effort to break the power of facts over the word, and to speak a language which is not the language of those who establish, enforce and benefit from the facts."[16] As even a quick glance at the longest entries for the late nineteenth and twentieth centuries in the PMLA bibliographies will testify, the "political" energy of avant-garde production, contained within the present academic system, leads to little more than the stockpiling of exegeses, restoring those texts back to propositional discourse. In fact, given this situation, the power of a *Les Guérillères* or a *Tell Me a Riddle* (to mention a non-French text)—distinguishing them from the "liberated texts" supposedly subverting "the traditional components of discourse," but in fact sharing "all the components of the most classic pornographic literature" (Benoîte Groult, p. 72)—is what they talk *about*, their *substantive* revision of, rather than their apparent *formal* allegiance to, the European avant-garde. This differential will stubbornly remain in the most "deconstructive" of readings.

The search for a discourse of woman is related not merely to a literary but also the philosophical avant-garde which I mentioned with reference to *About Chinese Women*. The itinerary of this group is set out in Jacques Derrida's "The Ends of Man."[17] Louis Althusser launched a challenge against Sartre's theory of humanistic practice and his anthropologistic reading of Marx with his own "Feuerbach's 'Philosophical Manifesto'" in 1960.[18] Althusser's position was *scientific* anti-humanism. The challenge in French philosophy described by Derrida in his essay (which makes a point of being written in 1968), again largely in terms of Sartre and his anthropologistic reading of Heidegger, can be called an *anti-scientific* anti-humanism. (Sartre does not remain the butt of the attack for long. An echo of the importance of Sartre as the chief philosopher of French humanism, however, is heard in Michèle Le Doeuff's "Simone de Beauvoir and Existentialism," presented on the occasion of the thirtieth anniversary of *The Second Sex* in New York.[19] Le Doeuff's essay reminds us that, just as the current anti-humanist move in French philosophy was "post-Sartrean" as well as "post-structuralist," so also the discourse-theorists in French feminism marked a rupture, precisely, from Simone de Beauvoir.)

In "Ends of Man," Derrida is describing a trend in contemporary French philosophy rather than specifically his own thoughts, though he does hint how his own approach is distinct from the others'. "Man" in this piece is neither distinguished from woman nor specifically inclusive of her. "Man" is simply the hero of philosophy:

> There is [in existentialism] no interruption in a metaphysical familiarity which so naturally relates the *we* of the philosopher to "we-men," the total horizon of humanity. Although the theme of history is eminently present . . . the history of the concept of man is never questioned. Everything takes place as though the sign "man" had no origin, no historical, cultural, linguistic limit (p. 35).

[handwritten: Derrida]

Any extended consideration of Derrida's description would locate the landmark texts. Here suffice it to point at Jean-François Lyotard's *Economie libidinale*, since it establishes an affinity with the French feminist use of Marx.[20]

For Lyotard, the Freudian pluralization of "the grounds of man" is still no more than a "political economy," plotted as it is in terms of investments (German *Besetzung*, English "cathexis," French *investissement*—providing a convenient analogy) of the libido. In terms of a "libidinal" economy as such, when the "libidinal Marx" is taken within this "libidinal cartography" (p. 117) what emerges is a powerful "literary-critical" exegesis under the governing allegory of the libido, cross-hatched with analogies between "a philosophy of alienation and a psychoanalysis of the signifier" (p. 158), or "capitalist society" and "prostitution" (p. 169) which has, admittedly, very little to do with the micrological and shifting specificities of the class-struggle and its complicity with the economic text of the world-market.[21]

[handwritten: Lyotard]

I have already spoken of the "New Philosophical" reaction to the possibility of a Left Coalition in 1978. Within this capsule summary such a reaction can be called anti-humanist (against the privileged subject), anti-scientific (against psychoanalysis and Marxism as specific or "regional" practices) and anti-revolutionary (against collectivities).

It is within this context of the deconstruction of the general sign of "man" as it exists within the "metaphysical" tradition (a deconstruction that can "produce"—Derrida commenting on Blanchot—"a 'female element,' which does not signify female person")[22] that the following statements by Kristeva about the specific sign "woman" should be read:

> On a deeper level [than advertisements or slogans for our demands], how-ever, a woman cannot "be"; it is something which does not even belong in the order of *being*. It follows that a feminist practice can only be negative, at odds with what already exists. . . . In "woman" I see something that cannot be represented, something above and beyond nomenclatures and ideologies. . . . Certain feminist demands revive a kind of naive roman-ticism, a belief in identity (the reverse of phallocentrism), if we compare them to the experience of both poles of sexual difference as is found in the economy of Joycian or Artaudian prose. . . . I pay close attention to the particular aspect of the work of the avant-garde which dissolves iden-tity, even sexual identities; and in my theoretical formulations I try to go against metaphysical theories that censure what I just labeled a "woman"—that is what, I think, makes my research that of a woman (pp. 137–38).

I have already expressed my dissatisfaction with the presupposition of the *necessarily* revolutionary potential of the avant-garde, literary or philosophical. There is something even faintly comical about Joyce rising above sexual identities and bequeathing the proper mind-set to the women's movement. The point might be to remark how, even if one knows how to undo identities, one does not necessarily escape the historical determinations of sexism.[23] Yet it must also be acknowledged that there is in Kristeva's text an implicit double program for women which we encounter in the best of French feminism: *against* sexism, where women unite as a biologically oppressed caste; and *for* feminism, where human beings train to prepare for a transformation of consciousness.

Within this group of male anti-humanist avant-garde philosophers, Derrida has most overtly investigated the possibilities of "the name of woman" as a corollary to the project of charging "the ends of man." In *Of Grammatology* he relates the privileging of the sovereign subject not only with phonocentrism (primacy of voice-consciousness) and logocentrism (primacy of the word as law), but also with phallocentrism (primacy of the phallus as arbiter of [legal] iden-tity).[24] In texts such as "La double séance"[25] (the figure of the hymen as both inside and outside), *Glas* (the project of philosophy as desire for the mother), *Eperons* (woman as affirmative deconstruction), "The Law of Genre" (the female element as double affirmation) and "Living On: Border Lines" (double invagin-ation as textual effect) a certain textuality of woman is established.

Hélène Cixous is most directly aware of this line of thought in Derrida. She mentions Derrida's work with approval in her influential "Laugh of the Medusa" (p. 258) and "Sorties" (p. 91). Especially in the latter, she uses the Derridian methodology of reversing and displacing hierarchized binary oppositions. The text begins with a series of these oppositions and Cixous says of women: "she does not enter into the oppositions, she is not coupled with the father (who is coupled with the son)." Later, Cixous deploys the Derridian notion of *restance* (remains) or minimal idealization, giving to woman a dispersed and differential identity: "She does not exist, she may be nonexistent; but there must be something of her" (p. 92).[26] She relates man to his particular "torment, his desire to be (at) the origin" (p. 92). She uses the theme of socio-political and ideological "textuality" with a sureness of touch that places her within the Derridian-Foucauldian problematic: "men and women are caught in a network of millennial cultural determinations of a complexity that is practically unanalyzable: we can no more talk about 'woman' than about 'man' without being caught within an ideological theater where the multiplication of representations, images, reflections, myths, identifications constantly transforms, deforms, alters each person's imaginary order and in advance, renders all conceptualization null and void" (p. 96).[27] "We can no more talk about 'woman' than about 'man.'" This sentiment is matched by the passage from Kristeva I quote above—to make my point that the decision *not* to search for a woman's identity but to speculate about a woman's discourse by way of the negative is related to the deconstruction—of man's insistence upon his own identity as betrayed by existing models of discourse—launched by mainstream French anti-humanism.

Cixous relates the idea of this over-determined ideological theater to the impossible heterogeneity of "each person's imaginary order." She is referring here to the Lacanian notion of the "irremediably deceptive" Imaginary, a "basically narcissistic relation of the subject to his [sic] ego"; a relationship to other subjects as my "counterparts"; a relationship to the world by way of ideological reflexes; a relationship to meaning in terms of resemblance and unity.[28] To change the stock of Imaginary counterparts which provides the material for sublation into the symbolic dimension is an important part of the project for a woman's discourse. "Assuming the *real* subjective position that corresponds to this discourse is another matter. One would cut through all the heavy layers of ideology that have borne down since the beginnings of the family and private property: that can be done only in the imagination. And that is precisely what feminist action is all about: to change the imaginary in order to be able to act on the real, to change the very forms of language which by its structure and history has been subject to a law that is patrilinear, therefore masculine" (Catherine Clément, pp. 130–31).[29] In the following remark by Antoinette Fouque, the space between the "ideological" and the "symbolic" is marked by the Imaginary order: "Women cannot allow themselves to deal with political problems while at the same time blotting out the unconscious. If they do, they become, at best, feminists capable of attacking patriarchy on the ideological level but not on a symbolic level" (p. 117).

Now Cixous, as the most Derridian of the French "anti-feminist" feminists, knows that the re-inscription of the Imaginary cannot be a project launched by a sovereign subject; just as she knows that "it is impossible to *define* a feminine practice of writing, and this is an impossibility that will remain" (p. 253). Therefore, in Cixous the Imaginary remains subjected to persistent alteration and the concept's grasp upon it remains always deferred. This is a classic argument within the French anti-humanist deconstruction of the sovereignty of the subject. It takes off from Freud's suggestion that the I (ego) constitutes itself in obligatory pursuit of the it (id): "I am" must be read as an anaseme of "where it was there shall I become" [*wo es war soll ich werden*]. Most obviously, of course, it relates to Lacan's admonition that the Symbolic order's grasp upon the stuff of the Imaginary is random and pointillist: like buttons in upholstery [*points de capiton*]. Yet, as Cixous begins the peroration of "The Laugh of the Medusa" she does take on Lacan. She questions the practice of deciphering every code as referring to the Name-of-the-Father or its alias, the mother-who-has-the-phallus: "And what about the libido? Haven't I read [Lacan's] the 'Signification of the Phallus.' . . ."[30] If the New Women, arriving now, dare to create outside the theoretical, they're called in by the cops of the Signifier, fingerprinted, remonstrated, and brought into the line of order that they are supposed to know; assigned by force of trickery to a precise place in the chain that's always formed for the benefit of a privileged 'signifier.' We are re-membered to the string that leads back, if not to the Name-of-the Father, then, for a new twist, to the place of the phallic mother" (pp. 262–63).[31] As she exposes the phallus to be the "privileged sig-nifier," she takes her place with Derrida's critique of the Lacanian phallus as the "transcendental signifier" in "The Purveyor of Truth," and with his artic-ulation of the phallic mother as the limit of man's enterprise in *Glas*.[32] I believe she is not speaking only of orthodox or neo-Freudian psychoanalysis when she writes: "Don't remain within the psychoanalytic enclosure" (p. 263). Indeed, the choice of the Medusa as her logo is a derisive takeoff on the notion that woman as object of knowledge or desire does not relate to the *subject*-object but to the *eye*-object dialectic. When she writes: "You only have to look at the Medusa straight on to see her" (p. 255), I believe she is rewriting the arrogance of "you only have to go and look at the Bernini statue in Rome to understand imme-diately she [St. Teresa] is coming."[33] For the passage is followed by an invocation of the male member in splendid isolation: "It's the jitters that give them a hard-on! for themselves! They need to be afraid of us. Look at the trembling Perseuses moving backward toward us, clad in apotropes."

The distance between a Cixous, sympathetic to the deconstructive morphol-ogy in particular and therefore critical of Lacan's phallocentrism and a Kristeva, sympathetic to French anti-humanism in general, may be measured, only half fancifully, by a juxtaposition like the following. Kristeva: "In 'woman' I see something that cannot be represented"; Cixous: "Men say there are two un-representable things: death and the feminine sex" (p. 255).

(In fact, Kristeva's association with Derridian thought dates back to the sixties. Derrida was a regular contributor to the early *Tel Quel*. Her project, however, has been, not to *deconstruct* the origin, but rather to *recuperate*, archeologically and formulaically, what she locates as the potential originary space *before* the sign. Over the years, this space has acquired names and inhabitants related to specific ideological sets: geno-text, Mallarméan avant-garde, ancient Asiatic lin-guistics, the Platonic *chora*; and now the European High Art of Renaissance and Baroque, Christian theology through the ages, and personal experience, as they cope with the mystery of pregnancy-infancy.)[34]

Like Kristeva, Cixous also seems not to ask what it means to say some "men," especially of the avant-garde, can be "women" in this special sense. In this respect, and in much of her argument for "bisexuality," she is sometimes reminiscent of the Freud who silenced female psychoanalysts by calling them as good as men.[35] The question of the political or historical and indeed ideological differential that irreducibly separates the male from the female critic of phallocentrism is not asked.[36] And, occasionally the point of Derrida's insistence that deconstruction is not a negative metaphysics and that one cannot practice free play is lost sight of: "To admit," Cixous writes, "that to write is precisely to work (in) the between, questioning the process of the same *and* of the other without which nothing lives, undoing the work of death—is first to want the two [*le deux*] and both, the ensemble of the one and the other not congealed in sequences of struggle and expulsion or some other form of death, but dynamized to infinity by an incessant process of exchange from one into the other different subject" (p. 254). Much of Derrida's critique of humanism-phallocentrism is concerned with a reminder of the limits of deconstructive power *as well as* with the impossibility of remaining in the in-between. Unless one is aware that one cannot avoid taking a stand, unwitting stands get taken. Further, "writing" in Derrida is not simply identical with the production of prose and verse. It is the name of "structure" which operates and fractures knowing (epistemology), being (ontology), doing (practice), history, politics, economics, institutions as such. It is a "structure" whose "origin" and "end" are necessarily provisional and absent. "The essential predicates in a minimal determination of the classical concept of writing" are presented and contrasted to Derrida's use of "writing" in "Signature Event Context."[37] Because Cixous seems often to identify the Derridian mode of writing about writing with merely the production of prose and verse, a statement like ". . . women are body. More body, hence more writing" (p. 258) remains confusing.

In a course on International Feminism, the question of Cixous's faithfulness to, or unquestioning acceptance of, Derrida, becomes quickly irrelevant. It suffices here to point out that the sort of anti-feminism that has its ties to anti-humanism understood as a critique of the name of man or of phallocentrism is to be distinguished from the other kinds of French anti-feminism, some of which the editors of *New French Feminisms* mention on page 32. Of the many varieties, I would mention the party-line anti-feminism with which Communist Parties associate themselves: "The 'new feminism' is currently developing the thesis that no society, socialist or capitalist, is capable of favorably responding to the aspirations of women. . . . If we direct against men the action necessary for women's progress, we condemn the great hopes of women to a dead end" (p. 128). Here the lesson of a double approach—against sexism and for feminism—is suppressed. I feel some sympathy with Christine Delphy's remark, even as she calls for "a materialist analysis of the oppression of women," that "the existence of this Marxist line had the practical consequence of being a brake on the [women's] movement, and this fact is obviously not accidental."[38]

Another variety of anti-"feminism" that should be yet further distinguished: "The social mode of being of men and women and of women is *in no way* linked with their nature as males and females nor with the shape of their sex organs" (p. 215; italics mine). These are the "radical feminists" who are interested in shaping a feminist materialism and who are not programmatically or methodologically influenced by the critique of humanism. Unlike them, I certainly would not reject the search for a woman's discourse out of hand. But I have, just as certainly, attended to the critique of such a search as expressed by the "radical feminists":

> The so-called explored language extolled by some women writers seems to be linked, if not in its content at least by its style, to a trend propagated by literary schools governed by its male masters. . . . To advocate a direct language of the body is . . . not subversive because it is equivalent to denying the reality and the strength of social mediations . . . that oppress us in our bodies (p. 219).

It would be a mistake (at least for those of us not directly embroiled in the French field) to ignore these astute warnings, although we should, of course, point out that the radical feminists' credo—"I will be neither a woman nor a man in the present historical meaning: I shall be some Person in the body of a woman" (p. 226)—can, if the wonderful deconstructive potential of *personne* in French (*some-one* and, at the same time no *one*) is not attended to, lead to the sort of obsession with one's proper identity as property that is both the self-duping and the oppressive power of humanism. This is particularly so because, neither in France nor in the U.S., apart from the curious example of Derrida, has mainstream academic anti-humanism had much to do with the practical critique of phallocentrism at all. In the U.S. the issue seems to be the indeterminacy of meaning and linguistic determination, in France the critique of identity and varieties of micrological and genealogical analyses of the structures of power.

We should also be vigilant, it seems to me, against the sort of gallic attitudinizing that has been a trend in Anglo-American literary criticism since the turn of the century. An American-style "French" feminist, eager to insert herself/himself into a Star Chamber, can at worst remind one of the tone of *The Symbolist Movement in Literature* by Arthur Symons.[39] It can emphasize our own tendency to offer grandiose solutions with little political specificity, couched in the strategic form of rhetorical questions.[40]

I can do no better than quote here part of the final exchange between Catherine Clément and Hélène Cixous in *La jeune née*, an exchange that is often forgotten:

> *H.* The class struggle is this sort of enormous machine whose system is described by Marx and which therefore functions today. But its rhythm is not always the same, it is a rhythm that is sometimes most attenuated.

One can sense the frustration in Clément's response, which could be directed equally well at a Lyotard or all of the "poetic revolutionaries":

C. It can *appear* attenuated, especially if one is bludgeoned into thinking so. But there is a considerable lag between the reality of the class struggle and the way in which it is lived mythically, especially by intellectuals for whom it is hard to measure the reality of struggles directly, because they are in a position where work on language and the imaginary has a primordial importance and can put blinkers on them (pp. 292, 294–95).

Cixous answers with a vague charge against the denial of poetry by advanced capitalism.

In the long run, the most useful thing that a training in French feminism can give us is politicized and critical examples of "Symptomatic reading" not always following the reversal-displacement technique of a deconstructive reading. The method that seemed recuperative when used to applaud the avant-garde is productively conflictual when used to expose the ruling discourse.

There are essays on Plato and Descartes in Irigaray's *Speculum de l'autre femme*, where the analysis brilliantly deploys the deconstructive *themes* of indeterminacy, critique of identity, and the absence of a totalizable analytic foothold, from a feminist point of view.[41] There are also the analyses of mainly eighteenth-century philosophical texts associated with work in progress at the feminist philosophy study group at the women's *École Normale* at Fontenay-aux-Roses. There is the long running commentary, especially on Greek mythemes—marked by an absence of questioning the history of the sign "myth," an absence, as I have argued in the case of *About Chinese Women*, which in its turn marks a historico-geographic boundary—to be found in *La jeune née*. The readings of Marx, generally incidental to other topics, suffer, as I have suggested above, from a lack of detailed awareness of the Marxian text. The best readings are of Freud. This is because Freud is at once the most powerful contemporary male philosopher of female sexuality, and the inaugurator, in *The Interpretation of Dreams*, of the technique of "symptomatic reading." Irigaray's "La Tache aveugle d'un vieux rêve de symétrie" (*Speculum*) has justifiably become a classic. More detailed, more scholarly, more sophisticated in its methodology, and perhaps more perceptive is Sarah Kofman's *L'énigme de la femme: la femme dans les textes de Freud*.[42]

This book exposes, even if it does not theorize upon, the possibility of being a deconstructor of the metaphysics of identity, and yet remaining caught within a masculist ideology; an awareness that I have found lacking in Kristeva and Cixous. Kofman comments on Freud's ideological betrayal of his own sympathy for women's mutism. She reveals the curious itinerary of Freud's progress towards his final thoughts upon female sexuality: three moments of the discovery of woman as the stronger sex—three subsequent long movements to sublate that strength into its unrecognizable contrary: the demonstration that woman is indeed the weaker sex. She deconstructs the "fact" of penis-envy through an analysis of the self-contradictory versions of the pre-oedipal stage. How is a sex possible that is despised by both sexes? This is the masculist enigma to which

Freud, like Oedipus, sought a solution. Like Oedipus's mask of blindness, biology, reduced to penis-envy, is Freud's screen-solution.

Using Freud's own method of oneirocritique to show its ideological limits, isolating seemingly marginal moments to demonstrate the ethico-political agenda in Freud's attempts at normalization, *L'énigme de la femme* is a fine example of French feminist critical practice of "symptomatic"—in this case deconstructive—reading. If we can move beyond the texts so far favored by the French feminists and relate the morphology of this critique with the "specificity" of other discourses that spell out and establish the power of the patriarchy, we will indeed have gained an excellent strategy for undermining the masculist vanguard.[43] This is no doubt a benefit for female academics, women who, by comparison with the world's women at large, are already infinitely privileged. And yet, since today the discourse of the world's privileged societies dictates the configuration of the rest, this is not an inconsiderable gift, even in a classroom.

As soon as one steps out of the classroom, if indeed a "teacher" ever fully can, the dangers rather than the benefits of academic feminism, French or otherwise, become more insistent. Institutional changes against sexism here or in France may mean nothing or, indirectly, further harm for women in the Third World.[44] This discontinuity ought to be recognized and worked at. Otherwise, the focus remains defined by the investigator as subject. To bring us back to my initial concerns, let me insist that here, the difference between "French" and "Anglo-American" feminism is superficial. However unfeasible and inefficient it may sound, I see no way to avoid insisting that there has to be a simultaneous other focus: not merely who am I? but who is the other woman? How am I naming her? How does she name me? Is this part of the problematic I discuss? Indeed, it is the absence of such unfeasible but crucial questions that makes the "colonized woman" as "subject" see the investigators as sweet and sympathetic creatures from another planet who are free to come and go; or, depending on her own socialization in the colonizing cultures, see "feminism" as having a vanguardist class fix, the liberties it fights for as luxuries, finally identifiable with "free sex" of one kind or another. Wrong, of course. My point has been that there is something equally wrong in our most sophisticated research, our most benevolent impulses.

"One of the areas of greatest verbal concentration among French feminists is the description of women's pleasure" (*New French Feminisms*, p. 37). Paradoxically enough, it is in this seemingly esoteric area of concern that I find a way of re-affirming the historically discontinuous yet common "object"-ification of the sexed subject as woman.

If it is indeed true that the best of French feminism encourages us to think of a double effort (*against* sexism and *for* feminism, with the lines forever shifting), that double vision is needed in the consideration of women's reproductive freedom as well. For to see women's liberation as identical with reproductive liberation is to make countersexism an end in itself, to see the establishment of women's subject-status as an unquestioned good and indeed not to heed the best lessons of French anti-humanism, which discloses the historical dangers of a subjectivist normativity; and it is also to legitimate the view of culture as general exchange of women, constitutive of kinship structures where women's object-status is clearly seen as identified with her reproductive function.[45]

The double vision that would affirm feminism as well as undo sexism suspects a pre-comprehended move *before* the reproductive coupling of man and woman, *before* the closing of the circle whose only productive excess is the child, and whose "outside" is the man's "active" life in society. It recognizes that "nature had programmed female sexual pleasure independently from the needs of production" (Evelyne Sullerot, p. 155).

Male and female sexuality are asymmetrical. Male orgasmic pleasure "normally" entails the male reproductive act—semination. Female orgasmic pleasure (it is not, of course, the "same" pleasure, only called by the same name) does not entail any one component of the heterogeneous female reproductive scenario: ovulation, fertilization, conception, gestation, birthing. The clitoris escapes reproductive framing. In legally defining woman as object of exchange, passage, or possession in terms of reproduction, it is not only the womb that is literally "appropriated"; it is the clitoris as the signifier of the sexed subject that is effaced. All historical and theoretical investigation into the definition of woman as legal *object*—in or out of marriage; or as politico-economic passageway for property and legitimacy would fall within the investigation of the varieties of the effacement of the clitoris.

Psychological investigation in this area cannot only confine itself to the effect of clitoridectomy on women. It would also ask why and show how, since an at least symbolic clitoridectomy has always been the "normal" accession to womanhood and the unacknowledged name of motherhood, it might be necessary to plot out the entire geography of female sexuality in terms of the imagined possibility of the dismemberment of the phallus. The arena of research here is not merely remote and primitive societies; the (sex) objectification of women by the elaborate attention to their skin and façade as represented by the immense complexity of the cosmetics, underwear, clothes, advertisement, women's magazine, and pornography networks, the double standard in the criteria of men's and women's aging; the public versus private dimensions of menopause as opposed to impotence, are all questions within this circuit. The pre-comprehended suppression or effacement of the clitoris relates to every move to define woman as sex object, or as means or agent of reproduction—with no recourse to a subject-function except in terms of those definitions or as "imitators" of men.

The woman's voice as Mother or Lover or Androgyne has sometimes been caught by great male writers. The theme of woman's *norm* as clitorally ex-centric from the reproductive orbit is being developed at present in our esoteric French group and in the literature of the gay movement. There is a certain melancholy exhilaration in working out the patriarchal intricacy of Tiresias's standing as a prophet—master of ceremonies at the Oedipal scene—in terms of the theme of the feminine norm as the suppression of the clitoris: "Being asked by Zeus and Hera to settle a dispute as to which sex had more pleasure of love, he decided for the female; Hera was angry and blinded him, but Zeus recompensed him by giving him long life and power of prophecy" (*Oxford Classical Dictionary*).[46]

Although French feminism has not elaborated these possibilities, there is some sense of them in women as unlike as Irigaray and the *Questions féministes* group. Irigaray: "In order for woman to arrive at the point where she can enjoy her pleasure as a woman, a long detour by the analysis of the various systems of oppression which affect her is certainly necessary. By claiming to resort to pleasure alone as the solution to her problem, she runs the risk of missing the reconsideration of a social practice upon which *her* pleasure depends" (p. 105). *Questions féministes*: "What we must answer is—not the false problem . . . which consists in measuring the 'role' of biological factors and the 'role' of social factors in the behavior of sexed individuals—but rather the following questions: (1) in what way is the biological political? In other words, what is the political function of the biological?" (p. 227).

If an analysis of the suppression of the clitoris in general as the suppression of woman-in-excess is lifted from the limitations of the "French" context and pursued in all its "historical," "political," and "social" dimensions, then *Questions féministes* would not need to make a binary opposition such as the following: "It is legitimate to expose the oppression, the mutilation, the 'functionalization' and the 'objectivation' of the female body, but it is also dangerous to put the female body at the center of a search for female identity" (p. 218). It would be possible to suggest that, the typology of the subtraction or excision of the clitoris in order to determine a biologico-political female identity is opposed, in discontinuous and indefinitely context-determined ways, by both the points of view above. It would also not be necessary, in order to share a detailed and ecstatic analysis of motherhood as "ultimate guarantee of sociality," to attack feminist collective commitments virulently: "A true feminine innovation . . . is not possible before maternity is clarified. . . . To bring that about, however, we must stop making feminism a new religion, an enterprise or a sect."[47]

The double vision is not merely to work against sexism and for feminism. It is also to recognize that, even as we reclaim the excess of the clitoris, we cannot fully escape the symmetry of the reproductive definition. One cannot write off what may be called a uterine social organization (the arrangement of the world in terms of the reproduction of future generations, where the uterus is the chief agent and means of production) *in favor of* a clitoral. The uterine social organization should, rather, be "situated" through the understanding that it has so far been established by excluding a clitoral social organization. (The restoration of a continuous bond between mother and daughter even *after* the "facts" of gestation, birthing, and suckling is, indeed, of great importance as a persistent effort against the sexism of millennia, an effort of repairing psychological damage through questioning norms that are supposedly self-evident and descriptive. Yet, for the sake of an affirmative feminism, this too should be "situated": to establish *historical* continuity by sublating a *natural* or *physiological* link as an end in itself is the idealistic subtext of the patriarchal project.) Investigation of the effacement of the clitoris—where clitoridectomy is a metonym for women's definition as "legal object as subject of reproduction"—would persistently seek to de-normalize uterine social organization. At the moment, the fact that the entire complex network of advanced capitalist economy hinges on home-buying, and that the philosophy of home-ownership is intimately linked to the sanctity of the nuclear family, shows how encompassingly the uterine norm of womanhood supports the phallic norm of capitalism. At the other end of the spectrum, it is this ideologico-material repression of the clitoris as the signifier of the sexed subject that operates the specific oppression of women, as the lowest level of the cheap labor that the multi-national corporations employ by remote control in the extraction of absolute surplus-value in the less developed countries. Whether the "social relations of patriarchy can be mapped into the social relations characteristic of a mode of production" or whether it is a "relatively autonomous structure written into family relations"; whether the family is a place of the production of socialization or the constitution of the subject of ideology; what such a heterogeneous sex-analysis would disclose is that the repression of the clitoris in the general or the narrow sense (the difference cannot be absolute) is presupposed by both patriarchy and family.[48]

I emphasize discontinuity, heterogeneity, and typology as I speak of such a sex-analysis, because this work cannot by itself obliterate the problems of race and class. It will not necessarily escape the inbuilt colonialism of First World feminism toward the Third. It might, one hopes, promote a sense of our common yet history-specific lot. It ties together the terrified child held down by her grandmother as the blood runs down her groin and the "liberated" heterosexual woman who, in spite of Mary Jane Sherfey and the famous page 53 of *Our Bodies, Ourselves*, in bed with a casual lover—engaged, in other words, in the "freest" of "free" activities—confronts, at worst, the "shame" of admitting to the "abnormality" of her orgasm: at best, the acceptance of such a "special" need; and the radical feminist who, setting herself apart from the circle of reproduction, systematically discloses the beauty of the lesbian body; the dowried bride—a body for burning—and the female wage-slave—a body for maximum exploitation.[49] There can be other lists; and each one will straddle and undo the ideological-material opposition. For me it is the best gift of French feminism, that it cannot itself fully acknowledge, and that we must work at; here is a theme that can liberate my colleague from Sudan, and a theme the old washerwomen by the river would understand.

For φst. thesis—▷

the relevance (&
theoretical potential)
of French feminism
(sp. Kristeva, Irigaray, &
Cixous) on Anglo-American
feminism(s).-

(sp. the body, desire,
"φs" writing)

10. Scattered Speculations on the Question of Value[1]

One of the determinations of the question of value is the predication of the subject. The modern "idealist" predication of the subject is consciousness. Labor-power is a "materialist" predication. Consciousness is not thought, but rather the subject's irreducible intendedness towards the object. Correspondingly, labor-power is not work (labor), but rather the irreducible possibility that the subject be more than adequate—super-adequate—to itself, labor-*power*: "it distinguishes itself [*unterscheidet sich*] from the ordinary crowd of commodities in that its use creates value, and a greater value than it costs itself" [Karl Marx, *Capital*, Vol. 1, 342; translation modified].

The "idealist" and the "materialist" are both exclusive predications. There have been attempts to question this exclusivist opposition, generally by way of a critique of the "idealist" predication of the subject: Nietzsche and Freud are the most spectacular European examples. Sometimes consciousness is *analogized* with labor-power as in the debates over intellectual and manual labor. Althusser's notion of "theoretical production" is the most controversial instance [*For Marx* 173–93]. The anti-Oedipal argument in France seems to assume a certain body without predication or without predication-function. (The celebrated "body without organs" is one product of this assumption—see Gilles Deleuze and Félix Guattari, *Anti-Oedipus: Capitalism and Schizophrenia*.) I have not yet been able to read this as anything but a last-ditch metaphysical longing. Since I remain bound by the conviction that subject-predication is methodologically necessary, I will not comment upon this anti-Oedipal gesture. The better part of my essay will concern itself with what the question of value becomes when determined by a "materialist" subject-predication such as Marx's.[2] This is a theoretical enterprise requiring a certain level of generality whose particular political implications I have tabulated in passing and in conclusion. Here it is in my interest to treat the theory-politics opposition as if intact.

Before I embark on the generalized project, I will set forth a practical deconstructivist-feminist-Marxist position on the question of value in a narrow disciplinary context. The issue of value surfaces in literary criticism with reference to canon-formation. From this narrowed perspective, the first move is a counter-question: *why* a canon? What is the ethico-political agenda that operates a canon? By way of a critique of phallogocentrism, the deconstructive impulse attempts to decenter the desire for the canon. Charting the agenda of phallocentrism involves the feminist, that of logocentrism the Marxist interested in patterns of *domination*. Yet for a deconstructive critic it is a truism that a full undoing of the canon-apocrypha opposition, like the undoing of any opposition, is impossible. ("The impossibility of a full undoing" is the curious definitive predication of deconstruction.) When we feminist Marxists are ourselves moved by a desire for alternative canon-formations, we work with varieties of and variations upon the old standards. Here the critic's obligation seems to be a scrupulous declaration of "interest."

We cannot avoid a kind of historico-political standard that the "disinterested" academy dismisses as "pathos." That standard emerges, mired in overdeterminations, in answer to the kinds of counter-questions of which the following is an example: What subject-effects were systematically effaced and trained to efface themselves so that a canonic norm might emerge? Since, considered from this perspective, literary canon-formation is seen to work within a much broader network of successful epistemic violence, questions of this kind are asked not only by feminist and Marxist critics, but also by anti-imperialist deconstructivists. Such counter-questions and declarations are often seen as constituting *the* new Marxist (feminist-deconstructivist) point of view on literary value. Since I share the point of view they subtend, I place them on the threshold of my essay as I move into my more generalized (more abstract?) concerns.

The first distinction to make, then, is that the point of view above focuses on *domination*. Concentrating on the desire for the canon, on the complicity with old standards, and on epistemic violence, the practical perspective of the discipline in the narrow sense need do no more than persistently clean up (or muddy) the "idealist" field as it nourishes the question of value. Any consideration of the question of value in its "materialist" predication must, however, examine Marx's investigation of *exploitation.*

On the level of intellectual-historical gossip, the story of Marx's investigation of exploitation is well-known. Around 1857, Marx set out to unpack the concept-phenomenon money in response to the analyses and crisis-managerial suggestions of Frédéric Bastiat and Henry Charles Carey, and to the utopian socialist projects endorsed by Proudhon. It is our task to suggest that, by lifting the lid of that seemingly unified concept-phenomenon, Marx uncovered the economic *text.* Sometimes it seems that cooking is a better figure than weaving when one speaks of the text, although the latter has etymological sanction. Lifting the lid, Marx discovers that the pot of the economic is forever on the boil. What cooks (in all senses of this enigmatic expression) is Value. It is our task also to suggest that, however avant-gardist it may sound, in this uncovering Value is seen to escape the onto-phenomenological question. It is also our task to emphasize that this is not merely asking ourselves to attend once again to the embarrassment of the final economic determinant but that, if the subject has a "materialist" predication, the question of value necessarily receives a textualized answer.[3]

Let us first deal with the continuist version of Marx's scheme of value.[4] Here is a crude summary: use-value is in play when a human being produces and uses up the product (or uses up the unproduced) immediately. Exchange-value emerges when one thing is substituted for another. Before the emergence of the money-form, exchange-value is ad hoc. Surplus-value is created when some value is produced for nothing. Yet even in this continuist version value seems to escape the onto-phenomenological question: what is it (*ti esti*). The usual answer—value is the representation of objectified labor—begs the question of use-value.

This continuist version is not absent in Marx, and certainly not absent in Engels. The intimations of discontinuity are most noticeably covered over in the move from the seven notebooks now collectively called the *Grundrisse* to the finished *Capital I*. It is a secondary revision of this version that yields the standard of measurement, indeed the calculus that emerges in the move from *Capital I* to *Capital III*. Vestiges of the "primary" continuist version linger in Derrida, whose version clearly animates Jean-Joseph Goux's *Numismatiques*, where most of the supporting evidence is taken from *Capital I*. Goux's reading, squaring the labor theory of value with the theories of ego-formation and signification in Freud and the early Lacan, is a rather special case of analogizing between consciousness and labor-power. Since my reading might seem superficially to resemble his, I will point at the unexamined presence of continuism in Goux in the next few paragraphs.

Goux's study seems ostensibly to issue from the French school of thought that respects discontinuities. Derrida gave *Numismatiques* his endorsement in "White Mythology," itself an important essay in the argument for discontinuity (see *Margins of Philosophy* 215 and passim). Goux takes the continuist version of the value-schema outlined above as given in Marx, though of course he elaborates upon it somewhat. Within that general continuist framework, then, Goux concentrates upon a unilinear version of the development of the money-form and draws an exact isomorphic analogy (he insists upon this) between it and the Freudian account of the emergence of genital sexuality. He concentrates next on Marx's perception that the commodity which becomes the universal equivalent must be excluded from the commodity function for that very reason. Here the analogy, again, resolutely isomorphic, is with Lacan's account of the emergence of the phallus as transcendental signifier. (For an early succinct account see Jacques Lacan, "The Signification of the Phallus.") Here is the claim: "It is the *same* genetic process, it is the *same* principle of discontinuous and progressive structuration which commands the accession to normative sovereignty of gold, the father and the phallus. The phallus is the universal equivalent of *subjects*; just as gold is the universal equivalent of *products*" [Goux 77; translation mine]. Goux's establishment of a relationship between Marx and Lacan in terms of gold and the phallus is based on his reading of exchange as mirroring and thus a reading of the origin of Value in the Lacanian "mirror-phase." Goux does notice that exchange value arises out of superfluity, but the question of use-value he leaves aside, perhaps even as an embarrassment.

Goux's argument is ingenious, but in the long run it seems to be an exercise in the domestication of Marx's analysis of Value. No doubt there are general morphological similarities between centralized sign-formations. But in order to see in those similarities the structural essence of the formations thus analogized, it is necessary to exclude the fields of force that make them heterogeneous, indeed discontinuous. It is to forget that Marx's critique of money is functionally different from Freud's attitude toward genitalism or Lacan's toward the phallus. It is to exclude those relationships between the ego/phallus and money that are attributive and supportive and not analogical. (Inheritance in the male line by way of patronymic legitimacy, indirectly sustaining the complex lines of class-formation, is, for example, an area where the case of the money-form, and that of the ego-form in the dialectic of the phallus, support each other and lend the subject the attributes of class- and gender-identity.) It is also to overlook the fact that Marx is a materialist dialectical thinker when he approaches the seemingly unified concept-phenomenon money. It is not the unilinear progressive account of the emergence of the money-form (Goux's model) that is Marx's main "discovery." It is in the full account of value-formation that the textuality of Marx's argument (rather than the recuperable continuist schema) and the place of use value is demonstrated, and the predication of the subject as labor-power (irreducible structural super-adequation—the subject defined by its capacity to produce more than itself) shows its importance.

(To draw an adequate analogy between the emergence of the money-form and the Oedipal scenario is also to conserve the European Marx. It is in my political interest to join forces with those Marxists who would rescue Marxism from its European provenance. It is not surprising that in a later book Goux argues for a kinship between Marx and Freud in terms of their Jewish heritage. This argument may well be cogent, but it should not be seen as clinching the question of the historical differential in the geopolitical situation of Marxism and psychoanalysis.)

In comparison to these problems, the problem of winning Marx over to structualist formalism would be a minor one, were it not that Anglo-U.S. continuist interests tend to lump together all attempts to read Marx in a structuralist way. The main enemy is here seen to be Althusser. Although I am critical of Althusser in many details of his argument, I would also pay tribute to a certain forgotten Althusser, precisely against the spirit of constructing phantom scapegoats, a personality-cultism in reverse.[5] Derrida innocently contributes to this by putting Althusser and Goux together in "White Mythology." If one looks up nothing but the references given by Derrida to certain passages in *Reading Capital*, one sees immediately that Althusser's attempt, for better or for worse, is to read Marx's text through the straining logic of the metaphors in the Marxian text. Goux's continuist reading proceeds by way of certain slippages. I will draw my discussion of Goux to a close by citing only one: It seems unwise to suggest, as Goux does, that because *exchange* springs up within what is superfluous to a person's use, the exclusion of the *universal symbol* of value (the money-material) from the commodity function is therefore due to being-in-excess. By the Marxian argument, all value is in excess of use-value. But Value is not therefore excluded. The universal symbol measures this excess (or "deficit," as Goux correctly notes) and is excluded from the commodity function so that it does not, inconveniently, operate on two registers at once, both measuring and carrying Value. (The only limited analogy here is that the *theory* of the phallus must exclude its penis-function.) This is to collapse value, exchange-value, surplus-value and money by way of an inflation of the concept of excess. In fact Goux, when he notices Marx's frequent metaphorizations of money as monarch, seems to elide the important differences between value-theory and theories of state formation.

In opening the lid of Money as a seemingly unitary phenomenon, Marx discovers a forever-seething chain in the pot: Value—Money—Capital. As in Hegel—of course Marx is not always a Hegelian but he seems to be here—those arrows are not irreversible. Logical schemes are not necessarily identical with chronological ones. But for purposes of philosophical cogitation and revolutionary agitation, the self-determination of the concept capital can be turned backward and forward every which way. (Perhaps it was the relative ease of the former and the insurmountable difficulties of the latter that led Marx to question philosophical justice itself.) Keeping this in mind, let us flesh the see-thing chain with names of relationships:

Value ^{representation} → Money ^{transformation} → Capital.

(My account here is a rough summary of "The Chapter on Money," and section 1 of "The Chapter on Capital" in the *Grundrisse*.) This chain is "textual" in the general sense on at least two counts.[6] The two ends are open, and the unified names of the relationships harbor discontinuities.

Exigencies of space will not permit elaboration of what is at any rate obvious—from the details of everyday life, through the practical mechanics of crisis-man-agement, to the tough reasonableness of a book like *Beyond the Waste Land* (eds. Samuel Bowles, et al.)—that the self-determination of capital as such is to date open-ended at the start. That moment is customarily sealed off in conventional Marxist political economic theory by extending the chain one step:

Labor ^{representation} → Value ^{representation} → Money ^{transformation} → Capital.

In fact, the basic premise of the recent critique of the labor theory of value is predicated on the assumption that, according to Marx, Value represents Labor.[7]

Yet the definition of Value in Marx establishes itself not only as a represen-tation but also a differential. What is represented or represents itself in the commodity-differential is Value: "In the exchange-relation of commodities their exchange-value appeared to us as totally independent of their use-value. But if we abstract their use-value from the product of labor, we obtain their value, as it has just been defined. The common element that represents itself (*sich darstellt*) in the exchange-relation of the exchange-value of the commodity, is thus value" [*Capital I* 128; translation modified]. Marx is writing, then, of a differential rep-resenting itself or being represented by an agency ("we") no more fixable than the empty and ad hoc place of the investigator or community of investigators (in the fields of economics, planning, business management). Only the contin-uist urge that I have already described can represent this differential as repre-senting labor, even if "labor" is taken only to imply "as objectified in the com-modity." It can be justly claimed that one passage in *Capital I* cannot be adduced to bear the burden of an entire argument. We must, however, remember that we are dealing here with *the* definitive passage on Value upon which Marx placed his imprimatur. For ease of argument and calculation, it is precisely the subtle open-endedness at the origin of the economic chain or text seen in this passage that Marx must himself sometimes jettison; or, for perspectivizing the argument, must "transform." (For a consideration of the "transformation" problem in this sense, see Richard D. Wolff, et al., "Marx's (Not Ricardo's) 'Transformation Problem': A Radical Conceptualization," *History of Political Economy* 14:4 [1982].)

I will presently go on to argue that the complexity of the notion of use-value also problematizes the origin of the chain of value. Let us now consider the discontinuities harbored by the unified terms that name the relationships between the individual semantemes on that chain. Such resident discontinuities also textualize the chain.

First, the relationship named "representation" between Value and Money. Critics like Goux or Marc Shell comment on the developmental narrative entailed by the emergence of the Money-form as the general representer of Value and establish an adequate analogy between this narrative on the one hand and narratives of psycho-sexuality or language-production on the other. (See Marc Shell, *Money, Language, and Thought: Literary and Philosophical Economies From the Medieval to the Modern Era.* It should be remarked that Shell's narrative account of the history of money is less subtle than Marx's analysis of it.) My focus is on Marx's effort to open up the seemingly unified phenomenon of Money through the radical methodology of the dialectic—opening up, in other words, the seemingly positive phenomenon of money through the work of the negative. At each moment of the three-part perspective, Marx seems to indicate the possibility of an indeterminacy rather than stop at a contradiction, which is the articulative driving force of the dialectical morphology. Here is the schema, distilled from the *Grundrisse*:

Position: The money commodity—the precious metal as medium of universal exchange—is posited through a process of separation from its own being as a commodity exchangeable for itself: "From the outset they represent superfluity, the form in which wealth originally appears [*ursprünglich erscheint*] [*Grundrisse* 166; translation modified]." As it facilitates commodity exchange "the simple fact that the commodity exists doubly, in one aspect as a specific product whose natural form of existence ideally contains (latently contains) its exchange value, and in the other aspect as manifest exchange value (money), in which all connection with the natural form of the product is stripped away again—this double, *differentiated* existence must develop into a *difference* [147]." When the traffic of exchange is in labor-power as a commodity, the model leads not only to difference but to indifference: "In the developed system of exchange . . . the ties of personal dependence, of distinctions, of education, etc. are in fact exploded, ripped up . . . ; and individuals *seem* independent (this is an independence which is at bottom merely an illusion, and it is more correctly called indifference [*Gleichgültgkeit—im Sinne der Indifferenz*—Marx emphasizes the philosophical quality of indifference]"[163].

Negation: Within circulation seen as a constantly repeated circle or totality, money is a vanishing moment facilitating the exchange of two commodities. Here its independent positing is seen as "a *negative* relation to circulation," for, "cut off from all relation to [circulation], it would not be money, but merely a simple natural object" [217]. In *this* moment of appearance its positive identity is negated in a more subtle way as well: "If a fake £ were to circulate in the place of a real one, it would render absolutely the same service in circulation as a whole as if it were genuine" [210]. In philosophical language: the self-adequation of the idea, itself contingent upon a negative relationship, here between the idea of money and circulation as totality, works in the service of a functional *in*-adequation (fake = real).

Negation of negation: Realization, where the actual quantity of money matters and capital accumulation starts. Yet here too the substantive specificity is contradicted (as it is not in unproductive hoarding). For, "to dissolve the things accumulated in individual gratification is to realize them" [234]. In other words, logical progression to accumulation can only be operated by its own rupture, releasing the commodity from the circuit of capital production into consumption in a simulacrum of use-value.

I am suggesting that Marx indicates the possibility of an indeterminacy rather than only a contradiction at each of these three moments constitutive of the chain

$$\text{Value} \xrightarrow{\textit{representation}} \text{Money} \xrightarrow{\textit{transformation}} \text{Capital}.$$

This textualization can be summarized as follows: the utopian socialists seemed to be working on the assumption that money is the root of all evil: a positive origin. Marx applies the dialectic to this root and breaks it up through the work of the negative. At each step of the dialectic something seems to lead off into the open-endedness of textuality: indifference, inadequation, rupture. (Here Derrida's implied critique of the dialectic as organized by the movement of semantemes and by the strategic exclusion of syncategoremes ["White Mythology" 270] would support the *conduct* of Marx's text.)

Let us move next to the relationship named "transformation between Money and Capital," a relationship already broached in the previous link. (This is not identical with the "transformation problem" in economics.) An important locus of discontinuity here is the so-called primitive or originary accumulation. Marx's own account emphasizes the discontinuity in comical terms, and then resolves it by invoking a process rather than an origin:

> We have seen how money is transformed into capital; how surplus-value is made through capital, and how more capital is made from surplus-value. But the accumulation of capital presupposes surplus-value; surplus-value presupposes capitalist production; capitalist production presupposes the availability of considerable masses of capital and labor-power in the hands of commodity producers. The whole movement, therefore, seems to turn around in a never-ending circle, which we can only get out of by assuming a "primitive" [ursprünglich: *originary*] accumulation . . . which precedes capitalist accumulation; an accumulation which is not the result of the capitalist mode of production but its point of departure. This primitive accumulation plays approximately the same role in political economy as original sin does in theology. Adam bit the apple, and thereupon sin fell on the human race. [Capital I 873]

Marx's resolution:

> The capital-relation presupposes a complete separation between the work-
> ers and the ownership of the conditions for the realization of their
> labor. . . . So-called primitive accumulation, therefore, is nothing else than
> the historical process of divorcing the producer from the means of pro-
> duction. Capital I 874–75]

This method of displacing questions of origin into questions of process is part
of Marx's general Hegelian heritage, as witness his early treatment, in the *Economic and Philosophical Manuscripts*, of the question: "Who begot the first man,
and nature in general?" [*Early Writings* 357].

When, however, capital is fully developed—the structural moment when the
process of extraction, appropriation, and realization of surplus-value begins to
operate with no extra-economic coercions—capital logic emerges to give birth
to capital as such. This moment does not arise either with the *coercive* extraction
of surplus-value in pre-capitalist modes of production, or with the accumulation
of interest capital or merchant's capital (accumulation out of buying cheap and
selling dear). The moment, as Marx emphasizes, entails the *historical* possibility
of the definitive predication of the subject as labor-power. Indeed, it is possible
to suggest that the "freeing" of labor-power may be a description of the social
possibility of this predication. Here the subject is predicated as structually super-
adequate to itself, definitively productive of surplus-labor over necessary labor.
And because it is this necessary possibility of the subject's definitive super-
adequation that is the origin of capital as such, Marx makes the extraordinary
suggestion that Capital consumes the *use*-value of labor-power. If the critique
of political economy were simply a question of restoring a society of use-value,
this would be an aporetic moment. "Scientific socialism" contrasts itself to a
"utopian socialism" committed to such a restoration by presupposing labor outside of capital logic or wage-labor. The radical heterogeneity entailed in that
presupposition was dealt with only very generally by Marx from the early *Economic and Philosophical Manuscripts* onwards. Indeed, it may perhaps be said that,
in revolutionary practice, the "interest" in social justice "unreasonably" introduces the force of illogic into the good use-value fit—*philosophical* justice—between Capital and Free Labor. If pursued to its logical consequence, revolutionary practice must be persistent because it can carry no theoretico-teleological
justification. It is perhaps not altogether fanciful to call this situation of open-
endedness an insertion into textuality. The more prudent notion of associated
labor in maximized social productivity working according to "those foundations
of the forms that are common to all social modes of production" is an alternative
that restricts the force of such an insertion [*Capital III* 1016].

In the continuist romantic anti-capitalist version, it is precisely the place of
use-value (and simple exchange or barter based on use-value) that seems to offer
the most secure anchor of social "value" in a vague way, even as academic
economics reduces use-value to mere physical co-efficients. This place can hap-

pily accommodate word-processors (of which more later) as well as independent commodity production (hand-sewn leather sandals), our students' complaint that they read literature for pleasure not interpretation, as well as most of our "creative" colleagues' amused contempt for criticism beyond the review, and mainstream critics' hostility to "theory." In my reading, on the other hand, it is use-value that puts the entire textual chain of Value into question and thus allows us a glimpse of the possibility that even textualization (which is already an advance upon the control implicit in linguistic or semiotic reductionism) may be no more than a way of holding randomness at bay.

For use-value, in the classic way of deconstructive levers, is both outside and inside the system of value-determinations (for a discussion of deconstructive "levers," see Derrida, *Positions* 71). It is outside because it cannot be measured by the labor theory of value—it is outside of the circuit of exchange: "A thing can be a use-value without being a value" [*Capital I* 131]. It is, however, not *altogether* outside the circuit of exchange. Exchange-value, which in some respects is the species-term of Value, is also a superfluity or a parasite of use-value: "This character (of exchange) does not yet dominate production as a whole, but concerns only its superfluity and is hence itself more or less *superfluous* . . . an accidental enlargement of the sphere of satisfactions, enjoyments. . . . It therefore takes place only at a few points (originally at the borders of the natural communities, in their contact with strangers)" [*Grundrisse* 204].

The part-whole relationship is here turned inside out. (Derrida calls this "invagination." See "The Law of Genre," *Glyph* 7 [1980]. My discussion of "invagination" is to be found in *Displacement: Derrida and After,* ed. Mark Krupnick 186–89). The parasitic part (exchange-value) is also the species term of the whole, thus allowing use-value the normative inside place of the host as well as banishing it as that which must be subtracted so that Value can be defined. Further, since one case of use-value can be that of the worker wishing to consume the (affect of the) work itself, that necessary possibility renders indeterminate the "materialist" predication of the subject as labor-power or super-adequation as calibrated and organized by the logic of capital. In terms of that necessarily possible "special case," this predication can no longer be seen as the excess of surplus labor over *socially* necessary labor. The question of *affectively* necessary labor brings in the attendant question of desire and thus questions in yet another way the mere philosophical justice of capital logic without necessarily shifting into utopian idealism.

If a view of *affectively* necessary labor (as possible within the present state of socialized consumer capitalism) as *labor* as such is proposed without careful attention to the international division of labor, its fate may be a mere political avant-gardism. This, in spite of its sincere evocations of the world economic system, is, I believe, a possible problem with Antonio Negri's theory of zero-work.[8] The resistance of the syncategoremes strategically excluded from the system so that the great semantemes can control its morphology (Derrida) can perhaps be related to the *heterogeneity* of use-value as a private grammar. For Derrida, however, capital is generally interest-bearing commercial capital. Hence surplus-value for him is the super-adequation of *capital* rather than a "materialist" predication of the *subject* as super-adequate to itself. This restricted notion can only lead to "idealist" analogies between capital and subject, or commodity and subject.

The concept of socially necessary labor is based on an identification of subsistence and reproduction. Necessary labor is the amount of labor required by the worker to "reproduce" himself in order to remain optimally useful for capital in terms of the current price-structure. Now if the dynamics of birth-growth-family-life reproduction is given as much attention as, let us say, the relationship between fixed and variable capitals in their several moments, the "materialist" predication of the subject as labor-power is rendered indeterminate in another way, without therefore being "refuted" by varieties of utopianism and "idealism." This expansion of the textuality of value has often gone unrecognized by feminists as well as mainstream Marxists, when they are caught within hegemonic positivism or orthodox dialectics.[9] They have sometimes tried to close off the expansion, by considering it as an opposition (between Marxism and feminism), or by way of inscribing, in a continuist spirit, the socializing or ideology-forming functions of the family as direct means of producing the worker and thus involved in the circuit of the production of surplus-value for the capitalist. They have also attempted to legitimize domestic labor within capital logic. Most of these positions arise from situational exigencies. My own involvement with them does not permit critical distance, as witness in the last page of this essay. That these closing off gestures are situationally admirable is evident from the practical difficulty of offering alternatives to them.

Let us consider the final item in the demonstration of the "textuality" of the chain of value. We have remarked that in circulation as totality, or the moment of negation in Marx's reading of money, money is seen as in a negative relation to circulation because, "cut off from all relation to (circulation) it would not be money, but merely a simple natural object." Circulation as such has the morphological (if not the "actual") power to insert Money back into *Nature*, and to *banish* it from the textuality of Value. Yet it is also circulation that *bestows* textuality upon the Money-form. Textuality as a structural description indicates the work of differentiation (both plus and minus) that opens up identity-as-adequation. Circulation in the following passage does precisely that with the restricted circuit of adequation within the money-form itself: "You may turn and toss an ounce of gold in any way you like, and it will never weigh ten ounces. But here in the process of circulation one ounce practically does weigh ten ounces." Marx describes this phenomenon as the "Dasein" of the coin as "value sign" [*Wertzeichen*]. "The circulation of money is an outer movement [*außere Bewegung*]. . . . In the friction with all kinds of hands, pouches, pockets, purses . . . the coin rubs off. . . . By being used it gets used up" [*A Contribution to the Critique of Political Economy* 108; the translation of "*Dasein*" as "the work it performs" seems puzzling].

If in its first dialectical "moment," circulation has the morphological potential of cancelling Money back into Nature, in its third "moment" it is shown to run the risk of being itself sublated into *Mind*: "The continuity of production presupposes that circulation time has been sublated [*aufgehoben*]. The nature of capital presupposes that it travels through the different phases of circulation not as it does in the idea-representation [*Vorstellung*] where one concept turns into the other at the speed of thought [*mit Gedankenschnelle*], in no time, but rather as situations which are separated in terms of time" [*Grundrisse* 548; translation modified]. By thus sublating circulation into Mind, production (of Value) as *continuous* totality would annul Value itself. For Value would not be value if it were not realized in consumption, strictly speaking, outside of the circuit of production. Thus capital, as the most advanced articulation of value "presupposes that it travels through different phases." The scheme is made problematic by the invagination of use-value, as discussed earlier in this essay.

Has circulation time of capital been sublated into the speed of Mind (and more) within telecommunication? Has (the labor theory of) Value become obsolete in micro-electronic capitalism? Let us mark these tantalizing questions here. I shall consider them at greater length below.

The consideration of the textuality of Value in Marx, predicated upon the subject as labor-power, does not answer the onto-phenomenological question "What is Value?," although it gives us a sense of the complexity of the mechanics of evaluation and value-formation. It shows us that the Value-form in the general sense and in the narrow—the economic sphere as commonly understood being the latter—are irreducibly complicitous. It implies the vanity of dismissing considerations of the economic as "reductionism." I have already indicated various proposed formulations that have the effect of neutralizing these suggestions: to find in the development of the money-form an adequate analogy to the psychoanalytic narrative; to see in it an analogy to metaphor or language; to subsume domestic or intellectual labor into a notion of the production of value expanded within capital logic. What narratives of value-formation emerge when consciousness itself is subsumed under the "materialist" predication of the subject?

If consciousness within the "idealist" analogy is seen as necessarily super-adequate to itself by way of intentionality, we can chart the emergence of ad hoc universal equivalents that measure the production of value in what we may loosely call "thought." Like the banishment of the money-commodity from the commodity-function, these equivalents can no longer themselves be treated as "natural examples." (Because these analogies are necessarily loose, one cannot be more specific in that last phrase.) One case of such a universal equivalent is "universal humanity"—both psychological and social—as the touchstone of value in literature and society. It is only half in jest that one would propose that the "credit" of certain "major" literatures is represented by capital-accumulation in terms of the various transformations of this universal equivalent. "Pure theory," within the Althusserian model of "theoretical production," may be seen as another case of a universal equivalent. The relativization of Value as a regression into the narrative stage where *any* commodity could be "cathected" as the value-form is, to follow Goux's analogy, the Freudian stage of polymorphous perversion, and can be channeled into aesthetics as varied as those of symbolism and post-modernism.

I have already commented on Goux's gloss on the Freudo-Lacanian narrative of the emergence of the phallus-in-the-genital-stage as the universal equivalent of value. Nietzsche in *The Genealogy of Morals* gives us two moments of the separation and transformation of an item from within the common circuit of exchange. They are worth mentioning because *The Genealogy of Morals* is Nietzsche's systematic attempt at a "critique of moral values," a "put[ting] in question [*in Frage stellen*]" of "the value of these values" [*Grundrisse* 348; translation modified]. The Nietzschean enterprise is not worked out on what I call a "materialist" subject-predication as labor-power, but rather by way of a critique of the "idealist" subject-predication as consciousness, through the double determinants of "philology" and "physiology" [Nietzsche, *On the Genealogy of Morals and Ecce Homo* 20]. Because it is a reinscription of the history of value as obliterated and discontinuous semiotic chains—ongoing sign-chains—disconnected references to money (guilt and punishment as systems of exchange), and to the inscription of coins, abound. The more crucial moment, the *separation* of the money-commodity, is touched upon once at the "beginning" and once at the inauguration of the "present," as the separation of the scapegoat and the sublation of that gesture into mercy respectively. That sublation is notoriously the moment of the creditor sacrificing himself for the debtor in the role of God's son in the Christ Story [*On the Genealogy of Morals and Ecce Homo* 77, 72]. (Any notions of "beginning" and "present" in Nietzsche are made problematic by the great warning against a successful genealogical method: "All concepts in which an entire process is semiotically concentrated elude definition; only that which has no history is definable" [ibid. 80].)

I think there can be no doubt that it is this separation rather than inscription or coining that is for Marx the philosophically determining moment in the discourse of value. Attention to Marx's concept-metaphor of the foreign language is interesting here. Often in our discussion of language the word seems to retain a capital "L" even when it is spelled in the lower case or re-written as *parole*. Using a necessarily pre-critical notion of language, which suggests that in the mother tongue "word" is inseparable from "reality," Marx makes the highly sophisticated suggestion that the development of the value-form separates "word" and "reality" (signifier and signified), a phenomenon that may be appreciated only in the learning of a foreign language: "To compare money with language is . . . erroneous. . . . Ideas which have first to be translated out of their mother tongue into a foreign language in order to circulate, in order to become exchangeable, offer a *somewhat better* analogy; but the analogy then lies not in language, but in the foreignness of language" [*Grundrisse* 163. If this were a technical discussion where it was necessary to respect the specificity of the vocabulary of linguistics, I would not of course, equate word/reality and signifier/signified.] It is certainly of interest that, using a necessarily post-monetary notion of Value-in-exchange, which must suggest that "political economy [is] . . . concerned with a system of equivalence [*système d'équivalence*] . . . [between a specific] labor and [a specific] wage [*un travail et un salaire*]," Saussure shows us that, even in the mother tongue, it is the work of difference that remains originary, that even as it is most "native," language is always already "foreign," that even in its "incorporeal essence," "the linguistic signifier . . . [is] constituted not by its material substance but only [*uniquement*] by the differences that separate its acoustic image from all others" [*Course in General Linguistics* 79, 118–19].

The binary opposition between the economic and the cultural is so deeply entrenched that the full implications of the question of Value posed in terms of the "materialist" predication of the subject are difficult to conceptualize. One cannot foresee a teleological moment when these implications are catastrophically productive of a new evaluation. The best one can envisage is the persistent undoing of the opposition, taking into account the fact that, first, the complicity between cultural and economic value-systems is acted out in almost every decision we make; and, secondly, that economic reductionism is, indeed, a very real danger. It is a paradox that capitalist humanism does indeed tacitly make its plans by the "materialist" predication of Value, even as its official ideology offers the discourse of humanism as such; while Marxist cultural studies in the First World cannot ask the question of Value within the "materialist" predication of the subject, since the question would compel one to acknowledge that the text of exploitation might implicate Western cultural studies in the international division of labor.[10] Let us, if somewhat fancifully, invoke the word-processor again. It is an extremely convenient and efficient tool for the production of writing. It certainly allows us to produce a much larger quantity of writing in a much shorter time and makes fiddling with it much easier. The "quality" of writing—the "idealist" question of value—as well as the use-value of manual composition—affectively necessary labor—are rendered irrelevant here. (It is of course not to be denied that the word-processor might itself generate affective use-value.) From within the "idealist" camp, one can even say, in the wake of a trend that runs from Professor A. B. Lord to Father Walter J. Ong, the following: we were not in on the "inception" of writing, and can copiously deplore the harm it did to the orality of the verbal world; we are, however, present at the inception of telecommunication, and, being completely encompassed by the historical ideology of efficiency, we are unable to reckon with the transformations wrought by the strategic exclusions of the randomness of *bricolage* operated by programming (see A. B. Lord, *The Singer of Tales*; Walter J. Ong, *Orality and Literacy*).

These are not the objections that I emphasize. I draw attention, rather, to the fact that, even as circulation time attains the apparent instantaneity of thought (and more), the continuity of production ensured by that attainment of apparent coincidence must be broken up by capital: its means of doing so is to keep the labor reserves in the comprador countries outside of this instantaneity, thus to make sure that multinational investment does not realize itself fully there through assimilation of the working class into consumerist-humanism.[11] It is one of the truisms of *Capital I* that technological inventions open the door to the production of relative rather than absolute surplus-value [*Capital I* 643–54. "Absolute surplus-value" is a methodologically irreducible theoretical fiction.] Since the production and *realization* of relative surplus-value, usually attendant upon technological progress *and* the socialized growth of consumerism, increase capital expenditure in an indefinite spiral, there is the contradictory drive within capitalism to produce more absolute and less relative surplus-value as part of its crisis management. In terms of this drive, it is in the "interest" of capital to preserve the comprador theater in a state of relatively primitive labor legislation and environmental regulation. Further, since the optimal relationship between fixed and variable capital has been disrupted by the accelerated rate of obsolescence of the former under the rapid progress within telecommunications research and the attendant competition, the comprador theater is also often obliged to accept scrapped and out-of-date machinery from the post-industrialist economies. To state the problem in the philosophical idiom of this essay: as the subject as super-adequation in labor-power seems to negate itself within telecommunication, a negation of the negation is continually produced by the shifting lines of the international division of labor. This is why any critique of the labor theory of value, pointing at the unfeasibility of the theory under post-industrialism, or as a calculus of economic indicators, ignores the dark presence of the Third World.[12]

It is a well-known fact that the worst victims of the recent exacerbation of the international division of labor are women. They are the true surplus army of labor in the current conjuncture. In their case, patriarchal social relations contribute to their production as the new focus of super-exploitation (see June Nash and María Patricia Fernández-Kelly, eds., *Women, Men, and the International Division of Labor*). As I have suggested above, to consider the place of sexual reproduction and the family within those social relations should show the pure (or free) "materialist" predication of the subject to be gender-exclusive.

The literary academy emphasizes when necessary that the American tradition at its best is one of individual Adamism and the loosening of frontiers.[13] In terms of political activism within the academy, this free spirit exercises itself at its best by analyzing and calculating predictable strategic effects of specific measures of resistance: boycotting consumer items, demonstrating against investments in countries with racist domestic politics, uniting against genocidal foreign policy. Considering the role of telecommunication in entrenching the international division of labor *and* the oppression of women, this free spirit should subject its unbridled passion for subsidizing computerized information retrieval and theoretical production to the same conscientious scrutiny. The "freeing" of the subject as super-adequation in labor-power entails an absence of extra-economic coercion. Because a positivist vision can only recognize the latter, that is to say, *domination*, within post-industrial cultures like the U.S., telecommunication seems to bring nothing but the promise of infinite liberty for the subject. Economic coercion as *exploitation* is hidden from sight in "the rest of the world."

These sentiments expressed at a public forum drew from a prominent U.S. leftist the derisive remark: "She will deny the workers their capuccino!" I am not in fact suggesting that literary critics should be denied word-processors. My point is that the question of Value in its "materialist" articulation must be asked as the capuccino-drinking worker and the word-processing critic actively forget the actual price-in-exploitation of the machine producing coffee and words. This is certainly not required of every literary critic. But if the literary critic in the U.S. today decides to ask the question of Value only within the frame allowed by an unacknowledged "nationalist" view of "productivity," she cannot be expected to be taken seriously everywhere. (The real problem is, of course, that she *will* be taken seriously, and the work of multinational ideology-reproduction will go on.) If my position here is mistaken for an embarrassing economic determinism, the following specification may be made: "There is a short-of and a beyond of [economic determinism]. To see to it that the beyond does not become the within is to recognize . . . the need of a communicating pathway (*parcours*). That pathway has to leave a wake (*sillage*) in the text. Without that wake or track, abandoned to the simple content of its conclusions, the ultra-transcendental text"—the discourse of textuality in the economic that I have been at pains to explicate and disclose—"will so closely resemble the pre-critical text"—economic determinism—"as to be indistinguishable from it. We must now meditate on upon the law of this resemblance" [Derrida, *Of Grammatology* 61]. I have done no more in this essay than to encourage such a meditation, to suggest that, following Marx, it is possible to put the economic text "under erasure," to see, that is, the unavoidable and pervasive *importance* of its operation and yet to question it as a concept of the *last resort*. (Incidentally, this also emphasizes that putting "under erasure" is as much an affirmative as a negative gesture.) In 1985, Walter Benjamin's famous saying, "there has never been a document of *culture* which was not at one and the same time a document of barbarism" [*Illuminations* 256] should be a starting rather than a stopping-point for Marxist axiological investigations. A "culturalism" that disavows the economic in its global operations cannot get a grip on the concomitant production of barbarism.

If, on the other hand, the suggestion is made that in the long run, through the multinationals, *everyone* will have word-processors *and* capuccino (not to mention guns and butter), the *evaluating* critic must be prepared to enter the debate between Samir Amin and the late Bill Warren, some of the broad strokes of which I have outlined above [see Warren, *Imperialism: Pioneer of Capitalism*; Amin, "Expansion or Crisis of Capitalism?"]. She must be prepared to admit that the unification churches being projected by the mechanisms of Euro-currency and "the globalization of markets" (we read it as "global crisis") do not lend much credibility to this uninstructed hope.

Perhaps a word on "The Globalization of Markets," an article by Theodore Levitt, Edward W. Carter Professor of Business Administration and head of the marketing area at the Harvard Business School, is in order here. The piece is exemplary of many of the attitudes I have tried to define. Since Professor Levitt writes from the point of view of big business ("people and nations" in the passage cited below) he is not concerned with the active divisiveness of the international division of labor. Here is his theory of the relationship between money and the division of labor, and his theory of money as a unified concept, reached in turn by way of "experience" as a fetishized concept: "Nobody takes scarcity lying down; everyone wants more. This in part explains division of labor and specialization of production. They enable people and nations to optimize their conditions [a deliberately vague word] through trade. The median [sic] is usually money. Experience teaches that money has three special qualities: scarcity, difficulty of acquisition, and transience. People understandably treat it with respect."[14] What I have been arguing is that this primitive notion of money must work complicitously with the contemporary sublation of money where it seems to question the "materialistic" predication of the subject; that the post-modern, in spite of all the cant of modernization, reproduces the "pre-modern" on another scene. In Professor Levitt's article the two views remain in an unresolved and distanced structural parataxis. To quote: "Today money is simply electronic impulses. With the speed of light [so much for Marx's impossible limit for circulation: speed of thought] it moves effortlessly between distant centers (and even lesser places). A change of ten basic points in the price of a bond causes an instant and massive shift of money from London to Tokyo. The system has profound impact on the way companies operate throughout the world" [Levitt 101].

The perspective here is unifocal and generally uncritically read (if read at all) by literary academics. I have been trying to explicate not only the parataxis above, but also the exploitation condensed and monumentalized in a seemingly scientific phrase such as "scale-efficient conditions" below (incidentally, "value" as used here is the unified continuist version that would be consonant with the Marxian definition of value relieved of its historical, ethical, or philosophical charge): "The most endangered companies in the rapidly-evolving world tend to be those that dominate rather small domestic markets with high value-added products for which there are smaller markets elsewhere. With transportation costs"—the only costs specified—"proportionately low, distant competitors will now enter the now-sheltered markets of those companies with goods produced more cheaply under scale-efficient conditions" [Levitt 94]. These "globalizers" also have their human universals: "an ancient motivation—to make one's money go as far as possible. This is universal—not simply a motivation but actually a need" [Levitt 96]. Yet, in an insane parody of the basic paradox of humanistic education, Levitt describes the epistemic violence of the universalizing global market: "The purpose of business is to get and keep a customer. Or, to use Peter Drucker's more refined construction, to create and keep a customer."[15]

This is how economic reductionism operates. The disavowal of the economic is its tacit and legitimizing collaborator. In its verdict on "the multinational mind" as opposed to the globalizing mind is to be heard the managerial version of shock at denying the workers of the First World their capuccino: "the multinational mind, warped into circumspection and timidity by years of stumbles and transnational troubles, now rarely challenges existing overseas practices. More often it considers any departure from inherited domestic routines as mindless, disrespectful, or impossible. *It is the mind of a bygone day*" [Levitt 101; italics mine].

I should like to construct a narrative here using "The Wiring of Wall Street," an article in the *New York Times* Sunday magazine for October 23, 1983. (I choose the *New York Times* because the broad spectrum that contains the Sunday supplements of newspapers, *Scientific American*, *Psychology Today*, as well as the *National Enquirer*, constitutes part of an ideological apparatus, through which the consumer becomes knowledgeable, the subject of "cultural" explanation. Could one suggest that organs such as the *Harvard Business Review* are also part of the apparatus, in that through them the investor-manager receives his "ideology"? As I suggest in note 15, feminist individualist consumerism is being appropriated within the same apparatus.)

After telecommunication, Wall Street seems to have been saved by reconcil-iation (rather than deconstruction) of the binary opposition between the im-mediate self-proximity of voice-consciousness and the visible efficiency of writ-ing. As Georg Simmel already observes of the stock exchange at the end of the last century, it is the place where the circulation of money can be most speeded up: the "twofold condensation of values into the money form and of monetary transactions into the form of the stock exchange makes it possible for values to be rushed through the greatest number of hands in the shortest possible time" [Simmel 506]. "The start of a solution of the market's major dilemma, *the man-agement of time*, appeared in 1972 when the New York Stock Exchange, the Amer-ican Stock Exchange, and their member firms organized the Securities Industries Automation Corporation. . . . Not long ago, the executives kept up with their investments on a monthly or weekly schedule; today, the reporting can be *in-stantaneous* because of the computer" ["The Wiring of Wall Street" 47]. It is worth remarking that, even as time is thus being *managed* on the post-industrial cap-italist front, high Marxist theory contests the labor theory of value by bracketing time as a vehicle of change: "No changes in output and . . . no changes in the proportions in which different means of production are used by an industry are considered, so that no question arises as to the variation or constancy of returns" [Sraffa, *Production of Commodities* v]. If money then circulates at the speed of *consciousness* by way of the computer, it *at the same time* accedes to the visible efficiency of writing. "'We had this amorphous, unorganized, mostly invisible market prior to 1971' says Gordon S. Macklin, president of the [National] As-sociation [of Securities Dealers]" ["Wiring" 73].

This reconciliation of the opposition between consciousness and writing ob-viously does not "refute" Freud's late proto-deconstructive model of the psyche as the *Wunderblok* or the mystic writing pad (see Derrida, "Freud and the Scene of Writing," *Writing and Difference*). If anything, the silicon chip appears to give "a plastic idea" to that pure virtuality, that difference as such which Derrida calls "the work of dead time" [the warning against the formation of a plastic idea is to be found in Freud, *The Standard Edition*, vol. 4, 281: the Derrida passage is in *Of Grammatology* 68].

But this is not the objection I emphasize here. I point out, rather, that the computer, even as it pushes the frontiers of rationalization, proves unable to achieve *bricolage*, to produce a program that will use an item for a purpose for which it was not designed. (This is the celebrated problem of programming a computer to build nests with random materials, as a bird does, that exercises Douglas Hofstadter and others.) And it is well-known that radical proto-decon-structive *cultural* practice instructs us precisely to work through *bricolage*, to "re-constellate" cultural items by wrenching them out of their assigned function. When Walter Benjamin writes: "What we require of the photographer is the ability to give his picture the caption that wrenches it from modish commerce and gives it a revolutionary use-value [*Gebrauschswert*]," he is implicitly "*bri-coling*" or tinkering with a continuist notion of use-value (I need not repeat my earlier argument) even as he recommends *bricolage* as cultural practice. This rec-ommendation can be traced from his earliest theory of allegory as the cathexis (or occupation) of ruins and fragments by the irreducible alterity of time [Benjamin, "The Author as Producer," *Reflections: Essays, Aphorisms, Autobiographical Writings* 230]. This is to be found in Deleuze and Guattari's bold notion of originarily unworkable machines. It can be said for Derrida that, by positioning citationality as originary, he has radicalized *bricolage* as the questioning of all ideologies of adequation and legitimacy.[16] These positions are now trickling down into a reckoning with the emergent ideological possibilities of the post-modern cultural phenomenon within a post-modern political economy.[17]

It is not even this possibility of a cultural theoretical practice, which sabotages the radically reconciling text of the post-modern stock exchange, that I emphasize within this narrative. My critique can find an allegorical summary in a passage about the old ticker-tape machine. "A holdover from the storied past is the old stock ticker. Fifteen minutes after trading has commenced, the ticker—a bit of technology that dates back to 1867—has already fallen behind the hectic trading by six minutes. Speed it up to match today's trading volume, and it would be a blur" ["Wiring" 47].

We cannot forget that *Capital I* is "a bit of technology that dates back to 1867," its date of publication. I have attempted to show that the Marxist historical narrative—"the storied past"—is far from a holdover. When it is expanded to accommodate the epistemic violence of imperialism as crisis-management, including its current displacements, it can allow us to read the text of political economy at large. When "speeded up" in this way it does not allow the irreducible rift of the International division of labor to blur. "The Wiring of Wall Street" speaks first of "time management" and next quotes Peter Solomon of Lehman Brothers "offer[ing] an explanation: 'Computers have shown us how to manage *risk*'" ["Wiring" 47]. The inconvenient and outdated ticker of Marxist theory discloses the excluded word between "time" and "risk" in the management game: crisis.

Let us retrieve the concept-metaphor of the text that we left behind a few pages back. Within this narrative replay of my argument in the previous pages it may be pointed out that, whereas Lehman Brothers, thanks to computers, "earned about $2 million for . . . 15 minutes of work," the entire economic text would not be what it is if it could not write itself as a palimpsest upon another text where a woman in Sri Lanka has to work 2,287 minutes to buy a t-shirt. The "post-modern" and "pre-modern" are inscribed together. It should also be remarked that Simmel argued nearly a hundred years ago that a developed money-form naturally promotes "the individual": "if freedom means only obeying one's own laws, then the distance between property and its owner that is made possible by the money form of returns provides a hitherto unheard-of freedom" [Simmel 334]. The best beneficiary of this "post-modernization" of Wall Street is, predictably, the individual small investor in the United States. And the apparently history-transcendent "individual subject" who will "have to hold to the truth of postmodernism . . . and have as its vocation the invention and projection of a global cognitive mapping" [Jameson, "Postmodernism, or the Cultural Logic of Late Capitalism" 92] will be, *as long as no attempt is made to specify the post-modern space-specific subject-production*, no other than a version of this unpromising individual.

It is within this framework of crisis-management and regulation, then, that I would propose to pursue the evaluation of the pervasive and tacit gesture that accepts the history of style-formations in Western European canonical literature as the evaluation of style as such. I am not recommending varieties of reactive nostalgia such as an unexamined adulation of working class culture, an ostentatious rejection of elitist standards, a devotion to all non-Judaeo-Christian mythologies, or the timid evocation of "poetry being written in Nicaragua." In fact, the version of historical narrative I am sketching here can be expanded to show that, in such nostalgic evaluative norms as the list above, the history of the epistemic violence of imperialism as crisis-management can still operate. Regular periodization should rather be seen in its role within the historical normalization required by the world-system of political economy, engaged in the production and realization of Value, the "post-modern" its latest symptom. Such evaluations would accommodate the "materialist" articulation of Value within what I described earlier as the practical position of Value in our discipline in the narrow sense, underlining the role of exploitation in understanding domination.[18]

In "Marx's (not Ricardo's) 'Transformation Problem,'" Richard A. Wolff, Bruce Brothers, and Antonino Collari suggest that when "Marx . . . considers a social object in which the processes of circulation constitute effective preconditions for the process of production, . . . the relevant magnitude must be the *price of production* of the consumed means of production and *not* the abstract labor time physically embodied in them" [Wolff et al., "Marx's 'Transformation Problem,'" 574]. I have so far been arguing, among other things, that to set the labor theory of value aside is to forget the textual and axiological implications of a materialist predication of the subject. The passage I quote, however, seems to be an appropriate description of the perspectival move which provisionally must set that theory aside. As a result of this move, "the equivalence of exchange *must be constructed* out of the processes specific to competitive capitalism which tend to establish a proportional distribution of unpaid labor time in the form of an average rate of profit on total capital, *no longer assumed* as in volume 1" ["Marx's 'Transformation Problem'" 572; italics mine, and I have conflated three sentences]. Thus the authors situate the specific arena of the labor theory of value but go on to suggest that, since "Marx's focus [was] on class relations as his object of discourse . . . simultaneously, however, the concept of value remains crucial to the quantification of prices of production. Price on production, as an absolute magnitude of labor time, *can be conceived only as a specific deviation from value*" ["Marx's 'Transformation Problem'" 575; italics mine].

I have not touched the topic of the value-price relationship in these pages. Further, I have questioned the mechanics of limiting the definition of value to the physical embodiment of abstract labor time. I would in fact argue that the premises of *Capital I* are themselves dependent upon a gesture of reduction that may be called a construction [*Capital I* 135]. Generalizing from Wolff's and his co-authors' position, I would find that Marx's focus on class (mode of production) must be made to accommodate his reach of crisis (world system). Yet Wolff and his co-authors' perspectival situation of the labor theory of value and concurrent definition of price of production as deviation or differential seem to us admirably just. Within the discipline of economics, which must keep any textualized notion of use-value out, it seems crucial to suggest that "Marx . . . affirms the interdependence of value and value form ([understood as] price of production), an interdependence which cannot be expressed by treating the relation between the two concepts as merely a functional relation between dependent and independent variables."[19] As I move more conclusively into the enclosure of my own disciplinary discourse, perhaps it might not be inappropriate to suggest that this essay does no more than point at the confused ideological space of some varieties of such an interdependence.

I will now appropriate yet another item on the threshold of this essay: the Derridean concept of "interest" as in "scrupulous declaration of interest." Derrida's own understanding of surplus-value as capital-appreciation or interest is, as I have suggested above, restricted. I simply wrest it back from that "false" metaphor and "literalize" it.[20] If and when we ask and answer the question of value, there seems to be no alternative to declaring one's "interest" in the text of the production of Value.

I offer this formula because the problem of "how to relate a critique of 'foundationalism,' which like its object is interminable and may always go astray, to a critique of ideology that allows for at least provisional endings and ends in research and 'political' practice" remains with us [Dominick LaCapra, Lecture given at Wesleyan University, 1984]. The early Derrida assured us that "deconstruction falls a prey to its own critique" and went largely unheeded [*Of Grammatology* 24]. The later Derrida, miming this precaution interminably, has been written off as, at best, a formal experimentalist or, at worst, uninteresting and repetitive. It should be clear from the last few pages that I can endorse Jean-François Lyotard's benevolent "paganism" as an axiological model as little as I can Jürgen Habermas's Europocentric rationalism. [Jean-François Lyotard, *Instructions païennes; Rudiments païens* with Jean-Loup Thébaud, *Au juste.* Jürgen Habermas, *Communication and the Evolution of Society.*] One of the more interesting solutions offered is Dominick LaCapra's "historiography as transference." Yet there, too, there are certain desires to appropriate the workings of the unconscious of which we should beware. For "repetition-displacement of the past into the present" (LaCapra's version of transferential historiography) may be too continuist and harmless a version of the transactions in transference. And it might not be enough simply to say that "it is a useful critical fiction to believe that the texts or phenomena to be interpreted may answer back and even be convincing enough to lead one to change one's mind" [LaCapra, *History and Criticism* 73]. Given Lacan's elaborate unfolding of the relationship between transference and the ethical moment, I can do no better here than to reiterate an earlier doubt, expressed not in terms of historiography but rather of literary criticism:

> Nor will the difference between text and person be conveniently effaced by refusing to talk about the psyche, by talking about the text as part of a self-propagating mechanism. The disjunctive, discontinuous metaphor of the subject, carrying and being carried by its burden of desire, does

systematically misguide and constitute the machine of text, carrying and
being carried by its burden of "figuration." One cannot escape it by dismissing the former as the residue of a productive cut, and valorizing the
latter as the only possible concern of a "philosophical" literary criticism.
This opposition too, between subject "metaphor" and text "metaphor,"
needs to be indefinitely deconstructed rather than hierarchized. [Spivak,
"The Letter as Cutting Edge," see pp. 3–14 above

The formula—"scrupulous declaration of interest in the text of the production
of Value"—that I offer comes out of the most problematic effect of the sovereign
subject, the so-called deliberative consciousness. Thus, there is no guarantee in
deconstruction for freezing this imperative into a coercive theoretical universal,
though it is of course subject to all the constraints of ethico-logical grounding.
The encroachment of the fictive (related, of course, to the textual) upon this
operation cannot be appreciated without passing through the seemingly deliberative, which, even in the most self-conscious transferential situation, can, at
any rate, only be resisted rather than fully avoided.

In closing, I will invoke the very threshold, the second paragraph of this essay,
where I write: "The 'idealist' and the 'materialist' are both exclusive predications." *All* predications are exclusive and thus operate on the metonymic principle of a part standing for the putative whole: "As soon as one retains only a
predicate of the circle (for example, return to the point of departure, closing off
the circuit), its signification is put into the position of a trope, of metonymy if
not metaphor" [Derrida, "White Mythology" 264]. In this sense, the "idealist"
and the "materialist" predications of the subject are metonyms of the subject.
Writing of the constitution of the subject as such, Lacan writes: "The double-
triggered mechanism of metaphor is the very mechanism by which the symptom
. . . is determined. And the enigmas that desire seems to pose for a 'natural
philosophy' . . . amount to no other derangement of instinct than that of . . .
metonymy" ["The Agency of the Letter in the Unconscious," *Ecrits* 166–67]. In
so far as the two predications are *concepts* of the subject, they are unacknowledged metaphoric substitute-presentations of the subject. Between metaphor
and metonymy, symptom and desire, the political subject distances itself from
the analyst-in-transference by declaring an "interest" by way of a "wild" rather
than theoretically grounded practice. Lest I seem, once again, to be operating
on an uncomfortable level of abstraction, let me choose a most non-esoteric
source. Here is the *McGraw-Hill Dictionary of Modern Economics* on the encroachment of the fictive upon the deliberative in the operation of the economic text:

Originally the Dow-Jones averages represented the average (arithmetical
mean) price of a share of stock in the group. As stocks split, the substitution of issues in the averages, and other factors occurred, however, a
formula was devised to compensate for these changes. Although the Dow-
Jones averages no longer represent the actual average prices of these stocks

in the groups, they still represent the levels and changes in the stock-prices reasonably well. [178]

I say above that "the full implications of the question of Value posed within the 'materialist' predication of the subject cannot yet be realized." I must now admit what many Marxist theoreticians admit today: that in any theoretical formulation, the horizon of full realization must be indefinitely and irreducibly postponed. On that horizon it is not utopia that may be glimpsed [see Jameson, *The Political Unconscious: Narrative As A Socially Symbolic Act* 103f]. For utopias are historical attempts at topographic descriptions that must become dissimulative if attempts are made to represent them adequately in actual social practice. The complicity between idealisms and materialisms in the production of theory is better acknowledged, even as one distances oneself from idealism, if one designates this open end by the name of the "apolcalyptic tone."[21] This tone announces the pluralized apocalypse of the practical moment, in our particular case the set or ensemble of ideology-critical, aesthetic-troping, economically-aware performative or operational value-judgment. My careful language here should make clear that the practical moment is not a "fulfillment." In the pluralized apocalypse, the body does not rise. There is no particular need to see this as the thematics of castration. Why not affirm as its concept-metaphor the performative and operational evaluation of the repeated moves of the body's survival and comfort, historically named woman's work or assigned to domestic labor when it is minimally organized? Why appropriate the irreducible non-fit between theory and practice (here in the grounding and making of Value judgments) into Oedipus's hobble?

I offer, then, no particular apology for this *deliberate* attempt to show the difference between pre-critical economism and the role of the economic text in the determination of Value; and, further, to plot some of the "interests" in its foreclosure.

1985

three

Entering the Third World

11. "Draupadi"

by Mahasweta Devi
Translated with a Foreword by Gayatri Chakravorty Spivak

Translator's Foreword

I translated this Bengali short story into English as much for the sake of its villain, Senanayak, as for its title character, Draupadi (or Dopdi). Because in Senanayak I find the closest approximation to the First-World scholar in search of the Third World, I shall speak of him first.

On the level of the plot, Senanayak is the army officer who captures and degrades Draupadi. I will not go so far as to suggest that, in practice, the instruments of First-World life and investigation are complicit with such captures and such a degradation.[1] The approximation I notice relates to the author's careful presentation of Senanayak as a pluralist aesthete. In *theory*, Senanayak can identify with the enemy. But pluralist aesthetes of the First World are, willy-nilly, participants in the production of an exploitative society. Hence in *practice*, Senanayak must destroy the enemy, the menacing other. He follows the necessities and contingencies of what he sees as his historical moment. There is a convenient colloquial name for that as well: pragmatism. Thus his emotions at Dopdi's capture are mixed: sorrow (theory) and joy (practice). Correspondingly, we grieve for our Third-World sisters; we grieve and rejoice that they must lose themselves and become as much like us as possible in order to be "free"; we congratulate ourselves on our specialists' knowledge of them. Indeed, like ours, Senanayak's project is interpretive: he looks to decipher Draupadi's song. For both sides of the rift within himself, he finds analogies in Western literature: Hochhuth's *The Deputy*, David Morrell's *First Blood*. He will shed his guilt when the time comes. His self-image for that uncertain future is Prospero.

I have suggested elsewhere that, when we wander out of our own academic and First-World enclosure, we share something like a relationship with Senanayak's doublethink.[2] When we speak for ourselves, we urge with conviction: the personal is also political. For the rest of the world's women, the sense of whose personal micrology is difficult (though not impossible) for us to acquire, we fall back on a colonialist theory of most efficient information retrieval. We will not be able to speak to the women out there if we depend completely on conferences and anthologies by Western-trained informants. As I see their photographs in women's-studies journals or on book jackets—indeed, as I look in the glass—it is Senanayak with his anti-Fascist paperback that I behold. In inextricably mingling historico-political specificity with the sexual differential in a literary discourse, Mahasweta Devi invites us to begin effacing that image.

My approach to the story has been influenced by "deconstructive practice" I clearly share an unease that would declare avant-garde theories of interpretation too elitist to cope with revolutionary feminist material. How, then, has the practice of deconstruction been helpful in this context?

The aspect of deconstructive practice that is best known in the United States is its tendency toward infinite regression.[3] The aspect that interests me most is, however, the recognition, within deconstructive practice, of provisional and intractable starting points in any investigative effort; its disclosure of complicities where a will to knowledge would create oppositions; its insistence that in disclosing complicities the critic-as-subject is herself complicit with the object of her critique; its emphasis upon "history" and upon the ethico-political as the "trace" of that complicity—the proof that we do not inhabit a clearly defined critical space free of such traces; and, finally, the acknowledgment that its own discourse can never be adequate to its example.[4] This is clearly not the place to elaborate each item upon this list. I should, however, point out that in my introductory paragraphs I have already situated the figure of Senanayak in terms of our own patterns of complicity. In what follows, the relationship between the tribal and classical characters of Draupadi, the status of Draupadi at the end of the story, and the reading of Senanayak's proper name might be seen as produced by the reading practice I have described. The complicity of law and transgression and the class deconstruction of the "gentlemen revolutionaries," although seemingly minor points in the interpretation of the story as such, take on greater importance in a political context.

I cannot take this discussion of deconstruction far enough to show how Dopdi's song, incomprehensible yet trivial (it is in fact about beans of different colors), and ex-orbitant to the story, marks the place of that other that can be neither excluded nor recuperated.[5]

"Draupadi" first appeared in *Agnigarbha* ("Womb of Fire"), a collection of loosely connected, short political narratives. As Mahasweta points out in her introduction to the collection, "Life is not mathematics and the human being is not made for the sake of politics. I want a change in the present social system and do not believe in mere party politics."[6]

Mahasweta is a middle-class Bengali leftist intellectual in her fifties. She has a master's degree in English from Shantiniketan, the famous experimental university established by the bourgeois poet Rabindranath Tagore. Her reputation as a novelist was already well established when, in the late '70s, she published *Hajar Churashir Ma* ("No. 1084's Mother"). This novel, the only one to be imminently published in English translation, remains within the excessively sentimental idiom of the Bengali novel of the last twenty-odd years.[7] Yet in *Aranyer Adhikar* ("The Rights [or, Occupation] of the Forest"), a serially published novel she was writing almost at the same time, a significant change is noticeable. It is a meticulously researched historical novel about the Munda Insurrection of 1899–1900. Here Mahasweta begins putting together a prose that is a collage of literary Bengali, street Bengali, bureaucratic Bengali, tribal Bengali, and the languages of the tribals.

Since the Bengali script is illegible except to the approximately twenty-five percent literate of the about ninety million speakers of Bengali, a large number of whom live in Bangladesh rather than in West Bengal, one cannot speak of the "Indian" reception of Mahasweta's work but only of its Bengali reception.[8] Briefly, that reception can be described as a general recognition of excellence;

skepticism regarding the content on the part of the bourgeois readership; some accusations of extremism from the electoral Left; and admiration and a sense of solidarity on the part of the nonelectoral Left. Any extended reception study would consider that West Bengal has had a Left-Front government of the united electoral Communist parties since 1967. Here suffice it to say that Mahasweta is certainly one of the most important writers writing in India today.

Any sense of Bengal as a "nation" is governed by the putative identity of the Bengali language.[9] (Meanwhile, Bengalis dispute if the purest Bengali is that of Nabadwip or South Calcutta, and many of the twenty-odd developed dialects are incomprehensible to the "general speaker.") In 1947, on the eve of its departure from India, the British government divided Bengal into West Bengal, which remained a part of India, and East Pakistan. Punjab was similarly divided into East Punjab (India) and West Pakistan. The two parts of Pakistan did not share ethnic or linguistic ties and were separated by nearly eleven hundred miles. The division was made on the grounds of the concentration of Muslims in these two parts of the subcontinent. Yet the Punjabi Muslims felt themselves to be more "Arab" because they lived in the area where the first Muslim emperors of India had settled nearly seven hundred years ago and also because of their proximity to West Asia (the Middle East). The Bengali Muslims—no doubt in a class-differentiated way—felt themselves constituted by the culture of Bengal.

Bengal has had a strong presence of leftist intellectualism and struggle since the middle of the last century, before, in fact, the word "Left" entered our political shorthand.[10] West Bengal is one of three Communist states in the Indian Union. As such, it is a source of considerable political irritation to the central government of India. (The individual state governments have a good deal more autonomy under the Indian Constitution than is the case in the U.S.) Although officially India is a Socialist state with a mixed economy, historically it has reflected a spectrum of the Right, from military dictatorship to nationalist class benevolence. The word "democracy" becomes highly interpretable in the context of a largely illiterate, multilingual, heterogeneous, and unpoliticized electorate.

In the spring of 1967, there was a successful peasant rebellion in the Naxalbari area of the northern part of West Bengal. According to Marcus Franda, "unlike most other areas of West Bengal, where peasant movements are led almost solely by middle-class leadership from Calcutta, Naxalbari has spawned an indigenous agrarian reform leadership led by the lower classes" including tribal cultivators.[11] This peculiar coalition of peasant and intellectual sparked off a number of Naxalbaris all over India.[12] The target of these movements was the long-established oppression of the landless peasantry and itinerant farm worker, sustained through an unofficial government-landlord collusion that too easily circumvented the law. Indeed, one might say that legislation seemed to have an eye to its own future circumvention.

It is worth remarking that this coalition of peasant and intellectual—with long histories of apprenticeship precisely on the side of the intellecual—has been recuperated in the West by both ends of the polarity that constitutes a "political spectrum." Bernard-Henri Lévy, the ex-Maoist French "New Philosopher," has implicitly compared it to the May 1968 "revolution" in France, where the students joined the workers.[13] In France, however, the student identity of the movement had remained clear, and the student leadership had not brought with it sustained efforts to undo the privilege of the intellectual. On the other hand, "in much the same manner as many American college presidents have described the protest of American students, Indian political and social leaders have explained the Naxalites (supporters of Naxalbari) by referring to their sense of alienation and to the influence of writers like Marcuse and Sartre which has seemingly dominated the minds of young people throughout the world in the 1960s."[14]

It is against such recuperations that I would submit what I have called the theme of class deconstruction with reference to the young gentlemen revolutionaries in "Draupadi." Senanayak remains fixed within his class origins, which are similar to those of the gentlemen revolutionaries. Correspondingly, he is contained and judged fully within Mahasweta's story; by contrast, the gentlemen revolutionaries remain latent, underground. Even their leader's voice is only heard formulaically within Draupadi's solitude. I should like to think that it is because they are so persistently engaged in undoing class containment and the opposition between reading (book learning) and doing—rather than keeping the two aesthetically forever separate—that they inhabit a world whose authority and outline no text—including Mahasweta's—can encompass.

In 1970, the implicit hostility between East and West Pakistan flamed into armed struggle. In 1971, at a crucial moment in the struggle, the armed forces of the government of India were deployed, seemingly because these were alliances between the Naxalites of West Bengal and the freedom fighters of East Bengal (now Bangladesh). "If a guerrilla-style insurgency had persisted, there forces would undoubtedly have come to dominate the politics of the movement. It was this trend that the Indian authorities were determined to pre-empt by intervention." Taking advantage of the general atmosphere of jubilation at the defeat of West Pakistan, India's "principal national rival in South Asia"[15] (this was also the first time India had "won a war" in its millennial history), the Indian prime minister was able to crack down with exceptional severity on the Naxalites, destorying the rebellious sections of the rural population, most significantly the tribals, as well. The year 1971 is thus a point of reference in Senanayak's career.

This is the setting of "Draupadi." The story is a moment caught between two deconstructive formulas: on the one hand, a law that is fabricated with a view to its own transgression, on the other, the undoing of the binary opposition between the intellectual and the rural struggles. In order to grasp the minutiae of their relationship and involvement, one must enter a historical micrology that no foreword can provide.

Draupadi is the name of the central character. She is introduced to the reader between two uniforms and between two versions of her name. Dopdi and Draupadi. It is either that as a tribal she cannot pronounce her own Sanskrit name (Draupadi), or the tribalized form, Dopdi, is the proper name of the ancient Draupadi. She is on a list of wanted persons, yet her name is not on the list of appropriate names for the tribal women.

The ancient Draupadi is perhaps the most celebrated heroine of the Indian epic *Mahabharata*. The *Mahabharata* and the *Ramayana* are the cultural credentials of the so-called Aryan civilization of India. The tribes predate the Aryan invasion. They have no right to heroic Sanskrit names. Neither the interdiction nor the significance of the name, however, must be taken too seriously. For this pious, domesticated Hindu name was given Dopdi at birth by her mistress, in the usual mood of benevolence felt by the oppressor's wife toward the tribal bond servant. It is the killing of this mistress's husband that sets going the events of the story.

And yet on the level of the text, this elusive and fortuitous name does play a role. To speculate upon this role, we might consider the *Mahabharata* itself in its colonialist function in the interest of the so-called Aryan invaders of India. It is an accretive epic, where the "sacred" geography of an ancient battle is slowly expanded by succeeding generations of poets so that the secular geography of the expanding Aryan colony can present itself as identical with it and thus justify itself.[16] The complexity of this vast and anonymous project makes it an incomparably more heterogeneous text than the *Ramayana*. Unlike the *Ramayana*, for example, the *Mahabharata* contains cases of various kinds of kinship structure and various styles of marriage. And in fact it is Draupadi who provides the only example of polyandry, not a common system of marriage in India. She is married to the five sons of the impotent Pandu. Within a patriarchal and patronymic context, she is exceptional, indeed "singular" in the sense of odd, unpaired, uncoupled.[17] Her husbands, since they are husbands rather than lovers, are *legitimately* pluralized. No acknowledgment of paternity can secure the Name of the Father for the child of such a mother. Mahasweta's story questions this "singularity" by placing Dopdi first in a comradely, activist, monogamous marriage and then in a situation of multiple rape.

In the epic, Draupadi's legitimized pluralization (as a wife among husbands) in singularity (as a possible mother or harlot) is used to demonstrate male glory. She provides the occasion for a violent transaction between men, the efficient cause of the crucial battle. Her eldest husband is about to lose her by default in a game of dice. He had staked all he owned, and "Draupadi belongs within that all" (*Mahabharata* 65:32). Her strange civil status seems to offer grounds for her predicament as well: "The Scriptures prescribed one husband for a woman; Draupadi is dependent on many husbands; therefore she can be designated a prostitute. There is nothing improper in bringing her, clothed or unclothed, into the assembly" (65:35–36). The enemy chief begins to pull at Draupadi's *sari*. Draupadi silently prays to the incarnate Krishna. The Idea of Sustaining Law (Dharma) materializes itself as clothing, and as the king pulls and pulls at her *sari*, there seems to be more and more of it. Draupadi is infinitely clothed and cannot be publicly stripped. It is one of Krishna's miracles.

Mahasweta's story rewrites this episode. The men easily succeed in stripping Dopdi—in the narrative it is the culmination of her political punishment by the representatives of the law. She remains publicly naked at her own insistence. Rather than save her modesty through the implicit intervention of a benign and divine (in this case it would have been godlike) comrade, the story insists that this is the place where male leadership stops.

It would be a mistake, I think, to read the modern story as a refutation of the ancient. Dopdi is (as heroic as) Draupadi. She is also what Draupadi—written into the patriarchal and authoritative sacred text as proof of male power—could not be. Dopdi is at once a palimpsest and a contradiction.

There is nothing "historically implausible" about Dopdi's attitudes. When we first see her, she is thinking about washing her hair. She loves her husband and keeps political faith as an act of faith toward him. She adores her fore*fathers* because they protected their women's honor. (It should be recalled that this is thought in the context of American soldiers breeding bastards.) It is when she crosses the sexual differential into the field of what could *only happen to a woman* that she emerges as the most powerful "subject," who, still using the language of sexual "honor," can derisively call herself "the object of your search," whom the author can describe as a terrifying superobject—"an unarmed target."

As a tribal, Dopdi is not romanticized by Mahasweta. The decision makers among the revolutionaries are, again, "realistically," bourgeois young men and women who have oriented their book learning to the land and thus begun the long process of undoing the opposition between book (theory or "outside") and spontaneity (practice or "inside"). Such fighters are the hardest to beat, for they are neither tribal nor gentlemen. A Bengali reader would pick them out by name among the characters: the one with the aliases who bit off his tongue; the ones who helped the couple escape the army cordon; the ones who neither smoke nor drink tea; and, above all, Arijit. His is a fashionable first name, tinsel Sanskrit, with no allusive paleonymy and a meaning that fits the story a bit too well: victorious over enemies. Yet it *is* his voice that gives Dopdi the courage to save not herself but her comrades.

Of course, this voice of male authority also fades. Once Dopdi enters, in the final section of the story, the postscript area of lunar flux and sexual difference, she is in a place where she will finally act *for* herself in *not* "acting," in challenging the man to (en)counter her as unrecorded or misrecorded objective historical monument. The army officer is shown as unable to ask the authoritative ontological question, What is this? In fact, in the sentence describing Dopdi's final summons to the *sahib*'s tent, the agent is missing. I can be forgiven if I find in this an allegory of the woman's struggle within the revolution in a shifting historical moment.

As Mahasweta points out in an aside, the tribe in question is the Santal, not to be confused with the at least nine other Munda tribes that inhabit India. They are also not to be confused with the so-called untouchables, who, unlike the tribals, are Hindu, though probably of remote "non-Aryan" origin. In giving the name *Harijan* ("God's people") to the untouchables, Mahatma Gandhi had tried to concoct the sort of pride and sense of unity that the tribes seem to possess. Mahasweta has followed the Bengali practice of calling each so-called untouchable caste by the name of its menial and unclean task within the rigid structural functionalism of institutionalized Hinduism.[18] I have been unable to reproduce this in my translation.

Mahasweta uses another differentiation, almost on the level of caricature: the Sikh and the Bengali. (Sikhism was founded as a reformed religion by Guru Nanak in the late fifteenth century. Today the roughly nine million Sikhs of India live chiefly in East Punjab, at the other end of the vast Indo-Gangetic Plain from Bengal. The tall, muscular, turbanned, and bearded Sikh, so unlike the slight and supposedly intellectual Bengali, is the stereotyped butt of jokes in the same way as the Polish community in North America or the Belgian in France.) Arjan Singh, the diabetic Sikh captain who falls back on the *Granth-sahib* (the Sikh sacred book—I have translated it "Scripture") and the "five Ks" of the Sikh religion, is presented as all brawn and no brains; and the wily, imaginative, corrupt Bengali Senanayak is of course the army officer full of a Keatsian negative capability.[19]

The entire energy of the story seems, in one reading, directed toward breaking the apparently clean gap between theory and practice in Senanayak. Such a clean break is not possible, of course. The theoretical production of negative capability is a practice; the practice of mowing down Naxalites brings with it a theory of the historical moment. The assumption of such a clean break in fact depends upon the assumption that the individual subject who theorizes and practices is in full control. At least in the history of the Indo-European tradition in general, such a sovereign subject is also the legal or legitimate subject, who is identical with his stable patronymic.[20] It might therefore be interesting that Senanayak is not given the differentiation of a first name and surname. His patronymic is identical with his function (not of course by the law of caste): the common noun means "army chief." In fact, there is the least hint of a doubt if it is a proper name or a common appellation. This may be a critique of the man's apparently self-adequate identity, which sustains his theory-practice juggling act. If so, it goes with what I see as the project of the story: to break this bonded identity with the wedge of an *unreasonable* fear. If our certitude of the efficient-information-retrieval and talk-to-the-accessible approach toward Third-World women can be broken by the wedge of an unreasonable uncertainty, into a feeling that what we deem gain might spell loss and that our practice should be forged accordingly, then we would share the textual effect of "Draupadi" with Senanayak.

The italicized words in the translation are in English in the original. It is to be noticed that the fighting words on both sides are in English. Nation-state politics combined with multinational economies produce war. The language of war—offense *and* defense—is international. English is standing in here for that nameless and heterogeneous world language. The peculiarities of usage belong to being obliged to cope with English under political and social pressure for a few centuries. Where, indeed, is there a "pure" language? Given the nature of the struggle, there is nothing bizarre in "Comrade Dopdi."[21] It is part of the undoing of opposites—intellectual-rural, tribalist-internationalist—that is the wavering constitution of "the underground," "the wrong side" of the law. On the right side of the law, such deconstructions, breaking down national distinctions, are operated through the encroachment of king-emperor or capital.

The only exception is the word *"sahib."* An Urdu word meaning "friend," it came to mean, almost exclusively in Bengali, "white man." It is a colonial word and is used today to mean "boss." I thought of Kipling as I wrote "Burra Sahib" for Senanayak.

In the matter of "translation" between Bengali and English, it is again Dopdi who occupies a curious middle space. She is the only one who uses the word "counter" (the "n" is no more than a nasalization of the diphthong "ou"). As Mahasweta explains, it is an abbreviation for "killed by police in an encounter," the code description for death by police torture. Dopdi does not understand English, but she understands this formula and the word. In her use of it at the end, it comes mysteriously close to the "proper" English usage. It is the menacing appeal of the objectified subject to its politico-sexual enemy—the provisionally silenced master of the subject-object dialectic—to encounter—"counter"—her. What is it to "use" a language "correctly" without "knowing" it?

We cannot answer because we, with Senanayak, are in the opposite situation. Although we are told of specialists, the meaning of Dopdi's song remains undisclosed in the text. The educated Bengali does not know the languages of the tribes, and no political coercion obliges him to "know" it. What one might falsely think of as a political "privilege"—knowing English properly—stands in the way of a deconstructive practice of language—using it "correctly" through a political displacement, or operating the language of the other side.

It follows that I have had the usual "translator's problems" only with the peculiar Bengali spoken by the tribals. In general we educated Bengalis have the same racist attitude toward it as the late Peter Sellers had toward our English. It would have been embarrassing to have used some version of the language of D. H. Lawrence's "common people" or Faulkner's blacks. Again, the specificity is micrological. I have used "straight English," whatever that may be.

Rather than encumber the story with footnotes, in conclusion I shall list a few items of information:

Page 188: The "five Ks" are *Kes* ("unshorn hair"); *kachh* ("drawers down to the knee"); *karha* ("iron bangle"); *kirpan* ("dagger"); *kanga* ("comb"; to be worn by every Sikh, hence a mark of identity).

Page 190: "Bibidha Bharati" is a popular radio program, on which listeners can hear music of their choice. The Hindi film industry is prolific in producing pulp movies for consumption in India and in all parts of the world where there is an Indian, Pakistani, and West Indian labor force. Many of the films are adaptations from the epics. Sanjeev Kumar is an idolized actor. Since it was Krishna who rescued Draupadi from her predicament in the epic, and, in the film the soldiers watch, Sanjeev Kumar encounters Krishna, there might be a touch of textual irony here.

Page 191: "Panchayat" is a supposedly elected body of village self-government.

Page 193: "Champabhumi" and "Radhabhumi" are archaic names for certain areas of Bengal. "Bhumi" is simply "land." All of Bengal is thus "Bangabhumi."

Page 194: The jackal following the tiger is a common image.

Page 194: Modern Bengali does not distinguish between "her" and "his." The "her" in the sentence beginning "No comrade will . . ." can therefore be considered an interpretation.[22]

Page 195: A *sari* conjures up the long, many-pleated piece of cloth, complete with blouse and underclothes, that "proper" Indian women wear. Dopdi wears a much-abbreviated version, without blouse or underclothes. It is referred to simply as "the cloth."

Draupadi

Name Dopdi Mejhen, age twenty-seven, husband Dulna Majhi (deceased), domicile Cherakhan, Bankrahjarh, information whether dead or alive and/or assistance in arrest, one hundred rupees . . .

An exchange between two liveried *uniforms.*

FIRST LIVERY: What's this, a tribal called Dopdi? The list of names I brought has nothing like it! How can anyone have an unlisted name?

SECOND: Draupadi Mejhen. Born the year her mother threshed rice at Surja Sahu (killed)'s at Bakuli. Surja Sahu's wife gave her the name.

FIRST: These officers like nothing better than to write as much as they can in English. What's all this stuff about her?

SECOND: *Most notorious* female. *Long wanted in many* . . .

Dossier: Dulna and Dopdi worked at harvests, *rotating* between Birbhum, Burdwan, Murshidabad, and Bankura. In 1971, in the famous *Operation* Bakuli, when three villages were *cordonned* off and *machine gunned*, they too lay on the ground, faking dead. In fact, they were the main culprits. Murdering Surja Sahu and his son, occupying upper-caste wells and tubewells during the drought, not surrendering those three young men to the police. In all this they were the chief instigators. In the morning, at the time of the body count, the couple could not be found. The blood-sugar level of Captain Arjan Singh, the *architect* of Bakuli, rose at once and proved yet again that diabetes can be a result of anxiety and depression. Diabetes has twelve husbands—among them anxiety.

Dulna and Dopdi went underground for a long time in a *Neanderthal* darkness. The Special Forces, attempting to pierce that dark by an armed search, compelled quite a few Santals in the various districts of West Bengal to meet their Maker against their will. By the Indian Constitution, all human beings, regardless of caste or creed, are sacred. Still, accidents like this do happen. Two sorts of reasons: (1), the underground couple's skill in self-concealment; (2), not merely the Santals but all tribals of the Austro-Asiatic Munda tribes appear the same to the Special Forces.

In fact, all around the ill-famed forest of Jharkhani, which is under the jurisdiction of the police station at Bankrajharh (in this India of ours, even a worm is under a certain police station), even in the southeast and southwest corners, one comes across hair-raising details in the eyewitness records put together on the people who are suspected of attacking police stations, stealing guns (since the snatchers are not invariably well educated, they sometimes say "give up your *chambers*" rather than give up your gun), killing grain brokers, landlords, moneylenders, law officers, and bureaucrats. A black-skinned couple ululated like police *sirens* before the episode. They sang jubilantly in a savage tongue, incomprehensible even to the Santals. Such as:

Samaray hijulenako mar goekope

and,

Hende rambra keche keche
Pundi rambra keche keche

This proves conclusively that they are the cause of Captain Arjan Singh's diabetes.

Government procedure being as incomprehensible as the Male Principle in Sankhya philosophy or Antonioni's early films, it was Arjan Singh who was sent once again on *Operation Forest* Jharkhani. Learning from Intelligence that the above-mentioned ululating and dancing couple was the escaped corpses, Arjan Singh fell for a bit into a *zombie*like state and finally acquired so irrational a dread of black-skinned people that whenever he saw a black person in a ball-bag, he swooned, saying "they're killing me," and drank and passed a lot of water. Neither uniform nor Scriptures could relieve that depression. At long last, under the shadow of a *premature and forced retirement*, it was possible to present him at the desk of Mr. Senanayak, the elderly Bengali specialist in com-bat and extreme-Left politics.

Senanayak knows the activities and capacities of the opposition better than they themselves do. First, therefore, he presents an encomium on the military genius of the Sikhs. Then he explains further: Is it only the opposition that should find power at the end of the barrel of a gun? Arjan Singh's power also explodes out of the *male organ* of a gun. Without a gun even the "five Ks" come to nothing in this day and age. These speeches he delivers to all and sundry. As a result, the fighting forces regain their confidence in the *Army Handbook*. It is not a book for everyone. It says that the most despicable and repulsive style of fighting is guerrilla warfare with primitive weapons. Annihilation at sight of any and all practitioners of such warfare is the sacred duty of every soldier. Dopdi and Dulna belong to the *category* of such fighters, for they too kill by means of hatchet and scythe, bow and arrow, etc. In fact, their fighting power is greater than the gentlemen's. Not all gentlemen become experts in the ex-plosion of "chambers"; they think the power will come out on its own if the gun is held. But since Dulna and Dopdi are illiterate, their kind have practiced the use of weapons generation after generation.

I should mention here that, although the other side make little of him, Senanayak is not to be trifled with. Whatever his *practice*, in *theory* he respects the opposition. Respects them because they could be neither understood nor demolished if they were treated with the attitude, "It's nothing but a bit of impertinent game-playing with guns." *In order to destroy the enemy, become one.* Thus he understood them by (*theoretically*) becoming one of them. He hopes to write on all this in the future. He has also decided that in his written work he will demolish the gentlemen and *highlight* the message of the harvest workers. These mental processes might seem complicated, but actually he is a simple man and is as pleased as his third great-uncle after a meal of turtle meat. In fact, he knows that, as in the old popular song, turn by turn the world will change. And in every world he must have the credentials to survive with honor. If necessary he will show the future to what extent he alone understands the matter in its proper perspective. He knows very well that what he is doing today the future will forget, but he also knows that if he can change color from world to world, he can represent the particular world in question. Today he is getting rid of the young by means of "*apprehension and elimination*," but he knows people will soon forget the memory and lesson of blood. And at the same time, he, like Shakespeare, believes in delivering the world's *legacy* into youth's hands. He is Prospero as well.

At any rate, information is received that many young men and women, *batch by batch* and on jeeps, have attacked police station after police station, terrified and elated the region, and disappeared into the forest of Jharkhani. Since after escaping from Bakuli, Dopdi and Dulna have worked at the house of virtually every landowner, they can efficiently inform the killers about their targets and announce proudly that they too are soldiers, *rank and file*. Finally the impenetrable forest of Jharkhani is surrounded by real soldiers, the *army* enters and splits the battlefield. Soldiers in hiding guard the falls and springs that are the only source of drinking water; they are still guarding, still looking. On one such search, army informant Dukhiram Gharari saw a young Santal man lying on his stomach on a flat stone, dipping his face to drink water. The soldiers shot him as he lay. As the .303 threw him off spread-eagled and brought a bloody foam to his mouth, he roared "Ma—ho" and then went limp. They realized later that it was the redoubtable Dulna Majhi.

What does "Ma—ho" mean? Is this a violent slogan in the tribal language? Even after much thought, the Department of Defense could not be sure. Two tribal-specialist types are flown in from Calcutta, and they sweat over the dictionaries put together by worthies such as Hoffmann-Jeffer and Golden-Palmer. Finally the omniscient Senanayak summons Chamru, the water carrier of the *camp*. He giggles when he sees the two specialists, scratches his ear with his "bidi," and says, the Santals of Maldah did say that when they began fighting at the time of King Gandhi! It's a battle cry. Who said "Ma—ho" here? Did someone come from Maldah?

The problem is thus solved. Then, leaving Dulna's body on the stone, the soldiers climb the trees in green camouflage. They embrace the leafy boughs like so many great god Pans and wait as the large red ants bite their private parts. To see if anyone comes to take away the body. This is the hunter's way, not the soldier's. But Senanayak knows that these brutes cannot be dispatched by the approved method. So he asks his men to draw the prey with a corpse as bait. All will come clear, he says. I have almost deciphered Dopdi's song.

The soldiers get going at his command. But no one comes to claim Dulna's corpse. At night the soldiers shoot at a scuffle and, descending, discover that they have killed two hedgehogs copulating on dry leaves. Improvidently enough, the soldiers' jungle scout Dukhiram gets a knife in the neck before he can claim the reward for Dulna's capture. Bearing Dulna's corpse, the soldiers suffer shooting pains as the ants, interrupted in their feast, begin to bite them. When Senanayak hears that no one has come to take the corpse, he slaps his *anti-Fascist paperback* copy of *The Deputy* and shouts, "What?" Immediately one of the tribal specialists runs in with a joy as naked and transparent as Archimedes' and says, "Get up, *sir*! I have discovered the meaning of that 'hende rambra' stuff. It's Mundari *language*."

Thus the search for Dopdi continues. In the forest *belt* of Jharkhani, the *Operation* continues—will continue. It is a carbuncle on the government's backside. Not to be cured by the tested ointment, not to burst with the appropriate herb. In the first phase, the fugitives, ignorant of the forest's topography, are caught easily, and by the law of confrontation they are shot at the taxpayer's expense. By the law of confrontation, their eyeballs, intestines, stomachs, hearts, genitals, and so on become the food of fox, vulture, hyena, wildcat, ant, and worm, and the untouchables go off happily to sell their bare skeletons.

They do not allow themselves to be captured in open combat in the next phase. Now it seems that they have found a trustworthy courier. Ten to one it's Dopdi. Dopdi loved Dulna more than her blood. No doubt it is she who is saving the fugitives now.

"They" is also a *hypothesis.*

Why?

How many went *originally?*

The answer is silence. About that there are many tales, many books in press. Best not to believe everything.

How many killed in six years' confrontation?

The answer is silence.

Why after confrontations are the skeletons discovered with arms broken or severed? Could armless men have fought? Why do the collarbones shake, why are legs and ribs crushed?

Two kinds of answer. Silence. Hurt rebuke in the eyes. Shame on you! Why bring this up? What will be will be. . . .

How many left in the forest? The answer is silence.

A *legion*? Is it *justifiable* to maintain a large battalion in that wild area at the taxpayer's expense?

Answer: *Objection*. "Wild area" is incorrect. The battalion is provided with supervised nutrition, arrangements to worship according to religion, opportunity to listen to "Bibidha Bharati" and to see Sanjeev Kumar and the Lord Krishna face-to-face in the movie *This Is Life*. No. The area is not wild.

How many are left?

The answer is silence.

How many are left? Is there anyone *at all*?

The answer is long.

Item: *Well, action* still goes on. Moneylenders, landlords, grain brokers, anonymous brothel keepers, ex-informants are still terrified. The hungry and naked are still defiant and irrepressible. In some *pockets* the harvest workers are getting a *better wage*. Villages sympathetic to the fugitives are still silent and hostile. These events cause one to think. . . .

Where in this picture does Dopdi Mejhen fit?

She must have connections with the fugitives. The cause for fear is elsewhere. The ones who remain have lived a long time in the primitive world of the forest. They keep company with the poor harvest workers and the tribals. They must have forgotten book learning. Perhaps they are *orienting* their book learning to the soil they live on and learning new combat and survival techniques. One can shoot and get rid of the ones whose only recourse is extrinsic book learning and sincere intrinsic enthusiasm. Those who are working practically will not be exterminated so easily.

Therefore *Operation* Jharkhani *Forest* cannot stop. Reason: the words of warning in the *Army Handbook*.

2.

Catch Dopdi Mejhen. She will lead us to the others.

Dopdi was proceeding slowly, with some rice knotted into her belt. Mushai Tudu's wife had cooked her some. She does so occasionally. When the rice is cold, Dopdi knots it into her waistcloth and walks slowly. As she walked, she picked out and killed the lice in her hair. If she had some *kerosene,* she'd rub it into her scalp and get rid of the lice. Then she could wash her hair with baking *soda.* But the bastards put traps at every bend of the falls. If they smell *kerosene* in the water, they will follow the scent.

Dopdi!

She doesn't respond. She never responds when she hears her own name. She has seen in the Panchayat office just today the notice for the reward in her name. Mushai Tudu's wife had said, "What are you looking at? Who is Dopdi Mejhen! Money if you give her up!"

"How much?"

"Two—hundred!"

Oh God!

Mushai's wife said outside the office: "A lot of preparation this time. A—ll new policemen."

Hm.

Don't come again.

Why?

Mushai's wife looked down. Tudu says that Sahib has come again. If they catch you, the village, our huts . . .

They'll burn again.

Yes. And about Dukhiram . . .

The Sahib knows?

Shomai and Budhna betrayed us.

Where are they?

Ran away by train.

Dopdi thought of something. Then said, Go home. I don't know what will happen, if they catch me don't know me.

Can't you run away?

No. Tell me, how many times can I run away? What will they do if they catch me? They will *counter* me. Let them.

Mushai's wife said, We have nowhere else to go.

Dopdi said softly, I won't tell anyone's name.

Dopdi knows, has learned by hearing so often and so long, how one can come to terms with torture. If mind and body give way under torture, Dopdi will bite off her tongue. That boy did it. They countered him. When they counter you, your hands are tied behind you. All your bones are crushed, your sex is a terrible wound. *Killed by police in an encounter . . . unknown male . . . age twenty-two . . .*

As she walked thinking these thoughts, Dopdi heard someone calling, Dopdi!

She didn't respond. She doesn't respond if called by her own name. Here her name is Upi Mejhen. But who calls?

Spines of suspicion are always furled in her mind. Hearing "Dopdi" they stiffen like a hedgehog's. Walking, she *unrolls the film* of known faces in her mind. Who? No Shomra, Shomra is on the run. Shomai and Budhna are also on the run, for other reasons. Not Golok, he is in Bakuli. Is it someone from Bakuli? After Bakuli, her and Dulna's names were Upi Mejhen, Matang Majhi. Here no one but Mushai and his wife knows their real names. Among the young gentlemen, not all of the previous *batches* knew.

That was a troubled time. Dopdi is confused when she thinks about it. *Operation* Bakuli in Bakuli. Surja Sahu arranged with Biddibabu to dig two tubewells and three wells within the compound of his two houses. No water anywhere, drought in Birbhum. Unlimited water at Surja Sahu's house, as clear as a crow's eye.

Get your water with canal tax, everything is burning.

What's my profit in increasing cultivation with tax money?

Everything's on fire.

Get out of here. I don't accept your Panchayat nonsense. Increase cultivation with water. You want half the paddy for sharecropping. Everyone is happy with free paddy. Then give me paddy at home, give me money, I've learned my lesson trying to do you good.

What good did you do?

Have I not given water to the village?

You've given it to your kin Bhagunal.

Don't you get water?

No. The untouchables don't get water.

The quarrel began there. In the drought, human patience catches easily. Satish and Jugal from the village and that young gentleman, was Rana his name?, said a landowning moneylender won't give a thing, put him down.

Surja Sahu's house was surrounded at night. Surja Sahu had brought out his gun. Surja was tied up with cow rope. His whitish eyeballs turned and turned, he was incontinent again and again. Dulna had said, I'll have the first blow, brothers. My greatgrandfather took a bit of paddy from him, and I still give him free labor to repay that debt.

Dopdi had said, His mouth watered when he looked at me. I'll put out his eyes.

Surja Sahu. Then a *telegraphic message* from Shiuri. *Special train. Army.* The *jeep* didn't come up to Bakuli. *March-march-march.* The *crunch-crunch-crunch* of gravel under hobnailed boots. *Cordon up. Commands* on the *mike.* Jugal Mandal, Satish Mandal, Rana *alias* Prabir *alias* Dipak, Dulna Majhi-Dopdi Mejhen *surrender surrender surrender. No surrender surrender. Mow-mow-mow down the village.* Putt-putt putt-putt—*cordite* in the air—putt-putt—*round the clock*—putt-putt. *Flame thrower.* Bakuli is burning. *More men and women, children . . . fire—fire. Close canal approach. Over-over-over by nightfall.* Dopdi and Dulna had crawled on their stomachs to safety.

They could not have reached Paltakuri after Bakuli. Bhupati and Tapa took them. Then it was decided that Dopdi and Dulna would work around the Jharkhani *belt.* Dulna had explained to Dopdi, Dear, this is best! We won't get family and children this way. But who knows? Landowner and moneylender and policemen might one day be wiped out!

Who called her from the back today?

Dopdi kept walking. Villages and fields, bush and rock—*Public Works Department* markers—sound of running steps in back. Only one person running. Jharkhani *Forest* still about two miles away. Now she thinks of nothing but entering the forest. She must let them know that the *police* have set up *notices* for her again. Must tell them that that bastard Sahib has appeared again. Must change *hideouts.* Also, the *plan* to do to Lakkhi Bera and Naran Bera what they did to Surja Sahu on account of the trouble over paying the field hands in Sandara must be cancelled. Shomai and Budhna knew everything. There was the *urgency* of great danger under Dopdi's ribs. Now she thought there was no shame as a Santal in Shomai and Budhna's treachery. Dopdi's blood was the pure unadulterated black blood of Champabhumi. From Champa to Bakuli the rise and set of a million moons. Their blood could have been contaminated; Dopdi felt proud of her forefathers. They stood guard over their women's blood in black armor. Shomai and Budhna are half-breeds. The fruits of the war. Contributions to Radhabhumi by the American soldiers stationed at Shiandanga. Otherwise, crow would eat crow's flesh before Santal would betray Santal.

Footsteps at her back. The steps keep a distance. Rice in her belt, tobacco leaves tucked at her waist. Arijit, Malini, Shamu, Mantu—none of them smokes or even drinks tea. Tobacco leaves and limestone powder. Best medicine for scorpion bite. Nothing must be given away.

Dopdi turned left. This way is the *camp.* Two miles. This is not the way to the forest. But Dopdi will not enter the forest with a cop at her back.

I swear by my life. By my life Dulna, by my life. Nothing must be told.

The footsteps turn left. Dopdi touches her waist. In her palm the comfort of a half-moon. A baby scythe. The smiths at Jharkhani are fine artisans. Such an edge we'll put on it Upi, a hundred Dukhirams—Thank God Dopdi is not a gentleman. Actually, perhaps they have understood scythe, hatchet, and knife best. They do their work in silence. The lights of the *camp* at a distance. Why is Dopdi going this way? Stop a bit, it turns again. Huh! I can tell where I am if I wander all night with my eyes shut. I won't go in the forest, I won't lose him that way. I won't outrun him. You fucking jackal of a cop, deadly afraid of death, you can't run around in the forest. I'd run you out of breath, throw you in a ditch, and finish you off.

Not a word must be said. Dopdi has seen the new *camp*, she has sat in the *bus station*, passed the time of day, smoked a "bidi" and found out how many *police convoys* had arrived, how many *radio vans*. Squash four, onions seven, peppers fifty, a straightforward account. This information cannot now be passed on. They will understand Dopdi Mejhen has been countered. Then they'll run. Arijit's voice. If anyone is caught, the others must catch the *timing* and *change* their *hideout*. If *Comrade* Dopdi arrives late, we will not remain. There will be a sign of where we've gone. No *comrade* will let the others be destroyed for her own sake.

Arijit's voice. The gurgle of water. The direction of the next *hideout* will be indicated by the tip of the wooden arrowhead under the stone.

Dopdi likes and understands this. Dulna died, but, let me tell you, he didn't lose anyone else's life. Because this was not in our heads to begin with, one was countered for the other's trouble. Now a much harsher rule, easy and clear. Dopdi returns—good; doesn't return—*bad. Change hideout.* The clue will be such that the opposition won't see it, won't understand even if they do.

Footsteps at her back. Dopdi turns again. These three and a half miles of land and rocky ground are the best way to enter the forest. Dopdi has left that way behind. A little level ground ahead. Then rocks again. The *army* could not have struck *camp* on such rocky terrain. This area is quiet enough. It's like a maze, every hump looks like every other. That's fine. Dopdi will lead the cop to the burning "ghat." Patitpaban of Saranda had been sacrificed in the name of Kali of the Burning Ghats.

Apprehend!

A lump of rock stands up. Another. Yet another. The elderly Senanayak was at once triumphant and despondent. *If you want to destroy the enemy, become one.* He had done so. As long as six years ago he could anticipate their every move. He still can. Therefore he is elated. Since he has kept up with the literature, he has read *First Blood* and seen approval of his thought and work.

Dopdi couldn't trick him, he is unhappy about that. Two sorts of reasons. Six years ago he published an article about information storage in brain cells. He demonstrated in that piece that he supported this struggle from the point of view of the field hands. Dopdi is a field hand. *Veteran fighter. Search and destroy.* Dopdi Mejhen is about to be *apprehended.* Will be *destroyed.* Regret.

Halt!

Dopdi stops short. The steps behind come around to the front. Under Dopdi's ribs the *canal* dam breaks. No hope. Surja Sahu's brother Rotoni Sahu. The two lumps of rock come forward. Shomai and Budhna. They had not escaped by train.

Arijit's voice. Just as you must know when you've won, you must also acknowledge defeat and start the activities of the next *stage*.

Now Dopdi spreads her arms, raises her face to the sky, turns toward the forest, and ululates with the force of her entire being. Once, twice, three times. At the third burst the birds in the trees at the outskirts of the forest awake and flap their wings. The echo of the call travels far.

3.

Draupadi Mejhen was apprehended at 6:53 P.M. It took an hour to get her to *camp*. Questioning took another hour exactly. No one touched her, and she was allowed to sit on a canvas camp stool. At 8:57 Senanayak's dinner hour approached, and saying, "Make her. *Do the needful*," he disappeared.

Then a billion moons pass. A billion lunar years. Opening her eyes after a million light years, Draupadi, strangely enough, sees sky and moon. Slowly the bloodied nailheads shift from her brain. Trying to move, she feels her arms and legs still tied to four posts. Something sticky under her ass and waist. Her own blood. Only the gag has been removed. Incredible thirst. In case she says "water" she catches her lower lip in her teeth. She senses that her vagina is bleeding. How many came to make her?

Shaming her, a tear trickles out of the corner of her eye. In the muddy moonlight she lowers her lightless eye, sees her breasts, and understands that, indeed, she's been made up right. Her breasts are bitten raw, the nipples torn. How many? Four-five-six-seven—then Draupadi had passed out.

She turns her eyes and sees something white. Her own cloth. Nothing else. Suddenly she hopes against hope. Perhaps they have abandoned her. For the foxes to devour. But she hears the scrape of feet. She turns her head, the guard leans on his bayonet and leers at her. Draupadi closes her eyes. She doesn't have to wait long. Again the process of making her begins. Goes on. The moon vomits a bit of light and goes to sleep. Only the dark remains. A compelled spread-eagled still body. Active *pistons* of flesh rise and fall, rise and fall over it.

Then morning comes.

Then Draupadi Mejhen is brought to the tent and thrown on the straw. Her piece of cloth is thrown over her body.

Then, after *breakfast*, after reading the newspaper and sending the radio message "Draupadi Mejhen apprehended," etc., Draupadi Mejhen is ordered brought in.

Suddenly there is trouble.

Draupadi sits up as soon as she hears "Move!" and asks, Where do you want me to go?

To the Burra Sahib's tent.

Where is the tent?

Over there.

Draupadi fixes her red eyes on the tent. Says, Come, I'll go.

The guard pushes the water pot forward.

Draupadi stands up. She pours the water down on the ground. Tears her piece of cloth with her teeth. Seeing such strange behavior, the guard says, She's gone crazy, and runs for orders. He can lead the prisoner out but doesn't know what to do if the prisoner behaves incomprehensibly. So he goes to ask his superior.

The commotion is as if the alarm had sounded in a prison. Senanayak walks out surprised and sees Draupadi, naked, walking toward him in the bright sunlight with her head high. The nervous guards trail behind.

What is this? He is about to cry, but stops.

Draupadi stands before him, naked. Thigh and pubic hair matted with dry blood. Two breasts, two wounds.

What is this? He is about to bark.

Draupadi comes closer. Stands with her hand on her hip, laughs and says, The object of your search, Dopdi Mejhen. You asked them to make me up, don't you want to see how they made me?

Where are her clothes?

Won't put them on, *sir*. Tearing them.

Draupadi's black body comes even closer. Draupadi shakes with an indomitable laughter that Senanayak simply cannot understand. Her ravaged lips bleed as she beings laughing. Draupadi wipes the blood on her palm and says in a voice that is as terrifying, sky splitting, and sharp as her ululation, What's the use of clothes? You can strip me, but how can you clothe me again? Are you a man?

She looks around and chooses the front of Senanayak's white bush shirt to spit a bloody gob at and says, There isn't a man here that I should be ashamed. I will not let you put my cloth on me. What more can you do? Come on, *counter* me—come on, *counter* me—?

Draupadi pushes Senanayak with her two mangled breasts, and for the first time Senanayak is afraid to stand before an unarmed *target*, terribly afraid.

1981

12. Subaltern Studies: Deconstructing Historiography

Change and Crisis

The work of the Subaltern Studies group offers a theory of change. The insertion of India into colonialism is generally defined as a change from semi-feudalism into capitalist subjection. Such a definition theorizes the change within the great narrative of the modes of production and, by uneasy implication, within the narrative of the transition from feudalism to capitalism. Concurrently, this change is seen as the inauguration of politicization for the colonized. The colonial subject is seen as emerging from those parts of the indigenous élite which come to be loosely described as "bourgeois nationalist." The Subaltern Studies group seems to me to be revising this general definition and its theorization by proposing at least two things: first, that the moment(s) of change be pluralized and plotted as confrontations rather than transition (they would thus be seen in relation to histories of domination and exploitation rather than within the great modes-of-production narrative) and, secondly, that such changes are signalled or marked by a functional change in sign-systems. The most important functional change is from the religious to the militant. There are, however, many other functional changes in sign-systems indicated in these collections: from crime to insurgency, from bondsman to worker, and so on.

The most significant outcome of this revision or shift in perspective is that the agency of change is located in the insurgent or the "subaltern."

(In fact their concern with function changes in sign-systems—the phrase "discursive displacements" is slightly shorter—extends beyond the arena of insurgent or subaltern activity. In more than one article Dipesh Chakrabarty discusses how the "self-consciously socialist discourse" of the left sector of the indigenous élite is, willy-nilly, attempting to displace the discourse of feudal authority and charge it with new functions.[1] Partha Chatterjee shows Gandhi "political[ly]) appropriat[ing] the popular in the evolving forms of the new Indian state" (3.156). The meticulously documented account of the emergence of Gandhi—far from a "subaltern"—as a political signifier within the social text, spanning many of the essays in the three collections, is one of the most stunning achievements of these studies.)

A functional change in a sign-system is a violent event. Even when it is perceived as "gradual," or "failed," or yet "reversing itself," the change itself can only be operated by the force of a crisis. What Paul de Man writes of criticism can here be extended to a subalternity that is turning things "upside down": "In periods that are not periods of crisis, or in individuals bent upon avoiding crisis at all cost, there can be all kinds of approaches to [the social] . . . but there can be no [insurgency]."[2] Yet, if the space for a change (necessarily also an addition) had not been there in the prior function of the sign-system, the crisis could not have made the change happen. The change in signification-function supplements the previous function. "The movement of signification adds something . . . but this addition . . . comes to perform a vicarious function, to supplement a lack on the part of the signified."[3] The Subaltern Studies collective scrupulously annotates this double movement.

They generally perceive their task as making a theory of consciousness or culture rather than specifically a theory of change. It is because of this, I think, that the force of crisis, *although never far from their argument*, is not systematically emphasized in their work, and sometimes disarmingly alluded to as "impingement," "combination," "getting caught up in a general wave," "circumstances for unification," "reasons for change," "ambiguity," "unease," "transit," "bringing into focus"; even as it is also described as "switch," "catching fire" and, pervasively, as "turning upside down"—all critical concept-metaphors that would indicate force.[4] Indeed, a general sobriety of tone will not allow them to emphasize sufficiently that they are themselves bringing hegemonic historiography to crisis. This leads them to describe the clandestine operation of supplementarity as the inexorable speculative logic of the dialectic. In this they seem to me to do themselves a disservice, for, as self-professed dialecticians, they open themselves to older debates between spontaneity and consciousness or structure and history. Their actual practice, which, I will argue, is closer to deconstruction, would put these oppositions into question. A theory of change as the site of the displacement of function between sign-systems—which is what they oblige me to read in them—is a theory of reading in the strongest possible general sense. The site of displacement of the function of signs is the name of reading as active transaction between past and future. This transactional reading as (the possibility of) action, even at its most dynamic, is perhaps what Antonio Gramsci meant by "elaboration," *e-laborare*, working out.[5] If seen in this way, the work of the Subaltern Studies group repeatedly makes it possible for us to grasp that the concept-metaphor of the "social text" is not the reduction of real life to the page of a book. My theoretical intervention is a modest attempt to remind us of this.

It can be advanced that their work presupposes that the entire socius, at least in so far as it is the object of their study, is what Nietzsche would call a *fortgesetzte Zeichenkette*—a "continuous sign-chain." The possibility of action lies in the dynamics of the disruption of this object, the breaking and relinking of the chain. This line of argument does not set consciousness over against the socius, but sees it as itself also constituted as and on a semiotic chain. It is thus an instrument of study which participates in the nature of the object of study. To see consciousness thus is to place the historian in a position of irreducible compromise. I believe it is because of this double bind that it is possible to unpack the aphoristic remark of Nietzsche's that follows the image of the sign-chain with reference to this double bind: "All concepts in which an entire process is comprehended [*sich zusammenfasst*] withdraws itself from [*sich entzieht*] definition; only that which has no history is definable."[6] At any rate these presuppositions are not, strictly speaking, consonant with a desire to find a consciousness (here of the subaltern) in a positive and pure state. My essay will also try to develop this discrepancy.

Cognitive Failure is Irreducible

All of the accounts of attempted discursive displacements provided by the group are accounts of failures. For the subaltern displacements, the reason for failure most often given is the much greater scope, organization, and strength of the colonial authorities. In the case of the nationalist movement for independence it is clearly pointed out that the bourgeoisie's "interested" refusal to recognize the importance of, and to ally themselves with, a politicized peasantry accounted for the failure of the discursive displacement that operated the peasants' politicization. Yet there is also an incipient evolutionism here which, trying perhaps to avoid a vulgar Marxist glorification of the peasant, lays the blame on "the existing level of peasant consciousness" for the fact "that peasant solidarity and peasant power were seldom sufficient or sustained enough" (3.52, 3.115). This contradicts the general politics of the group—which sees the élite's hegemonic access to "consciousness" as an interpretable construct.

To examine this contradiction we must first note that discursive displacements wittingly or unwittingly operated from above are also failures. Chakrabarty, Das, and Chandra chart the failures of trade union socialism, functionalist entrepreneurialism and agrarian communism to displace a semi-feudal into a "modern" discourse. Chatterjee shows how Gandhi's initial dynamic transaction with the discursive field of the Hindu religious Imaginary had to be travestied in order that his ethics of resistance could be displaced into the sign-system of bourgeois politics.[7] (No doubt if an "entity" like "bourgeois politics" were to be opened up to discursive analysis the same micro-dynamics of displacements would emerge.) My point is, simply, that failures or partial successes in discursive-field displacement do not necessarily relate, following a progressivist scale, to the "level of consciousness" of a class.

Let us now proceed to note that what has seemingly been thoroughly successful, namely élite historiography, on the right or the left, nationalist or colonialist, is itself, by the analysis of this group, shown to be constituted by cognitive failures. Indeed, if the theory of change as the site of the displacement of a discursive field is their most pervasive argument, this comes a close second. Here too no distinction is made, quite properly in my estimation, between witting and unwitting lapses. Hardiman points at the Nationalists' persistent (mis)cognition of discursive field-displacement on the part of the subaltern as the signature of Sanskritization (3.214). He reads contemporary analysis such as Paul Brass's study of factionalism for the symptoms of what Edward Said has called "orientalism" (1.227). It is correctly suggested that the sophisticated vocabulary of much contemporary historiography *successfully* shields this cognitive *failure* and that this success-in-failure, this sanctioned ignorance, is inseparable from colonial domination. Das shows rational expectation theory, that hegemonic yet defunct (successful cognitive failure once again) mainstay of neo-colonialism, at work in India's "Green Revolution to Prevent A Red One" (2.198–9).

Within this tracking of successful cognitive failure, the most interesting manoeuvre is to examine the production of "evidence," the cornerstone of the edifice of historical truth (3.231–70), and to anatomize the mechanics of the construction of the self-consolidating Other—the insurgent and insurgency. In this part of the project, Guha seems to radicalize the historiography of colonial India through a combination of Soviet and Barthesian semiotic analysis. The discursivity (cognitive failure) of disinterested (successful and therefore true) historiography is revealed. The Muse of History and counter-insurgency are shown to be complicit (2.1–42 & *EAP*).

I am suggesting, of course, that an implicitly evolutionist or progressivist set of presuppositions measuring failure or success in terms of level of consciousness is too simple for the practice of the collective. If we look at the varieties of activity treated by them, subaltern, insurgent, nationalist, colonialist, historiographic, it is a general field of failures that we see. In fact the work of the collective is making the distinction between success and failure indeterminate—for the most successful historical record is disclosed by them to be crosshatched by cognitive failure. Since in the case of the subaltern they are considering consciousness (however "negative") and culture (however determining); and in the case of the élite, culture and manipulation—the subaltern is also operating in the theatre of "cognition." At any rate, where does cognition begin and end? I will consider later the possible problems with such compartmentalized views of consciousness. Here suffice it to say that by the ordinary standards of coherence, and in terms of their own methodology, the possibility of failure cannot be derived from any criterion of success unless the latter is a theoretical fiction.[8]

A word on "alienation," as used by members of this group, to mean "a failure of *self*-cognition," is in order here.

> To overestimate . . . [the] lucidity or depth [of the subaltern consciousness] will be . . . ill-advised . . . This characteristic expression of a negative consciousness on the insurgent's part matched its other symptom, that is, his self-alienation. He was still committed to envisaging the coming war on the Raj as the project of a will independent of himself and his own role in it as no more than instrumental . . . [In their own] parwana [proclamation] . . . the authors did not recognize even their own voice, but heard only that of God (*EAP* 28).

To be sure, within his progressivist narrative taxonomy Hegel describes the march of history in terms of a diminution in the self-alienation of the so-called world historical agent. Kojève and his followers in France distinguished between this Hegel, the narrator of (a) history, and the speculative Hegel who outlined a system of logic.[9] Within the latter, alienation is irreducible in any act of consciousness. Unless the subject separates from itself to grasp the object there is no cognition, indeed no thinking, no judgment. Being and Absolute Idea, the first and last sections of *The Science of Logic*, two accounts of simple unalienability, are not accessible to individual or personal consciousness. From the strictly philosophical point of view, then, (a) élite historiography (b) the bourgeois nationalist account, as well as (c) re-inscription by the Subaltern Studies group, are operated by alienation—*Verfremdung* as well as *Entäußerung*. Derrida's reading of Hegel as in *Glas* would question the argument for the inalienability even of Absolute Necessity and Absolute Knowledge, but here we need not move that far. We must ask the opposite question. How shall we deal with Marx's suggestion that man must strive toward self-determination and unalienated practice and Gramsci's that "the lower classes" must "achieve self-awareness via a series of negations"?[10]

Formulating an answer to this question might lead to far-reaching practical effects if the risks of the irreducibility of cognitive "failure" and of "alienation" are accepted. The group's own practice can then be graphed on this grid of "failures," with the concept of failure generalized and re-inscribed as I have suggested above. This subverts the inevitable vanguardism of a theory that otherwise criticizes the vanguardism of theory. This is why I hope to align them with deconstruction: "Operating necessarily from the inside, borrowing all the strategic and economic resources of subversion from the old structure, borrowing them structurally, that is to say without being able to isolate their elements and atoms, the enterprise of deconstruction always in a certain way falls prey to its own work."[11]

This is the greatest gift of deconstruction: to question the authority of the investigating subject without paralysing him, persistently transforming conditions of impossibility into possibility.[12] Let us pursue the implications of this in our particular case.

The group, as we have seen, tracks failures in attempts to displace discursive fields. A deconstructive approach would bring into focus the fact that they are themselves engaged in an attempt at displacing discursive fields, that they themselves "fail" (in the general sense) for reasons as "historical" as those they adduce for the heterogeneous agents they study; and would attempt to forge a practice that would take this into account. Otherwise, refusing to acknowledge the implications of their own line of work because that would be politically incorrect, they would, willy-nilly, "insidiously objectify" the subaltern (2.262), control him through knowledge even as they restore versions of causality and self-determination to him (2.30), become complicit, in their desire for totality (and therefore totalization) (3.317), with a "law [that] assign[s] a[n] undifferentiated [proper] name" (*EAP* 159) to "the subaltern as such."

Subaltern Studies and the European Critique of Humanism

A "religious idiom gave the hillmen [of the Eastern Ghats] a framework, within which to conceptualize their predicament and to seek solutions to it" (1.140–1). The idiom of recent European theories of interpretation seems to offer this collective a similar framework. As they work their displacement, they are, as I suggest above, expanding the semantic range of "reading" and "text," words that are, incidentally, not prominent in their vocabulary. This is a bold transaction and can be compared favorably to some similar attempts made by historians in the United States.[13] It is appropriately marked by attempts to find local parallels, as in the concept of *atideśa* in Guha's work, and to insert the local into the general, as in the pervasive invocation of English, French, German, and occasionally Italian insurgency in *EAP*, and in the invocation of the anthropology of Africa in Partha Chatterjee's work on modes of power.

It is the force of a crisis that operates functional displacements in discursive fields. In my reading of the volumes of *Subaltern Studies*, this critical force or bringing-to-crisis can be located in the energy of the questioning of humanism in the post-Nietzschean sector of Western European structuralism, for our group Michel Foucault, Roland Barthes, and a certain Lévi-Strauss. These structuralists question humanism by exposing its hero—the sovereign subject as author, the subject of authority, legitimacy, and power. There is an affinity between the imperialist subject and the subject of humanism. Yet the crisis of anti-humanism—*like all crises*—does not move our collective "fully." The rupture shows itself to be also a repetition. They fall back upon notions of consciousness-as-agent, totality, and upon a culturalism, that are discontinuous with the critique of humanism. They seem unaware of the historico-political provenance of their various Western "collaborators." Vygotsky and Lotman, Victor Turner and Lévi-Strauss, Evans-Pritchard and Hindess and Hirst can, for them, fuel the same fire as Foucault and Barthes. Since one cannot accuse this group of the eclecticism of the supermarket consumer, one must see in their practice a repetition of as well as a rupture from the colonial predicament: the transactional quality of inter-conflicting metropolitan sources often eludes the (post)colonial intellectual.

I remind the reader that, in my view, such "cognitive failures" are irreducible. As I comment on the place of "consciousness" in the work of Subaltern Studies, it is therefore not my intent to suggest a formula for correct cognitive moves.

The Problem of Subaltern Consciousness

I have been trying to read the work of the group against the grain of their theoretical self-representation. Their figuration of peasant or subaltern consciousness makes such a reading particularly productive.

To investigate, discover, and establish a subaltern or peasant consciousness seems at first to be a positivistic project—a project which assumes that, if properly prosecuted, it will lead to firm ground, to some *thing* that can be disclosed. This is all the more significant in the case of recovering a consciousness because, within the post-Enlightenment tradition that the collective participates in as interventionist historians, consciousness is *the* ground that makes all disclosures possible.

And, indeed, the group is susceptible to this interpretation. There *is* a certain univocal reflection or signification-theory presupposed here by which "peasant action in famine as in rebellion" is taken to "reflect . . . a single underlying consciousness" (3.112); and "solidarity" is seen as a "signifier of consciousness," where signification is representation, figuration, propriation (stringent de-limitation within a unique and self-adequate outline), and imprinting (*EAP* 169).

Yet even as "consciousness" is thus entertained as an indivisible self-proximate signified or ground, there is a force at work here which would contradict such a metaphysics. For consciousness here is not consciousness-in-general, but a historicized political species thereof, subaltern consciousness. In a passage where "transcendental" is used as "transcending, because informing a hegemonic narrative" rather than in a strictly philosophical sense, Guha puts this admirably: "Once a peasant rebellion has been assimilated to the career of the Raj, the Nation or the people [the hegemonic narratives], it becomes easy for the historian to abdicate the responsibility he has of exploring and describing the consciousness specific to that rebellion and be content to ascribe to it a transcendental consciousness . . . representing them merely as instruments of some other will" (2.38).

Because of this bestowal of a historical specificity to consciousness in the narrow sense, even as it implicitly operates as a metaphysical methodological presupposition in the general sense, there is always a counterpointing suggestion in the work of the group that subaltern consciousness is subject to the cathexis of the élite, that it is never fully recoverable, that it is always askew from its received signifiers, indeed that it is effaced even as it is disclosed, that it is irreducibly discursive. It is, for example, chiefly a matter of "negative consciousness" in the more theoretical of these essays. Although "negative consciousness" is conceived of here as an historical stage peculiar to the subaltern, there is no logical reason why, given that the argument is inevitably historicized, this "negative," rather than the grounding positive view of consciousness, should not be generalized as the group's methodological presupposition. One view of "negative consciousness," for instance, sees it as the consciousness not of the being of the subaltern, but of that of the oppressors (*EAP* chap. 2, 3.183). Here, in vague Hegelian limnings, is the anti-humanist and anti-positivist position that it is always the desire for/of (the power of the Other) that produces an image of the self. If this is generalized, as in my reading of the "cognitive failure" argument, it is the subaltern who provides the model for a general theory of consciousness. And yet, since the "subaltern" cannot appear without the thought of the "élite," the generalization is by definition incomplete—in philosophical language "non-originary," or, in an earlier version of "*unursprünglich,*" non-primordial. This "instituted trace at the origin" is a representation of the deconstructive critique of simple origins. Of the practical consequences of recognizing the traces of this strategy in the work of the group I will speak below.

Another note in the counterpoint deconstructing the metaphysics of consciousness in these texts is provided by the reiterated fact that it is only the texts of counter-insurgency or élite documentation that give us the news of the consciousness of the subaltern. "The peasants' view of the struggle will probably never be recovered, and whatever we say about it at this stage must be very tentative" (1.50); "Given the problems of documenting the consciousness of the jute mill workers, their will to resist and question the authority of their employers can be read only in terms of the sense of crisis it produced among the people in authority" (3.121); "It should be possible to read the presence of a rebel consciousness as a necessary and pervasive element within that body of evidence" (*EAP* 15). To be sure, it is the vocabulary of "this stage," "will to resist," and "presence." Yet the language seems also to be straining to acknowledge that the subaltern's view, will, presence, can be no more than a theoretical fiction to entitle the project of reading. It cannot be recovered, "it will probably never be recovered." If I shifted to the slightly esoteric register of the language of French post-structuralism, I could put it thus: "Thought [here the thought of subaltern consciousness] is here for me a perfectly neutral name, the blank part of the text, the necessarily indeterminate index of a future epoch of difference."[14]

Once again, in the work of this group, what had seemed the historical predicament of the colonial subaltern can be made to become the allegory of the predicament of *all* thought, *all* deliberative consciousness, though the élite profess otherwise. This might seem preposterous at first glance. A double take is in order. I will propose it in closing this section of my paper.

The definitive accessibility of subaltern consciousness is counterpointed also by situating it in the place of a difference rather than an identity: "The terms 'people' and 'subaltern classes' have been used as synonymous throughout this [introductory] note [to 1]. The social groups and elements included in this category represent the *demographic difference between the total Indian population and all those whom we have described as the 'élite'*" (1.82; italics author's). I refer the reader to an essay where I have commented extensively on the specific counterpointing here: between the ostensible language of quantification—*demographic difference*—which is positivistic, and the discourse of a definitive difference—demographic *difference*—which opens the door to deconstructive gestures.[15]

I am progressively inclined, then, to read the retrieval of subaltern consciousness as the charting of what in post-structuralist language would be called the subaltern subject-effect.[16] A subject-effect can be briefly plotted as follows: that which seems to operate as a subject may be part of an immense discontinuous network ("text" in the general sense) of strands that may be termed politics, ideology, economics, history, sexuality, language, and so on. (Each of these strands, if they are isolated, can also be seen as woven of many strands.) Different knottings and configurations of these strands, determined by heterogeneous determinations which are themselves dependent upon myriad circumstances, produce the effect of an operating subject. Yet the continuist and homogenist deliberative consciousness symptomatically requires a continuous and homogeneous cause for this effect and thus posits a sovereign and determining subject. This latter is, then, the effect of an effect, and its positing a metalepsis, or the substitution of an effect for a cause. Thus do the texts of counter-insurgency locate, in the following description, a "will" as the sovereign cause when it is no more than an effect of the subaltern subject-effect, itself produced by the particular conjunctures called forth by the crises meticulously described in the various *Subaltern Studies*:

> It is of course true that the reports, despatches, minutes, judgements, laws, letters, etc. in which policemen, soldiers, bureaucrats, landlords, usurers and others hostile to insurgency register their sentiments, amount to a representation of their will. But these documents do not get their content from that will alone, for the latter is predicated on another will—

that of the insurgent. It should be possible therefore to read the presence
of a rebel consciousness as a necessary and pervasive element within that
body of evidence (*EAP* 15).

Reading the work of Subaltern Studies from within but against the grain, I
would suggest that elements in their text would warrant a reading of the project
to retrieve the subaltern consciousness as the attempt to undo a massive historiographic metalepsis and "situate" the effect of the subject as subaltern. I
would read it, then, as a *strategic* use of positivist essentialism in a scrupulously
visible political interest. This would put them in line with the Marx who locates
fetishization, the ideological determination of the "concrete," and spins the narrative of the development of the money-form; with the Nietzsche who offers us
genealogy in place of historiography, the Foucault who plots the construction
of a "counter-memory," the Barthes of semiotropy and the Derrida of "affirmative deconstruction." This would allow them to use the critical force of anti-
humanism, in other words, even as they share its constitutive paradox: that the
essentializing moment, the object of their criticism, is irreducible.

The strategy becomes most useful when "consciousness" is being used in the
narrow sense, as self-consciousness. When "consciousness" is being used in
that way, Marx's notion of un-alienated practice or Gramsci's notion of an "ideologically *coherent*," "spontaneous philosophy of the multitude" are plausible
and powerful.[17] For class-consciousness does not engage the ground-level of
consciousness—consciousness in general. "Class" is not, after all, an inalienable
description of a human reality. Class-consciousness on the *descriptive* level is
itself a strategic and artificial rallying awareness which, on the *transformative*
level, seeks to destory the mechanics which come to construct the outlines of
the very class of which a collective consciousness has been situationally developed. "Any member of the insurgent community"—Guha spends an entire
chapter showing how that collective consciousness of community develops—
"who chooses to continue in such subalternity is regarded as hostile towards
the inversive process initiated by the struggle and hence as being on the enemy's
side" (*EAP* 202). The task of the "consciousness" of class or collectivity within
a social field of exploitation and domination is thus necessarily self-alienating.
The tradition of the English translations of Marx often obliterates this. Consider,
for example, the following well-known passage from the *Communist Manifesto*:
"If the proletariat in struggle [*im Kampfe*] against the bourgeoisie is compelled
to unite itself in a class [*sich notwendig zum Klasse vereint*], and, by means of a
revolution, it makes itself the ruling class, and, as such, sweeps away by force
the old conditions of production, it thus sweeps away the conditions of class
oppositions [*Klassengegensatz*] and of classes generally, and abolishes its own
lordship [*Herrschaft*] as a class."[18] The phrases translated as "sweeps away,"
"sweeps away," and "abolishes" are, in Marx's text "aufhebt." "'Aufheben'
has a twofold meaning in the language: on the one hand it means to preserve,
to maintain, and equally it also means to cause to cease, to put an end to. . . .
The two definitions of 'Aufheben' which we have given can be quoted as two

dictionary *meanings* of this word.''[19] In this spirit of ''maintain *and* cause to cease,'' we would rewrite ''inversive'' in the passage from *EAP* as ''displacing.''

It is within the framework of a strategic interest in the self-alienating displacing move of and by a consciousness of collectivity, then, that self-determination and an unalienated self-consciousness can be broached. In the definitions of ''consciousness'' offered by the Subaltern Studies group there are plenty of indications that they are in fact concerned with consciousness not in the general, but in this crucial narrow sense.

Subaltern consciousness as self-consciousness of a sort is what inhabits ''the whole area of independent thought and conjecture and speculation . . . on the part of the peasant'' (1.188), what offers the ''clear proof of a distinctly independent interpretation of [Gandhi's] message'' (3.7), what animates the ''parley[s] among . . . the principal [insurgents] seriously to weigh the pros and cons of any recourse to arms'' (2.1), indeed underwrites all invocations of the will of the subaltern.

Subaltern consciousness as emergent collective consciousness is one of the main themes of these books. Among the many examples that can be found, I will cite two: ''what is indubitably represented in these extracts from Abdul Majid [a weaver]'s diary is a consciousness of the 'collective'—the community. Yet this consciousness of community was an ambiguous one, straddling as it did the religious fraternity, class *qasba*, and mohalla'' (3.269). ''[The tribe's] consciousness of itself as a body of insurgents was thus indistinguishable from its recognition of its ethnic self'' (*EAP* 286). The group places this theory of the emergent collective subaltern consciousness squarely in the context of that tendency within Western Marxism which would refuse class-consciousness to the pre-capitalist subaltern, especially in the theatres of Imperialism. Their gesture thus confronts E. J. Hobsbawm's notion of the ''pre-political'' as much as functionalist arguments from ''reciprocity and moral economy'' between ''agrarian labourers'' and ''peasant proprietors,'' which are ''an attempt to deny the relevance of class identities and class conflict to agrarian relations in Asia until a very recent date'' (3.78). Chakrabarty's analysis of how historically unsound it is simply to reverse the gesture and try to impose a Marxian *working*-class consciousness upon the urban proletariat in a colonial context and, by implication, as Guha shows, upon the rural subaltern, takes its place within this confrontation.

For readers who notice the points of contact between the Subaltern Studies group and critics of humanism such as Barthes and Foucault, the confusion arises because of the use of the word ''consciousness,'' unavoidably a post-phenomenological and post-psychoanalytic issue with such writers. I am not trying to clear the confusion by revealing through analysis that the Subaltern Studies group is not entertaining ''consciousness'' within that configuration at all, but is rather working exclusively with the second-level collective consciousness to be encountered in Marx and the classical Marxist tradition. I am suggesting, rather, that although the group does not wittingly engage with the post-structuralist understanding of ''consciousness,'' our own transactional reading of them is enhanced if we see them as *strategically* adhering to the essentialist notion of consciousness, that would fall prey to an anti-humanist critique, within a historiographic practice that draws many of its strengths from that very critique.

Historiography as Strategy

Can a strategy be unwitting? Of course not fully so. Consider, however, statements such as the following: "[a] discrepancy . . . is necessarily there at certain stages of the class struggle between the level of its objective articulation and that of the consciousness of its subjects"; or, "with all their practical involvement in a rebellion the masses could still be tricked by a false consciousness into trusting the magical faculties of warrior heroes . . ."; or yet, "the peasant rebel of colonial India could do so [learn his very first lesson in power] only by translating it backwards into the semi-feudal language of politics to which he was born" (*EAP* 173, 270, 76). A theory which allows a partial lack of fit in the fabrication of any strategy cannot consider itself immune from its own system. It must remain caught within the possibility of that predicament in its own case. If in translating bits and pieces of discourse theory and the critique of humanism back into an essentialist historiography the historian of subalternity aligns himself to the pattern of conduct of the subaltern himself, it is only a progressivist view, that diagnoses the subaltern as necessarily inferior, that will see such an alignment to be without interventionist value. Indeed it is in their very insistence upon the subaltern as the subject of history that the group acts out such a translating back, an interventionist strategy that is only partially unwitting.

If it were embraced as a strategy, then the emphasis upon the "sovereignty, . . . consistency and . . . logic" of "rebel consciousness" (*EAP* 13) can be seen as "affirmative deconstruction": knowing that such an emphasis is theoretically non-viable, the historian then breaks his theory in a scrupulously delineated "political interest."[20] If, on the other hand, the restoration of the subaltern's subject-position in history is seen by the historian as the establishment of an inalienable and final truth of things, then any emphasis on sovereignty, consistency, and logic will, as I have suggested above, inevitably objectify the subaltern and be caught in the game of knowledge as power. Even if the discursivity of history is seen as a *fortgesetzte Zeichenkette*, a restorative genealogy cannot be undertaken without the strategic blindness that will entangle the genealogist in the chain. Seeing this, Foucault in 1971 recommended the "historical sense," much like a newscaster's persistently revised daily bulletin, in the place of the arrogance of a successful genealogy.[21] It is in this spirit that I read *Subaltern Studies* against its grain and suggest that its own subalternity in claiming a *positive* subject-position for the subaltern might be reinscribed as a strategy for our times.

What good does such a re-inscription do? It acknowledges that the arena of the subaltern's persistent emergence into hegemony must always and by definition remain heterogeneous to the efforts of the disciplinary historian. The historian must persist in *his* efforts in this awareness, that the subaltern is necessarily the absolute limit of the place where history is narrativized into logic. It is a hard lesson to learn, but not to learn it is merely to nominate elegant solutions to be correct theoretical practice. When has history ever contradicted that practice norms theory, as subaltern practice norms official historiography in this case? If that assumption, rather than the dissonant thesis of the subaltern's infantility were to inhabit *Subaltern Studies*, then their project would be proper to itself in recognizing that it can never be proper to "subaltern consciousness"; that it can never be continuous with the subaltern's situational and uneven entry into political (not merely disciplinary, as in the case of the collective) hegemony as the content of an after-the-fact description. This is the always asymmetrical relationship between the interpretation and transformation of the world which Marx marks in the eleventh thesis on Feuerbach. There the contrast is between the words *haben interpretiert* (present participle—a completed action—of *interpretieren*—the Romance verb which emphasizes the establishment of a meaning that is commensurate with a phenomenon through the metaphor of the fair exchange of prices) and *zu verändern* (infinitive—always open to the future—of the German verb which "means" strictly speaking, "to make other"). The latter expression matches *haben interpretiert* neither in its Latinate philosophical weight nor in its signification of propriety and completion, as *transformieren* would have done. Although not an unusual word, it is not the most common word for "change" in German—*verwandeln*. In the open-ended "making-other"—*Ver-änderung*—of the properly self-identical—adequately *interpretiert*—lies an allegory of the theorist's relationship to his subject-matter. (There is no room here to comment on the richness of "es kommt darauf an," the syntactical phrase that joins the two parts of the Eleventh Thesis.) It is not only *"bad"* theory but *all* theory that is susceptible to this open-endedness.

Theoretical descriptions cannot produce universals. They can only ever produce provisional generalizations, even as the theorist realizes the crucial importance of their persistent production. Otherwise, because they desire perhaps to claim some unspecified direct hand in subaltern practice, the conclusions to the essays become abrupt, inconclusive, sometimes a series of postponements of some empirical project. One striking example of this foreclosed desire is where Das, in an otherwise brilliant essay, repudiates *formalization* as thwarting for practice, even as he deplores the lack of sufficient *generalization* that might have allowed subaltern practice to flourish (2.227).

Louis Althusser spoke of the limit of disciplinary theoretical production in the following way: "[A] new practice of philosophy can transform philosophy. And in addition it can in its way *help* [*aider a sa mesure*] in the transformation of the world. Help only. . . ."[22] In his trivializing critique of Althusser, E. P. Thompson privileges the British style of history-teaching as against the French style of philosophy-teaching.[23] Whatever position we take in the ancient quarrel between history and philosophy, it is incumbent upon us to realize that as *disciplines* they must both remain heterogeneous to, and discontinuous with, subaltern social practice. To acknowledge this is not to give way to functionalist abdication. It is a curious fact of Michel Foucault's career that, in a certain phase of his influential last period, he performed something like an abdication, refused to "represent" (as if such a refusal were possible), and privileged the oppressed subject, who could seemingly speak for himself.[24] The Subaltern Studies group, methodical trackers of representation, cannot follow that route. Barthes, after he "situated" semiology, turned in large measure to autobiography and a celebration of the fragment. Not only because of their devotion to semiotics, but also because they are trying to assemble a historical *bio*-graphy of those whose active lives are only disclosed by a deliberately fragmentary record produced elsewhere, the Subaltern Studies group cannot follow Barthes here. They must remain committed to the subaltern as the subject of his history. As they choose this strategy, they reveal the limits of the critique of humanism as produced in the West.

The radical intellectual in the West is either caught in a deliberate choice of subalternity, granting to the oppressed either that very expressive subjectivity which s/he criticizes or, instead, a total unrepresentability. The logical negation of this position is produced by the discourse of post-modernism, where the "mass is only the mass because its social energy has already frozen. It is a cold reservoir, capable of absorbing and neutralizing any hot energy. It resembles those half-dead systems into which more energy is injected than is withdrawn, those paid-out deposits exorbitantly maintained in a state of artificial exploitation." This negation leads to an emptying of the subject-position: "Not to arrive at the point where one no longer says I, but at the point where it's no longer of any importance whether one says I or not."[25] Although some of these Western intellectuals express genuine concern about the ravages of contemporary neocolonialism in their own nation-states, they are not knowledgeable in the history of imperialism, in the epistemic violence that constituted/effaced a subject that was obliged to cathect (occupy in response to a desire) the space of the Imperialists' self-consolidating other. It is almost as if the force generated by their crisis is separated from its appropriate field by a sanctioned ignorance of that history.

It is my contention that, if the Subaltern Studies group saw their own work of subject-restoration as crucially strategic, they would not miss this symptomatic blank in contemporary Western anti-humanism. In his innovative essay on modes of power, Partha Chatterjee quotes Foucault on the eighteenth century and writes:

> Foucault has sought to demonstrate the complexities of this novel regime of power in his studies of the history of mental illness, of clinical practice, of the prison, of sexuality and of the rise of the human sciences. When one looks at regimes of power in the so-called backward countries of the world today, not only does the dominance of the characteristically 'modern' modes of exercise of power seem limited and qualified by the persistence of older modes, but by the fact of their combination in a particular state and formation, it seems to open up at the same time an entirely new range of possibilities for the ruling classes to exercise their domination (3.348–9).

I have written earlier that the force of crisis is not systematically emphasized in the work of the group. The Foucauldian example being considered here, for instance, can be seen as marking a crisis *within* European consciousness. A few months before I had read Chatterjee's essay, I wrote a few sentences uncannily similar in sentiment upon the very same passage in Foucault. I write, of course, within a workplace engaged in the ideological production of neo-colonialism even through the influence of such thinkers as Foucault. It is not therefore necessarily a mark of extraordinary acumen that what I am calling the crisis in European consciousness is much more strongly marked in my paragraph, which I take the liberty of quoting here. My contention below is that the relationship between First World anti-humanist post-Marxism and the history of imperialism is not merely a question of "enlarging the range of possibilities," as Chatterjee soberly suggests above.

Although Foucault is a brilliant thinker of power-in-spacing, the awareness of the topographic reinscription of imperialism does not inform his presuppositions. He is taken in by the restricted version of the West produced by that reinscription and thus helps to consolidate its effects. Notice, for example, the omission of the fact, in the following passage, that the new mechanism of power in the seventeenth and eighteenth centuries (the extraction of surplus-value without extra-economic coercion is its Marxist description) is secured *by means of* territorial imperialism—the Earth and its products—'elsewhere.' The representation of sovereignty is crucial in those theatres: 'In the seventeenth and eighteenth centuries, we have the production of an important phenomenon, the emergence, or rather the invention, of a new mechanism of power possessed of highly specific procedural techniques . . . which is also, I believe, absolutely incompatible with the relations of sovereignty. . . .' I am suggesting that to buy a self-contained version of the West is symptomatically to ignore its production by the spacing-timing of the imperialist project. Sometimes it seems as if the very brilliance of Foucault's analysis of the centuries of European imperialism produces a miniature version of that heterogeneous phenomenon: management of space—but by doctors, development of administrations—but in asylums, considerations of the periphery—but in terms of the insane, prisoners, and children. The clinic, the asylum, the prison, the university, seem screen-allegories that foreclose a reading of the broader narratives of imperialism.[26]

Thus the discourse of the unified consciousness of the subaltern *must* inhabit the strategy of these historians, even as the discourse of the micrologized or "situated" subject must mark that of anti-humanists on the other side of the international division of labor. The two following remarks by Ranajit Guha and Louis Althusser can then be seen as marking not a contradiction but the fracture of a discontinuity of philosophic levels, *as well as* a strategic asymmetry: "Yet we propose," writes Guha in the eighties, "to focus on this consciousness as our central theme, because it is not possible to make sense of the experience of insurgency merely as a history of events without a subject" (4.11). Precisely, "it is not possible." And Althusser, writing in 1967:

Undeniably, for it has passed into his works, and *Capital* demonstrates it, Marx owes to Hegel the decisive philosophical category of process. He owes him yet more, that Feuerbach himself did not suspect. He owes him the concept of the process *without subject* . . . The origin, indispensable to the teleological nature of the process . . . must be *denied* from the start, so that the process of alienation may be a process without subject. . . . Hegel's logic is of the affirmed-denied Origin: first form of a concept that Derrida has introduced into philosophical reflection, the *erasure*.[27]

As Chakrabarty has rightly stated, "Marx thought that the logic of capital could be best deciphered only in a society where 'the notion of human equality has already acquired the fixity of a popular prejudice'" (2.263). The first lesson of ideology is that a "popular prejudice" mistakes itself for "human nature," the original mother-tongue of history. Marxist historiography can be caught within the mother-tongue of a history and a culture that had graduated to bourgeois individualism. As groups such as the Subaltern Studies collective attempt to open up the texts of Marx beyond his European provenance, beyond a homogeneous internationalism, to the persistent recognition of heterogeneity, the very goal of "forget-[ting] his original [or 'rooted'—*die ihm angestammte Sprache*] language while using the new one" must be reinscribed.[28] A repeated acknowledgment of the complicity of the new and the "original" is now on the agenda. I have tried to indicate this by deconstructing the opposition between the collective and their object of investigation—the subaltern—on the one hand; and by deconstructing the seeming continuity between them and their anti-humanist models on the other. From this point of view, it would be interesting if, instead of finding their only internationalism in European *history* and African *anthropology* (an interesting disciplinary breakdown), they were also to find their lines of contact, let us say, with the *political economy* of the independent peasant movement in Mexico.[29]

You can only read against the grain if misfits in the text signal the way. (These are sometimes called "moments of transgression.") I should like to bring the body of my argument to a close by discussing two such moments in the work of this group. First, the discussion of rumor; and, second, the place of woman in their argument.

Rumor

The most extensive discussion of rumors, to be found in *EAP*, is not, strictly speaking, part of the work of the group. I think I am correct, however, in maintaining that Guha's pages make explicit an implicit set of assumptions about the nature and role of subaltern means of communication, such as rumor, in the mobilization of insurgency, present in the work of the entire group. It also points up the contradiction inherent in their general practice, which leans toward post-structuralism, and their espousal of the early semiological Barthes, Lévi-Strauss, Greimas, and taxonomic Soviet structuralists such as Vygotsky, Lotman, and Propp.

Steven Ungar plots Barthes's trajectory from semiology through semioclasty to semiotropy in *Roland Barthes: the Professor of Desire*.[30] Any use of the Barthes of the first period would have to refute, however briefly, Barthes's own refutation and rejection of his early positions.

One of the enterprises made problematic by the critique of the subject of knowledge identified with post-structuralist anti-humanism is the desire to produce exhaustive taxonomies, "to assign names by a metalinguistic operation" (2.10). I have already discussed this issue lengthily in another part of my essay. All of the figures listed above would be susceptible to this charge. Here I want to point at their common phonocentrism, the conviction that speech is a direct and immediate representation of voice-consciousness and writing an indirect transcript of speech. Or, as Guha quotes Vygotsky, "'The speed of oral speech is unfavourable to a complicated process of formulation—it does not leave time for deliberation and choice. Dialogue implies immediate unpremeditated utterance'" (*EAP* 261).

By this reckoning the history of writing is coincident with the inauguration and development of exploitation. Now there is no reason to question this well-documented story of what one might call writing in the "narrow" or "restricted" sense. However, over against this restricted model of writing one must not set up a model of speech to which is assigned a total self-identity based on a psychological model so crude as to imply that the space of "premeditation" is confined to the deliberative consciousness, and on empirical "evidence" so impressionistic as "the speed of oral speech."

By contrast, post-structuralist theories of consciousness and language suggest that all possibility of expression, spoken or written, shares a common distancing from a self so that meaning can arise—not only meaning for others but also the meaning of the self to the self. I have advanced this idea in my discussion of "alienation." These theories suggest further that the "self" is itself always production rather than ground, an idea I have broached in my discussion of the "subject-effect." If writing is seen in terms of its historical predication, the production of our sense of self as ground would seem to be structured like writing:

> The essential predicates in a minimal determination of the classical concept of writing . . . [are that] a written sign . . . is a mark that remains [*reste*], . . . [that] carries with it a force that breaks with its context, . . . [and that] this force of rupture is tied to the spacing . . . which separates it from other elements of the internal contextual chain . . . Are these three predicates, together with the entire system they entail, limited, as is often believed, strictly to 'written' communication in the narrow sense of the word? Are they not to be found in all language, in spoken language for instance, and ultimately in the totality of 'experience' insofar as it is inseparable from this field of the mark, which is to say, from the network of effacement and of difference, of units of iterability, which are separable

from their internal and external context and also from themselves, inasmuch as the very iterability which constituted their identity does not permit them ever to be a unit of self-identity?[31]

For the burden of the extended consideration of how the exigencies of theory forbid an ideological manipulation of *naive* psychologism and empiricism, we should turn to Derrida's "Signature Event Context," from where the long passage above is taken. Here suffice it to say that this line of thinking can be made consonant with the argument that the abstract determines the "concrete."[32] That argument is not about chronological but logical priority. And it is a pity that, thanks to Engels's noble efforts to make Marx accessible, "determination" in it is most often reduced to "causality." I cannot belabor this historical situation here. Suffice it further to say that by this line of argument it would not only appear that to "describe speech as the immediate expression of the self" marks the site of a desire that is obliged to overlook the complexity of the production of (a) sense(s) of self. One would, by this, also have to acknowledge that no speech, no "natural language" (an unwitting oxymoron), not even a "language" of gesture, can signify, indicate, or express without the mediation of a preexisting code. One would further begin to suspect that the most authoritative and potentially exploitative manifestations of writing in the narrow sense—the codes of law—operate on an implicit phonocentrism, the presupposition that speech is the immediate expression of the self.

I would submit that it is more appropriate to think of the power of rumor in the subaltern context as deriving from its participation in the structure of illegitimate writing rather than the authoritative writing of the law—itself sanctioned by the phonocentric model of the spirit of the law. "Writing, the outlaw, the lost son. It must be recalled here that Plato always associates speech and law, *logos* and *nomos*. Laws speak. In the personification of *Crito*, they speak to Socrates directly."[33]

Let us now consider *EAP* 259–64, where the analysis of rumor is performed. (These pages are cited in 3.112, n. 157.) Let us also remember that the mindset of the peasants is as much affected by the phonocentrism of a tradition where śruti—that which is heard—has the greatest authority, as is the mind-set of the historian by the phonocentrism of Western linguistics. Once again, it is a question of complicity rather than the distance of knowledge.

If, then, "rumor is spoken utterance *par excellence*" (*EAP* 256), it must be seen that its "functional immediacy" is its non-belonging to any *one* voice-consciousness. This is supposed to be the signal characteristic of writing. Any reader can "fill" it with her "consciousness." Rumor evokes comradeship because it belongs to every "reader" or "transmitter." No one is its origin or source. Thus rumor is not error but primordially (originarily) errant, always in circulation with no assignable source. This illegitimacy makes it accessible to insurgency. Its "absolute" (we would say "indefinite," since "fictive source[s] may be assigned to it") "transitivity," collapsed at origin and end (a clear picture of writing) can be described as the received model of *speech* in the narrow sense ("the collaterality of word and deed issuing from a common will") only under the influence of phonocentrism. In fact the author himself comes closer to the case about fifteen pages later, when he notices the open verbality of rumor being restricted by the insurgents—who are also under the influence of phonocentrism—by an apocalyptic horizon. Subaltern, élite authority, and critic of historiography become complicit here. Yet the description of rumor in its "distinctive features [of] . . . anonymity and transitivity" (*EAP* 260) signal a contradiction that allows us to read the text of *Subaltern Studies* against its grain.

The odd coupling of Soviet structuralism and French anti-humanism sometimes produces a misleading effect. For example, the applicability to rumor of Barthes's suggestion that ascription of an author closes up *writing*, should alert us to rumor's writing-like (*scriptible*) character rather than oblige us to displace Barthes's remark to speech via Vygotsky. Dialogue, Vygotsky's example, is the privileged example of the so-called communication of direct verbality, of two immediately self-present sources or "authors." Dialogue is supposed to be "unpremeditated" (although theories of subject-effect or the abstract determination of the concrete would find this a dubious claim). Rumor is a relay of something always assumed to be pre-existent. In fact the mistake of the colonial authorities was to take rumor for speech, to impose the requirements of speech in the narrow sense upon something that draws its strength from participation in writing in the general sense.

The Subaltern Studies group has here led us to a theme of great richness. The cross-hatching of the revolutionary non-possessive possibilities in the structure of writing in general and its control by subaltern phonocentrism gives us access to the micrology or minute-scale functioning of the subaltern's philosophical world. The matter of the "blank paper falling from heaven" or the use of apparently "random" material "to . . . convey . . . the Thakur's own command in writing" (*EAP* 248–9), for instance, can provide us a most complex text for the use of the structure of writing in the fable of "insurgent consciousness." The matter of the role of "the reading aloud of newspapers" in the construction of Gandhi as a signifier is perhaps too quickly put to rest as a reliance on "spoken language," when, through such an act, "a story acquires its authentication from its motif and the name of its place of origin rather than the authority of the correspondent" (3.48–9). I have dwelt on this point so long that it might now suffice to say no more than that the newspaper is exploitative writing in the narrow sense, "spoken language" is a phonocentric concept where authority is supposed to spring directly from the voice-consciousness of the self-present speaker, and the reading out of someone else's text as "an actor does on the stage" is a setting-in-motion of writing in the general sense. To find corroboration of this, one can see the contrast made between speaker and rhetor in the Western tradition from the Platonic Socrates through Hobbes and Rousseau to J. L. Austin.[34] When newspapers start reporting rumors (3.88), the range of speculative possibilities becomes even more seductive. The investigator seems herself beckoned by the circuit of "absolute transitivity."

Without yielding to that seduction, the following question can be asked: what is the use of noticing this misfit between the suggested structure of writing-in-general and the declared interest in phonocentrism? What is the use of pointing out that a common phonocentrism binds subaltern, élite authority, and disciplinary-critical historian together, and only a reading against the grain discloses the espousal of illegitimacy by the first and the third? Or, to quote Terry Eagleton:

> Marx is a metaphysician, and so is Schopenhauer, and so is Ronald Reagan. Has anything been gained by this manoeuvre? If it is true, is it informative? What is ideologically at stake in such homogenizing? What differences does it exist to suppress? Would it make Reagan feel uncomfortable or depressed? If what is in question for deconstructionism is metaphysical discourse, and if this is all-pervasive, then there is a sense in which in reading against the grain we are subverting everything and nothing.[35]

Not all ways of understanding the world and acting upon it are *equally* metaphysical or phonocentric. If, on the other hand, there *is* something shared by élite (Reagan), colonial authority, subaltern and mediator (Eagleton/Subaltern Studies) that we would rather not acknowledge, any elegant solution devised by means of such a refusal would merely mark a site of desire. It is best to attempt to forge a practice that can bear the weight of that acknowledgment. And, using the buried operation of the structure of writing as a lever, the strategic reader can reveal the asymmetry between the three groups above. Yet, since a "reading against the grain" must forever remain strategic, it can never claim to have established the authoritative truth of a text, it must forever remain dependent upon practical exigencies, never legitimately lead to a theoretical orthodoxy. In the case of the Subaltern Studies group, it would get the group off the dangerous hook of claiming to establish the truth-knowledge of the subaltern and his consciousness.

Woman

The group is scrupulous in its consideration towards women. They record moments when men and women are joined in struggle (1.178, *EAP* 130), when their conditions of work or education suffer from gender or class discrimination (2.71, 2.241, 243, 257, 275). But I think they overlook how important the concept-metaphor woman is to the functioning of their discourse. This consideration will bring to an end the body of my argument.

In a certain reading, the figure of woman is pervasively instrumental in the shifting of the function of discursive systems, as in insurgent mobilization. Questions of the mechanics of this instrumentality are seldom raised by our group. "Femininity" is as important a discursive field for the predominantly male insurgents as "religion." When cow-protection becomes a volatile signified in the re-inscription of the social position of various kinds of subaltern, semi-subaltern, and indigenous élite groups, the cow is turned into a female figure of one kind or another. Considering that in the British nineteenth century the female access to "possessive individualism" is one of the most important social forces, what does it mean to imply that "femininity" has the same discursive sense and force for all the heterogeneous groups meticulously documented by Pandey? Analogous research into the figure of the "worker" is performed by Chakrabarty. No such luck for the "female."

On the most "ancient and indigenous" religious level, a level that "perhaps gave [the rebellious hillmen] an extra potency [*sic*] in times of collective distress and outside oppression" (1.98), all the deities are man-eating goddesses. As this pre-insurgent level of collectivity begins to graduate into revolt, the sacrifices continue to be made to goddesses rather than gods. And, even as this level of subaltern-led revolt is contrasted to the "élite struggles of the earlier period" (1.124), we notice that in that earlier period the struggles began on two occasions because men would not accept female leadership:

> With the deposition in 1836 of Ananta Bhupati, the 17th Zamindar of Golgonda, the Collector of Vishakhapatnam installed Jamma Devamma, widow of the 15th Zamindar, in his place. This was an affront to the *muttadars* and *mokhasadars* of Gudem who were not consulted . . . and who protested that they had never before been ruled by a woman. . . . In Rampa, the death of the Mansabdar Ram Bhupati Dev in March 1835 was followed by a revolt of *muttadars* against the daughter who had been appointed as the successor (1.102).

In terms of social semiosis, what is the difference between man-eating goddesses, objects of reverence and generators of solidarity on the one hand, and secular daughters and widows, unacceptable as leaders, on the other? On the occasion of the "culture of sugarcane" in Eastern UP, Shahid Amin speaks of the deliberate non-coincidence created between natural inscription (script as used when referring to a play) of the harvest calendar and the artificial inscription of the circuit of colonial monopoly capital. It is of course of great interest to wonder in what ways the composition of the peasantry and landownership would have developed had the two been allowed to coincide. Yet I think it should also be noticed that it is dowry that is the invariably mentioned *social* demand that allowed the demands of nature to devastate the peasant via the demands of empire. Should one trouble about the constitution of the subaltern as (sexed) subject when the exploitation of sexual difference seems to have so crucial a role on so many fronts? Should one notice that the proverb on 1.53 is sung by a young daughter who will deny her lover's demands in order to preserve her father's fields? Should one notice this metaphoric division of sexuality (in the woman's case, sex is of course identical with selfhood or consciousness) as property to be passed on or not from father to lover? Indeed, in a collective where so much attention is rightly paid to the subjectivity or subject-positioning of the subaltern, it should be surprising to encounter such indifference to the subjectivity, not to mention the indispensable presence, of the woman as crucial instrument. These four sentences should illustrate my argument:

It was not uncommon for a 'superior' Patidar to spend his dowry money and return his wife to her father so that he could marry for a new dowry. Amongst Patidars, it was considered very shameful to have to take back a daughter [!] . . . *Gols* were formed to prevent ruinous hypergamous marriages with 'superior' Patidar lineages. . . . Here, therefore, we discover a strong form of subaltern organization within the Patidar caste which provided a check on the power of the Patidar élite. . . . Even Mahatma Gandhi was unable to break the solidarity of the Patidar *gol* of twenty-one villages.

I do not see how the crucial instrumentality of woman as symbolic object of exchange can be overlooked here. Yet the conclusion is: "the solidarity of the *Gols* was a form of *class* solidarity" (1.202, 203, 207). As in the case of the insurgent under colonial power, the condition of the woman gets "bettered" as a by-product, but what's the difference? Male subaltern and historian are here united in the common assumption that the procreative sex is a species apart, scarcely if at all to be considered a part of civil society.

These are not unimportant questions in the context of contemporary India. Just as the *ulgulan* of 1899–1901 dehegemonized millennarian Christianity in the Indian context, so also did the Adivasis seem to have tapped the emergent possibilities of a goddess-centered religion in the Devi movement of 1922–3, a movement that actively contested the re–inscription of land into private property.[36] In the current Indian context, neither religion nor femininity shows emergent potential of this kind.

I have left till last the two broad areas where the instrumentality of woman seems most striking: notions of territoriality and of the communal mode of power.

Concept-metaphors of Territoriality and of Woman

The concept of territoriality is implicit in most of the essays of the three volumes of *Subaltern Studies*. Here again the explicit theoretical statement is to be found in *EAP*. Territoriality is the combined "pull of the primordial ties of kinship, community" which is part "of the actual mechanics of . . . autonomous mobilization" (*EAP* 118). On the simplest possible level, it is evident that notions of kinship are anchored and consolidated by the exchange of women. This consolidation, according to Guha, cuts across the religious division of Hindu and Muslim. "In Tamil Nadu . . . with all four [subdivisions of the Muslim community] endogamy helps to reinforce their separate identities in both kinship and territorial terms" (*EAP* 299). In "Allahabad . . . the Mewati . . . effect[ed] a massive mobilization of their close knit exogamous villages" (*EAP* 316). In all these examples woman is the neglected syntagm of the semiosis of subalternity of insurgency.

Throughout these pages it has been my purpose to show the complicity between subject and object of investigation—the Subaltern Studies group and subalternity. Here too, the historians' tendency, not to ignore, but to re-name the semiosis of sexual difference "class" or "caste-solidarity" (*EAP* 316), bears something like a relationship with the peasants' general attempt to undo the distinction between consanguinity and co-residence. Here, as in the case of the brutal marriage customs of the Patidars, the historian mentions, but does not pause to reflect upon, the significance of the simple exclusion of the subaltern as female (sexed) subject: "In each of these [rebel villages] nearly all the population, *barring females acquired by marriage*, claimed descent from a common patrilineage, consanguinal or mythical, and regarded themselves as members of the same clan or gotra. This belief in a shared ancestry made the village assert itself positively by acting as a solidarity unit and negatively by operating an elaborate code of discrimination against aliens" (*EAP* 314; italics mine).

Although it was unemphatically and trivially accepted by everyone that it was the woman, without proper identity, who operated this consanguinal or mythic patrilineage; and although, in the historian's estimation, "these village-based primordial ties were the principal means of rebel mobilization, mauza by mauza, throughout northern and central India in 1857" (*EAP* 315), it seems that we may not stop to investigate the subject-deprivation of the female in the operation of this mobilization and this solidarity. It seems clear to me that, if the question of female subaltern consciousness, whose instrumentality is so often seen to be crucial, is a red herring, the question of subaltern consciousness as such must be judged a red herring as well.

"Territoriality acted to no small extent in putting the brakes on resistance against the Raj" (*EAP* 331). What was needed for this resistance was a concept of "nation." Today, after the computerization of global economics, concepts of nationhood are themselves becoming problematic in specific ways:

> The mode of integration of underdeveloped countries into the international economy has shifted from a base relying exclusively on the exploitation of primary resources and labor to one in which manufactures have gained preponderance. This movement has paralleled the proliferation of export-processing zones (EPZs) throughout the world. More than a uniformly defined or geographically delimited concept, the export-processing zone provides a series of incentives and loosened restrictions for multinational corporations by developing countries in their effort to attract foreign investment in export oriented manufacturing. This has given rise to new ideas about development which *often question preexisting notions of national sovereignty*.[37]

If the peasant insurgent was the victim and the unsung hero of the first wave of resistance against territorial imperialism in India, it is well known that, for reasons of collusion between pre-existing structures of patriarchy and transnational capitalism, it is the urban sub-proletarian female who is the paradigmatic subject of the current configuration of the International Division of Labor.[38] As we investigate the pattern of resistance among these "permanent casual"-s, questions of the subject-constitution of the subaltern female gain a certain importance.

The Communal Mode of Power and the Concept of Woman

Although Partha Chatterjee's concept of the communal mode of power is not as pervasively implicit in all the work of the group, it is an important sustaining argument for the enterprise of Subaltern Studies. Here the importance of communal power structures, based largely on kin and clan, are shown to embrace far-flung parts of the pre-capitalist world. And, once again, the crucial syntagmatic and micrologically prior defining importance of sexual difference in the deployment of such power is foreclosed so that sexuality is seen only as one element among the many that drive this "social organization of production" (2.322). The making-visible of the figure of woman is perhaps not a task that the group should fairly be asked to perform. It seems to this reader, however, that a feminist historian of the subaltern must raise the question of woman as a structural rather than marginal issue in each of the many different types and cultures that Chatterjee invokes in "More on Modes of Power and the Peasantry."

If in the explanation of territoriality I notice a tension between consanguinal and spatial accounts shared by subaltern and historian alike, in the case of "the communal mode of power" we are shown a clash between explanations from kinship and "political" perceptions. This is a version of the same battle—the apparent gender-neutralizing of the world finally explained through reason, domestic society sublated and subsumed in the civil.

The clash between kinship and politics is one of Chatterjee's main points. What role does the figure of woman play here? In the dispersal of the field of power, the sexual division of labor is progressively defined from above as power-sharing. That story is the underside of the taxonomy of power that Chatterjee unfolds.

Thus there might be other ways of accounting for the suggestion that "the structure of communal authority must be located primarily in ideology." Our account would notice the specifically patriarchal structures producing the discursive field of the unity of the "community as a whole." "It is the community as a whole which is the source of all authority, no one is a permanent repository of delegated powers" (2.341). If the narrative of "the institutionalization of communal authority" (2.323) is read with this in mind, the taxonomy of modes of power can be made to interact with the history of sexuality.

Chatterjee quotes Victor Turner, who suggests that the resurgence of communal modes of power often generates ways to fight feudal structures: "resistance or revolt often takes on the form of . . . *communitas*" (2.339). This is particularly provocative in the case of the dehegemonization of monarchy. In this fast-paced fable of the progress of modes of power, it can be seen that the idea of one kind of a king may have supplemented a built-in gap in the ideology of community-as-a-whole: "a new kind of chief whom Tacitus calls 'king' (*rex*) who was elected from within a 'royal clan'" (2.323). The figure of the exchanged woman still produces the cohesive unity of a "clan," even as what emerges is a "king." And thus, when the insurgent *community* invokes monarch against *feudal* authority, the explanation that they are re-cathecting or re-filling the king with the old patriarchal ideology of consanguinity, never far from the metaphor of the King as Father, seems even less surprising (3.344).

My point is, of course, that through all of these heterogeneous examples of territoriality and the communal mode of power, the figure of the woman, moving from clan to clan, and family to family as daughter/sister and wife/mother, syntaxes patriarchal continuity even as she is herself drained of proper identity. In this particular area, the continuity of community or history, for subaltern and historian alike, is produced on (I intend the copulative metaphor—philosophically and sexually) the dissimulation of her discontinuity, on the repeated emptying of her meaning as instrument.

If I seem to be intransigent here, perhaps the distance travelled between high structuralism and current anti-humanism can best be measured by two celebrated passages by two famous men. First the Olympian dismissal, ignoring the role of representation in subject-constitution:

> These results can be achieved only on one condition: considering marriage regulations and kinship systems as a kind of language. . . . That the 'message' ['*message*'] should be constituted by the *women of the group*, which are circulated between class, lineages, or families, in place of the *words of the group*, which are *circulated* between individuals, does not at all change the identity of the phenomenon considered in the two cases . . . This ambiguity [between values and signs] is clearly manifested in the critique sometimes addressed to the *Elementary Structures of Kinship* as an 'anti-feminist' book by some, because women are there treated as objects. . . . [But] words do not speak, while women do. The latter are signs and producers of signs; as such, they cannot be reduced to the status of symbols or tokens.[39]

And, second, the recognition of a limit:

> The significations or conceptual values which apparently form the stakes or means of all Nietzschean analyses on sexual difference, on the 'unceasing war between the sexes', on the 'mortal hatred of the sexes' and 'love', eroticism, etc., are all on the vector of what might be called the process of *propriation* (appropriation, expropriation, taking, taking possession, gift and exchange, mastery, servitude, etc.). Through numerous analyses, that I cannot follow here, it appears, by the law already formalized, that sometimes the woman is woman by giving, *giving herself*, while the man takes, possesses, takes possession, and sometimes by contrast the woman by giving herself, gives-herself-as, and thus simulates and assures for herself possessive mastery. . . . As a sexual operation pro-

priation is more powerful, because undecidable, than the question *ti esti* [what is it], than the question of the veil of truth or the meaning of Being. All the more—and this argument is neither secondary nor supplementary—because the process of propriation organizes the totality of the process of language and symbolic exchange in general, including, therefore, all ontological statements [*enoncés*].[40]

I quote these passages, by Lévi-Strauss and Derrida, and separated by twenty years, as a sign of the times. But I need not add that, in the latter case, the question of being and the ontological statement would relate to the phenomenality of subaltern consciousness itself.

Envoi

In these pages, I have repeatedly emphasized the complicity between subject and object of investigation. My role in this essay, as subject of investigation, has been entirely parasitical, since my only object has been the *Subaltern Studies* themselves. Yet I am part of their object as well. Situated within the current academic theatre of cultural imperialism, with a certain *carte d'entrée* into the élite theoretical *ateliers* in France, I bring news of power-lines within the palace. Nothing can function without us, yet the part is at least historically ironic.

What of the post-structuralist suggestion that *all* work is parasitical, slightly to the side of that which one wishes adequately to cover, that critic (historian) and text (subaltern) are always "beside themselves"? The chain of complicity does not halt at the closure of an essay.

1985

13. Breast-Giver

by Mahasweta Devi
Translated by Gayatri Chakravorty Spivak

My aunties they lived in the woods, in the forest their home they did make.
Never did Aunt say here's a sweet dear, eat, sweetie, here's a piece of cake.

Jashoda doesn't remember if her aunt was kind or unkind. It is as if she were
Kangalicharan's wife from birth, the mother of twenty children, living or dead,
counted on her fingers. Jashoda doesn't remember at all when there was no
child in her womb, when she didn't feel faint in the morning, when Kangali's
body didn't *drill* her body like a geologist in a darkness lit only by an oil-lamp.
She never had the time to calculate if she could or could not bear motherhood.
Motherhood was always her way of living and keeping alive her world of count-
less beings. Jashoda was a mother by profession, *professional mother*. Jashoda
was not an *amateur* mama like the daughters and wives of the master's house.
The world belongs to the professional. In this city, this kingdom, the amateur
beggar-pickpocket-hooker has no place. Even the mongrel on the path or side-
walk, the greedy crow at the garbage don't make room for the upstart *amateur*.
Jashoda had taken motherhood as her profession.

The responsibility was Mr. Haldar's new son-in-law's Studebaker and the
sudden desire of the youngest son of the Haldar-house to be a driver. When
the boy suddenly got a whim in mind or body, he could not rest unless he had
satisfied it instantly. These sudden whims reared up in the loneliness of the
afternoon and kept him at slave labor like the khalifa of Bagdad. What he had
done so far on that account did not oblige Jashoda to choose motherhood as a
profession.

One afternoon the boy, driven by lust, attacked the cook and the cook, since
her body was heavy with rice, stolen fishheads, and turnip greens, and her body
languid with sloth, lay back, saying, "Yah, do what you like." Thus did the
incubus of Bagdad get off the boy's shoulders and he wept repentant tears,
mumbling, "Auntie, don't tell." The cook—saying, "What's there to tell?"—
went quickly to sleep. She never told anything. She was sufficiently proud that
her body had attracted the boy. But the thief thinks of the loot. The boy got
worried at the improper supply of fish and fries in his dish. He considered that
he'd be fucked if the cook gave him away. Therefore on another afternoon,
driven by the Bagdad djinn, he stole his mother's ring, slipped it into the cook's
pillowcase, raised a hue and cry, and got the cook kicked out. Another afternoon
he lifted the radio set from his father's room and sold it. It was difficult for his
parents to find the connection between the hour of the afternoon and the boy's
behavior, since his father had created him in the deepest night by the astrological
calendar and the tradition of the Haldars of Harisal. In fact you enter the sixteenth century as you enter the gates of this house. To this day you take your
wife by the astrological almanac. But these matters are mere blind alleys. Motherhood did not become Jashoda's profession for these afternoon-whims.

One afternoon, leaving the owner of the shop, Kangalicharan was returning home with a handful of stolen samosas and sweets under his dhoti. Thus he returns daily. He and Jashoda eat rice. Their three offspring return before dark and eat stale samosas and sweets. Kangalicharan stirs the seething vat of milk in the sweet shop and cooks and feeds "food cooked by a good Brahmin" to those pilgrims at the Lionseated goddess's temple who are proud that they are not themselves "fake Brahmins by sleight of hand." Daily he lifts a bit of flour and such and makes life easier. When he puts food in his belly in the afternoon he feels a filial inclination toward Jashoda, and he goes to sleep after handling her capacious bosom. Coming home in the afternoon, Kangalicharan was thinking of his imminent pleasure and tasting paradise at the thought of his wife's large round breasts. He was picturing himself as a farsighted son of man as he thought that marrying a fresh young thing, not working her overmuch, and feeding her well led to pleasure in the afternoon. At such a moment the Haldar son, complete with Studebaker, swerving by Kangalicharan, ran over his feet and shins.

Instantly a crowd gathered. It was an accident in front of the house after all, "otherwise I'd have drawn blood," screamed Nabin, the pilgrim-guide. He guides the pilgrims to the Mother goddess of Shakti-power, his temper is hot in the afternoon sun. Hearing him roar, all the Haldars who were at home came out. The Haldar chief started thrashing his son, roaring, "You'll kill a Brahmin, you bastard, you unthinking bull?" The youngest son-in-law breathed relief as he saw that his Studebaker was not much damaged and, to prove that he was better human material than the money-rich, *culture*-poor in-laws, he said in a voice as fine as the finest muslin, "Shall we let the man die? Shouldn't we take him to the hospital?"—Kangali's boss was also in the crowd at the temple and, seeing the samosas and sweets flung on the roadway was about to say, "Eh Brahmin!! Stealing food?" Now he held his tongue and said, "Do that *sir*." The youngest son-in-law and the Haldar-chief took Kangalicharan quickly to the hospital. The master felt deeply grieved. During the Second War, when he helped the anti-Fascist struggle of the Allies by buying and selling scrap iron— then Kangali was a mere lad. Reverence for Brahmins crawled in Mr. Haldar's veins. If he couldn't get chatterjeebabu in the morning he would touch the feet of Kangali, young enough to be his son, and put a pinch of dust from his chapped feet on his own tongue. Kangali and Jashoda came to his house on feast days and Jashoda was sent a gift of cloth and vermillion when his daughters-in-law were pregnant. Now he said to Kangali—"Kangali! don't worry son. You won't suffer as long as I'm around." Now it was that he thought that Kangali's feet, being turned to ground meat, he would not be able to taste their dust. He was most unhappy at the thought and he started weeping as he said, "What has the son of a bitch done." He said to the doctor at the hospital, "Do what you can! Don't worry about cash."

But the doctors could not bring the feet back. Kangali returned as a lame Brahmin. Haldarbabu had a pair of crutches made. The very day Kangali returned home on crutches, he learned that food had come to Jashoda from the Haldar house every day. Nabin was third in rank among the pilgrim-guides. He could only claim thirteen percent of the goddess's food and so had an inferiority complex. Inspired by seeing Rama-Krishna in the movies a couple of times, he called the goddess "my crazy one" and by the book of the Kali-worshippers kept his consciousness immersed in local spirits. He said to Kangali, "I put flowers on the crazy one's feet in your name. She said I have a share in Kangali's house, he will get out of the hospital by that fact." Speaking of this to Jashoda, Kangali said, "What? When I wasn't there, you were getting it off with Nabin?" Jashoda then grabbed Kangali's suspicious head between the two hemispheres of the globe and said, "Two maid servants from the big house slept here every day to guard me. Would I look at Nabin? Am I not your faithful wife?"

In fact Kangali heard of his wife's flaming devotion at the big house as well. Jashoda had fasted at the mother's temple, had gone through a female ritual, and had travelled to the outskirts to pray at the feet of the local guru. Finally the Lionseated came to her in a dream as a midwife carrying a *bag* and said, "Don't worry. Your man will return." Kangali was most overwhelmed by this. Haldarbabu said, "See, Kangali? The bastard unbelievers say, the Mother gives a dream, why togged as a midwife? I say, she creates as mother, and preserves as midwife."

Then Kangali said, "Sir! How shall I work at the sweetshop any longer. I can't stir the vat with my kerutches.* You are god. You are feeding so many people in so many ways. I am not begging. Find me a job."

Haldarbabu said, "Yes Kangali! I've kept you a spot. I'll make you a shop in the corner of my porch. The Lionseated is across the way! Pilgrims come and go. Put up a shop of dry sweets. Now there's a wedding in the house. It's my bastard seventh son's wedding. As long as there's no shop, I'll send you food."

Hearing this, Kangali's mind took wing like a rainbug in the rainy season. He came home and told Jashoda, "Remember Kalidasa's pome? You eat because there isn't, wouldn't have got if there was? That's my lot, chuck. Master says he'll put up a shop after his son's wedding. Until then he'll send us food. Would this have happened if I had legs? All is Mother's will, dear!"

Everyone is properly amazed that in this fallen age the wishes and wills of the Lionseated, herself found by a dream-command a hundred and fifty years ago, are circulating around Kangalicharan Patitundo. Haldarbabu's change of heart is also Mother's will. He lives in independent India, the India that makes no distinctions among people, kingdoms, languages, varieties of Brahmins, varieties of Kayasthas and so on. But he made his cash in the British era, when *Divide and Rule* was the policy. Haldarbabu's mentality was constructed then. Therefore he doesn't trust anyone—not a Panjabi-Oriya-Bihari-Gujarati-Marathi-Muslim. At the sight of an unfortunate Bihari child or a starvation-ridden Oriya beggar his flab-protected heart, located under a forty-two inch Gopal brand vest, does not itch with the rash of kindness. He is a successful son of Harisal. When he sees a West Bengali fly he says, "Tchah! at home even the flies were fat—in the bloody West everything is pinched-skinny." All the temple people are struck that such a man is filling with the milk of humankindness toward the West Bengali Kangalicharan. For some time this news is the general

---

* *Underclass Bengali pronunciation for "crutches." [GCS]*

talk. Haldarbabu is such a patriot that, if his nephews or grandsons read the lives of the nation's leaders in their schoolbook, he says to his employees, "Nonsense! why do they make 'em read the lives of characters from Dhaka, Mymansingh, Jashore? Harisal is made of the bone of the martyr god. One day it will emerge that the *Vedas* and the *Upanishads* were also written in Harisal." Now his employees tell him, "You have had a *change of heart*, so much kindness for a West Bengali, you'll see there is divine *purpose* behind this." The Boss is delighted. He laughs loudly and says, "There's no East or West for a Brahmin. If there's a sacred thread around his neck you have to give him respect even when he's taking a shit."

Thus all around blow the sweet winds of sympathy-compassion-kindness. For a few days, whenever Nabin tries to think of the Lionseated, the heavy-breasted, languid-hipped body of Jashoda floats in his mind's eye. A slow rise spreads in his body at the thought that perhaps she is appearing in his dream as Jashoda just as she appeared in Jashoda's as a midwife. The fifty percent pilgrim-guide says to him, "Male and female both get this disease. Bind the root of a white forget-me-not in your ear when you take a piss."

Nabin doesn't agree. One day he tells Kangali, "As the Mother's son I won't make a racket with Shakti-power. But I've thought of a plan. There's no problem with making a Hare Krishna racket. I tell you, get a Gopal in your dream. My Aunt brought a stony Gopal from Puri. I give it to you. You announce that you got it in a dream. You'll see there'll be a to-do in no time, money will roll in. Start for money, later you'll get devoted to Gopal."

Kangali says, "Shame, brother! Should one joke with gods?"

"Ah get lost, " Nabin scolds. Later it appears that Kangali would have done well to listen to Nabin. For Haldarbabu suddenly dies of heart failure. Shakespeare's *welkin* breaks on Kangali and Jashoda's head.

2.

Haldarbabu truly left Kangali in the lurch. Those wishes of the Lionseated that were manifesting themselves around Kangali *via-media* Haldarbabu disappeared into the blue like the burning promises given by a political party before the elections and became magically invisible like the heroine of a fantasy. A European witch's *bodkin* pricks the colored balloon of Kangali and Jashoda's dreams and the pair falls in deep trouble. At home, Gopal, Nepal, and Radharani whine interminably for food and abuse their mother. It is very natural for children to cry so for grub. Ever since Kangalicharan's loss of feet they'd eaten the fancy food of the Haldar household. Kangali also longs for food and is shouted at for trying to put his head in Jashoda's chest in the way of Gopal, the Divine Son. Jashoda is fully an Indian woman, whose unreasonable, unreasoning, and unintelligent devotion to her husband and love for her children, whose unnatural renunciation and forgiveness have been kept alive in the popular consciousness by all Indian women from Sati-Savitri-Sita through Nirupa Roy and Chand Osmani. The creeps of the world understand by seeing such women that the old Indian tradition is still flowing free—they understand that it was with such women in mind that the following aphorisms have been composed—"a female's life hangs on like a turtle's"—"her heart breaks but no word is uttered"—"the woman will burn, her ashes will fly / Only then will we sing her / praise on high." Frankly, Jashoda never once wants to blame her husband for the present misfortune. Her mother-love wells up for Kangali as much as for the children. She wants to become the earth and feed her crippled husband and helpless children with a fulsome harvest. Sages did not write of this motherly feeling of Jashoda's for her husband. They explained female and male as Nature and the Human Principle. But this they did in the days of yore—when they entered this *peninsula* from another land. Such is the power of the Indian soil that all women turn into mothers here and all men remain immersed in the spirit of holy childhood. Each man the Holy Child and each woman the Divine Mother. Even those who deny this and wish to slap *current posters* to the effect of the *"eternal she"*—"Mona Lisa"—"La passionaria"—"Simone de Beauvoir," et cetera, over the old ones and look at women that way are, after all, Indian cubs. It is notable that the educated Babus desire all this from women outside the home. When they cross the threshold they want the Divine Mother in the words and conduct of the revolutionary ladies. The *process* is most complicated. Because he understood this the heroines of Saratchandra always fed the hero an extra mouthful of rice. The apparent simplicity of Saratchandra's and other similar writers' writings is actually very complex and to be thought of in the evening, peacefully after a glass of wood-apple juice. There is too much influence of fun and games in the lives of the people who traffic in studies and intellectualism in West Bengal and therefore they should stress the wood-apple correspondingly. We have no idea of the loss we are sustaining because we do not stress the wood-apple-type-herbal remedies correspondingly.

However, it's incorrect to cultivate the habit of repeated incursions into *bye-lanes* as we tell Jashoda's life story. The reader's patience, unlike the cracks in Calcutta streets, will not widen by the decade. The real thing is that Jashoda was in a cleft stick. Of course they ate their fill during the Master's funeral days, but after everything was over Jashoda clasped Radharani to her bosom and went over to the big house. Her aim was to speak to the Mistress and ask for the cook's job in the vegetarian kitchen.

The Mistress really grieved for the Master. But the lawyer let her know that the Master had left her the proprietorship of this house and the right to the rice warehouse. Girding herself with those assurances, she has once again taken the rudder of the family empire. She had really felt the loss of fish and fish-head.* Now she sees that the best butter, the best milk sweets from the best shops, heavy cream, and the best variety of bananas can also keep the body going somehow. The Mistress lights up her easychair. A six-months' babe in her lap, her grandson. So far six sons have married. Since the almanac approves of the taking of a wife almost every month of the year, the birth rooms in a row on the ground floor of the Mistress's house are hardly ever empty. The *lady doctor* and Sarala the midwife never leave the house. The Mistress has six daughters.

---

* *Hindu widows become vegetarians in West Bengal as a sign of lifelong mourning.* [GCS]

They too breed every year and a half. So there is a constant *epidemic* of blanket-quilt-feeding spoon-bottle-oilcloth-*Johnson's baby powder*-bathing basin.

The Mistress was out of her mind trying to feed the boy. As if relieved to see Jashoda she said, "You come like a god! Give her some milk, dear, I beg you. His mother's sick—such a brat, he won't touch a bottle." Jashoda immediately suckled the boy and pacified him. At the Mistress's special request Jashoda stayed in the house until nine p.m. and suckled the Mistress's grandson again and again. The Cook filled a big bowl with rice and curry for her own household. Jashoda said as she suckled the boy, "Mother! The Master said many things. He is gone, so I don't think of them. But Mother! Your Brahmin-son does not have his two feet. I don't think for myself. But thinking of my husband and sons I say, give me any kind of job. Perhaps you'll let me cook in your household?"

"Let me see dear! Let me think and see." The Mistress is not as sold on Brahmins as the Master was. She does not accept fully that Kangali lost his feet because of her son's afternoon whims. It was written for Kangali as well, otherwise why was he walking down the road in the blazing sun grinning from ear to ear? She looks in charmed envy at Jashoda's *mammal projections* and says, "The good lord sent you down as the legendary Cow of Fulfillment. Pull the teat and milk flows! The ones I've brought to my house, haven't a quarter of this milk in their nipples!"

Jashoda says, "How true Mother! Gopal was weaned when he was three. This one hadn't come to my belly yet. Still it was like a flood of milk. Where does it come from, Mother? I have no good food, no pampering!"

This produced a lot of talk among the women at night and the menfolk got to hear it too at night. The second son, whose wife was sick and whose son drank Jashoda's milk, was particularly uxorious. The difference between him and his brothers was that the brothers created progeny as soon as the almanac gave a good day, with love or lack of love, with irritation or thinking of the accounts at the works. The second son impregnates his wife at the same *frequency*, but behind it lies deep love. The wife is often pregnant, that is an act of God. But the second son is also interested in that the wife remains beautiful at the same time. He thinks a lot about how to *combine* multiple pregnancies and beauty, but he cannot fathom it. But today, hearing from his wife about Jashoda's surplus milk, the second son said all of a sudden, "Way found."

"Way to what?"

"Uh, the way to save you pain."

"How? I'll be out of pain when you burn me. Can a year-breeder's health mend?"

"It will, it will, I've got a divine engine in my hands! You'll breed yearly *and* keep your body."

The couple discussed. The husband entered his Mother's room in the morning and spoke in heavy whispers. At first the Mistress hemmed and hawed, but then she thought to herself and realized that the proposal was worth a million rupees. Daughters-in-law *will* be mothers. When they are mothers, they will suckle their children. Since they will be mothers as long as it's possible—progressive suckling will ruin their shape. Then if the sons look outside, or harass the maidservants, she won't have a voice to object. Going out because they can't get it at home—this is just. If Jashoda becomes the infants' suckling-mother, her daily meals, clothes on feast days, and some monthly pay will be enough. The Mistress is constantly occupied with women's rituals. There Jashoda can act as the fruitful Brahmin wife. Since Jashoda's misfortune is due to her son, that sin too will be lightened.

Jashoda received a portfolio when she heard her proposal. She thought of her breasts as most precious objects. At night when Kangalicharan started to give her a feel she said, "Look. I'm going to pull our weight with these. Take good care how you use them." Kangalicharan hemmed and hawed that night, of course, but his Gopal frame of mind disappeared instantly when he saw the amount of grains—oil—vegetables coming from the big house. He was illuminated by the spirit of Brahma the Creator and explained to Jashoda, "You'll have milk in your breasts only if you have a child in your belly. Now you'll have to think of that and suffer. You are a faithful wife, a goddess. You will yourself be pregnant, be filled with a child, rear it at your breast, isn't this why Mother came to you as a midwife?"

Jashoda realized the justice of these words and said, with tears in her eyes, "You are husband, you are guru. If I forget and say no, correct me. Where after all is the pain? Didn't Mistress-Mother breed thirteen? Does it hurt a tree to bear fruit?"

So this rule held. Kangalicharan became a professional father. Jashoda was by *profession* Mother. In fact to look at Jashoda now even the skeptic is convinced of the profundity of that song of the path of devotion. The song is as follows:

> Is a Mother so cheaply made?
> Not just by dropping a babe!

Around the paved courtyard on the ground floor of the Haldar house over a dozen auspicious milch cows live in some state in large rooms. Two Biharis look after them as Mother Cows. There are mountains of rind-bran-hay-grass-molasses. Mrs. Haldar believes that the more the cow eats, the more milk she gives. Jashoda's place in the house is now above the Mother Cows. The Mistress's sons become incarnate Brahma and create progeny. Jashoda preserves the progeny.

Mrs. Haldar kept a strict watch on the free flow of her supply of milk. She called Kangalicharan to her presence and said, "Now then, my Brahmin son? You used to stir the vat at the shop, now take up the cooking at home and give her a rest. Two of her own, three here, how can she cook at day's end after suckling five?"

Kangalicharan's intellectual eye was thus opened. Downstairs the two Biharis gave him a bit of chewing tobacco and said, "Mistress Mother said right. We serve the Cow Mother as well—your woman is the Mother of the World."

From now on Kangalicharan took charge of the cooking at home. Made the children his assistants. Gradually he became an expert in cooking plantain curry, lentil soup, and pickled fish, and by constantly feeding Nabin a head-curry with the head of the goat dedicated to the Lionseated he tamed that ferocious cannabis-artist and drunkard. As a result Nabin inserted Kangali into the temple of Shiva the King. Jashoda, eating well-prepared rice and curry every day, became as inflated as the *bank account* of a Public Works Department *officer*. In addition, Mistress-Mother gave her milk gratis. When Jashoda became pregnant, she would send her preserves, conserves, hot and sweet balls.

Thus even the skeptics were persuaded that the Lionseated had appeared to Jashoda as a midwife for this very reason. Otherwise who has ever heard or seen such things as constant pregnancies, giving birth, giving milk like a cow, without a thought, to others' children? Nabin too lost his bad thoughts. Devotional feelings came to him by themselves. Whenever he saw Jashoda he called out "Mother! Mother! Dear Mother!" Faith in the greatness of the Lionseated was rekindled in the area and in the air of the neighborhood blew the *electrifying* influence of goddess-glory.

Everyone's devotion to Jashoda became so strong that at weddings, showers, namings, and sacred-threadings they invited her and gave her the position of chief fruitful woman. They looked with a comparable eye on Nepal-Gopal-Neno-Boncha-Patal etc. because they were Jashoda's children, and as each grew up, he got a sacred thread and started catching pilgrims for the temple. Kangali did not have to find husbands for Radharani, Altarani, Padmarani and such daughters. Nabin found them husbands with exemplary dispatch and the faithful mother's faithful daughters went off each to run the household of her own Shiva! Jashoda's worth went up in the Haldar house. The husbands are pleased because the wives' knees no longer knock when they riffle the almanac. Since their children are being reared on Jashoda's milk, they can be the Holy Child in bed at will. The wives no longer have an excuse to say "no." The wives are happy. They can keep their figures. They can wear blouses and bras of "European cut." After keeping the fast of Shiva's night by watching all-night picture shows they are no longer obliged to breast-feed their babies. All this was possible because of Jashoda. As a result Jashoda become vocal and, constantly suckling the infants, she opined as she sat in the Mistress's room, "A woman breeds, so here medicine, there bloodpeshur,* here doctor's visits. Showoffs! Look at me! I've become a year-breeder! So is my body failing, or is my milk drying? Makes your skin crawl? I hear they are drying their milk with injishuns.* Never heard of such things!"

The fathers and uncles of the current young men of the Haldar house used to whistle at the maidservants as soon as hair grew on their upper lips. The young ones were reared by the Milk-Mother's milk, so they looked upon the maid and the cook, their Milk-Mother's friends, as mothers too and started walking around the girls' school. The maids said, "Joshi! You came as The Goddess! You made the air of this house change!" So one day as the youngest son was squatting to watch Jashoda's milking, she said, "There dear, my Lucky! All

---

* *Underclass Bengali pronunciation for "blood pressure" and "injections." [GCS]*

this because you swiped him in the leg! Whose wish was it then?" "The Lion-seated's," said Haldar junior.

He wanted to know how Kangalicharan could be Brahma without feet? This encroached on divine area, and he forgot the question.

All is the Lionseated's will!

3.

Kangali's shins were cut in the fifties, and our narrative has reached the present. In twenty-five years, sorry in thirty, Jashoda has been confined twenty times. The maternities toward the end were profitless, for a new wind entered the Haldar house somehow. Let's finish the business of the twenty-five or thirty years. At the beginning of the narrative Jashoda was the mother of three sons. Then she became gravid seventeen times. Mrs. Haldar died. She dearly wished that one of her daughters-in-law should have the same good fortune as her mother-in-law. In the family the custom was to have a second wedding if a couple could produce twenty children. But the daughters-in-law called a halt at twelve-thirteen-fourteen. By evil counsel they were able to explain to their husbands and make arrangements at the hospital. All this was the bad result of the new wind. Wise men have never allowed a new wind to enter the house. I've heard from my grandmother that a certain gentleman would come to her house to read the liberal journal *Saturday Letter*. He would never let the tome enter his home. "The moment wife, or mother, or sister reads that paper," he would say, "she'll say 'I'm a woman! Not a mother, not a sister, not a wife.'" If asked what the result would be, he'd say, "They would wear shoes while they cooked." It is a perennial rule that the power of the new wind disturbs the peace of the women's quarter.

It was always the sixteenth century in the Haldar household. But at the sudden significant rise in the *membership* of the house the sons started building new houses and splitting. The most objectionable thing was that in the matter of motherhood, the old lady's granddaughters-in-law had breathed a completely different air before they crossed her threshold. In vain did the Mistress say that there was plenty of money, plenty to eat. The old man had dreamed of filling half Calcutta with Haldars. The granddaughters-in-law were unwilling. Defying the old lady's tongue, they took off to their husbands' places of work. At about this time, the pilgrim-guides of the Lionseated had a tremendous fight and some unknown person or persons turned the image of the goddess around. The Mistress's heart broke at the thought that the Mother had turned her back. In pain she ate an unreasonable quantity of jackfruit in full summer and died shitting and vomiting.

4.

Death liberated the Mistress, but the sting of staying alive is worse than death. Jashoda was genuinely sorry at the Mistress's death. When an elderly person dies in the neighborhood, it's Basini who can weep most elaborately. She is an old maidservant of the house. But Jashoda's meal ticket was offered up with the Mistress. She astounded everyone by weeping even more elaborately.

"Oh blessed Mother!," Basini wept. "Widowed, when you lost your crown, you became the Master and protected everyone! Whose sins sent you away Mother! Ma, when I said, don't eat so much jackfruit, you didn't listen to me at all Mother!"

Jashoda let Basini get her breath and lamented in that pause, "Why should you stay, Mother! You are blessed, why should you stay in this sinful world! The daughters-in-law have moved the throne! When the tree says I won't bear, alas it's a sin! Could you bear so much sin, Mother! Then did the Lionseated turn her back, Mother! You knew the abode of good works had become the abode of sin, it was not for you Mother! Your heart left when the Master left Mother! You held your body only because you thought of the family. O mistresses, o daughters-in-law! take a vermillion print of her footstep! Fortune will be tied to the door if you keep that print! If you touch your forehead to it every morning, pain and disease will stay out!"

Jashoda walked weeping behind the corpse to the burning ghat and said on return, "I saw with my own eyes a chariot descend from heaven, take Mistress-Mother from the pyre, and go on up."

After the funeral days were over, the eldest daughter-in-law said to Jashoda, "Brahmin sister! the family is breaking up. Second and Third are moving to the house in Beleghata. Fourth and Fifth are departing to Maniktala-Bagmari. Youngest will depart to our Dakshireswar house."

"Who stays here?"

"I will. But I'll let the downstairs. Now must the family be folded up. You reared everyone on your milk, food was sent every day. The last child was weaned, still Mother sent you food for eight years. She did what pleased her. Her children said nothing. But it's no longer possible."

"What'll happen to me, elder daughter-in-law-sister?"

"If you cook for my household, your board is taken care of. But what'll you do with yours?"

"What?"

"It's for you to say. You are the mother of twelve living children! The daughters are married. I hear the sons call pilgrims, eat temple food, stretch out in the courtyard. Your Brahmin-husband has set himself up in the Shiva temple, I hear. What do you need?"

Jashoda wiped her eyes. "Well! Let me speak to the Brahmin."

Kangalicharan's temple had really caught on. "What will you do in my temple?" he asked.

"What does Naren's niece do?"

"She looks after the temple household and cooks. You haven't been cooking at home for a long time. Will you be able to push the temple traffic?"

"No meals from the big house. Did that enter your thieving head? What'll you eat?"

"You don't have to worry," said Nabin.

"Why did I have to worry for so long? You're bringing it in at the temple, aren't you? You've saved everything and eaten the food that sucked my body."

"Who sat and cooked?"

"The man brings, the woman cooks and serves. My lot is inside out. Then you ate my food, now you'll give me food. Fair's fair."

Kangali said on the beat, "Where did you bring in the food? Could you have gotten the Haldar house? Their door opened for *you* because *my* legs were cut off. The Master had wanted to set *me* up in business. Forgotten everything, you cunt?"

"Who's the cunt, you or me? Living off a wife's carcass, you call that a man?"

The two fought tooth and nail and cursed each other to the death. Finally Kangali said, "I don't want to see your face again. Buzz off!"

"All right."

Jashoda too left angry. In the meantime the various pilgrim-guide factions conspired to turn the image's face forward, otherwise disaster was imminent. As a result, penance rituals were being celebrated with great ceremony at the temple. Jashoda went to throw herself at the goddess's feet. Her aging, milkless, capacious breasts are breaking in pain. Let the Lionseated understand her pain and tell her the way.

Jashoda lay three days in the courtyard. Perhaps the Lionseated has also breathed the new wind. She did not appear in a dream. Moreover, when, after her three days' fast, Jashoda went back shaking to her place, her youngest came by. "Dad will stay at the temple. He's told Naba and I to ring the bells. We'll get money and holy food every day."

"I see! Where's dad?"

"Lying down. Golapi-auntie is scratching the prickly heat on his back. Asked us to buy candy with some money. So we came to tell you."

Jashoda understood that her usefulness had ended not only in the Haldar house but also for Kangali. She broke her fast in name and went to Nabin to complain. It was Nabin who had dragged the Lionseated's image the other way. After he had settled the dispute with the other pilgrim-guides re the overhead income from the goddess Basanti ritual, the goddess Jagaddhatri ritual, and the autumn Durgapuja, it was he who had once again pushed and pulled the image the right way. He'd poured some liquor into his aching throat, had smoked a bit of cannabis, and was now addressing the local electoral candidate: "No offerings for the Mother from you! Her glory is back. Now we'll see how you win!"

Nabin is the proof of all the miracles that can happen if, even in this decade, one stays under the temple's power. He had turned the goddess's head himself and had himself believed that the Mother was averse because the pilgrim-guides were not organizing like all the want-votes groups. Now, after he had turned the goddess's head he had the idea that the Mother had turned on her own.

Jashoda said, "What are you babbling?"

Nabin said, "I'm speaking of Mother's glory."

Jashoda said, "You think I don't know that you turned the image's head yourself?"

Nabin said, "Shut up, Joshi. God gave me ability, and intelligence, and only then could the thing be done through me."

"Mother's glory has disappeared when you put your hands on her."

"Glory disappeared! If so, how come, the fan is turning, and you are sitting under the fan? Was there ever an elettiri* fan on the porch ceiling?"

"I accept. But tell me, why did you burn my luck? What did I ever do to you?"

"Why? Kangali isn't dead."

"Why wait for death? He's more than dead to me."

"What's up?"

Jashoda wiped her eyes and said in a heavy voice, "I've carried so many, I was the regular milk-mother at the Master's house. You know everything. I've never left the straight and narrow."

"But of course. You are a portion of the Mother."

"But Mother remains in divine fulfillment. Her 'portion' is about to die for want of food. Haldar-house has lifted its hand from me."

"Why did you have to fight with Kangali? Can a man bear to be insulted on grounds of being supported?"

"Why did you have to plant your niece there?"

"That was divine play. Golapi used to throw herself in the temple. Little by little Kangali came to understand that he was the god's companion-incarnate and she *his* companion."

"Companion indeed! I can get my husband from her clutches with one blow of a broom!"

Nabin said, "No! that can't be any more. Kangali is a man in his prime, how can he be pleased with you any more? Besides, Golapi's brother is a real hoodlum, and he is guarding her. Asked *me* to *get out*. If I smoke ten pipes, he smokes twenty. Kicked me in the midriff. I went to speak for you. Kangali said, don't talk to me about her. Doesn't know her man, knows her master's house. The master's house is her household god, let her go there."

"I will."

Then Jashoda returned home, half-crazed by the injustice of the world. But her heart couldn't abide the empty room. Whether it suckled or not, it's hard to sleep without a child at the breast. Motherhood is a great addiction. The addiction doesn't break even when the milk is dry. Forlorn Jashoda went to the Haldaress. She said, "I'll cook and serve, if you want to pay me, if not, not. You must let me stay here. That sonofabitch is living at the temple. What disloyal sons! They are stuck there too. For whom shall I hold my room?"

"So stay. You suckled the children, *and* you're a Brahmin. So stay. But sister, it'll be hard for you. You'll stay in Basini's room with the others. You mustn't fight with anyone. The master is not in a good mood. His temper is rotten because his third son went to Bombay and married a local girl. He'll be angry if there's noise."

Jashoda's good fortune was her ability to bear children. All this misfortune happened to her as soon as that vanished. Now is the downward time for Jash-

---

* *Underclass Bengali pronunciation for "electric." [GCS]*

oda, the milk-filled faithful wife who was the object of the reverence of the local houses devoted to the Holy Mother. It is human nature to feel an inappropriate vanity as one rises, yet not to feel the *surrender* of "let me learn to bite the dust since I'm down" as one falls. As a result one makes demands for worthless things in the old way and gets kicked by the weak.

The same thing happened to Jashoda. Basini's crowd used to wash her feet and drink the water. Now Basini said easily, "You'll wash your own dishes. Are you my master, that I'll wash your dishes. You are the master's servant as much as I am."

As Jashoda roared, "Do you know who I am?" she heard the eldest daughter-in-law scold, "This is what I feared. Mother gave her a swelled head. Look here, Brahmin sister! I didn't call you, you begged to stay, don't break the peace."

Jashoda understood that now no one would attend to a word she said. She cooked and served in silence and in the late afternoon she went to the temple porch and started to weep. She couldn't even have a good cry. She heard the music for the evening worship at the temple of Shiva. She wiped her eyes and got up. She said to herself, "Now save me, Mother! Must I finally sit by the roadside with a tin cup? Is that what you want?"

The days would have passed in cooking at the Haldar-house and complaining to the Mother. But that was not enough for Jashoda. Jashoda's body seemed to keel over. Jashoda doesn't understand why nothing pleases her. Everything seems confused inside her head. When she sits down to cook she thinks she's the milk-mother of this house. She is going home in a showy sari with a free meal in her hand. Her breasts feel empty, as if wasted. She had never thought she wouldn't have a child's mouth at her nipple.

Joshi became bemused. She serves nearly all the rice and curry, but forgets to eat. Sometimes she speaks to Shiva the King, "If Mother can't do it, you take me away. I can't pull any more."

Finally it was the sons of the eldest daughter-in-law who said, "Mother! Is the milk-mother sick? She acts strange."

The eldest daughter-in-law said, "Let's see."

The eldest son said, "Look here? She's a Brahmin's daughter, if anything happens to her, it'll be a sin for us."

The eldest daughter-in-law went to ask. Jashoda had started the rice and then lain down in the kitchen on the spread edge of her sari. The eldest daughter-in-law, looking at her bare body, said, "Brahmin sister! Why does the top of your left tit look so red? God! flaming red!"

"Who knows? It's like a stone pushing inside. Very hard, like a rock."

"What is it?"

"Who knows? I suckled so many, perhaps that's why?"

"Nonsense! One gets breast-stones or pus-in-the-tit if there's milk. Your youngest is ten."

"That one is gone. The one before survived. That one died at birth. Just as well. This sinful world!"

"Well the doctor comes tomorrow to look at my grandson. I'll ask. Doesn't look good to me."

Jashoda said with her eyes closed, "Like a stone tit, with a stone inside. At first the hard ball moved about, now it doesn't move, doesn't budge."

"Let's show the doctor."

"No, sister daughter-in-law, I can't show my body to a male doctor."

At night when the doctor came the eldest daughter-in-law asked him in her son's presence. She said, "No pain, no burning, but she is keeling over."

The doctor said, "Go ask if the *nipple* has shrunk, if the armpit is swollen like a seed."

Hearing "swollen like a seed," the eldest daughter-in-law thought, "How crude!" Then she did her field investigations and said, "She says all that you've said has been happening for some time."

"How old?"

"If you take the eldest son's age she'll be about about fifty-five."

The doctor said, "I'll give medicine."

Going out, he said to the eldest son, "I hear your *Cook* has a problem with her *breast*. I think you should take her to the *cancer hospital*. I didn't see her. But from what I heard it could be *cancer* of the *mammary gland*."

Only the other day the eldest son lived in the sixteenth century. He has arrived at the twentieth century very recently. Of his thirteen offspring he has arranged the marriages of the daughters, and the sons have grown up and are growing up at their own speed and in their own way. But even now his grey cells are covered in the darkness of the eighteenth- and the pre-Bengal-Renaissance nineteenth centuries. He still does not take smallpox vaccination and says, "Only the lower classes get smallpox. I don't need to be vaccinated. An upper-caste family, respectful of gods and Brahmins, does not contract that disease."

He pooh-poohed the idea of cancer and said, "Yah! Cancer indeed! That easy! You misheard, all she needs is an ointment. I can't send a Brahmin's daughter to a hospital just on your word."

Jashoda herself also said, "I can't go to hospital. Ask me to croak instead. I didn't go to hospital to breed, and I'll go now? That corpse-burning devil returned a cripple because he went to hospital!"

The elder daughter-in-law said, "I'll get you a herbal ointment. This ointment will surely soothe. The hidden boil will show its tip and burst."

The herbal ointment was a complete failure. Slowly Jashoda gave up eating and lost her strength. She couldn't keep her sari on the left side. Sometimes she felt burning, sometimes pain. Finally the skin broke in many places and sores appeared. Jashoda took to her bed.

Seeing the hang of it, the eldest son was afraid, if at his house a Brahmin died! He called Jashoda's sons and spoke to them harshly, "It's your mother, she fed you so long, and now she is about to die! Take her with you! She has everyone and she should die in a Kayastha* household?"

Kangali cried a lot when he heard this story. He came to Jashoda's almost-dark room and said, "Wife! You are a blessed auspicious faithful woman! After I spurned you, within two years the temple dishes were stolen, I suffered from

---

* *Second caste [GCS]*

boils in my back, and that snake Golapi tricked Napla, broke the safe, stole everything and opened a shop in Tarakeswar. Come, I'll keep you in state."

Jashoda said, "Light the lamp."

Kangali lit the lamp.

Jashoda showed him her bare left breast, thick with running sores and said, "See these sores? Do you know how these sores smell? What will you do with me now? Why did you come to take me?"

"The Master called."

"Then the Master doesn't want to keep me."—Jashoda sighed and said, "There is no solution about me. What can you do with me?"

"Whatever, I'll take you tomorrow. Today I clean the room. Tomorrow for sure."

"Are the boys well? Noblay and Gaur used to come, they too have stopped."

"All the bastards are selfish. Sons of my spunk after all. As inhuman as I."

"You'll come tomorrow?"

"Yes—yes—yes."

Jashoda smiled suddenly. A heart-splitting nostalgia-provoking smile.

Jashoda said, "Dear, remember?"

"What, wife?"

"How you played with these tits? You couldn't sleep otherwise? My lap was never empty, if this one left my nipple, there was that one, and then the boys of the Master's house. How I could, I wonder now!"

"I remember everything, wife!"

In this instant Kangali's words are true. Seeing Jashoda's broken, thin, suffering form even Kangali's selfish body and instincts and belly-centered consciousness remembered the past and suffered some empathy. He held Jashoda's hand and said, "You have fever?"

"I get feverish all the time. I think by the strength of the sores."

"Where does this rotten stink come from?"

"From these sores."

Jashoda spoke with her eyes closed. Then she said, "Bring the holy doctor. He cured Gopal's *typhoid* with *homeopathy*."

"I'll call him. I'll take you tomorrow."

Kangali left. That he went out, the tapping of his crutches, Jashoda couldn't hear. With her eyes shut, with the idea that Kangali was in the room, she said spiritlessly, "If you suckle you're a mother, all lies! Nepal and Gopal don't look at me, and the Master's boys don't spare a peek to ask how I'm doing." The sores on her breast kept mocking her with a hundred mouths, a hundred eyes. Jashoda opened her eyes and said, "Do you hear?"

Then she realized that Kangali had left.

In the night she sent Basini for *Lifebuoy* soap and at dawn she went to take a bath with the soap. Stink, what a stink! If the body of a dead cat or dog rots in the garbage can you get a smell like this. Jashoda had forever scrubbed her breasts carefully with soap and oil, for the master's sons had put the nipples in their mouth. Why did those breasts betray her in the end? Her skin burns with the sting of soap. Still Jashoda washed herself with soap. Her head was ringing, everything seemed dark. There was fire in Jashoda's body, in her head. The black floor was very cool. Jashoda spread her sari and lay down. She could not bear the weight of her breast standing up.

As Jashoda lay down, she lost sense and consciousness with fever. Kangali came at the proper time: but seeing Jashoda he lost his grip. Finally Nabin came and rasped, "Are these people human? She reared all the boys with her milk and they don't call a doctor? I'll call Hari the doctor."

Haribabu took one look at her and said, "Hospital."

Hospitals don't admit people who are so sick. At the efforts and recommendations of the eldest son, Jashoda was admitted.

"What's the matter? O Doctorbabu, what's the problem?"—Kangali asked, weeping like a boy.

"Cancer."

"You can get cancer in a tit?"

"Otherwise how did she get it?"

"Her own twenty, thirty boys at the Master's house—she had a lot of milk—"

"What did you say? How many did she *feed*?"

"About fifty for sure."

"Fif-ty!"

"Yes sir."

"She had twenty children?"

"Yes sir."

"*God!*"

"Sir!"

"What?"

"Is it because she suckled so many—?"

"One can't say why someone gets cancer, one can't say. But when people breast-feed too much—didn't you realize earlier? It didn't get to this in a day?"

"She wasn't with me, sir. We quarreled—"

"I see."

"How do you see her? Will she get well?"

"Get well! See how long she lasts. You've brought her in the last stages. No one survives this stage."

Kangali left weeping. In the late afternoon, harassed by Kangali's lamentations, the eldest son's second son went to the doctor. He was minimally anxious about Jashoda—but his father nagged him and he was financially dependent on his father.

The doctor explained everything to him. It happened not in a day, but over a long time. Why? No one could tell. How does one perceive breast cancer? A hard lump inside the breast toward the top can be removed. Then gradually the lump inside becomes large, hard, and like a congealed pressure. The skin is expected to turn orange, as is expected a shrinking of the nipple. The gland in the armpit can be inflamed. When there is *ulceration*, that is to say sores, one can call it the final stages. Fever? From the point of view of seriousness it falls in the second or third category. If there is something like a sore in the body, there can be fever. That is *secondary*.

The second son was confused with all this specialist talk. He said, "Will she live?"

"No."

"How long will she suffer?"

"I don't think too long."

"When there's nothing to be done, how will you treat her?"

"Painkiller, sedative, antibiotic for the fever. Her body is very, very *down."*

"She stopped eating."

"You didn't take her to a doctor?"

"Yes."

"Didn't he tell you?"

"Yes."

"What did he say?"

"That it might be cancer. Asked us to take her to the hospital. She didn't agree."

"Why would she? She'd die!"

The second son came home and said, "When Arun-doctor said she had *cancer,* she might have survived if treated then."

His mother said, "If you know that much then why didn't you take her? Did I stop you?"

Somewhere in the minds of the second son and his mother an unknown sense of guilt and remorse came up like bubbles in dirty and stagnant water and vanished instantly.

Guilt said—she lived with us, we never took a look at her, when did the disease catch her, we didn't take it seriously at all. She was a silly person, reared so many of us, we didn't look after her. Now, with everyone around her she's dying in hospital, so many children, husband living, when she clung to us, then we had _____! What an alive body she had, milk leaped out of her, we never thought she would have this disease.

The disappearance of guilt said—who can undo Fate? It was written that she'd die of *cancer*—who'd stop it? It would have been wrong if she had died here— her husband and sons would have asked, how did she die? We have been saved from that wrongdoing. No one can say anything.

The eldest son assured them, "Now Arun-doctor says no one survives *cancer.* The cancer that Brahmin-sister has can lead to cutting of the tit, removing the uterus, even after that people die of *cancer*. See, Father gave us a lot of reverence toward Brahmins—we are alive by father's grace. If Brahmin-sister had died in our house, we would have had to perform the penance-ritual."

Patients much less sick than Jashoda die much sooner. Jashoda astonished the doctors by hanging on for about a month in hospital. At first Kangali, Nabin, and the boys did indeed come and go, but Jashoda remained the same, comatose, cooking with fever, spellbound. The sores on her breast gaped more and more and the breast now looks like an open wound. It is covered by a piece of thin *gauze* soaked in *antiseptic lotion,* but the sharp smell of putrefying flesh is cir- culating silently in the room's air like incense-smoke. This brought an ebb in the enthusiasm of Kangali and the other visitors. The doctor said as well, "Is she not responding? All for the better. It's hard to bear without consciousness, can anyone bear such death-throes consciously?"

"Does she know that we come and go?"

"Hard to say."

"Does she eat."

"Through tubes."

"Do people live this way?"

"Now you're very _____"

The doctor understood that he was unreasonably angry because Jashoda was in this condition. He was angry with Jashoda, with Kangali, with women who don't take the signs of breast-cancer *seriously* enough and finally die in this dreadful and hellish pain. Cancer constantly defeats patient and doctor. One patient's cancer means the patient's death and the defeat of science, and of course of the doctor. One can medicate against the secondary symptom, if eating stops one can *drip glucose* and feed the body, if the lungs become incapable of breathing there is *oxygen*—but the advance of *cancer*, its expansion, spread, and killing, remain unchecked. The word *cancer* is a general signifier, by which in the different parts of the body is meant different *malignant growths*. Its characteristic properties are to destroy the infected area of the body, to spread by *metastasis*, to return after *removal*, to create *toximeia*.

Kangali came out without a proper answer to his question. Returning to the temple, he said to Nabin and his sons, "There's no use going any more. She doesn't know us, doesn't open her eyes, doesn't realize anything. The doctor is doing what he can."

Nabin said, "If she dies?"

"They have the *telephone number* of the old Master's eldest son, they'll call."

"Suppose she wants to see you. Kangali, your wife is a blessed auspicious faithful woman! Who would say the mother of so many. To see her body—but she didn't bend, didn't look elsewhere."

Talking thus, Nabin became gloomily silent. In fact, since he'd seen Jashoda's infested breasts, many a philosophic thought and sexological argument have been slowly circling Nabin's drug-and-booze-addled dim head like great rutting snakes emptied of venom. For example, I lusted after her? This is the end of that intoxicating bosom? Ho! Man's body's a zero. To be crazy for that is to be crazy.

Kangali didn't like all this talk. His mind had already *rejected* Jashoda. When he saw Jashoda in the Haldar-house he was truly affected and even after her admission into hospital he was passionately anxious. But now that feeling is growing cold. The moment the doctor said Jashoda wouldn't last, he put her out of mind almost painlessly. His sons are his sons. Their mother had become a distant person for a long time. Mother meant hair in a huge topknot, blindingly white clothes, a strong personality. The person lying in the hospital is someone else, not Mother.

Breast *cancer* makes the *brain comatose*, this was a solution for Jashoda.

Jashoda understood that she had come to hospital, she was in the hospital, and that this desensitizing sleep was a medicated sleep. In her weak, infected, dazed brain she thought, has some son of the Haldar-house become a doctor? No doubt he sucked her milk and is now repaying the milk-debt? But those boys entered the family business as soon as they left high school! However, why don't the people who are helping her so much free her from the stinking presence of her chest? What a smell, what treachery? Knowing these breasts to be the rice-winner, she had constantly conceived to keep them filled with milk. The breast's job is to hold milk. She kept her breast clean with perfumed soap, she never wore a top, even in youth, because her breasts were so heavy.

When the *sedation* lessens, Jashoda screams, "Ah! Ah! Ah!"—and looks for the *nurse* and the doctor with passionate bloodshot eyes. When the doctor comes, she mutters with hurt feelings, "You grew so big on my milk, and now you're hurting me so?"

The doctor says, "She sees her milk-sons all over the world."

Again injection and sleepy numbness. Pain, tremendous pain, the cancer is spreading *at the expense of the human host*. Gradually Jashoda's left breast bursts and becomes like the *crater* of a volcano. The smell of putrefaction makes approach difficult.

Finally one night, Jashoda understood that her feet and hands were getting cold. She understood that death was coming. Jashoda couldn't open her eyes, but she understood that some people were looking at her hand. A needle pricked her arm. Painful breathing inside. Has to be. Who is looking? Are these her own people? The people whom she suckled because she carried them, or those she suckled for a living? Jashoda thought, after all, she had suckled the world, could she then die alone? The doctor who sees her every day, the person who will cover her face with a sheet, will put her on a cart, will lower her at the burning ghat, the untouchable who will put her in the furnace, are all her milk-sons. One must become Jashoda* if one suckles the world. One has to die friendless, with no one left to put a bit of water in the mouth. Yet someone was supposed to be there at the end. Who was it? It was who? Who was it?

Jashoda died at 11 p.m.

The Halder-house was called on the phone. The phone didn't ring. The Haldars *disconnected* their phone at night.

Jashoda Devi, Hindu female, lay in the hospital morgue in the usual way, went to the burning ghat in a van, and was burnt. She was cremated by an untouchable.

Jashoda was God manifest, others do and did whatever she thought. Jashoda's death was also the death of God. When a mortal masquerades as God here below, she is forsaken by all and she must always die alone.

1987

---

* *The mythic mother of Krishna, and in that sense the suckler of the world.* [GCS]

14. A Literary Representation of The Subaltern: A Woman's Text From the Third World[1]

A historian confronts a text of counterinsurgency or gendering where the subaltern has been represented. He unravels the text to assign a new subject-position to the subaltern, gendered or otherwise.

A teacher of literature confronts a sympathetic text where the gendered subaltern has been represented. She unravels the text to make visible the assignment of subject-positions.

These two operations are similar but not identical. By way of a teaching strategy for Mahasweta Devi's "Stanadayini" [Breast-Giver], this paper circulates among the similarities and differences.[2] By its end, I will hope to have importuned the reader at least to entertain the following propositions:

a. The performance of these tasks, of the historian and the teacher of literature, must critically "interrupt" each other, bring each other to crisis, in order to serve their constituencies; especially when each seems to claim all for its own.

b. The teacher of literature, because of her institutional subject-position, can and must "re-constellate" the text to draw out its use. She can and must wrench it out of its proper context and put it within alien arguments.

c. If thus placed in the arguments from Western Marxist-Feminism, Western Liberal Feminism, and French high theory of the Female Body, "Stanadayini" can show us some of their limits and limitations.

d. This might have implications for the current and continued subalternization of so-called "third world" literatures.

The paper will also touch upon the always tendentious question of elite methodologies and subaltern material. I suppose it needs to be said that the problem of "what to *do*" about the gendered subaltern cannot be solved in any interpretive essay, historical or literary. A paper such as this one can perhaps give an idea of the extent and politics of the problem somewhat more soberly than invocations of the immediacy of the need for social justice or the ineluctability of a woman's domain.

1. The Historian and the Teacher of Literature

The production of historical accounts is the discursive narrativization of events. When historiography is self-consciously "non-theoretical," it sees its task, with respect to rival historical accounts of the same period, as bringing forth "what really happened" in a value-neutral prose. Since the incursion of "theory" into the discipline of history, and the uncomfortable advent of Michel

Foucault, it is no longer too avant-garde to suspect or admit that "events" are never not discursively constituted and that the language of historiography is always also language.

> The fact that every object is constituted as an object of discourse has *nothing to do* with whether there is a world external to thought, or with the realism/ idealism opposition. An earthquake or the falling of a brick is an event that certainly exists. . . . But whether their specificity as objects is constructed in terms of "natural phenomena" or "expressions of the wrath of God" depends upon the structure of a discursive field. What is denied is not that such objects exist externally to thought, but the rather different assertion that they would constitute themselves as objects outside any discursive condition of emergence.[3]

The thought of "how events exist" can itself be complicated in different ways via say, Heidegger or particle physics; and I remain troubled by anything that claims to have nothing to do with its opposition.[4] Avoiding these perils, however, one might still posit an active relationship between historical and literary representation as discursive formations. With this in mind, let us consider a celebrated passage in the early Foucault, which establishes "discourse" in the sense in which Laclau and Mouffe use it above.

The problem examined in the Foucauldian passage is not merely if *events* exist outside of discourse but also if language (sentences, propositions, signs) exists only to report events. Foucault is making a distinction between language as sentence, proposition, and sign and what he calls "statement" [*énonciation*].

Among other things, a statement is "a function of existence" of language "on the basis of which one may . . . decide . . . whether or not [it] 'make[s] sense'."[5] A "statement" involves the positioning of a subject (the place of the "I"):

> The subject of the statement should not be regarded as identical with the author of the formulation. It is not in fact the cause, origin, or starting-point of the phenomenon of the written or spoken articulation of a sentence . . . it is not the constant, motionless, unchanging arena [*foyer*] of a series of operations . . . It is a determined [*determinée*] and vacant place that may in fact be filled by different individuals. . . . If a proposition, a sentence, a group of signs can be called "statement," it is not in so far as there had been [*dans la mesure ou il y a eu*] one day someone to utter [*proférer*] them or to deposit somewhere their provisional mark [*en deposer quelque part la trace provisoire*]; it is in so far as [*dans la mesure ou*] *the position of the subject can be assigned.* To describe a formulation qua statement does not consist in analyzing the relations between the author and what he says (or wanted to say, or said without wanting to); but in determining what position can and must be occupied by any individual if he is to be the subject of it.[6]

This understanding of a statement does not entail ignoring what it is that sentences report or tell. It is the precondition for the analysis of how the what is made. That is what a "discursive formation" is: "the formation of objects, the formation of enunciative modalities, the formation of concepts, the formation of strategies."[7] Not even the simplest reporting or telling can avoid these maneuvers. Foucault asks us to remember that what is reported or told is also reported or told and thus entails a positioning of the subject. Further, that anyone dealing with a report or a tale (the material of historiography or literary pedagogy) can and must occupy a certain "I"-slot in these dealings. The particularity of this "I"-slot is a sign. It may for instance signify a sociopolitical, psycho-sexual, disciplinary-institutional or ethno-economic provenance. Hence, Foucault uses the word "assigned": "the position of the subject can be assigned." There may be a hidden agenda in covering over this rather obvious thing. For the purposes of this essay, the "I"-slots (subject-positions) to be kept in mind are: author, reader, teacher, subaltern, historian.

It is well-known that Foucault was finally disaffected from this project.[8] But many of the subalternist historians are, in my judgment wisely, working within its wider implications. One of these implications is that the archival or archaeological work of historiography might resemble a certain work of reading which is usually associated with literary interpretation if it is detached from its psychologistic or characterological orthodoxy. In this view, it is as if the narrativizations of history are structured or textured like what is called literature. Here one must re-think the notion that fiction derives from truth as its negation. In the context of archival historiography, the possibility of fiction cannot be derived.[9]

That history deals with real events and literature with imagined ones may now be seen as a difference in degree rather than in kind. The difference between cases of historical and literary events will always be there as a differential moment in terms of what is called "the effect of the real".[10] What is called history will always seem more real to us than what is called literature. Our very uses of the two separate words guarantees that.[11] This difference can never be exhaustively systematized. In fact, the ways in which the difference is articulated also has a hidden agenda. The historians' resistance to fiction relates to the fact that the writing of history and of literature has a social connotation even when these activities do not resemble what we understand by them today; and that historiography and literary pedagogy are disciplines.

Mahasweta Devi's own relationship to historical discourse seems clear. She has always been gripped by the individual in history. Up to and including *Hajar Churashir Ma* (1973–74) her prose belonged to the generally sentimental style of the mainstream Bengali novel of the fifties and the sixties. To this reader it seems as if the vision of *Hajar Churashir Ma*—the bringing-to-crisis of the personal through a political event of immediate magnitude (the "climactic phase of the annihilation of the urban naxalites") pushed Mahasweta from what was perceived as "literary" or "subjective" into an experiment with a form perceived as "historical."[12] The stories of *Agnigarbha* (collected in 1978) mark the site of this difficult move. In *Aranyer Adhikar* (1977) the prose is beginning to bend into full-fledged "historical fiction," history imagined into fiction. The division between fact (historical event) and fiction (literary event) is operative in all these moves. Indeed, her repeated claim to legitimacy is that she researches thoroughly everything she represents in fiction.

Fiction of this sort relies for its effect on its "effect of the real." The plausibility of a Jashoda ("Stanadayini"), a Draupadi ("Draupadi," *Agnigarbha*), a Birsha Munda (*Aranyer Adhikar*) is that they could have existed as subalterns in a specific historical moment imagined and tested by orthodox assumptions. When the subalternist historian imagines a historical moment, within which shadowy named characters, backed up by some counter-insurgent or dominant-gender textual material, have their plausible being, in order that a historical narrative can coherently take shape, the assumptions are not very different. Those who read or write literature can claim as little of subaltern status as those who read or write history. The difference is that the subaltern as object is supposed to be imagined in one case and real in another. I am suggesting that it is a bit of both in both cases. The writer acknowledges this by claiming to do research (my fiction is also historical). The historian might acknowledge this by looking at the mechanics of representation (my history is also fictive). It is with this suggestion that I submit the following pages to the Subaltern Studies collective. I hope it will be admitted that my brief is very different from saying that history is only literature.

2. The Author's Own Reading: A Subject Position

By Mahasweta Devi's own account, "Stanadayini" is a parable of India after decolonization.[13] Like the protagonist Jashoda, India is a mother-by-hire. All classes of people, the post-war rich, the ideologues, the indigenous bureaucracy, the diasporics, the people who are sworn to protect the new state, abuse and exploit her. If nothing is done to sustain her, nothing given back to her, and if scientific help comes too late, she will die of a consuming cancer. I suppose if one extended this parable the end of the story might come to "mean" something like this: the ideological construct "India" is too deeply informed by the goddess-infested reverse sexism of the Hindu majority. As long as there is this hegemonic cultural self-representation of India as a goddess-mother (dissimulating the possibility that this mother is a slave), she will collapse under the burden of the immense expectations that such a self-representation permits.

This interesting reading is not very useful from the perspective of a study of the subaltern. Here the representation of India is by way of the subaltern as metaphor. By the rules of a parable the logic of the connection between the tenor and the vehicle of the metaphor must be made absolutely explicit.[14] Under the imperatives of such a reading, the "effect of the real" of the vehicle must necessarily be underplayed. The subaltern must be seen only as the vehicle of a greater meaning. The traffic between the historian and the writer that I have been proposing could not be justified if one devoted oneself to this reading. In order that Mahasweta's parable be disclosed, what must be excluded from the story is precisely the attempt to represent the subaltern as such. I will therefore take the risk of putting to one side that all too neat reading, and unravel the text to pick up the threads of the excluded attempt.

This takes me to a general argument implicit within the study of the subaltern in the context of decolonization: if the story of the rise of nationalist resistance to imperialism is to be disclosed coherently, it is the role of the indigenous subaltern that must be strategically excluded. Then it can be argued that, in the initial stages of the consolidation of territorial imperialism, no organized political resistance was forthcoming. Through access to the cultural aspects of imperialism, the colonized countries acceded to sentiments of nationhood. It was then that genuine anti-imperialist resistance developed.[15]

As in the case of the opposition between fact and fiction, there is a certain paratheoretical good sense in this. The exclusions that must operate in order to preserve that good sense are at least two-fold. First, if nationalism is the *only* discourse credited with emancipatory possibilities in the imperialist theater, then one must ignore the innumerable subaltern examples of resistance throughout the imperialist and pre-imperialist centuries, often suppressed by those very forces of nationalism which would be instrumental in changing the geo-political conjuncture from territorial imperialism to neo-colonialism, and which seem particularly useless in current situations of struggle.[16] Secondly, if *only* the emancipatory possibilities of the culture of imperialism are taken into account, the distortions in the ideals of a national culture when imported into a colonial theater would go unnoticed.[17]

Citizens of the nation must give something to the nation rather than merely take from it, the gist of Mahasweta's own reading of "Stanadayini," is one of the many slogans of a militant nationalism. It can accommodate sentiments extending from "*sat koti santanere he mugdha janani, rekhechho bangali kore manush karoni.* ['Fond mother, you have kept your seventy million children Bengalis but haven't made them human"—Tagore] to "Ask not what your country can do for you" (John F. Kennedy, Inaugural Address). In spite of the best possible personal politics, the reading Mahasweta Devi offers of her own story, entailing her subject-position as writer, signifies that narrative of nationalism that is perceived as a product of the culture of imperialism. This too obliges me to set it aside and to wonder what her text, as statement, articulates that must in its turn be set aside so that her reading can emerge.

3. The Teacher and Reader(s): More Subject-Positions

Mahasweta's text might show in many ways how the narratives of nationalism have been and remain irrelevant to the life of the subordinate. The elite culture of nationalism participated and participates with the colonizer in various ways.[18] In Mahasweta's story we see the detritus of that participation. In a certain sense, we witness there the ruins of the ideas of parliamentary democracy and of the nation when bequeathed to the elite of a colonized people outside the supposedly "natural" soil of the production of those ideas. Some of us would speculate that, used as a teaching tool (from within the subject-position of the teacher in a certain discursive formation), stories such as this can deconstruct those ideas even in their natural habitat. It is for us important that, in "Stanadayini," the piece of flotsam least susceptible to those ideas is the subaltern as gendered subject, a subject-position different from the subaltern as class-subject. In orthodox literary-critical circles, the authority of the author's reading still holds a certain glamor. By way of Foucault, I have therefore taken some pains to explain why I focus on the subaltern as gendered subject rather than as an allegorical seme for Mother India.

If "the need to make the subaltern classes the subject of their own history [has, among other] themes . . . provided a fresh critical thrust to much recent writing on modern Indian history and society," then a text about the (im)possibility of "making" the subaltern gender the subject of its own story seems to me to have a certain pertinence.[19] Toward the end of this essay, I will discuss the need to put the "im" of "impossible" in parentheses.

Accounts of history and literary pedagogy, as they appropriate and disseminate reports and tales, are two ways in which mind-sets are set.[20] The reading of "Stanadayini" presented here, assigning the subject-position to the teacher/reader, can be helpful in combating a certain tendency in literary pedagogy that still shapes, by remote control, the elite in the most prestigious Indian educational institutions: the so-called radical teaching of literary criticism and literature in the United States and perhaps also in Britain.

This dominant *radical* reader in the Anglo-U.S. reactively homogenizes the Third World and sees it only in the context of nationalism and ethnicity. The dominant reader in India who is resistant to such homogenization, and who is to be distinguished from students of reading theory in elite Indian institutions, inhabits a reading practice that is indistinguishable from the *orthodox* position in the Anglo-U.S. The Indian reader, a faceless person within the sphere of influence of a post-colonial humanistic education (I use this awkward terminology because sociologists, economists, doctors, scientists, et cetera are not outside of this sphere), takes this orthodox position to be the "natural" way to read literature. The position is undergirded by the author's account of her "original vision." In this particular case, that account (the reading of the story as a parable) would forbid the fulfillment of another assumption implicit in the orthodox position, the psychologistic or characterological assumption that we "feel" the story as if it is gossip about nonexistent people. The general reader can straddle such contradictions easily. The historians, anthropologists, sociologists, and doctors among them can know or show that any group's perception of the "natural" meanings of things may be discursively constructed through an erring common sense. When, however, it comes to their own presuppositions about the "natural" way to read literature, they cannot admit that this might be a construction as well, that this subject-position might also be assigned. Given that this way of reading has been in control for at least a couple of centuries in post-Enlightenment Europe, and has served to distinguish our indigenous elite from the uneducated, to read thus certainly engages our affects.[21] I will not enter the abstruse arguments about the historicity or phenomenality of affects.[22] Nor will I suggest that there is a correct way to train our affects. Indeed, it is not only "false consciousness" that is "ideological." A Foucauldian or, in this case, deconstructive position would oblige us to admit that "truths" are constructions as well, and that we cannot avoid producing them.

Without venturing up to the perilous necessity of asking the question of true readings or true feelings, then, I will propose an alternative. Let us jealously guard the orthodoxy's right to be "moved" by literature "naturally," and tremble before the author's authority. By a slightly different argument, let us consider "literature" as a use of language where the transactional quality of reading is socially guaranteed. A literary text exists between writer and reader. This makes literature peculiarly susceptible to didactic use. When literature is used didactically, it is generally seen as a site for the deployment of "themes," even the theme of the undoing of thematicity, of unreadability, of undecidability.[23] This is not a particularly "elite" approach, although it may be called "unnatural." On the one hand, Marxist literary criticism as well as a remark like Chinua Achebe's "all art is propaganda, though not all propaganda is art" can be taken as cases of such a "thematic" approach.[24] On the other hand, some "elite" approaches (deconstructive, structuralist, semiotic, structuralist-psychoanalytic, phenomenological, discourse-theoretical; though not necessarily feminist, reader-responsist, intertextual, or linguistic) can also be accommodated here.

(Any reader nervous about the fact that Mahasweta Devi has probably not read much of the material critically illuminated by her text should stop here.)

4. (Elite) Approaches: "Stanadayini" in Marxist Feminism

An allegorical or parabolic reading of "Stanadayini" such as Mahasweta's own would reduce the complexity of the signals put up by the text. Let us consider another reductive allegorical or parabolic reading. This reading can be uncovered in terms of a so-called Marxist-feminist thematics. Peculiar to the orthodoxy of U.S. Marxist-feminism and some, though not all, British varieties, these thematics unfold in a broadly pre-Althusserian way.[25]

Here is a representative generalization: "It is the provision by men of means of subsistence to women during the child-bearing period, and not the sex division of labor in itself, that forms the material basis for women's subordination in class society."[26]

If one were teaching "Stanadayini" as the site of a critical deployment of Marxist-feminist thematics, one would point out that the text reverses this generalization. The protagonist subaltern Jashoda, her husband crippled by the youngest son of a wealthy household, becomes a wet-nurse for them. Her repeated gestation and lactation support her husband and family. By the logic of the production of value, they are both means of production. By the logic of sexual reproduction, he is her means of production (though not owned by her) as the field-beast or the beast of burden is the slave's. In fact, even as it reverses the Marxist-feminist generalization I quote above, Jashoda's predicament also undoes, by placing within a gender-context, the famous Roman distinction, invoked by Marx, between *instrumentum vocale* ("the speaking tool"—Jashoda, the woman-wife-mother) and *instrumentum semi-vocale* (the working beast—Kangali, the man-husband-father).[27] This is worth noticing because one of the most important Marxist-feminist critiques of the labor theory of value is that it does not take sexual reproduction into account when speaking of social reproduction or the reproduction of labor-power.[28]

The political economy or the sexual division of labor changes considerably by the sale of Jashoda's labor-power, which is specific to the female of the species. One may even call this a moment of transition from one mode of social reproduction to another. Or perhaps one could call it the moment of the emergence of value and its immediate extraction and appropriation. These changes take place within extended domestic economy. One might therefore call it a transition from the domestic to the "domestic." "Stanadayini" stalls the classic Engelsian-feminist narrative, which sees the family as the agent of transition from domestic to civil, private to public, home to work, sex to class. It should be pointed out that it also displaces the new Marxist-feminist critique of such a position (which I quote below) by bringing back the focus on the mothering female: "The identification of the family as the sole site of maintenance of labor power overstates its role at the level of immediate production. It fetishizes the family at the level of total social reproduction, by representing generational replacement as the only source of renewal of society's labor force."[29]

The emergence of (exchange) value and its immediate appropriation in "Stanadayini" may be thematized as follows:

The milk that is produced in one's own body for one's own children is a use-value. When there is a superfluity of use values, exchange values arise. That which cannot be used is exchanged. As soon as the (exchange) value of Jashoda's milk emerges, it is appropriated. Good food and constant sexual servicing are provided so that she can be kept in prime condition for optimum lactation. The milk she produces for her children is presumably through "necessary labor." The milk that she produces for the children of her master's family is through "surplus labor." Indeed, this is how the origin of this transition is described in the story: "But today, hearing from his wife about Jashoda's *surplus* [in English in the original] milk, the second son said all of a sudden, 'way found'" (227).

In order to keep her in prime condition to produce surplus, the sexual division of labor is easily reversed. Her husband is relegated to housework. "Now take up the cooking at home and give her a rest," says the Mistress. "Two of her own, three here, how can she cook at day's end after suckling five?" (p. 228) This particular parabolic or allegoric reading is not necessarily disqualified by the fact that Jashoda's body produces a surplus that is fully consumed by the owners of her labor-power and leads to no *capital* accumulation (as it would have if the milk had been bottled and sold in the open market at a profit), although rearing children is indirectly an "investment in the future." Like the economy of the temple (which will provide the husband a patriarchal escape route), this domestic/"domestic" transition survives in a relatively autonomous way in the pores of a comprador capitalism whose outlines are only shadowily indicated in Mahasweta's story. If within this pre-capitalist surplus-appropriation we assumed Jashoda's milk to be standing in for the "universal equivalent" in the restricted "domestic" sphere, we might get away with pronouncing that the situation is what Marx, with obviously unwitting irony, would describe as "simple reproduction."[30]

This account of the deployment of some Marxist-feminist "themes" introduces a stutter in the pre-supposition that women's work is typically non-productive of value. I am not considering women's insertion into the labor-process. In that narrative woman is less than the norm of "free labor." I am half-fantasizing, rather, about an area where the product of a woman's body has been historically susceptible to idealization—just as, in the classical Marxian argument, the reason why the free (male) laborer becomes a "proletarian" under capitalism is not that he has nothing but his body but that, his product, being a value-term, is susceptible to idealization. The commodity, by the same token, is susceptible to being transformed to commodity-capital.[31] Yet the word "proletarian"—"one who serves the state with nothing but his [sic] offspring" (OED)—continues to carry an effaced mark of sexuality. Am I then proposing to endorse some weird theory where labor-power is replaced by the power of gestation and lactation? Or am I suggesting that the study of this particular female activity, professional mothering, as it is to be found, for example, in Fanny Fay-Sallois's excellent *Les Nourrices à Paris aux XIX siècle*, be included in any study of the subaltern?[32]

I am suggesting both less and more. I see no particular reason to curtail the usefulness of classical Marxist analysis, within its own limits, by a tendentious requirement for uncritical inclusiveness. Any critique of strategic exclusions should bring analytical presuppositions to crisis. Marxism and feminism must become persistent interruptions of each other. The "mode of existence" of literature, as of language, is where "the task of understanding does not basically amount to *recognizing* the form used, but . . . to understanding its novelty and *not* to recognizing its identity . . . The understander, belonging to the same language community, is attuned to the linguistic form *not* as a fixed, self-identical signal, but as a changeable and adaptable sign. . . . The ideal of mastering a language is absorption of signality by pure semioticity."[33]

As the user, occupying different instituted "I"-slots, understands the supposedly self-identical signal, always supposedly indicating the same thing, she persistently distances herself, in heterogeneous ways, from that monumentalized self-identity, the "proper meaning."[34] We can use "Stanadayini," a discursive literary production, from the perspective of Marxist-feminist thematics by considering how it helps us distance ourselves from two self-identical propositions that ground much of subalternist analysis implicitly:

a. that the free worker as such is male (hence the narrative of value-emergence and value-appropriation; the labor power specific to the female body is susceptible to the production of value in the strict sense);

b. that the *nature* of woman is physical, nurturing and affective (hence the professional-mother).

A good deal of feminist scholarship has reasonably and soberly analyzed and revised these propositions in recent years.[35] I will consider two provocative examples at the end of this section. Such painstaking speculative scholarship, though invaluable to our collective enterprise does, however, *reason* gender into existing paradigms.[36] By contrast, emphasizing the literariness of literature, pedagogy invites us to take a distance from the continuing project of reason. Without this supplementary distancing, a position and its counter-position, both held in the discourse of reason, will keep legitimizing each other. Feminism and masculism, benevolent or militant, might not then be able to avoid becoming opposing faces of each other.[37]

Resuming, then, our fabulation with Marxist-feminist thematics on the occasion of "Stanadayini," let us consider Jashoda's "alienation" from her breasts:

> She thought of her breasts as most precious objects. At night when Kangalicharan [her husband] started to give her a feel she said "Look. I'm going to pull our weight with these. Take good care how you use them." Jashoda had forever scrubbed her breasts carefully with soap and oil, for the master's sons had put the nipples in their mouth. Why did these breasts betray her in the end? . . . . Knowing these breasts to be the rice-winner she had constantly conceived to keep them filled with milk (pp. 228, 236, 240).

Just as the wage-worker cannot distinguish between necessary and surplus labor, so the gendered "proletarian"—serving the *oikos* rather than the *polis* with nothing but her (power to produce) offspring—comes to call the so-called sanctity of motherhood into question. At first Mahasweta broaches it derisively:

> Is a Mother so cheaply made?
> Not just by dropping a babe. (p. 228)

Finally it becomes part of Jashoda's last sentient judgment: " 'If you suckle you're a mother, all lies! Nepal and Gopal [her own sons] don't look at me, and the Master's boys don't spare a peek to ask how I'm doing.' The sores on her breast kept mocking her with a hundred mouths, a hundred eyes" (p. 236).

By contrast, her final judgment, the universalization of foster-motherhood, is a "mistake": "The doctor who sees her every day, the person who will cover her face with a sheet, will put her on a cart, will lower her at the burning ghat, the untouchable who will put her in the furnace, are all her milk-sons" (p. 240). Such a judgment can only be "right" within the pieties of Mahasveta's own nationalist reading.

The Marxian fable of a transition from the domestic to the "domestic" mode of social reproduction has no more than a strained plausibility here. In order to construct it, one must entertain a grounding assumption, that the originary state of "necessary labor" is where the lactating mother produces a use value. For whose use? If you consider her in a subject-position, it is a situation of exchange, with the child, for immediate and future psycho-social affect. Even if we read the story as a proto-nationalist parable about Mother India, it is the failure of this exchange that is the substance of the story. It is this failure, the absence of the child as such, that is marked by the enigmatic answer-question-parataxis toward the conclusion: "Yet someone was supposed to be there at the end. Who was it? It was who? Who was it? Jashoda died at 11 p.m." (p. 240).

By dismantling (professional) motherhood and suckling into their minute particulars, "Stanadayini" allows us to differentiate ourselves from the axiomatics of a certain "Marxist-feminism" which is obliged to ignore the subaltern woman as subject.

If Lise Vogel, from whom I drew my representative generalization, signals a certain orthodoxy, Anne Ferguson, in "On Conceiving Motherhood," shows us a way out of it via the question of affect:

> Although different societies have had different modes of sex/affective production at different times, a cross-cultural constant is involved in different modes of bourgeois patriarchal sex/affective production. This is that women as mothers are placed in a structural bind by mother-centered infant and small child care, a bind that ensures that mothers will give more than they get in the sex/affective parenting triangle in which even lesbian and single parents are subjected.[38]

"Mothers will give more than they get." If this broad generalization is broadened so that the distinction between domestic ("natural" mother) and "domestic" (waged wet-nurse) disappears, this can certainly serve as a constant for us and can be a good tool for our students.[39] Yet it should also be acknowledged that such a broadening might make us misrepresent important details. A text such as "Stanadayini," even if taught as nothing but sociological evidence, can show how imprecise it is to write: "In stratified class and caste societies, different economic classes and racial/ethnic groups may hold different sex/gender ideals, although when this happens the lower classes are usually categorized as inferior male and female types by nature."[40] (I am referring, of course, to the class-subalternity of the Brahmin and the grotesque functioning of caste markers within subalternity. Jashoda is a complicit victim of all these factors.) It is possible that it is not only "the relationship between the three domination systems [class, racial/ethnic, and sex/gender]" that is "dialectical" but that in the theaters of decolonization, the relationship between indigenous and imperialist systems of domination are also "dialectical," even when they are variously related to the Big Three Systems cited above. Indeed, the relationship might not be "dialectical" at all but discontinuous, "interruptive."

It is often the case that revisionist socialist-feminism trivializes basic issues in the Marxist system.[41] Ferguson writes, for example: "My theory, unlike one tendency within classic marxist theory, does not privilege the economic realm (the production of *things* to meet human material needs and the manner in which

the social surplus gets appropriated) as the material base for all human domination relations. . . . The production of things and the production of people . . .
interpenetrate."[42]

This is an excellent advance on generalizations such as Vogel's. But it is an
oversimplification of Marx's view of the economic sphere. That sphere is the
site of the production of *value*, not *things*. As I have mentioned earlier, it is the
body's susceptibility to the production of value which makes it vulnerable to
idealization and therefore to insertion into the economic. This is the ground of
the labor theory of value. It is here that the story of the emergence of value
from Jashoda's labor-power infiltrates Marxism and questions its gender-specific
presuppositions. The production of people through sexual reproduction and
affective socialization, on the other hand, presupposes mothers embodied not
as female humans but only as mothers and belongs properly speaking to the
sphere of politics and ideology (domination).[43] Of course it interpenetrates the
economic sphere (exploitation), the sphere of the production of value, of the
sustained alienation of the body to which the very nature of labor-power makes
the body susceptible. In spite of the greatest sympathy for the mother, Ferguson's ignoring of the mother's body obliges her to ignore the woman as subject
of the production of value. "Stanadayini"'s lesson may be simply this: when
the economic as such (here shown in terms of the woman's body) enters in,
mothers are divided, women can exploit, not merely dominate. Ideology sustains and interpenetrates this operation of exploitation.

Anna Davin's meticulous "Imperialism and Motherhood" shows us the development of sex/affective control within the context of class-struggle. ("Imperialism" and "War" here are political signifiers used for ideological mobilization.)[44] In Davin's account, the great narrative of the development of
capitalism is untroubled by discontinuities and interruptions. She describes the
construction of the British National Subject on the bodies of British mothers.[45]
Public opinion is under active construction so that the working of the privates
may be adjudicated. *Mutatis mutandis*, echoes of these arguments from eugenics
and educated mothercraft can be heard among the Indian indigenous elite today.
The space where Jashoda, burdened by her ideological production, nourishes
her cancer, is not accessible to that narrative.

In Davin's essay, the central reference point is class. The *oikos* is fully a metaphor for the *polis*. Foster-mothers are Virgin Mothers. Christianity, the official
religion, gives a little help to the ideology of the secular state.

The lack of fit between this neat narrative and the bewildering cacophony of
"Stanadayini" permits us to ask: why globalize? Why should a sociological study
that makes astute generalizations about sex/affective production in the United
States feel obliged to produce a "cross-cultural constant"? Why should a study
that exposes gender-mobilization in Britain purport to speak on the relationship
between imperialism and motherhood? Why, on the contrary, does "Stanadayini" invoke the singularity of the gendered subaltern? What is at stake here?
How are these stakes different from those of imperialism as such? The story will
make us come back to these questions.

5. Elite Approaches: "Stanadayini" in Liberal Feminism

There is a tendency in the U.S. towards homogenizing and reactive critical descriptions of Third World literatures. There is a second tendency, not necessarily related to the first, to pedagogic and curricular appropriation of Third World women's texts in translation by feminist teachers and readers who are vaguely aware of the race-bias within mainstream feminism: "Black and Third World feminist organizations are thus developing within different racial and ethnic communities as an attempt to resolve intra-community the social crisis of the family and personal intimacy presently occurring across racial/ethnic lines. Influential members and groups within the white women's movements are presently seeking to make coalitions with black feminists, in part by dealing with the racism within the white women's movement."[46]

There are problems with this basically benevolent impulse which are increasingly under scrutiny.[47] The ravenous hunger for Third World literary texts in English translation is part of the benevolence and the problem. Since by translating this text I am contributing to both, I feel obliged to notice the text's own relationship to the thematics of liberal feminism. This will permit me also to touch directly the question of elite approaches to subaltern material.

Resisting "elite" methodology for "subaltern" material involves an epistemological/ontological confusion. The confusion is held in an unacknowledged analogy: just as the subaltern *is* not elite (ontology), so must the historian not *know* through elite method (epistemology).

This is part of a much larger confusion: can men theorize feminism, can whites theorize racism, can the bourgeois theorize revolution and so on.[48] It is when *only* the former groups theorize that the situation is politically intolerable. Therefore it is crucial that members of these groups are kept vigilant about their assigned subject-positions. It is disingenuous, however, to forget that, as the collectivities implied by the second group of nouns start participating in the production of knowledge about themselves, they must have a share in some of the structures of privileges that contaminate the first group. (Otherwise the ontological errors are perpetuated: it is unfortunate simply to *be* a woman—now a man; to *be* a black—now a white; and to *be* subaltern—now elite—is only the fault of the individual.) Therefore did Gramsci speak of the subaltern's rise into hegemony; and Marx of associated labor benefitting from "the forms that are common to all social modes of production."[49] This is also the reason behind one of the assumptions of subalternist work: that the subaltern's own idiom did not allow him to *know* his struggle so that he could articulate himself as its subject.

If the woman/black/subaltern, possessed through struggle of some of the structures previously metonymic as men/white/elite, continues to exercise a self-marginalized purism, and if the benevolent members of the man/white/elite participate in the marginalization and thus legitimate the bad old days, we have a caricature of correct politics that leaves alone the field of continuing subalternization. It is the *loneliness* of the gendered subaltern that is staged in "Stanadayini."

(The position that only the subaltern can know the subaltern, only women can know women and so on, cannot be held as a theoretical presupposition either, for it predicates the possibility of knowledge on identity. Whatever the political necessity for holding the position, and whatever the advisability of attempting to "identify" (with) the other as subject in order to know her, knowledge is made possible and is sustained by irreducible difference, not identity. What is known is always in excess of knowledge. Knowledge is never adequate to its object. The theoretical model of the ideal knower in the embattled position we are discussing is that of the person identical with her predicament. This is actually the figure of the impossibility and non-necessity of knowledge. Here the relationship between the practical—need for claiming subaltern identity—and the theoretical—no program of knowledge production can presuppose identity as origin—is, once again, of an "interruption" that persistently brings each term to crisis.)

By drawing attention to the complicity between hegemonic (here U.S.) and orthodox (here Indian) readings, I have been attempting to attend to the continuing subalternization of Third World material. At this point, I hope it will come as no surprise that a certain version of the elite vs. subaltern position is perpetuated by non-Marxist anti-racist feminism in the Anglo-U.S. toward Third World women's texts in translation. (The group covers the spectrum from anti-Marxism through romantic anti-capitalism into corporatism—I will call the ensemble "liberal feminism" for terminological convenience.) The position is exacerbated by the fact that liberal feminist Third Worldist criticism often chooses as its constituency the indigenous post-colonial elite, diasporic or otherwise.

If Mahasweta's text displaces the Marxist-feminist terms of the analysis of domestic labor, it also calls into question this liberal-feminist choice. It dramatizes indigenous class-formation under imperialism and its connection to the movement towards women's social emancipation. In the strong satiric voice of authorial comment she writes of the patriarch Haldarkarta: "He made his cash in the British era, when *Divide and Rule* was the policy. Haldarbabu's mentality was constructed then. . . . During the Second War . . . he helped the anti-Fascist struggle of the Allies by buying and selling scrap iron" (224, 223). The mindset of the imperialist is displaced and replicated in the comprador capitalist. If "East and West" meant a global division for the imperialist, within the minute heterogeneous cartography of this post-colonial space, the phrase comes to indicate East and West Bengal. East Bengal (today's Bangladesh) has a phantasmatic status as a proper name, an indigenous division now merely alluding to the imperial and pre-imperial past. Haldarkarta identifies in no way with the parts of "India" outside of this "Bengal":—"he doesn't trust anyone—not a Punjabi-Oriya-Bihari-Gujarati-Marathi-Muslim" (p. 224).

This sentence is an echo of a well-known line from the Indian national anthem, an obvious cultural monument: "Punjab-Sindhu-Gujarat-Maratha-Dravida-Utkala [Orissa]-Banga [Bengal]." A national anthem is a regulative metonym for the identity of a nation. Mahasweta's mocking enumeration, describing the country metonymically even as it alludes to that regulative metonym, the anthem, measures the distance between regulation and constitution. This measure then reflects back upon the declarative sentence about secular India that opens the passage we are reading: "He lives in independent India, the India that makes no distinctions among people, kingdoms, languages . . ." (p. 224). The reader cannot find a stable referent for the ill-treated Mother India of Mahasweta's reading.

Even in the archaic "East Bengal" that seems to be the space of Haldarkarta's "national" identity (Mahasweta's word is "patriotism"), Dhaka, Mymensingh, Jashor—the celebrated cities, towns, areas are found wanting. "Harisal," the man's birthplace, is claimed as the fountainhead of that most hegemonic construct, the cultural heritage of ancient India: "One day it will emerge that the Vedas and the Upanishads were also written in Harisal" (p. 225). Of course a lot of this relies for effect on the peculiar humor of the two Bengals. But surely to tie, as "Stanadayini" does, this kind of molecular chauvinism to the divisive operations of imperialism is to warn against its too-quick definition as Hegel's "childhood of history," transferred to Adorno's caution in *Minima Moralia* against "pre-capitalist peoples," percolated into Habermas's careless admission that his defense of the ethico-politics of modernism had to be, alas, Eurocentric, or into Kristeva's impassioned call to protect the future of the European illusion against the incursions of a savage Third World.[50]

This appropriation of a "national" identity is not the "taking on [of] an essentialist temptation for internationalist purposes."[51] Internationalist stakes are a remote presence here. This "national" self-situation is marked by a contradiction, a failure of the desire for essence. First it seeks to usurp the origins of Brahminism, the *Vedas* and the *Upanishads*. Next it declares itself dissolved by a Brahmin: "There's no East or West for a Brahmin. If there's a sacred thread around his neck [the sign of being a Brahmin] you have to give him respect even when he's taking a shit" (225). This two-step standing in for identity, is a cover for the brutalizing of the Brahmin when the elite in caste is subaltern in class. (In the case of class-manipulation, "poverty [is] the fault of the individuals, not an intrinsic part of a class society"; in the case of caste-manipulation, the implicit assumption is the reverse: the Brahmin is systemically excellent, not necessarily so as an individual.)[52]

I have gone through the rich texture of the description of Haldarkarta as "patriot" (nationalism reduced to absurdity) because, although he is a patriarch, it is through their access to the circuit of his political, economic, and ideological production ("he had made his cash in the British era . . . [his] mentality was constructed then") that the Haldar women move into a species of reproductive emancipation seemingly outside of patriarchal control. Jashoda the "proletarian" is only useful at the first stage:

Jashoda's worth went up in the Haldar house. The husbands are pleased because the wives' knees no longer knock when they riffle the almanac. Since their children are being reared on Jashoda's milk, they can be the Holy Child in bed at will. The wives no longer have an excuse to say "no."

The wives are happy. They can keep their figures. They can wear blouses
and bras of "European cut." After keeping the fast of Shiva's night by
watching all-night picture shows they are no longer obliged to breast-feed
their babies. (p. 229)

But the transition from domestic to "domestic" has no place in the greater narrative where women's ideological liberation has its class fix: "In the matter of
motherhood, the old lady's granddaughters-in-law had breathed a completely
different air before they crossed her threshold. . . . The old man had dreamed
of filling half Calcutta with Haldars. The granddaughters-in-law were unwilling.
Defying the old lady's tongue, they took off to their husbands' places of work"
(p. 230).

Another step, and we are free to fantasize an entry into the world of many
of Bharati Mukherjee's heroines, Indian wives whose husbands' places of work
are in the United States.[53] If they start going to school on the side, we have the
privileged native informants of liberal third worldist feminism. Can we not imagine the Haldar *daughters* of this generation going off to graduate school on their
own, rebels and heroines suckled on Jashoda's milk, full fledged feminists, writing pieces such as "The Betrayal of Superwoman":

We must learn to be vocal in expressing, without guilt or embarrassment,
what our careers mean to us. It is not something on the side that we can
abandon at will to take up career moves of a husband that we were not
included in discussing. . . . We must reach out to other women who think
they are alone, share our experiences and be each other's support. We
need to accept ourselves as Women Who Never Learned To Do Macramé
and Do Not Plan Their Weekend Social Life until Friday Afternoon. We
are sad. But we are glad. This is what we will always be.[54]

There is a complete absence of a sense of history or of subject position in this
passage written by a woman of the Indian diaspora in the United States. Mahasweta's Jashoda dies in the 1980s, of the history that allows this diasporic
woman to say "this is what we will *always* be." The critical deployment of liberal
feminist thematics in Mahasweta's text obliges us to remember that "we" in this
passage might be parasitical not only upon imperialism (Haldarkarta) but upon
the gendered subaltern (Jashoda) as well. Fiction and its pedagogy can here
perform the ideological mobilization of a moral economy that a mere benevolent
tracing of the historical antecedents of the speaker might not be able to. The
two must go together as each other's "interruption," for the burden of proof
lies upon historical research. It is to belabor the obvious to say that structures
of logical and legal-model scholarly demonstrations alone cannot bring about
counter-hegemonic ideological production.

It might be worth mentioning here that the left fringe of liberal feminism
would like to correct Marxism by defining woman as a sexual class.[55] Again, it

is possible to appreciate the situational force of this as an attempt to ensure that women's problems are not demeaned. But if this so-called correction is entertained theoretically, then the call to unity might carry the imprint of the academic or corporatist class among women.

In this context, Mahasweta's own reading can be extended into plausibility. The granddaughters-in-law leave the household (a relic of imperialism) and thus deprive Jashoda of her means of livelihood, however grotesque. This can be decoded as the post-Independence Indian diaspora, specifically as part of the "brain drain." It is a tribute to the story that no direct "logical" or "scientific" connection exists between this departure and Jashoda's disease and death, just as nor.e can be established between the nature of Jashoda's labor and her end. Strictly speaking, *whatever the pathology of her disease*, what would have saved her is better medical care. I have tried to show so far that the pre-history and peculiar nature of her disease, since they involve unequal gendering, are crucial if "Stanadayini" is to become a text for use.

Jashoda's story is thus not that of the development of a feminine subjectivity, a female *Bildungsroman*, which is the ideal of liberal feminist literary criticism. This is not to say that Jashoda is a "static" character. To go back to my opening remarks, the development of character or the understanding of subjectivity as growth in consciousness is beside the point of this parable or of this representation of the subaltern. That road not taken is marked by the progress of the granddaughters-in-law. To place the subaltern in a subject-position in her history is not necessarily to make her an individualist.

Inhabiting the shifting line between parable and representation, undoing the opposition between tenor and vehicle, Mahasweta's Jashoda also expands the thematics of the woman's political body. Within liberal feminism, the feminist body politic is defined by the struggle for reproductive rights.

It is of course of central importance to establish women's right to practice or withhold reproduction. A text such as "Stanadayini," by posing the double scene of Jashoda as both subaltern (representation rather than character) and parabolic sign, reminds us that the crucial struggle must be situated within a much larger network where feminism is obliged to lose the clear race- and class-specific contours which depend upon an *exclusive* identification of woman with the reproductive or copulating body. (Black and Hispanic working-class women in the U.S. have already made this point with reference to the ignoring of enforced sterilization in favor of the right to abortion; but this is still to remain within the identification of woman with the body defined minimally.) When the woman's body is used only as a metaphor for a nation (or anything else) feminists correctly object to the effacement of the materiality of that body. Mahasweta's own reading, taken too literally, might thus transgress the power of her text. But, in that shadow area where Jashoda is a signifier for subalternity as such, as well as a metaphor for the predicament of the decolonized nation-state

"India," we are forced, once again, to distance ourselves from the identity of Woman with the female copulative and reproductive body.

In the story, having children is also accession to free labor, the production of surplus that can be appropriated with no apparent extra-economic coercion. (Almost incidentally, "Stanadayini" undoes the line between consenting and coercive sexual intercourse (rape) without the facile reference to free libidinal choice.[56]) As such the solution to Jashoda's problem cannot be mere reproductive rights but productive rights as well. And these rights are denied her not just by men, but by elite women as well. This is the underlying paradox of population control in the Third World.[57] To oppose reproductive rights with the casuistical masculist pseudo-concern about the "right to life" cannot be relevant here or elsewhere.[58] Yet to oppose productive rights with the so-called "right to work" laws cannot be the only issue either, precisely because the subject here is female, and the question is not only of class but of gender.

Again, "Stanadayini" can offer no precise answers, no documented evidence. Taught as a text for use, it can raise constructive questions, corrective doubts.

6. "Elite" Approaches: "Stanadayini" in a Theory of Woman's Body

Used as a teachable text, "Stanadayini" calls into question that aspect of Western Marxist feminism which, from the point of view of work, trivializes the theory of value and, from the point of view of mothering as work, ignores the mother as subject. It calls into question that aspect of Western Liberal Feminism which privileges the indigenous or diasporic elite from the Third World and identifies Woman with the reproductive or copulative body. So-called Feminist "Theory," generally associated with developments in France of the last thirty years, is perceived as unrealistic and elitist by the two former groups.[59] I do not wish to enter that sterile quarrel. I submit that if "Stanadayini" is made to intervene in some thematics of this esoteric theoretical area, it can show up some of the limits of that space as well.

I will keep myself restricted to the question of *jouissance* as orgasmic pleasure. If to identify woman with her copulative or reproductive body can be seen as minimalizing and reductive, woman's orgasmic pleasure, taking place in excess of copulation or reproduction, can be seen as a way out of such reductive identifications. There is a great deal of rather diverse writing on the subject.[60] Mahasweta's text seems to be silent on the issue. I have heard a Bengali woman writer remark in public, "Mahasweta Devi writes like a man." I will therefore consider a man's text about women's silence: "A Love Letter," by Jacques Lacan.[61]

In this essay Lacan gives a rather terse formulation of a point of view that he developed throughout his career: "The unconscious presupposes that *in* the speaking being there is something, somewhere, which knows more than he does."[62] If this is taken to mean that the subject (speaking being) is more like a map or graph of knowing rather than an individual self that knows, a limit to the claim to power of knowledge is inscribed. The formulation belongs with such experiments as those epistemographs (maps of stages of knowing rather than the story of the growth of an individual mind that knows) of Hegel that the early Lukács used so brilliantly as charts of "immanent meaning"; the Marxian notion of ideology; and the Barthesian notion of the writable text that is not readable as such.[63] Fredric Jameson has recently expanded this specifically Lacanian position into the "political unconscious."[64]

If we take Lacan at his word here, this knowing-place, writing itself and writing us, "others" the self. It is a map of the speaking being that is beyond its own grasp as other. Thought is where this knowing-program, the mapping of knowledge, exceeds itself into and thus outlines the deliberative consciousness. Since this epistemograph is also what constitutes the subject (as well as "others" it), knowing in this para-subjective sense is also being. (If we understand this being-that-is-a-map-of-the-known as the socio-political and historical ensemble, collectively constituting the subject but not fully knowable, this would produce materiality preceding or containing consciousness.)[65] It is in this sense that Lacan writes: "As against the being upheld by philosophical tradition, that is the being residing in thought and taken to be its correlate, I argue that we are played by *jouissance*. Thought is *jouissance*. . . . There is a *jouissance* of being."[66]

Thought, as *jouissance*, is not orgasmic pleasure genitally defined, but the excess of being that escapes the circle of the reproduction of the subject. It is the mark of the Other in the subject. Now psychoanalysis can only ever conceive of thought as possible through those mechanics of signification where the phallus comes to *mean* the Law by positing castration as punishment as such. Although the point is made repeatedly by Lacan that we are not speaking of the actual male member but of the phallus as the signifier, it is still obviously a gendered position. Thus when thought thinks itself a place that cannot be known, that always escapes the proof of reproduction, it thinks according to Lacan, of the *jouissance* of the woman.[67]

If one attempted to figure this out without presupposing the identity of the male-gendered position and the position of the thinking (speaking) subject, the singularity and asymmetry of woman's *jouissance* would still seem undeniable in a heterosexually organized world. It would still escape the closed circle of the theoretical fiction of pleasured reproduction-in-copulation as use-value.[68] It would still be the place where an unexchangeable excess can be imagined and figured forth. *This*, rather than male-gendered thought, is woman's *jouissance* in the general sense.

I cannot agree with Lacan that woman's *jouissance* in the narrow sense, "the opposition between [so-called] vaginal satisfaction and clitoral orgasm," is "fairly trivial."[69] We cannot compute the line where *jouissance* in the general sense shifts into *jouissance* in the narrow sense. But we can propose that, because *jouissance* is where an unexchangeable excess is tamed into exchange, where "what is this" slides into "what is this worth" slides into "what does this mean?" *it* (rather than castration) is where signification emerges. Women's liberation, women's access to autobiography, women's access to the ambivalent arena of thought, must remain implicated in this taming. Thus, to call Mahasweta's preoccupation in "Stanadayini" with *jouissance* in the general sense "writing like a man" is to reduce a complex position to the trivializing simplicity of a hegemonic gendering.

Jouissance in general: Jashoda's body

In "Stanadayini" Jashoda's body, rather than her fetishized deliberative consciousness (self or subjectivity), is the *place* of knowledge, rather than the instrument of knowing. This cannot be an argument. Literary language, as it is historically defined, allows us no more than to take a persistent distance from the rationalist project, shared by the social sciences, radical or otherwise. This distancing is a supplement to the project. It could never have the positive role of an opposition. The role of Jashoda's body as the place where the sinister knowledge of decolonization as failure of foster-mothering is figured forth produces cancer, an excess very far from the singularity of the clitoral orgasm.

The speech of the Other is recorded in a cryptic sentence. It is a response to Jashoda's last "conscious" or "rational" judgment: "'If you suckle you're a mother, all lies'. . . . The sores on her breast kept mocking her with a hundred mouths, a hundred eyes." (236)

This is the only time the Other "speaks." The disease has not been diagnosed or named yet. The Other inhabits a hundred eyes and mouths, a transformation of the body's inscription into a disembodied yet anthropomorphic agency, which makes of the breast, the definitive female organ within the circle of reproduction, (a) pluralized almost-face.[70] (The metonymic construction common in Bengali colloquial usage should literally be translated "in a hundred mouths" et cetera, "meaning," of course, also *with*.) Does the Other agree or disagree with Jashoda's judgment about the identity of the mother, so crucial to the story? "Mocking" tells us nothing.

Consider for a moment the phrase that I have translated, "kept mocking": *Byango korte thaklo.*

The first noticeable thing here is the lack of synchronization between Jashoda's judgment and the response. The latter is sustained—"*kept* mocking"—as if Jashoda's remarks were merely an interruption. (We recall that the remarks had been made in the mistaken assumption that her husband was still in the room. Even as normal intersubjective exchange, it is a failure.) One may put discourse into the mouth and eyes of a displaced and disembodied Other. One cannot fabricate an intersubjective dialogue with it. The status of the cancer as the figuring of the *jouissance* of the subaltern female body as thought-in-decolonization is thus kept intact here.

Let us focus on the word *byango*—translatable loosely as "mock[ery]". The word *ango*—body (with organs) as opposed to *deho*—the body as a whole—makes itself felt within it. The Sanskrit source word *vyangya* meant, primarily, deformed. The secondary meaning—mockery—indicated the specific mockery that is produced by a contortion of the body, by deforming one's form. Modern Bengali has lost the sense that, in Sanskrit, would consolidate the reading that I am trying to produce: the implicit meaning that can only be understood through (gestural) suggestion.[71] When language de-forms itself and gestures at you, mocking signification, there is *byango*. The limit of meaning, the *jouissance* of the female body politic, is marked in this sentence.

This is altogether different from using the cancer simply as another metaphor invading the metaphor of the sexually undifferentiated body politic, listed in

Susan Sontag's *Illness As Metaphor*.[72] It is interesting to see how different the history of cancer as metaphor is in the context of the last couple of centuries in the Anglo-U.S. The emphasis there is basically psychologistic: "the disease is what speaks through the body, language for dramatizing the *mental*."[73] From within this history, Sontag calls for a "de-metaphorization" of the disease. This brings up two widely separated issues: philosophically, can anything be absolutely de-metaphorized? and politically, is it necessary in order to bring the theatre of decolonization into such a de-metaphorized arena of reality, to drag it through the various stages of comprador capitalism, until it can graduate into "expressive individualism" so that it can begin to qualify for demetaphorization? In other words, the political aspect of this suggestion must confront us with the argument for "development." There can be no doubt that situational agents of "development," especially counter-diasporic indigenous service professionals like "Stanadayini"'s doctor, are often selfless and good. Yet it must be noticed that, if we were to read him characterologically, he would be the only character who had so internalized bureaucratic egalitarianism as to judge Jashoda by an absolute standard: "The doctor understood that he was unreasonably angry because Jashoda was in this condition. He was angry with Jashoda, with Kangali, with women who don't take the signs of breast cancer *seriously* enough and finally die in this dreadful and hellish pain" (p. 239).

Engaging the thematics of the *jouissance* of the female body, "Stanadayini" can be read not only to show (a race-and-class-specific) gendering at work in Lacanian theory. It can also make visible the limits of a merely structural psychoanalytic strategy of reading.

In "A Love Letter," Lacan rewrites "I think, therefore I am" in the following way: "There is . . . an animal which finds himself speaking [taken to presume or entail 'thinking'], and for whom it follows that, by inhabiting [occupying with desire and mastery, *besetzend*, cathecting] the signifier, he is its subject."[74] If one is sympathetic to the critique of the sovereign subject, one does not have trouble accepting this as a persistent caution. "From then on, everything is played out for him on the level of fantasy, but a fantasy which can perfectly well be taken apart so as to allow for the fact that he knows a great deal more than he thinks when he acts."

Knowledge is played out or mapped out on the entire map of the speaking being, thought is the *jouissance* or excess of being. We have already drawn out the implications of this position in our discussion of Jashoda's body as the *place* of knowing in the text. But, in order "to take apart" the fantasy inhabiting this text "perfectly" one would have to part company with the psychoanalytic scenario.

I have speculated elsewhere that a narrative of sanctioned suicide (rather than castration) might begin to limn a "Hindu" phantasmatic order.[75] Rather than the stories of Oedipus (signification) and Adam (salvation), the multiple narratives of situated suicide might then regulate a specifically "Hindu" sense of the progress of life. (These narratives are "regulative psychobiographies.") When we begin to consider the question of a "perfect" analysis, we have to analyze the subalternization of indigenous psychobiographic narratives. The institutionalization of psychoanalysis, the establishment of its claim to scientificity (within which one must situate Lacan's critique), and its imposition upon the colonies, has its own history.[76] A question similar to some I have already posed emerges here also: should the access to hegemony of an indigenous (here "Hindu") regulative psychobiography lie through the necessary access to an institutionalization, like that of psychoanalysis, entailing the narrative of imperialist political economy? Within feminist "theory," we are caught in only the *gendering* rather than the overtly imperialist politics of psychoanalysis.

Given such matters, it might be interesting to measure the distance between Lacan's connecting of woman's *jouissance* and the naming of God on the one hand, and the end of "Stanadayini" on the other. Lacan moves the question, "can the woman say anything about *jouissance*?" asked by a man, to the point where the woman also confronts the question of the Other:

> for in this she is herself subjected to the Other just as much as the man. Does the Other know? . . . If God does not know hatred, it is clear for Empedocles that he knows less than mortals. . . . which might lead one to say that the more man may ascribe to the woman in confusion with God, that is, in confusion with what it is she comes from, the less he hates, the lesser he is, and since after all, there is no love without hate, the less he loves.[77]

At the end of Mahasweta's story Jashoda herself is said to "be God manifest." This is inconsistent with the logic of the rest of the narrative, where Jashoda is clearly being played by the exigencies of the Haldar household. It is also a sudden and serious introduction of the discourse of philosophical monotheism in what has so far been a satiric indexing of the ideological use of goddesses (*Singhabahini* or the Lionseated) and mythic god-women (the "original" Jashoda of Hindu mythology). Here at the conclusion the gender of the agent is unspecified. (The English translation obliges us to choose a gender.) Is it possible that, because Mahasweta Devi does not present this conclusion from a male-gendered position, we are not reduced to man's affective diminution when he puts woman in the place of God? Is it possible that we have here, not the discourse of castration but of sanctioned suicide? "Jashoda was God manifest, others do and did whatever she thought. Jashoda's death was also the death of God" (p. 240). Does Jashoda's death spell out a species of *icchamrityu*—willed death—the most benign form of sanctioned suicide within Hindu regulative psychobiography? Can a woman have access to *icchamrityu*—a category of suicide arising out of *tatvajnana* or the knowledge of the "it"-ness of the subject? The question of gendering here is not psychoanalytic or counterpsychoanalytic. It is the question of woman's access to that paradox of the knowledge of the limits of knowledge where the strongest assertion of agency, to negate the possibility of agency, cannot be an example of itself as suicide.[78] "Stanadayini" affirms this access through the (dis)figuring of the Other in the (woman's) body rather than the possibility of transcendence in the (man's) mind. Read in the context of *icchamrityu*, the last sentence of the text becomes deeply ambivalent. Indeed, the positive or negative value of the statement becomes undecidable: "When a mortal plays God here below, she is forsaken by all and she must always die alone."

Over against what might be seen as the "serious" laying out of the thematics of woman's *jouissance* in the general sense, there is rather a strange moment that might be read as indicating the inscrutability of woman's *jouissance* in the narrow sense.

"Stanadayini" opens with a general description of Jashoda as a professional mother. Immediately following, there is a brief narrative sequence, embedded in other, even briefer, references, the logical irrelevance of which the text is at pains to point out: "But these matters are mere blind alleys. Motherhood did not become Jashoda's profession for these afternoon-whims." (p. 222).

The sequence deals with the cook. Like Jashoda, she loses her job as a result of the youngest Haldar-son's clandestine activities: "He stole his mother's ring, slipped it into the cook's pillowcase, raised a hue and cry, and got the cook kicked out" (p. 222). We do not know the end of her story. In terms of narrative value, the cook is the real marginal. It is in her voice that the inscrutability of woman's pleasure announces itself: "One afternoon the boy, driven by lust, attacked the cook and the cook, since her body was heavy with rice, stolen fishheads and turnip greens and her body languid with sloth, lay back, saying, 'Yah, do what you like.' [Afterwards] . . . he wept repentant tears, mumbling 'Auntie, don't tell.' The cook—saying, 'What's there to tell?'—went quickly to sleep" (p. 222).

(I am not suggesting that we should give in to our body's depradations and refuse to testify—just as, at the other end of the scale of cultural control—no one would suggest that the text about sex-affective production called *King Lear* invites people to go mad and walk about in storms. If what we are combating as teachers is liberal-nationalist-universalist humanism with its spurious demands for the autonomy of art and the authority of the author, we must be ready to admit that the demand that plots be directly imitable in politically correct action leads to the extravagances of "socialist" or "feminist" realism and a new Popular Front.)

In the voice of the marginal who disappears from the story, in between the uncaring "do what you like" and "what's there to tell," Mahasweta might be marking the irreducible inscrutability of the pleasure of the woman's body.[79] This is not the rhapsodic high artistic language of elite feminist literary experimentation. Escaping the reducible logic (including the authorial reading *and* the pedagogic interventions) of the story, this exchange is clothed in slang. As Gautam Bhadra has pointed out, it is in the unfreezable dynamic of slang that subaltern semiosis hangs out.[80]

What, indeed, is there to tell? The cook, a non-character in the story, could not have *intended* the rhetorical question *seriously*. It is almost as if what is told, the story of Jashoda, is the result of an obstinate misunderstanding of the rhetorical question that transforms the condition of the (im)-possibility of answering—of telling the story—into the condition of its possibility.[81] Every production of experience, thought, knowledge, all humanistic disciplinary production, perhaps especially the representation of the subaltern in history or literature, has this double bind at its origin.

The influential French feminist theorist Julia Kristeva has proposed a rewriting of the Freudian version of the Oedipal family romance. She theorizes an "abject" mother who, unequally coupled with the "imaginary" father, offers a primary narcissistic model which allows the infant to speak.[82] The focus here is unwaveringly on the child—and, since Kristeva is an apologist for Christianity—upon the Holy Child. If some details of the iconography of the abject mother seem to fit Jashoda's predicament, we should, I think, resist the seduction of a lexicon that beckons to a coherent reading by strategically excluding the entire political burden of the text. There can be no similarity between Kristeva's positing of a pre-originary space where sexual difference is annulled—so that a benignly Christian *agape* can be seen to pre-date *Eros* on the one hand, and the sinister vision of the failure of social cement in a decolonized space where questions of genital pleasure or social affect are framed, on the other.[83]

One cannot of course compare analytical discussions of ideology with psychoanalytical reconstructions of interpellation.[84] Kristeva's discussions of the place of the Virgin within cultural Subject-representation and constitution are, however, so close to isomorphic generalizations that I think they might be productively contrasted to Mahasweta's critique of the nationwide patriarchal mobilization of the Hindu Divine Mother and Holy Child. Her treatment of an active polytheism focusses the possibility that there are many accesses to the mother-child scene.   The story plays itself out between two cultural uses of it. The figure of the all-willing Lionseated, whose official icon of motherhood triumphant is framed by her many adult divine children, democratically dividing the governance of the many sectors of the manifest world, is reflected in the temple quarter of Calcutta. The figure of the all-nurturing Jashoda provides the active principle of patriarchal sexual ideology. As in the case of her earlier short story "Draupadi," Mahasweta mobilizes the figure of the mythic female as opposed to the full-fledged goddess. Kristeva points at the Virgin's asymmetrical status as the Mother of God by constructing the imaginary father and the abject mother.[85] Mahasweta introduces exploitation/domination into that detail in the mythic story which tells us that Jashoda is a *foster*-mother. By turning fostering into a profession, she sees mothering in its materiality beyond its socialization as affect, beyond psychologization as abjection, or yet transcendentalization as the vehicle of the divine.

7. Considerations Specifically of Gendering

A few more remarks on the economy of the Lionseated and Jashoda are in order here.

A basic technique of representing the subaltern as such (of either sex) is as the object of the gaze "from above."[86] It is noticeable that whenever Jashoda is represented in this way in "Stanadayini," the eye-object situation is deflected into a specifically religious discourse. In Hindu polytheism the god or goddess, as indeed, *mutatis mutandis* the revered person, is also an object of the gaze, "from below." Through a programmed confounding of the two kinds of gaze goddesses can be used to dissimulate women's oppression.[87] The transformation of the final cause of the entire chain of events in the first part of the narrative into the will of the Lionseated is an example of how the latter is used to dissimulate Jashoda's exploitation. For the sufficient cause is, as we well know, the cheating and spoiled youngest Haldar son with the genital itch. In the following passage, it is he who is the *subject* of the gaze, the object being the suckling Jashoda, a sort of living icon of the mythic Jashoda the Divine (Foster) Mother suckling the Holy Child. The man (the one above) thus masquerades as the one below, so that the subaltern can be dissimulated into an icon. Displaced into that iconic role, she can then be used to declare the will of the dominant Female, the goddess Lionseated: "One day as the youngest son was squatting to watch Jashoda's milking, she said, 'There dear, my Lucky. All this because you swiped him in the leg. Whose wish was it then?' 'The Lionseated's,' said Haldar junior" (pp. 229–30).

Mahasweta presents Jashoda as constituted by patriarchal ideology. In fact, her outspoken self-confidence in the earlier part of the story comes from her ideological conviction.[88] If the text questions the distinction between rape and consenting intercourse, Jashoda the subaltern does not participate in this questioning. "You are husband," she will say, "you are guru. If I forget and say no, correct me. Where after all is the pain? . . . Does it hurt a tree to bear fruit?" (p. 228) (She is given the same metaphor of the "naturalness" of woman's reproductive function—one ideological cornerstone of gendering—when she reproaches the granddaughters-in-law for "causing" the Old Mistress's death through their refusal to bear children.) She also accepts the traditional sexual division of labor: "The man brings, the woman cooks and serves. My lot is inside out. . . . Living off a wife's carcass, you call that a man?" (p. 232).

Indeed, Mahasweta uses Jashoda the subaltern as a measure of the dominant sexual ideology of "India." (Here gender uniformity is more encompassing than class difference.) Over against this is a list of Western stereotypes, where a certain Western feminism ("Simone de Beauvoir" serves Mahasweta as a metonym) is also situated:

> Jashoda is fully an Indian woman, whose unreasonable, unreasoning, and unintelligent devotion to her husband and love for her children, whose unnatural renunciation and forgiveness have been kept alive in the popular consciousness by all Indian women. . . . Her mother-love wells up as much for Kangali as for the children. . . . Such is the power of the Indian soil that all women turn into mothers here and all men remain immersed in the spirit of holy childhood. Each man the Holy Child and each woman the Divine Mother. Even those who wish to deny this and wish to slap *current posters* to the effect of the "eternal she,"—"Mona Lisa,"—"La passionaria,"—"Simone de Beauvoir"—et cetera over the old ones and look at women that way are, after all, Indian cubs. It is notable that the educated Babus desire all this from women outside the home. When they cross the threshold they want the Divine Mother in the words and conduct of the revolutionary ladies (pp. 225–26).

Here the authority of the author-function is elaborately claimed. We are reminded that the story is no more than the author's construction. The allusion
to another school of Bengali fiction places the story in literary history rather than
the stream of reality. In an ostentatious gesture, the author recovers herself and
resumes her story: "However, it's incorrect to cultivate the habit of repeated
incursions into *bye-lanes* as we tell Jashoda's life story" (p. 226). That Jashoda's
name is also an interpellation into patriarchal ideology is thus given overt authorial sanction through the conduct of the narrative. In terms of that ideology,
the fruit of Jashoda's fostering is the Krishna whose flute-playing phallocentric
eroticism, and charioteering logocentric sublation of militarism into a model of
correct karma, will be embraced in nineteenth- and twentieth-century Bengali
nationalism as images of the private and the public.[89]

The end of the story undoes this careful distancing of the author from the
gender-ideological interpellation of the protagonist. Even when Mahasweta Devi
predicates her at the end by way of the defilement of institutional English on
the name-tag for unclaimed corpses in the morgue ("Jashoda Devi, Hindu female"), a certain narrative irony, strengthening the author-function, seems still
intact.[90] It is the three propositions at the very end that call into question the
strategically well-advertised ironic stance of the author-function.

The language and terminology of these conclusive propositions remind us of
those high Hindu scriptures where a merely narrative religion shifts, through
the register of theology, into a species of speculative philosophy: "Jashoda was
God manifest, others do and did whatever she thought. Jashoda's death was
also the death of God. When a mortal plays God here below, she is forsaken
by all and she must always die alone" (p. 240).

It is a common argument that the subaltern as historical subject persistently
translates the discourse of religion into the discourse of militancy. In the case
of the subaltern as gendered subject, "Stanadayini" recounts the failure of such
a translation. It undoes the hierarchical opposition between the Hinduism of
philosophical monotheism (largely bred in its contemporary outlines by way of
the culture of imperialism) and that of popular polytheism. It suggests that the
arrogance of the former may be complicitous with the ideological victimage of
the latter. This is managed through making indeterminate the distinction between the author-function and the protagonist's predicament. If, therefore, the
story (*énoncé*) tells us of the failure of a translation or discursive displacement
from religion to militancy, the text as statement (*énonciation*) participates in such
a translation (now indistinguishable from its "failure") from the discourse of
religion into that of political critique.

"Stanadayini" as statement performs this by compromising the author's
"truth" as distinct from the protagonist's "ideology." Reading the solemn as-
senting judgment of the end, we can no longer remain sure if the "truth" that
has so far "framed" the ideology has any resources without it or outside it. Just
as in the case of the cook's tale, we begin to notice that the narrative has, in
fact, other frames that lie outside a strictly authorial irony. One of these frames,
we remember, renders the world's foster mother motherless within the text. The
text's epigraph comes from the anonymous world of doggerel and the first word
invokes *mashi pishi*—aunts—not mothers, not even aunts by marriage, but aunts

suspended before kinship inscription, the sisters of the two unnamed parents, suspended also on the edge of nature and culture, in *Bangan*, a place whose name celebrates both forest and village.[91] If the narrative recounts the failure of affect, a counter-narrative (yet another non-story) of these curious, affectless, presumably fostering aunts threatens the coherence of our interpretation in yet another way.

It is the powerful title which holds together the reading that we have been developing in these pages. It is not "Stanyadayini," the word we expect, meaning "the suckler" or "wet-nurse." It is, rather, "Stanadayini,"—the giver of the breast, of the alienated means of production, the part-object, the distinguishing organ of the female as mother. The violence of this neologism allows the cancer to become the signifier of the oppression of the gendered subaltern. It is the parasite feeding on the breast in the name of affect, consuming the body politic, "flourishing at the expense of the human host" (p. 240). The sentence is in English in the Bengali text, which allows for the word "human." The representative or defining human case, given in English and the objective language of science, is here female.

"Much third world fiction is still caught in realism" (whereas the international literatures of the First World have graduated into language games) is a predictable generalization. This is often the result of a lack of acquaintance with the language of the original. Mahasweta's prose is an extraordinary melange of street slang, the dialect of East Bengal, the everyday household language of family and servant, and the occasional gravity of elegant Bengali. The deliberately awkward syntax conveys by this mixture an effect far from "realistic," although the individual elements are representationally accurate to the last degree. (I have not been able to reproduce this in the translation.) In addition, the structural conduct of the story has a fabulistic cast: the telescoped and improbable list of widespread changes in the household and locality brought about by the transition from domestic to "domestic," and the quick narrative of the thirty years of decolonization with its exorbitant figures, are but two examples.

What is most interesting for my purposes, however, is that the text's own comment on realism in literature should be given in terms of gendering. Just as a naive understanding of a realistic style is that it is true to life, so is it politically naive and pernicious understanding of gendering that it is true to nature. Mahasweta's rendering of the truth of gendering in realism is so deliberately mysterious and absurd that it is almost incomprehensible even to the native speaker. The reference is to Saratchandra Chatterjee, the greatest sentimental realist in Bengali literature. No ethnographic or sociological explication of the "connotation" of "wood apple nectar" would do the disciplinary trick here:

Because he understood this the heroines of Saratchandra always fed the hero an extra mouthful of rice. The apparent simplicity of Saratchandra's and other similar writers' writings is actually very complex and to be thought of in the evening, peacefully after a glass of wood apple nectar. There is too much influence of fun and games in the lives of the people who traffic in studies and intellectualism in West Bengal and therefore they should stress the wood apple correspondingly. We have no idea of the loss we are sustaining because we do not stress the wood apple-type herbal remedies correspondingly (p. 226).

Speaking in code, then, we might say that to diagnose all Third World literature in English translation, by way of a sanctioned ignorance of the original, as a realism not yet graduated into language-games, is a species of "stress upon the wood-apple-type-herbal remedies correspondingly." Such a minimalizing reading would docket Mahasweta's story as nothing more than a "realistic" picture of Indian gendering.

In his account of the Subaltern Studies Conference (January 1986) where an earlier version of this paper was read, and where Mahasweta presented her own reading of "Stanadayini," David Hardiman comes to the following conclusion: "[Mahasweta's] down-to-earth style made for excellent theatre, with Gayatri being upstaged."[92] I have obviously taken Mahasweta's reading, "not unsurpisingly," as Hardiman writes, "greatly at variance with Gayatri Spivak's," seriously enough to engage with it in writing; and I have commented elsewhere on the implicit benevolent sexism of some subalternist work.[93] Yet I must point out that Hardiman's gesture is explicitly masculist: turning women into rivals by making them objects of the gaze. Beyond this particular male voyeurism, beyond the ontological/epistemological confusion that pits subaltern being against elite knowing, beyond the nativist's resistance to theory when it is recognizably different from her or his own unacknowledged theoretical position, I hope these pages have made clear that, in the *mise-en-scène* where the text persistently rehearses itself, writer and reader are both upstaged. If the teacher clandestinely carves out a piece of action by using the text as a tool, it is only in celebration of the text's apartness (*être-à-l'écart*). Paradoxically, this apartness makes the text susceptible to a history larger than that of the writer, reader, teacher. In that scene of writing, the authority of the author, however seductively down-to-earth, must be content to stand in the wings.

1987

Notes

1. The Letter as Cutting Edge

[1] Jacques Lacan, "A Jakobson," *Le Séminaire de Jacques Lacan*, ed. Jacques-Alain Miller, Livre XX, *Encore* (1972–1973), Paris, 1975, p. 25. All references to Lacan are in my translation.

[2] Paul de Man, "Form and Intent in the American New Criticism," *Blindness and Insight: Essays in the Rhetoric of Contemporary Criticism* (New York: Oxford University Press, 1971), p. 21.

[3] Ivor Armstrong Richards, *Coleridge on Imagination* (Bloomington: Indiana University Press, 1960), p. 44. On Coleridge's central role in propagating "organistic formalism," the received opinion is nicely stated in the passage below: "This organistic formalism has many antecedents: it started in Germany late in the eighteenth century and came to England with Coleridge. . . . Coleridge, Croce, and French symbolism are the immediate antecedents of modern English and American so-called New Criticism." René Wellek, *Concepts of Criticism*, ed. Stephen G. Nichols, Jr. (New Haven and London: Yale University Press, 1963), p. 354.

[4] Lacan, "Analysis and truth," *The Four Fundamental Concepts of Psychoanalysis*, trans. Alan Sheridan (New York: W.W. Norton, 1981), pp. 144–145. The discrepancy between the object *a* and the unconscious is contained in Lacan's optic metaphor, which accommodates the idea of the *angle* of incidence.

[5] "Introduction," Samuel Taylor Coleridge, *Biographia Literaria*, ed. J. Shawcross, (Oxford: Oxford University Press, 1907), vol. 1 (hereafter cited in the text by page reference alone), p. v.

[6] Lacan, "La Subversion," *Ecrits* (New York: W.W. Norton, 1977), p. 303.

[7] Ibid., p. 294.

[8] Ibid., p. 824.

[9] "Le Savoir et la vérité," *Encore*, p. 87.

[10] Ibid., p. 91. My deliberately clumsy translation tries to, but does not quite catch the play in French: both, "Is to have the *a* being?" and, "Is to have the *a*, to be the *a*?" The (sup)posing of the subject for the subject relates to what is in question in Coleridge's text here.

[11] "Ronds de ficelle," Ibid., p. 109.

[12] "Subversion," *Ecrits*, pp. 314–15.

[13] Ibid., p. 324. I am moved by Derrida's argument, general rather than psychoanalytic, for rewriting the thematics of castration as the thematics of the

hymen ("The Double Session," *Dissémination*, trans. Barbara Johnson (Chicago: University of Chicago Press, 1981), or of "anthérection" (*Glas* [Paris, 1974]). But since this essay is the story of a common critic armed with a specifically psychoanalytic vocabulary, I do not broach that re-inscription here.

[14] Serge Leclaire, *Psychanalyser: un essai sur l'ordre de l'inconscient et la pratique de la lettre* (Paris: Seuil, 1968), pp. 184–85.

[15] For a typical reading that has not been alerted to the importance of letters and cuttings, see Owen Barfield, *What Coleridge Thought* (Middletown: Wesleyan University Press, 1971), pp. 26–27.

[16] Lacan, "Analyse du discours et analyse du moi," *Séminaire*, ed. Miller, Livre I, *Les Écrits techniques de Freud* (1953–1954), Paris, 1975, p. 80. Again, our critic would probably not enter into the sweeping commentary-critique of the position implied by Lacan's remark launched by Gilles Deleuze and Félix Guattari in *Anti-Oedipus: Capitalism and Schizophrenia*, trans. Robert Hurley, et al. (New York: Viking, 1977) or by schizo-analysis in general.

[17] "From Interpretation to transference," *Fundamental Concepts*, pp. 255–56.

[18] "Analysis and Truth," *Fundamental Concepts*, pp. 145–46.

[19] "La direction de la cure," *Ecrits*, pp. 228–29.

[20] "From Interpretation," *Fundamental Concepts*, pp. 250–51.

[21] "Subversion," *Ecrits*, pp. 296, 300–301.

[22] Shoshana Felman, "La Méprise et sa chance," *L'Arc* 58 (*Lacan*), p. 46.

[23] "From Interpretation," *Fundamental Concepts*, pp. 253–254.

[24] Generally in the first part of *Of Grammatology*, trans. Gayatri Chakravorty Spivak (Baltimore: Johns Hopkins University Press, 1976), and more specifically, apropos of Husserl, in *Speech and Phenomena: And Other Essays on Husserl's Theory of Signs*, trans. David B. Allison (Evanston: Northwestern University Press, 1973), Chapter VII.

[25] Lacan, "Ronds de ficelle," *Encore*, p. 114. The curious construction leads into the labyrinth by denying the very gift it offers. Need I mention that this formula—taken from one of Lacan's recent seminars—invokes the entire Lacanian thematics of the unconscious producing its own slippage as it positions the subject by the production of the sliding signifier? The *locus classicus* is still the much earlier "L'instance de la lettre dans l'inconscient ou la raison depuis Freud," *Ecrits*, pp. 146–173 (translated by Jan Miel as "The Insistence of the Letter in the Unconscious," *Structuralism*, ed. Jacques Ehrmann [New York: Doubleday, 1970], pp. 101–37).

2. *Finding Feminist Readings: Dante-Yeats*

[1] *Dante's Vita nuova: A Translation and an Essay*, trans. Mark Musa (Bloomington: Indiana University Press, 1973); further references are given as page

numbers in my text. *La Vita nuova di Dante: con le illustrazioni di Dante Gabriele Rossetti* (Torino-Roma, 1903); cited in my text as D. I thank Ms. Gianna Kirtley for helping me with the Italian text.

[2] Ignoring the ethico-political charge of such "minimal idealizations" some-times affects the very finest readings with a formalist prejudice. In Shoshana Felman's brilliant treatment of *The Turn of the Screw*, for example ("Turning the Screw of Interpretation," *Yale French Studies* 55/56, 1977), it is overlooked that the irony against the reading-enterprise is operated specifically through a female employee of a gentleman master. When Felman writes: "the 'governess' does *govern*" (p. 170), or that "the governess becomes, indeed, the *Master* of the ship, the Master of the meaning of the story (a master-reader)" (p. 173), we cannot help recalling the socio-sexual usage that fixes a great gulf between governess and Governor, mistress and Master. Indeed, in writing "In James's text as well as in Sophocles's, the self-proclaimed detective ends up discovering that he [!] himself is the author of the crime he is investigating: that the crime is his, that he is, himself, the criminal he seeks" (p. 175), Felman's otherwise impressively acute glance seems to miss that the governess in the James story is *not* allowed access to the Oedipal scene; unlike Oedipus, she does *not* know she is the crim-inal; and certainly is *not* allowed the privilege of punishing herself to save man-kind, or even the story's world. Indeed Felman's essay does point out, although in a "sex-neutral" way, that the text's irony is against a governess who clutches the helm (phallus) too hard. Because she traces out in the text the intricate allegory of the flight of meaning, does she herself become a victim of the text's trap? We look in vain for a reading of the exclusion of Mrs. Grose (the illiterate housekeeper) and Flora (the girl-child) from The *Turn's* allegory. Felman takes her place in the august company of the book's best readership: the Master-Author (Lacan, who is Master enough to forbid acknowledgement—"Lacan's works will be periodically referred to, not so much as an *authoritative* [italics mine] body of theoretical knowledge, but as a remarkably rich and complex analytical *text*" [p. 119]), the Author-Master (James, who is cited as authority against the critics' vulgar errors throughout the essay, and is finally shown as Master/dupe of his own fiction [p. 205]); and the governess, herself.

[3] In "*Glas*-Piece: A Compte-rendu," *Diacritics* 8:3 (Fall 1977).

[4] "What must be included in the description, i.e., in *what* is described, but also in the practical discourse, in the *writing that* describes, is not merely the factual reality of corruption and of alternation [*de l'écart*], but corrupt*ability*" (Jacques Derrida, "Limited Inc," trans. Samuel Weber, *Glyph* II [1977], p. 218).

[5] Jacques Derrida, "ME—PSYCHOANALYSIS: An introduction to the Trans-lation of 'The Shell and the Kernel' by Nicolas Abraham," trans. Richard Klein, *Diacritics* 9:1 (Spring 1979), pp. 6, 4, 12. Italics mine.

[6] Ibid., p. 8.

[7] A pre-deconstructive model of this is to be found in Heidegger's notion of the constitutive status of the necessary conflict between labor's worlding of a

world and the self-secluding being of the earth; a non-deconstructive one in Deleuze and Guattari's formulation of the productive status of the ruptures between desire-production, disjunctive synthesis, recording, and conjunctive synthesis. Cf. Martin Heidegger, "Origin of the Work of Art," *Poetry, Language, Thought*, trans. Albert Hofstadter (New York: Harper & Row, 1971); and Gilles Deleuze and Félix Guattari, *Anti-Oedipus: Capitalism and Schizophrenia*, trans. Robert Hurley, et al. (New York: Viking, 1977).

[8] The Rev. H. F. Cary's translation of the *Commedia* (New York, 1816), which Yeats is known to have used, was entitled *The Vision*. Yeats thought of himself as a subject, like Dante, of phase seventeen of the moon. Cf. Richard Ellman, *Yeats: the Man and the Masks* (New York: W.W. Norton, 1948), pp. 236–37. The relationship between the definite and indefinite articles in the two titles is worth nothing.

[9] A reading such as Felman's expertly describes the scenario but does not see the sexist charge.

[10] *A Vision* (New York, 1961), p. 44.

[11] It is difficult to find systematic definition in Lacan. I therefore quote Anthony Wilden, "Culture and Identity: the Canadian Question, Why?", *Ciné-Tracts* 2. ii (Spring 1979), p. 6. I feel a certain solidarity with Mr. Wilden. As I translated the early Derrida, so he the early Lacan. He too seems to resist the elitist championship of his author, and to transpose the author's work into overtly political and situational categories that often lack "refinement of style."

[12] The classic argument for enabling incorporation-identifications is "Mourning and Melancholia," *The Complete Psychological Works of Sigmund Freud*, trans. James Strachey (London: Hogarth Press, 1957), vol. 14; *Gesammelte Werke* (London, 1940), vol. 10. Incorporation as verbal cryptomania, traces of which one may find in Dante's text, is discussed in Nicolas Abraham and Maria Torok, *Cryptomanie: le verbier de l'homme-au-loup* (Paris: Flammarion, 1976). Derrida's introduction to this book has been translated as "Fors: The Anglish Words by Nicolas Abraham and Maria Torok," trans. Barbara Johnson, *Georgia Review* XXXI:1 (1977). *La Vita nuova* may be considered Dante's act of mourning for Beatrice, incorporating her as a facet of his own ego-identification as poet. In that case, the mirror-image of Beatrice performing precisely that gesture of mourning for Dante's loss is a pertinent fantasy.

[13] Melanie Klein developed the argument that the part-object, rather than necessarily an entire person, may be the object of affects. "My main conclusions on this theme: the primal internalized objects form the basis of complex processes of identification. . . . The inner world consists of objects, first of all the mother, internalized in various aspects and emotional situations. . . . In my view, the processes which Freud describes imply that this loved object is felt to contain the split-off, loved, and valued part of the self, which in this way continues its existence inside the object. It thereby becomes an extension of the self" ("On Identification," *New Directions in Psycho-analysis: the Significance of*

Infant conflict in the Pattern of Adult Behaviour, ed. Melanie Klein, et al. [London: Tavistock, 1955], pp. 310, 313). The part-object that is metonymic of the mother is of course the breast, as here the phallus is the metonym of the male. The curious thing, as I mention in note 11, is that Dante "object"-ifies himself so that Beatrice can be filled with his distanced "subject"-ivity.

[14] Trans. Jeffrey Mehlman, *Yale French Studies* 48 (1972); "Le Séminaire sur *La Lettre volée*," *Ecrits* (Paris, 1966). The question Lacan does not ask would be: what is Freud that he needed to describe the woman's desire in this way? It is a question asked by Luce Irigaray in "La Tache aveugle d'un vieux rêve de symétrie," *Speculum: de l'autre femme* (Paris, 1974). Maria Torok's essay "La Signification de 'l'envie du penis' chez la femme," in Nicolas Abraham, *L'écorce et le noyau* (Paris: Flammarion, 1978), seems, in the final analysis, unable to ask this question. She certainly takes the work of Melanie Klein and Ernest Jones forward by suggesting that the penis is no more than an idealized part-object, that although its fetishization requires the complicity of the woman its institutionalization is to man's advantage. But she never questions the sociality of what she seems to assume is the universally vicious imago of the mother—anal or phallic—and ends her piece praising analysis because "it is meant to serve the cure" of penis-envy in women, with the highly ambiguous and possibly ironic condition that "the analyst be herself free from the phallo-centric prejudice, *as old as humanity*" (p. 171, italics mine).

[15] For the deconstructive singularity of the frame or margin, see Jacques Derrida, "The Purveyor of Truth," trans. Willis Domingo, et al., *Yale French Studies* 52 (1975); "Le Facteur de la vérité," *Poétique* 21 (1975); and "Le Parergon," in *La Vérité en peinture* (Paris, 1978).

[16] I am referring to the symbological fantasmagoria developed by Yeats in *A Vision* and most of his mature poetry.

[17] As evinced, for example, in a title such as the following: Henry Walcott Boynton, *The World's Leading Poets: Homer, Virgil, Dante, Shakespeare, Milton, Goethe* (New York: Ayer Co. Pubs., 1912). Hugo and Verlaine on the matter of Troy might provide occasion for a comparable feminist excursus.

[18] It seems pertinent to mention the completion of one such project since this essay was written: a long article entitled "Displacement and the Discourse of Women," in Mark Krupnick, ed., *Displacement: Derrida and After* (Bloomington: Indiana Univ. Press, 1983).

[19] Michel Foucault, "History of Systems of Thought," in *Language, Counter-Memory, Practice: Selected Essays and Interviews*, trans. Donald F. Bouchard and Sherry Simon (Ithaca: Cornell University Press, 1977), p. 199.

[20] Jacques Derrida, *Of Grammatology*, trans. Gayatri Chakravorty Spivak (Baltimore: Johns Hopkins University Press, 1976), p. 24.

[21] Ellman, *Yeats*, p. 197.

3. *Unmaking and Making in* to the Lighthouse

[1] Virginia Woolf, *To the Lighthouse* (New York: Harcourt, Brace & Company, 1927), p. 310. Subsequent page references are included in my text.

[2] Quentin Bell, *Virginia Woolf: A Biography* (New York: Harcourt Brace Jovanovich, 1972), p. 65.

[3] Virginia Woolf, *The Letters of Virginia Woolf*, ed. Nigel Nicholson, vol. II: 1912–1922 (New York: Harcourt Brace Jovanovich, 1976), p. 462. Subsequent references to the *Letters* are given in the text. Volumes I and II are indicated as L I and L II respectively.

[4] Virginia Woolf, *Moments of Being*: unpublished autobiographical writings, ed. Jeanne Schulkind (Sussex: Sussex University Press, 1976), p. 124.

[5] Virginia Woolf, *A Room of One's Own*, Harbinger Books edition (New York: Harcourt, Brace and World, 1929), p. 108.

[6] Stephen Heath, "Difference," *Screen* 19.3. (Autumn 1978): pp. 56–57.

[7] Jacques Derrida, *Glas* (Paris: Galilée, 1974), p. 290b.

[8] Luce Irigaray, "La tâche aveugle d'un vieux rêve de symétrie," *Speculum: de l'autre femme* (Seuil, Paris, 1974). Subsequent references to this essay are included in my text. For a critique of Irigaray's position, read Monique Plaza, "'Phallomorphic Power' and the Psychology of 'Woman': a Patriarchal Chain," *Ideology and Consciousness* 4 (1978): 5–36.

[9] Sigmund Freud, "Femininity," *The Complete Psychological Works of Sigmund Freud*, ed. James Strachey (London: The Hogarth Press, 1961), XXII, p. 132.

[10] Ibid., p. 114.

[11] Interview with Michel Foucault, *Politique-Hébdo*, no. 247 (Nov. 29–Dec. 6, 1976), p. 33. Trans. by Colin Gordon, "The Political Function of the Intellectual," *Radical Philosophy*, no. 17 (Summer 1977).

4. *Sex and History in* The Prelude (1805): *Books Nine to Thirteen*

[1] Wallace W. Douglas, *Wordsworth: The Construction of a Personality* (Kent: Kent State University Press, 1968), pp. 3–4.

[2] Legouis's approach is so sexist and politically reactionary that the reader feels that it was Annette's good fortune to have been used by Wordsworth, Wordsworth's good sense to have treated her with exemplary pious indifference and no financial assistance, and his magnanimity to have given his daughter money in her adult life, to have allowed this daughter, by default, to use his name, and to have probably addressed her as "dear Girl" in "It is a beauteous evening," when, on the eve of his marriage to sweet Mary Hutchinson, Dorothy and William were walking with ten-year-old Caroline, *without* Annette, because

the latter, "although inexhaustibly voluble when she pours out her heart, . . . seems to be devoid of intellectual curiosity" (Emile Legouis, *William Wordsworth and Annette Vallon* [London: J. M. Dent, 1922], pp. 68, 33). Critical consensus has taken Wordsworth's increasingly brutal evaluation of the Annette affair at face value: "In retrospect [his passion for Annette] seemed to him to have been transient rather than permanent in its effects upon him, and perhaps to have arrested rather than developed the natural growth of his poetic mind. . . . Consequently, however vital a part of his biography as a man, it seemed less vital in the history of his mind" (*The Prelude, or Growth of A Poet's Mind*, ed. Ernest de Selincourt [Oxford: Clarendon Press, 1926], p. 573; this is the edition of *The Prelude* that I have used. References to book and line numbers in the 1805 version are included in my text.) Female critics have not necessarily questioned this evaluation: "What sort of girl was Annette Vallon that she could arouse such a storm of passion in William Wordsworth?" (Mary Moorman, *William Wordsworth: A Biography* [Oxford: Clarendon Press, 1957] p. 178.) More surprisingly, "it would not be possible to read *The Prelude* without wondering why on earth Vaudracour and Julia suddenly crop up in it, or why Wordsworth does not make any more direct mention of Annette Vallon. Nevertheless, although one cannot help wondering about these things, they are not really what the poem is about" (Margaret Drabble, *Wordsworth* [London: Evans Brothers, 1966], p. 79). Herbert Read did in fact put a great deal of emphasis on Annette's role in the production of Wordsworth's poetry (*Wordsworth*, The Clark Lectures, 1929–30 [London: Jonathan Cape, 1930]). His thoroughly sentimental view of the relationship between men and women—"the torn and anguished heart [Wordsworth] brought back to England at the end of this year 1792"—and his discounting of politics—"he was transferring to this symbol France the effects of his cooling affection for Annette"—make it difficult for me to endorse his reading entirely (pp. 102, 134).

[3] Read, pp. 205–06. "It is impossible to date *Vaudracour and Julia* accurately; we know of no earlier version than that in MS. 'A' of the *Prelude*, but it is possible that the episode was written some time before 1804" (F. M. Todd, "Wordsworth, Helen Maria Williams, and France," *Modern Language Review*, 43 [1948], p. 462).

[4] Richard J. Onorato, *The Character of the Poet: Wordsworth in* the Prelude (Princeton: Princeton University Press, 1971), p. 409.

[5] I refer the reader to my essay, partially on a passage from *The Prelude*, "Allégorie et histoire de la poésie: hypothèse de travail" (*Poétique*, 8 [1971]), for a working definition of the "iconic" style. An "icon" is created in "passages where the [putative] imitation of real time is momentarily effaced for the sake of a descriptive atemporality [*achronie*]" (p. 430). Such passages in Romantic and post-Romantic allegory characteristically include moments of a "temporal menace . . . resulting in a final dislocation" (p. 434). This earlier essay does not relate Wordsworth's "iconic" practice to a political program. Geoffrey Hartman's definition of the concept of a "spot of time," also unrelated to a political argument, is provocative: "The concept is . . . very rich, fusing not only time and place but also stasis and continuity" (*Wordsworth's Poetry 1787–1814* [New Haven: Yale University Press, 1964], p. 212).

[6] *Sophocles I,* ed. David Grene (Chicago: University of Chicago Press, 1954), p. 42.

[7] For the sort of practical but unacknowledged use that Wordsworth made of Dorothy, see Drabble, pp. 111 and passim. The most profoundly sympathetic account of the relationship between William and Dorothy is to be found in F. W. Bateson, *Wordsworth: A Re-interpretation,* second ed. (London: Longmans, Green, 1954).

[8] "Femininity," in *The Standard Edition of the Complete Psychological Works of Sigmund Freud,* trans. James Strachey (London: Hogarth Press, 1964), vol. XXII.

[9] Gilles Deleuze and Félix Guattari, *Anti-Oedipus: Capitalism and Schizophrenia,* trans. Mark Seem, et al. (New York: Viking Press, 1977), p. 161.

[10] A sense of the field may be gleaned from A. V. Dicey, *The Statesmanship of Wordsworth: An Essay* (Oxford: Clarendon Press, 1917); Crane Brinton, *The Political Ideas of the English Romanticists* (New York: Russell & Russell, 1926); Kenneth MacLean, *Agrarian Age: A Background for Wordsworth* (New Haven: Yale University Press, 1950); E. P. Thompson, "Disenchantment or Default? A Lay Sermon," in *Power and Consciousness,* ed. Conor Cruise O'Brien and William Dean Vanech (London: University of London Press, 1969); George Watson, "The Revolutionary Youth of Wordsworth and Coleridge," John Beer, "The 'Revolutionary Youth' of Wordsworth and Coleridge: Another View," David Ellis, "Wordsworth's Revolutionary Youth: How We Read *The Prelude,*" in *Critical Quarterly,* 18, 19, Nos. 3, 2, 4 (1976, 1977; I am grateful to Sandra Shattuck for drawing my attention to this exchange); and Kurt Heinzelman, *The Economics of the Imagination* (Amherst: University of Massachusetts Press, 1980).

[11] Karl Marx and Friedrich Engels, *The German Ideology,* in *Collected Works,* ed. Jack Cohen, et al. (New York: International Publishers, 1976) V, pp. 39–40. I do not say Marx and Engels here because the passage is from Part I of *The German Ideology.* "It gives every appearance of being the work for which the 'Theses on Feuerbach' served as an outline; hence we may infer that it was written by Marx" (*The Marx-Engels Reader,* ed. Robert C. Tucker [New York: Norton, 1972], p. 110).

[12] Karl Marx, "The Eighteenth Brumaire of Louis Bonaparte," in *Surveys from Exile,* ed. David Fernbach (New York: Vintage Books, 1974), pp. 146–47.

[13] E. P. Thompson, *The Making of the English Working Class* (New York: Vintage Books, 1966), p. 105.

[14] Ibid., p. 107.

[15] Ibid., p. 79; only first ellipsis mine.

[16] A contrast is to be encountered in Rousseau. "A man is not planted, in one place like a tree, to stay there the rest of his life" (*Emile,* trans. Barbara Foxley [London: Modern Library, 1911], p. 20). Although Derrida (*Of Grammatology,* trans. Gayatri Chakravorty Spivak [Baltimore: Johns Hopkins University Press, 1976], pp. 222–23) shows us how even "this criticism of the empirical

Europe" can be used in the service of ethnocentric anthropology, it is certainly a less insulated world view than Wordsworth's. It is in this spirit that, at the end of *Emile*, the hero is encouraged to travel in order to choose that system of government under which he would find greatest fulfillment. He does of course come back to woman and mother country.

[17] See "The Origin of the Work of Art," in *Poetry, Language, Thought*, trans. Albert Hofstadter (New York: Harper & Row, 1971), pp. 44ff.

[18] "From the context, Wordsworth clearly means 'statist' not only in the sense of 'a politician, statesman' (*OED* 1, which cites as example a Wordsworthian usage from 1799) but also in the sense of a political economist (which might include *OED* 2, 'one who deals with statistics,' the earliest usage of which is given as 1803)" (Heinzelman, p. 305, n. 18).

[19] Adam Smith, *An Inquiry into the Nature and Causes of the Wealth of Nations*, ed. Edwin Cannan (New York: Modern Library, 1937), p. 30.

[20] Ibid., p. 14.

[21] Karl Marx, *Capital*, trans. Ben Fowkes (New York: Vintage Books, 1977), I, p. 300.

[22] "Wordsworth as a social poet would seem to have preferred to be faithful to the experience of his own northern counties rather than to the greater experience of England, which he certainly knew about" (MacLean, p. 95).

[23] Marx, *German Ideology*, p. 39; italics mine.

[24] MacLean, p. 89.

[25] "Feeling as imagination he reserved for himself and the child, our 'best philosopher'; feeling as affection he conferred, with just a slight air of condescension and shame, upon the peasant world" (MacLean, p. 96). "He obviously no longer believed [in Michel Beaupuy's philosophy], and he perhaps had convinced himself that there was a difference between English and French beggary, but this does not justify him in rationalizing beggary, no matter how eloquently, as a fundamental good" (Edward E. Bostetter, *The Romantic Ventriloquists: Wordsworth, Coleridge, Keats, Shelley, Byron* [Seattle: University of Washington Press, 1963], p. 56).

[26] Karl Marx, *Grundrisse: Foundations of the Critique of Political Economy*, trans. Martin Nicolaus (New York: Vintage Books, 1973), p. 273.

[27] Northrop Frye, *Anatomy of Criticism: Four Essays* (Princeton: Princeton University Press, 1957), p. 348.

5. *Feminism and Critical Theory*

[1] For an explanation of this aspect of deconstruction, see Gayatri Chakravorty Spivak, "Translator's Preface" to Jacques Derrida, *Of Grammatology* (Baltimore: Johns Hopkins University Press, 1976).

[2] It seems appropriate to note, by using a masculine pronoun, that Marx's standard worker is male.

[3] I am not suggesting this by way of what Harry Braverman describes as "that favorite hobby horse of recent years which has been taken from Marx without the least understanding of its significance" in *Labor and Monopoly Capital: the Degradation of Work in the Twentieth Century* (New York and London: Monthly Review Press, 1974, pp. 27, 28). Simply put, alienation in Hegel is that structural emergence of negation which allows a thing to sublate itself. The worker's alienation from the product of his labor under capitalism is a particular case of alienation. Marx does not question its specifically *philosophical* justice. The revolutionary upheaval of this philosophical or morphological justice is, strictly speaking, also a harnessing of the principle of alienation, the negation of a negation. It is a mark of the individualistic ideology of liberalism that it understands alienation as *only* the pathetic predicament of the oppressed worker.

[4] In this connection, we should note the metaphors of sexuality in *Capital*.

[5] I remember with pleasure my encounter, at the initial presentation of this paper, with Mary O'Brien, who said she was working on precisely this issue, and who later produced the excellent book *The Politics of Reproduction* (London: Routledge and Kegan Paul, 1981). I should mention here that the suggestion that mother and daughter have "the same body" and therefore the female child experiences what amounts to an unalienated pre-Oedipality argues from an individualist-pathetic view of alienation and locates as *discovery* the essentialist *presuppositions* about the sexed body's identity. This reversal of Freud remains also a legitimation.

[6] See Jack Goody, *Production and Reproduction: A Comparative Study of the Domestic Domain* (Cambridge: Cambridge University Press, 1976), and Maurice Godelier, "The Origins of Male Domination," *New Left Review* 127 (May/June 1981): pp. 3–17.

[7] Collected in *Karl Marx on Education, Women, and Children* (New York: Viking Press, 1977).

[8] No feminist reading of this text is now complete without Jacques Derrida's "Spéculer—sur Freud," *La Carte postale: de Socrate à Freud et au-delà* (Paris: Aubier-Flammarion, 1980).

[9] *The Standard Edition of the Complete Psychological Works of Sigmund Freud*, trans. James Strachey et al. (London: Hogarth Press, 1964), vol. 22.

[10] Luce Irigaray, "La tâche aveugle d'un vieux rêve de symmétrie," in *Speculum de l'autre femme* (Paris: Minuit, 1974).

[11] I have moved, as I explain later, from womb-envy, still bound to the closed circle of coupling, to the suppression of the clitoris. The mediating moment would be the appropriation of the vagina, as in Derrida (see Gayatri Chakravorty Spivak, "Displacement and the Discourse of Women," in Mark Krupnick, ed., *Displacement: Derrida and After* (Bloomington: Indiana University Press, 1983).

[12] One way to develop notions of womb-envy would be in speculation about a female fetish. If, by way of rather obvious historico-sexual determinations, the typical male fetish can be said to be the phallus, given to and taken away from the mother (Freud, "Fetishism," *Standard Edition*, trans. James Strachey, et al., vol. 21), then, the female imagination in search of a name from a revered sector of masculist culture might well fabricate a fetish that would operate the giving and taking away of a womb to a father. I have read Mary Shelley's *Frankenstein* in this way. The play between such a gesture and the Kantian socio-ethical framework of the novel makes it exemplary of the ideology of moral and practical imagination in the Western European literature of the nineteenth century. See Gayatri Chakravorty Spivak, "Three Women's Texts and a Critique of Imperialism," *Critical Inquiry* 12, no. 1 (Autumn 1985).

[13] As I have repeatedly insisted, the limits of hegemonic ideology are larger than so-called individual consciousness and personal goodwill. See "The Politics of Interpretations," pp. 118–33 above; and "A Response to Annette Kolodny," widely publicized but not yet published.

[14] This critique should be distinguished from that of Gilles Deleuze and Félix Guattari, *Anti-Oedipus: Capitalism and Schizophrenia*, trans. Robert Hurley, et al. (New York: Viking Press, 1977), with which I am in general agreement. Its authors insist that the family-romance should be seen as inscribed within politico-economic domination and exploitation. My argument is that the family romance-effect should be situated within a larger familial formation.

[15] "French Feminism in an International Frame," pp. 134–53 above.

[16] Pat Rezabek, unpublished letter.

[17] What in man exceeds the closed circle of coupling in sexual reproduction is the entire "public domain."

[18] I understand Lise Vogel is currently developing this analysis. One could analogize directly, for example, with a passage such as Karl Marx, *Grundrisse: Foundations of the Critique of Political Economy*, trans. Martin Nicolaus (New York: Vintage Books, 1973), p. 710.

[19] Antonio Negri, *Marx Beyond Marx*, trans. Harry Cleaver, et al. (New York: J. F. Bergen, 1984). For another perspective on a similar argument, see Jacques Donzelot, "Pleasure in Work," *I & C* 9 (Winter 1981–82).

[20] An excellent elucidation of this mechanism is to be found in James O'-Connor, "The Meaning of Crisis," *International Journal of Urban and Regional Research* 5, no. 3 (1981): pp. 317–29.

[21] Jean-François Lyotard, *Instructions païens* (Paris: Union générale d'éditions, 1978). Tony Bennett, *Formalism and Marxism* (London: Methuen, 1979), pp. 145 and passim. Marx, *Grundrisse*, p. 326. The self-citation is from "Woman in Derrida," unpublished lecture, School of Criticism and Theory, Northwestern University, July 6, 1982.

[22] See Gayatri Chakravorty Spivak, "Love Me, Love My Ombre, Elle," *Diacritics* (Winter 1984), pp. 19–36.

[23] Michael Ryan, *Marxism and Deconstruction: A Critical Articulation* (Baltimore: Johns Hopkins University Press, 1982), p. xiv.

[24] Margaret Drabble, *The Waterfall* (Harmondsworth: Penguin, 1971). Subsequent references are included in the text. Part of this reading has appeared in a slightly different form in *Union Seminary Quarterly Review* 35 (Fall–Winter 1979–80): 15–34.

[25] As in Paul de Man's analysis of Proust in *Allegories of Reading: Figural Language in Rousseau, Nietzsche, Rilke, and Proust* (New Haven: Yale University Press, 1979), p. 18.

[26] For definitions of "overdetermination," see Freud, *Standard Edition*, trans. James Strachey, et al., vol. 4, pp. 279–304; Louis Althusser, *For Marx*, trans. Ben Brewster (New York: Vintage Books, 1970), pp. 89–128.

[27] See Gayatri Chakravorty Spivak, response, "Independent India: Women's India," forthcoming in a collection edited by Dilip Basu.

[28] "Was Headquarters Responsible? Women Beat Up at Control Data, Korea," *Multinational Monitor* 3, no. 10 (September 1982): 16.

[29] Perry Anderson, *Passages from Antiquity to Feudalism* (London: Verso Editions, 1978), pp. 24–25.

[30] Ibid., pp. 39–40.

[31] Spivak, "Love Me, Love My Ombre, Elle."

[32] I have already made the point that "clitoris" here is not meant in a physiological sense alone. I had initially proposed it as the reinscription of a certain physiological emphasis on the clitoris in some varieties of French feminism. I use it as a name (close to a metonym) for women in excess of coupling-mothering. When this excess is in competition in the public domain, it is suppressed in one way or another. I can do no better than refer to the very end of my earlier essay, where I devise a list that makes the scope of the metonym explicit. "French Feminism," p. 184.

[33] *Ms.* 10, no. II (May 1982):30. In this connection, it is interesting to note how so gifted an educator as Jane Addams misjudged nascent socialized capital. She was wrong, of course, about the impartiality of commerce: "In a certain sense commercialism itself, at least in its larger aspect, tends to educate the working man better than organized education does. Its interests are certainly world-wide and democratic, while it is absolutely undiscriminating as to country and creed, coming into contact with all climes and races. If this aspect of commercialism were utilized, it would in a measure counterbalance the tendency which results from the subdivision of labor" (*Democracy and Social Ethics*, Cambridge, Mass.: Harvard University Press, 1964), p. 216.

6. *Reading the World: Literary Studies in the Eighties*

[1] I apologize for this awkward sentence. The production of language is our practice. The received dogma asks that our language be pleasant and easy, that it slip effortlessly into things as they are. Our point of view is that it should be careful, and not take the current dogmatic standard of pleasure and ease as natural norms. As for Bacon, I am rueful that, given his spotty record, that is the best one can do for the American literary-critical sensibility. As Stuart Hall has argued, "The concept of 'ideology' has never been fully absorbed into Anglo-Saxon social theory. . . . An interesting essay could be written on what concepts did duty, in American social theory, for the absent concept of 'ideology': for example, the notion of norms in structural functionalism, and of 'values' and the 'central value system' in Parsons" ("The Hinterland of Science: Ideology and the 'Sociology of Knowledge,'" *Working Papers in Cultural Studies*, 10 [1977], p. 9). As for the "New Philosophy," I hastily disclaim any connection with the young philosophical aesthetes in Paris whose passionate effusions are sometimes known by that name. It is "active" that I want to stress, and "science" in the sense of "state or fact of knowing" (OED).

[2] Because the essay was too long, those pages outlining the argument were edited out. That decision in itself might provide food for thought on the norms of pertinence for scholarly journals. I hope to include the argument in my forthcoming book on theory and practice in the humanities.

[3] I understand and sympathize with that part of the impulse behind New Criticism which wanted to focus attention upon deciphering the text in its context. My point is that, as with my Plan II students, the dominant ideology, slipping in through the back door, has a lot to do with determining a seemingly "free choice"; and that a degree of freedom of choice can be achieved if that determination is recognized.

[4] The effort is minor also because, since we are gathered here together to discuss the problems for our profession, questions of race, sex, and class—the common threads of the social fabric—have had to be laid aside. I am reminded of a two-and-a-half hour-long conversation I had with a group of feminist women and some men on the West Coast earlier this year. Many of them were students of English or French literature. They spoke to me emphatically of an issue of faculty development. Our most prestigious professors, they said, will have nothing to do with so "localized" an issue as "feminism," at least not in the matter of reading the canon. Since we must try to pass our examinations, get recommendation letters, and to get jobs in this impossible market, we write our papers with our feminist consciousness and conscience strangulated, with a deliberate and self-contemptuous cynicism. If an advanced degree in literary studies requires and trains in such divisive compromise, its "humanistic" value comes to very little. Even this is a restricted example. The larger questions—Who can make use of a method such as I outline? Where?—must always loom as immediate correctives for the delusion that "to defend the autonomy of culture [provisionally defined as the total body of imaginative hypothesis in a society

and its tradition] seems to me the social task of the 'intellectual' in the modern world" (Northrop Frye, *Anatomy of Criticism* [Princeton: Princeton University Press, 1957], p. 127).

[5] If I admit that the simple expression "break down" is doing duty for the often trivialized word "deconstruct," the possibility of reading my speech as being about deconstructive practice in the academy may be entertained.

7. Explanation and Culture: Marginalia

[1] Stirrings of such a point of view can be seen in Mary Wollstonecraft, *Vindication of the Rights of Woman* (1972), by way of the apparently converse argument that reason, the animating principle of civil society, must become the guiding principle of domestic society as well.

[2] Paul Ricoeur, *Freud and Philosophy: An Essay on Interpretation*, trans. Denis Savage (New Haven: Yale University Press, 1970), pp. 32–36.

[3] Edmund Husserl, *Ideas: General Introduction to Pure Phenomenology*, trans. W. R. Boyce Gibson (New York: Collier Books, 1962), p. 12.

[4] As I argue elsewhere, Derrida's "playfulness" is in fact a "serious" and practical critique of pure seriousness. Here suffice it to point out that the disciplinary unease that is the straight reaction to the later Derrida can be described in the following way: "Here [is] a *new object*, calling for new conceptual tools, and for fresh theoretical foundations. . . . [Here] is a true monster . . . [not someone who is] committing no more than a disciplined error." (Italics mine.) Michel Foucault, *The Archaeology of Knowledge*, trans. A. M. Sheridan Smith (London: Tavistock, 1972), p. 224.

[5] *Speech and Phenomena: And Other Essays on Husserl's Theory of Signs*, trans. David B. Allison (Evanston: Northwestern University Press, 1973), p. 102.

[6] Sigmund Freud, *The Standard Edition of the Complete Psychological Works of Sigmund Freud*, trans. James Strachey (London: Hogarth Press, 1964), XXII; pp. 116–17.

[7] *Ms.* 8 (September 1979): p. 43.

[8] By "technocracy" I am not referring to the "technocracy movement [which] was a short-lived episode of the thirties" and "was rooted in the nineteenth-century strand of thought that identified technology as the dominant force capable of fulfilling the American dream." I am referring rather to the practical sellout of this dream which is a condition of the possibility of the theory of technocracy: "The modern postindustrial state—with its centralization, its emphasis on replacing politics with administrative decisions, and its meritocratic elite of specially trained experts—bears a more striking resemblance to the progressive formulation, which was the starting point for the technocrats. The progressive intellectuals, progressive engineers, and scientific managers of the early

twentieth century saw the outlines of the future political economy with amazing clarity. But the 'immensely enriched and broadened life within reach of all,' which Harlow Person predicted, remains a dream that technology and engineering rationality seem incapable of fulfilling." William F. Akin, *Technocracy and the American Dream: The Technocrat Movement, 1900–1941* (Berkeley and Los Angeles: University of California Press, 1977), pp. xi, xiii, 170. My essay speculates in a very minor way about the theoretical humanists' unselfconscious role in sustaining this inevitable sellout. For preliminary information on some of the major actors in this drama, see Ronald Radosh and Murray N. Rothbard, eds., *A New History of Leviathan: Essays on the Rise of the American Corporate State* (New York, 1972).

[9] I am simply referring as "masculism" to old-fashioned humanism, which considers the study of woman to be a special interest and defines woman invariably in terms of man. Among the many studies of the relationship between capitalism and masculism, I cite two here: *Feminism and Materialism: Women and Modes of Production*, ed. Annette Kuhn and AnnMarie Wolpe (London: Routledge & Kegan Paul, 1978); and *Capitalist Patriarchy and the Case for Socialist Feminism*, ed. Zillah R. Eisenstein (New York: Monthly Review Press, 1979).

[10] A simple test case of how politics-economics-technology (i.e., technocracy) becomes a collective determinant where "the last instance" can only be situated provisionally, temporarily, and in a slippery way, is the revisions of Edison's technological systems as recorded in the publications of the Edison Electric Institute. A humanist analysis of technology, choosing to ignore this transformation in the definition of technology, situates *technè* as the dynamic and undecidable middle term of the triad *theoria-technè-praxis*. The *loci classici* are, say, Aristotle's *Metaphysics* (1.1 and 2) and *Nicomachean Ethics* (6). For extensive documentation, Nikolaus Lobkowicz, *Theory and Practice: History of a Concept from Aristotle to Marx* (Notre Dame: University Press of America, 1967), is useful. Heidegger's "The Question Concerning Technology," in *The Question Concerning Technology and Other Essays*, trans. William Lovitt (New York, 1977) may be cited as a case of a modern humanist study of the question. I am suggesting, of course, that such a text as the last can be made to produce a reading "against itself" if technology is understood as the disruptive middle term between politics and economics, or between science and society, making arguments from binary oppositions or "the last instance" productively undecidable.

[11] I am leaving out of the argument the fact that this very "scholarly life" is sustained by bands of workers—secretarial and janitorial staff—who inhabit another world of pay scale and benefits and whose existence as labor is often, as at my own university, denied by statute.

[12] I have so internalized the power of this phrase that I had forgotten in the first draft that Professor Norman Rudich had said with great passion at the Marxist Literary Group Summer Institute (1979): "They are trashing the humanities. . . ."

[13] The last suggestion was offered by the executive secretary of the Modern

Language Association at an unpublished lecture at the University of Texas-Austin in October, 1979.

[14] That the poststructuralists have developed a vocabulary that is on principle somewhat fluid has offended three groups who have no interest in studying them carefully. One group (represented by E. P. Thompson, E. J. Hobsbawm, as well as, curiously enough, Terry Eagleton) would seek to establish the disciplinary privilege of history over philosophy, or of an ultimately isomorphic theory of material and literary form over a theory that questions the convenience of isomorphism. "If we deny the determinate properties of the object, then no discipline remains." Thompson, *The Poverty of Theory and Other Essays* (New York: Monthly Review Press, 1978), p. 41. This book, containing some astute criticism of Althusser, seems finally to claim—as Althusser claims that Marx had not developed an adequate (philosophical) theory—that Marx had not developed an adequate (historical) theory. The real issue seems to be to *keep the disciplines going* so that theory can endorse "enlightened practice." For a lexical analysis of Thompson's text, see Sande Cohen, *Historical Culture* (Berkeley: University of California Press, 1986), pp. 185–229. As that thinker of a rather different persuasion, Barrington Moore, Jr., wrote in 1965: "Objective here means simply that correct and unambiguous answers, independent of individual whims and preferences, are in principle possible." *A Critique of Pure Tolerance*, ed. Robert Paul Wolff, et al. (Boston: Beacon Press, 1965), p. 70. The second group is made up of conservative academic humanists like Gerald Graff (*Literature Against Itself: Literary Ideas in Modern Society*, Chicago: University of Chicago Press, 1979) or Peter Shaw ("Degenerate Criticism," *Harper's*, October 1979). These literary disciplinarians refuse to recognize that the poststructuralist vocabulary emerges in response to the problem of practice in the discourse of the human sciences. The fault is not altogether theirs for, given the ideology of American literary criticism (hinted at cryptically by way of Wallace Stevens in my final section), American deconstructivism seems repeatedly to demonstrate that theory as such is defunct and there make an end. A Derrida or a Foucault would and do ask, if theory *as such* is defunct, what are the conditions of possibility of a practice that is not merely practice *as such*? The academic conservatives would rather argue, if a deconstructive view of things threatens business as usual, no one should be allowed to think deconstructive thoughts. In Thompson's words, the situation can be represented as a refusal to "argue with inconvenient evidence" (*Poverty*, p. 43). The third group is the resolutely anti-intellectual communalist political activists whose slogan seems to be "if you think too much about words, you will do no deeds."

[15] All the quotations in this section, unless otherwise indicated, are from the typed material by all the participants circulated among us before the symposium.

[16] Karl Marx, *Capital: A Critique of Political Economy*, trans. Ben Fowkes (New York: Vintage Books, 1977), I: pp. 89–90.

[17] As representative figures of the two sides of this exceedingly complex debate, let us choose the Althusser of *For Marx*, trans. Ben Brewster (London:

Monthly Review Press, 1969) and the Paul K. Feyerabend of *Against Method: Outline of An Anarchistic Theory of Knowledge* (London: New Left Books, 1975).

[18] Such a generalization would be able to include the Pierre Bourdieu of *Outline of A Theory of Practice*, trans. Richard Nice (Cambridge: Cambridge University Press, 1977) and the Jürgen Habermas of *Theory and Practice*, trans. John Viertel (Boston, 1973), and *Knowledge and Human Interests*, trans. Jeremy J. Shapiro (Boston: Beacon Press, 1971).

[19] Jacques Derrida, "Signature Event Context," *Glyph* 1 (1977): p. 179. In this passage Derrida is questioning a naive critique of ideology that assumes an isomorphic and continuous relationship between things of the mind and things of the world. I should add that I am indebted to this and its companion essay "Limited Inc," *Glyph* 2 (1977) for much of my understanding of deconstructive practice.

[20] I refer the reader to the play of disciplinary allegiances broadly outlined in note 14. Michel Foucault's work on the genealogy of disciplines is of interest here. I have already cited "The Discourse on Language" (see note 4). Pertinent also are *The Birth of the Clinic: An Archaeology of Medical Perception*, trans. A. M. Sheridan Smith (New York: Pantheon Books, 1973) and *Discipline and Punish: the Birth of the Prison*, trans. Alan Sheridan (New York: Random House, 1977). One could do worse than cite the young Marx and Engels: "*The occupation assumes an independent existence owing to division of labour.* Everyone believes his craft to be the true one. Illusions regarding the connection between craft and reality are the more likely to be cherished by them because of the very nature of the craft." Karl Marx and Friedrich Engels, *Collected Works* (New York: International Publishers, 1976), vol. 5, p. 92.

[21] One could ponder, for example, the splintering of Students for A Democratic Society: Progressive Labor, the New American Movement, Democratic Socialist Organizing Committee. Each splinter has taken on certain idioms permitted by American sociopolitical discourse as it has moved from a politics of personal freedom (even in a collective guise) to a politics of social justice.

[22] Herbert Marcuse, "Repressive Tolerance," in *Critique of Pure Tolerance*, p. 82.

[23] Wallace Stevens, "The Idea of Order at Key West," in *The Collected Poems of Wallace Stevens* (New York: Knopf, 1954), p. 130.

[24] Rosalind Coward and John Ellis, *Language and Materialism: Developments in Semiology and the Theory of the Subject* (London: Routledge & Kegan Paul, 1977), p. 23.

[25] Wordsworth, Coleridge, T. S. Eliot, and Matthew Arnold, of course.

[26] Such a "making use" Foucault would call "the task [of] beco[ming] a curative science" based on a "historical sense" linked to Nietzsche's "active forgetfulness," which must make a "cut" in knowledge in order to act. "Nietzsche, Genealogy, History," in *Language, Counter-Memory, Practice*, trans. Donald F.

Bouchard and Sherry Simon (Ithaca: Cornell University Press, 1977), pp. 156, 154. *Defeminates* is used as *emasculates*.

[27] *The New Science of Giambattista Vico*, trans. Thomas Goddard Bergin and Max Harold Fisch (Ithaca: Cornell University Press, 1948), pp. 100, 109–110, 107, 106, 105, 155, 85. I am grateful to Professors Sidney Monas and James Schmidt for invoking these problematic passages.

[28] Jean Bethke Elshtain, "The Social Relation of the Classroom: A Moral and Political Perspective," in *Studies in Socialist Pedagogy*, ed. T. M. Norton and Bertell Ollman (New York: Monthly Review Press, 1978). I am grateful to Professor Michael Ryan for calling my attention to this essay.

8. *The Politics of Interpretations*

[1] Stuart Hall, "The Hinterland of Science: Ideology and the 'Sociology of Knowledge,'" *On Ideology*, Working Papers in Cultural Studies, no. 10 (Birmingham, 1977), p. 9. See also Douglas Kellner, "A Bibliographical Note on Ideology and Cultural Studies," *Praxis* 5 (1981): 84–88, and John B. Thompson, ed. *Studies in Theory of Ideology* (Berkeley and Los Angeles: University of California Press, 1985).

[2] See Newton Garver, introduction to Jacques Derrida, *"Speech and Phenomena" and Other Essays on Husserl's Theory of Signs*, trans. David B. Allison (Evanston: Northwestern University Press, 1973), for a summary of the opposition between logic and rhetoric in the disciplinary ideology of philosophy. Not only does Garver parallel Toulmin but he also describes Derrida's work as seeking to undo that opposition. Whatever the validity of Garver's broader analysis, it is interesting to speculate what Toulmin would make of such a suggestion of propinquity. I should perhaps add here that Derrida is suspicious of the concept of ideology because, in his view, it honors too obstinate a binary opposition between mind and matter.

[3] Karl Marx, "The Eighteenth Brumaire of Louis Bonaparte," *Karl Marx, Frederick Engels: Collected Works*, trans. Richard Dixon et al., fifteen vols. (New York: International Publishers, 1975–), 2:103; all translated material has been modified when necessary.

[4] Armand Hammer, "A Primer for Doing Business in China," *New York Times*, 11 April 1982.

[5] Pierre Macherey, *A Theory of Literary Production*, trans. Geoffrey Wall (London: Routledge & Kegan Paul, 1978), p. 60; italics mine.

[6] See Cavell, "Politics as Opposed to What?" (p. 173). For a discussion of this difference, see my review of Jacques Derrida, *Memoires: For Paul de Man* in *boundary* 2 (forthcoming). See also my "Revolutions That as Yet Have no Model: Derrida's *Limited Inc*," *Diacritics* 10 (Winter 1980): 47–48.

[7] For an articulation of deconstruction as syntactic or micrological resistance against the hegemony of semantics or macrology, see Derrida, "White Mythology: Metaphor in the Text of Philosophy," in Alan Bass, trans. *Margins of Philosophy* (Chicago: University of Chicago Press, 1983), pp. 270–71.

[8] Derrida, "Signature Event Context," trans. Jeffrey Mehlman and Samuel Weber, *Glyph* 1 (1977): 179, 177.

[9] Macherey, *Theory of Literary Production*, p. 86.

[10] See Michael Harrington, "Getting Restless Again," *New Republic*, 1 and 8 Sept. 1979, and David B. Richardson, "Marxism in U.S. Classrooms," *U.S. News and World Report*, 25 January 1982.

[11] "On/Against Mass Culture III: Opening Up the Debate," *Tabloid* 5 (Winter 1982): 1.

[12] A similar problem is encountered with White's offer of a running narrative as a critique of the narrativization of the discipline of history.

[13] See my "Il faut s'y prendre en se prenant à elle," in *Les Fins de l'homme*, ed. Philippe Lacoue-Labarthe and Jean-Luc Nancy (Paris, 1981).

[14] See, e.g., Joel Feinberg, ed., *The Problem of Abortion* (Belmont, Calif., 1973), and Marshall Cohen et al., eds., *Rights and Wrongs of Abortion* (Princeton: Princeton University Press, 1974).

[15] I have analyzed this in my "Explanation and Culture: Marginalia," pp. 103–17 above.

[16] Giovanni Battista Vico, *The New Science*, trans. Thomas Goddard Bergin and Max Harold Fisch (Ithaca: Cornell University Press, 1968), p. 175. Said refers to the Viconian passage on the origin of the patricians without any reference to its sex-fix ("Opponents, Audiences, Constituencies, and Community," pp. 10–11).

[17] I will give Davie a start. See Elaine Marks and Isabelle de Courtivron, eds., *New French Feminisms: An Anthology* (Amherst: University of Massachusetts Press, 1980); *Signs* 3 (Autumn 1977), special issue on *Women and National Development*; Julia Kristeva, *About Chinese Women*, trans. Anita Barrows (New York, 1977); Nawal El Saadawi, *The Hidden Face of Eve: Women in the Arab World*, trans. and ed. Sherif Hetata (London: Zed Press, 1980); Lesley Caldwell, "Church, State, and Family: The Women's Movement in Italy," in *Feminism and Materialism: Women and Modes of Production*, ed. Annette Kuhn and AnnMarie Wolpe (London: Routledge & Kegan Paul, 1978); Gail Omvedt, *We Will Smash This Prison! Indian Women in Struggle* (London: Zed Press, 1980); Cherríe Moraga and Gloria Anzaldúa, eds., *This Bridge Called My Back: Writings by Radical Women of Color* (Watertown, Mass., 1981); and Spivak, "Three Feminist Readings: McCullers, Drabble, Habermas," *Union Seminary Quarterly Review* 35 (Fall–Winter 1979–80): 15–34, "French Feminism in an International Frame," *Yale French Studies* 62 (1981): 154–84, and "'Draupadi' by Mahasweta Devi," *Critical Inquiry* 8

(Winter 1981): 381–402. Since the first publication of this essay a great deal of additional material has appeared in the area. [For the last two see pp. 134–53 and 179–96 below.]

[18] And to verify the extension of that turf, Davie might consult an essay by a respected male anthropologist who is not necessarily a feminist, Maurice Godelier, "The Origins of Male Domination," *New Left Review* 127 (May–June 1981): 3–17. A similar objection could be brought to Davie's insistence that there was nothing of the colonizer in the behavior of the British officer. Situationally and personally, perhaps not. But it is not without significance that it was the British rather than the Palestinian who had the power to decide.

[19] Terry Eagleton, *Walter Benjamin; or, Towards a Revolutionary Criticism* (London: New Left Books, 1981), p. 98.

[20] It is a place—the end of the line of the evolution of Marxist criticism—previously named with his own patronymic: "Let us review some of the names of the major Marxist aestheticians of the century to date: Lukács, Goldmann, Sartre, Caudwell, Adorno, Marcuse, Della Volpe, Macherey, Jameson, Eagleton" (Eagleton, ibid., p. 96). It should be mentioned that Eagleton surrounds the implicit evolutionism of his argument with many apologies to the contrary.

[21] Ken Wissoker, "The Politics of Interpretation," *Chicago Grey City Journal*, 24 November 1981.

9. *French Feminism in an International Frame*

[1] Bert F. Hoselitz, "Development and the Theory of Social Systems," in M. Stanley, ed., *Social Development* (New York: Basic Books, 1972), pp. 45 and passim. I am grateful to Professor Michael Ryan for drawing my attention to this article.

[2] Nawal El Saadawi, *The Hidden Face of Eve: Women in the Arab World* (London: Zed Press, 1980), p. 5.

[3] Julia Kristeva, *About Chinese Women*, trans. Anita Barrows (London: Marion Boyars, 1977).

[4] As is indicated by Philippe Sollers, "On n'a encore rien vu," *Tel Quel* 85, Autumn 1980, this interest has now been superseded.

[5] For an astute summary and analysis of this problem in terms of electoral Communism and Social Democracy, see Adam Przeworski, "Social Democracy as a Historical Phenomenon," *New Left Review* 122, July–August 1980.

[6] For Kristeva's argument that the literary intellectual is the fulcrum of dissent see "Un nouveau type d'intellectuel: le dissident," *Tel Quel* 74, Winter 1977.

[7] Joseph Needham's attitudes toward the curious fact of feminine symbolism

in Taoism, as expressed in *The Grand Titration: Science and Society in East and West* (Toronto: University of Toronto Press, 1969) are altogether tentative.

[8] Stanford University Press, 1970. See *Chinese Women*, p. 98n, p. 145n.

[9] For a somewhat dated and dogmatic view of this movement, see Michael Ryan and Spivak, "Anarchism Revisited: A New Philosophy?" *Diacritics* 8, no. 2, Summer 1978.

[10] *The Standard Edition of the Psychological Works of Sigmund Freud* (London: Hogarth Press, 1964) vol. 23; Gilles Deleuze and Félix Guattari, *Anti-Oedipus: Capitalism and Schizophrenia*, vol. 1, trans. Robert Hurley, et al. (New York: Viking Press, 1972).

[11] Amherst: University of Massachusetts Press, 1980. In this part of my essay, I have quoted liberally from *New French Feminisms*, giving the name of the author of the particular piece and the page number.

[12] I hope to present a discussion of such an appropriation in a forthcoming book on deconstruction, feminism, and Marxism.

[13] Irigaray, *This Sex Which Is Not One*, trans. Catherine Porter (Ithaca: Cornell Univ. Press, 1985); Cixous, *Préparatifs de noces au delà de l'abîme* (Paris: des femmes, 1978); Wittig, *Lesbian Body*, trans. David Le Vay (New York: William Morrow, 1975).

[14] (London: New Left Books, 1973.)

[15] Cf. Ernst Bloch, et al., *Aesthetics and Politics*, trans. Ronald Taylor (London: New Left Books, 1977).

[16] *Reason and Revolution: Hegel and the Rise of Social Theory* (Boston: Beacon Press, 1960), p. x.

[17] Tr. Edouard Morot-Sir, et al., *Philosophy and Phenomenological Research*, 30, no. 1, September, 1969.

[18] In *For Marx*, trans. Ben Brewster (New York: Vintage, 1970).

[19] Trans. Colin Gordon, *Feminist Studies* 6, no. 2, Summer, 1980.

[20] (Paris: Minuit), 1974, p. 10.

[21] For a discussion of the lack of specificity in the privileged metaphorics of political economy, especially in some texts of Derrida, see Spivak, "Il faut s'y prendre en s'en prenant à elles," in *Les fins de l'homme* (Paris: Galilée, 1981).

[22] "The Law of Genre," *Glyph* 7, 1980, p. 225.

[23] Percy Shelley's treatment of Harriet and Mary is a case in point; a "life" is not necessarily "outside the text." I have discussed the question in greater detail in "Finding Feminist Readings: Dante-Yeats" [see pp. 15–29 above] and "Displacement and the Discourse of Woman" in Mark Krupnick, ed., *Displacement: Derrida and After* (Bloomington: Indiana University Press, 1983), pp. 169–95.

[24] Derrida, *Of Grammatology*, trans. Spivak (Baltimore: Johns Hopkins University Press, 1976).

[25] "La double séance," *La dissémination* (Paris: Seuil, 1972); *Glas* (Paris: Galilée, 1976); "The Law of Genre" (op. cit.); "Living On: Border Lines," in Harold Bloom, et al., *Deconstruction & Criticism* (New York: Seabury Press, 1979).

[26] For a discussion of the importance of *restance* or minimal idealization in Derrida, see Spivak, "Revolutions that as Yet Have No Model: Derrida's *Limited Inc.*"

[27] Cf. Clément, "La Coupable," in *La jeune née* (Paris: Union Générale d'Editions, 1975), p. 15. This network-web-*tissu*-text is the untotalizable yet always grasped "subject" of "textuality." In Barthes it is the "writable," where we are written into this fuller text. Derrida speaks of it most compellingly in "Ja, ou le faux-bond," *Digraphes* 11, March 1977. It is in these terms that Foucault's notion of the microphysics of power should be understood. It is a mistake to think of such a thematic of textuality as a mere reduction of history to language.

[28] J. Laplanche and J.-B. Pontalis, *The Language of Psycho-Analysis*, trans. Donald Nicholson-Smith (New York: Norton, 1973), p. 210. The gap between this distilled definition and its use in the feminist context reminds us yet once again that the use of a dictionary has its own attendant dangers.

[29] Clément's use of "imaginary" and "symbolic" here inclines towards the colloquial, perhaps because of situational reasons. Clément is addressing irate feminists who are disaffected from what they see as Marxist-feminist theoreticism.

[30] Lacan, *Ecrits*, trans. Alan Sheridan (New York: Norton, 1977).

[31] Cixous is referring to the two axes of the male subject: the Oedipal norm (discovering the Name-of-the-Father) and the fetishist deviation (fetishizing the Mother as possessing a fantasmatic phallus).

[32] "The Purveyor of Truth," trans. Willis Domingo, et al., *Yale French Studies*, 52, 1975.

[33] Lacan, "God and the Jouissance of the Woman," in *Feminine Sexuality: Jacques Lacan and the école freudienne*, trans. Juliet Mitchell and Jacqueline Rose (London: Routledge and Kegan Paul, 1982). Also cited in Stephen Heath's excellent essay "Difference," *Screen* 19, no. 8, Autumn, 1978.

[34] "L'engendrement de la formule," *Tel Quel* 37 & 38, Spring & Summer, 1969; *Révolution du langage poétique* (Paris: Seuil, 1974); "Motherhood According to Bellini," *Desire in Language: A Semiotic Approach to Literature and Art*, trans. Thomas Gora, et al. (New York: Columbia Univ. Press, 1980); "Héréthique de l'amour," *Tel Quel* 74, Winter, 1977. And passim.

[35] Cf. *La jeune née*, p. 160. "Femininity," *Standard Edition*, vol. 22, pp. 116–117.

[36] I attempt to discuss this question in detail in "Displacement and the Discourse of Woman" (see n. 29).

[37] Trans. Samuel Weber and Jeffrey Mehlman, *Glyph* I, 1977, p. 181.

[38] "The Main Enemy," *Feminist Issues* I, no. 1 (1980), pp. 24–25.

[39] London: Heinemann, 1899.

[40] As revealed in *Chinese Women*, pp. 200–01, or the juxtaposition of Cixous, *To Live the Orange* (Paris: Des femmes, 1979), pp. 32–34 and p. 94.

[41] *Speculum* (Paris: Minuit, 1974).

[42] Paris: Galilée, 1980. A portion of this book has been published as "The Narcissistic Woman: Freud and Girard" in *Diacritics* 10.3, Fall 1980.

[43] I have attempted to develop the implications of such a strategy in "Displacement and the Discourse of Woman" (see n. 23, 36). As the reader may have surmised, that piece is in many ways a companion to this one.

[44] To take the simplest possible American examples, even such innocent triumphs as the hiring of more tenured women or adding feminist sessions at a Convention might lead, since most U.S. universities have dubious investments, and most Convention hotels use Third World female labor in a most oppressive way, to the increasing proletarianization of the women of the less developed countries.

[45] Claude Lévi-Strauss, "Structural Study of Myth," in *Myth: A Symposium*, ed. Thomas A. Sebeok (Bloomington: Indiana University Press, 1958), p. 103. The classic defense, to be found in *Structuralist Anthropology*, trans. Claire Jacobson and Brooke Grundfest Schoepf (New York: Basic Books, 1963), vol. 1, pp. 61–62, against the feminist realization that this was yet another elaboration of the objectification of women, seems curiously disingenuous. For if women had indeed been symbolized, on that level of generality, as *users* of signs rather than as signs, the binary opposition of exchanger and exchanged, founding structures of kinship, would collapse.

[46] For further ironies of the prohibitions associated with Hera's pleasure, see C. Kerényi, *Zeus and Hera: Archetypal Image of Father, Husband, and Wife*, trans. Christopher Holme (Princeton: Princeton University Press, 1975), pp. 97, 113.

[47] "Un nouveau type d'intellectuel: le dissident," p. 71.

[48] *Feminism and Materialism: Women and Modes of Production*, ed. Annette Kuhn and AnnMarie Wolpe (London: Routledge and Kegan Paul, 1978), pp. 49, 51. For an eloquent reverie on the ethic of penetration as it denies the clitoris see Irigaray, *New French Feminisms*, p. 100. In "Displacement," I suggest that such a gesture of penetrative appropriation is not absent from Derrida's reach for the "name of woman."

[49] Sherfey, *The Nature and Evolution of Female Sexuality* (New York: Vintage,

1973); *Our Bodies, Ourselves: A Book by and for Women* (New York: Simon and Schuster, second edition, 1971).

10. *Scattered Speculations on the Question of Value*

[1] I am deeply grateful to Professor John Fekete for a thorough criticism of this piece.

[2] Any serious consideration of this question must take into account Georg Simmel's monumental *Philosophy of Money* (trans. Tom Bottomore and David Frisby, London: Routledge and Kegan Paul, 1978). My differences with Simmel are considerable. He writes in a brilliantly analogical vein that cannot acknowledge the discontinuity between "idealist" and "materialist" predications. Although he is technically aware of the argument from surplus-value, he is basically interested in value-in-exchange. His anti-socialism is thus directed against a pre-Marxian socialism. His few references to Marx, as the translators note in their admirable introduction, do not betray knowledge of the Marxian text. Yet I have also been deeply influenced by his meditations upon the relationship between money and individualism and upon the beginnings of what Volosinov later called "behavioral ideology"; in a certain way even by his cogitation upon woman as commodity. In these respects, he should be distinguished from both the Engels of the *Origin of the Family* and the Weber of *The Protestant Ethic and the Spirit of Capitalism*.

[3] I am obliged here to admit that the "answer" that follows in this essay can in no way be considered definitive. This is my third attempt at working over these questions. The first, "Marx after Derrida," is to be found in William E. Cain, ed., *Philosophical Approaches to Literature: New Essays on Nineteenth- and Twentieth-Century Texts* (Lewisburg: Bucknell University Press, 1984). The second, an extended version of "the same piece," is forthcoming in Derek Attridge, et al., eds., *Post-Structuralism and the Question of History* (Cambridge: Cambridge University Press).

[4] If we think of Marx, Freud, Nietzsche (Derrida includes Heidegger) as the crucial Western thinkers of discontinuity, betrayed or obliged by their method to unbridgeable gaps and shifts in planes, a deconstructivist reading shows their texts to be a battleground between the intimations of discontinuity and the strong pull toward constructing a continuous argument with a secure beginning (arché), middle (historical enjambement), and end (telos). By and large, scholarship attempts to establish the continuity of the argument. It is therefore the continuist versions that are generally offered as the real Marx, the real Freud, the real Nietzsche.

[5] One of the chief complaints against Althusser is his privileging of "science" over "ideology," and his cutting up Marx into an earlier ideological and a later scientific thinker. I would submit that, in the spirit of a critique of positivism, Althusser *bricole*-s or tinkers with the name of science itself, re-constellates it

by spinning it out [*filer*] as a convenient metaphor even as he establishes Marx's claim to be a scientist rather than merely a philosopher of history: "When I say that Marx organized a theoretical system of scientific concepts in the domain previously monopolized by philosophies of history, I am spinning out [*filons*] a metaphor which is no more than a metaphor." This allows him to chart out the two great continents of science: physics (nature) and mathematics (idea). Marx inaugurates a science of history (humankind) because he proposes rules by which the metaleptic semiosis of history as account might be deciphered. It is not seen by Althusser as an authoritative inductive leap: "Obviously this epistemological break is not exactly locatable [*ponctuel*] . . . [it] inaugurates a history that will never come to an end." According to Althusser, Lenin consolidates this into a clear-cut program: "Lenin thus defines the ultimate essence of philosophical practice as an *intervention* in the theoretical domain. This intervention takes a double form: it is theoretical in its formulation of definite categories; and practical in the function of these categories." This is a "wild practice" ([*pratique sauvage*] on the analogy of "*la psychanalyse sauvage*" or pop psych). Althusser "generalizes this" into a (new) practice of philosophy, which recognizes that traditional philosophy is the arena of a denegation and a game played for the high stakes of scientificity. In this context, the terms "ideology" and "science," far from being a frozen and loaded binary opposition, are terms that must be thought over again and again (*Lenin and Philosophy*, trans. Ben Brewster [New York: Monthly Review Press, 1971], pp. 38–40, 61, 66). The relationship between the theory of subject-formation in Lacanian psychoanalysis and the Althusserian critique of ideology, or between Freudian notions of overdetermination and Althusser's emendation of the theory of contradictions, is established by way of a developed argument, not, as in Goux, by an isomorphic analogy.

[6] Textual criticism of this sort assumes, a) in the narrow sense, that even "theoretical" texts are produced in language, and, b) that "reality" is a fabrication out of discontinuities and constitutive differences with "origins" and "ends" that are provisional and shifting. "One no longer has a tripartition between a field of reality, the world, a field of representation, the book, and a field of subjectivity, the author. But an arrangement [*agencement*] puts in connection certain multiplicities drawn in each of these orders, so much that a book does not have its continuation in the following book nor its object in the world, nor yet its subject in one or more authors" [Deleuze and Guattari, *Mille plateaux*, Paris: 1980, p. 34; translation mine].

[7] I refer to this critique at greater length below. Here a brief checklist will suffice: Piero Sraffa, *Production of Commodities by Means of Commodities* (Cambridge: Cambridge University Press, 1960); Samir Amin, *The Law of Value and Historical Materialism* (New York: Monthly Review Press, 1978); Diane Elson, ed., *Value: The Representation of Labor in Capitalism* (Atlantic Highlands, NJ: Humanities Press, 1979); Ian Steedman, *Marx After Sraffa* (London: Verso Edition, 1981); Ian Steedman, et al., *The Value Controversy* (London: Verso Edition, 1981).

[8] For excellent elaborations of this theory, see the "Introduction"-s and indeed the entire issues of *Zerowork: Political Materials 1 & 2* (December 1975 and

Fall 1977). One of the most revolutionary suggestions of this thought is that the working class includes the unwaged as well as the waged. I am suggesting that the unwaged under socialized capital has a different status and definition from the unwaged in the peripheral capitalisms.

[9] One striking exception is Diane Elson, "The Value Theory of Labour," in Elson, ed. *Value*. I propose something similar in "Feminism and Critical Theory," pp. 77–92 above.

[10] Hazel Carby, et al., eds., *The Empire Strikes Back: Race and Racism in 70s Britain* (London: Hutchinson, 1982) is a significant exception. Not only are the authors aware of the connection between racism in Britain and the international division of labor; they are also aware that a study of race relations in Britain cannot pretend to be a general study of the Third World.

[11] There is a steadily growing body of work dealing with this phenomenon, a glimpse of which may be found in journals such as *NACLA, The Bulletin of Concerned Asian Scholars*, and *Economic and Political Weekly*. A bibliographical starting point would be Kathleen Gough and Hari P. Sharma, eds., *Imperialism and Revolution in South Asia* (New York: Monthly Review Press, 1973), Part I; Samir Amin, *Unequal Development: An Essay on the Social Formations of Peripheral Capitalism*, trans. Brian Pearce (New York: Monthly Review Press, 1976); and Cheryl Payer, *The Debt Trap: The IMF and the Third World* (New York: Monthly Review Press, 1974) and *The World Bank: A Critical Analysis* (New York: Monthly Review Press, 1982).

[12] See Deborah Fahy Bryceson, "Use Value, The Law of Value and the Analysis of Non-Capitalist Production," *Capital & Class* 20 (Summer 1983). (I have differences of theoretical detail with Bryceson which are immaterial to my argument here.) My account of the "Third World" here is of the predominant "peripheral capitalist model of development," which works through "an alliance of imperialism with the local exploiting classes" (Samir Amin, *The Future of Maoism*, trans. Norman Finkelstein [New York: Monthly Review Press, 1982], 9–10).

[13] In spite of necessary qualifications, this argument underlies much of the criticism relating to the U.S. nineteenth century and a certain twentieth century. A general line may be traced from F. O. Matthiessen, *American Renaissance: Art and Expression in The Age of Emerson and Whitman* (London: Oxford University Press, 1941), through R. W. B. Lewis, *The American Adam: Innocence, Tragedy and Tradition in the 19th Century* (Chicago: University of Chicago Press, 1955), to, say, Sherman Paul's *The Lost America of Love* (Baton Rouge: Louisiana State University Press, 1981).

[14] Theodore Levitt, "The Globalization of Markets," *Harvard Business Review* 61:3 (May–June, 1983), 95. I am indebted to Dennis Dworkin for bringing this piece to my attention.

[15] Ibid., 101. In terms of the ideological interpellation of the subject as consumer, it is worth remarking that the semiotic field here reproduces capitalist

as well as patriarchal social relations faithfully: "The Customer" (who is male) does not know what he wants; "Managers [should not be] confidently wedded to a distorted version of the marketing concept according to which you give the customer what he says he wants." But, since the item under discussion here is an automatic washer, the actual target is, of course, "the homemaker" (who is female): "Hoover's media message should have been: This is the machine that you, the homemaker, deserve to have to reduce the repetitive heavy daily household burdens, so that you may have more constructive time to spend with your children and your husband. The promotion should also have targeted the husband to give him, preferably in the presence of his wife, a sense of obligation to provide an automatic washer for her even before he bought an automobile for himself. An aggressively low price, combined with heavy promotion of this kind, would have overcome previously expressed preferences for particular features" [98]. There is something like a relation between this ideological reproduction and reinforcement of the international division of labor in the discourse of patriarchal relations in consumerism, and the reproduction and reinforcement of the international division of labor in the discourse of feminist individualism within socialized capital. Examine, for instance, the following convincingly innocent and unproblematic evaluation of telecommunication in *Ms* in light of the axiology suggested by considerations of the "materialist" predication of the subject, which the readers of *Ms* cannot be expected to know since that magazine too is an ideological apparatus within the social arena under consideration. (Incidentally, it is interesting to see how the time-problematic is reversed within a "narrative" context, how the language of narrative-production in telecommunication seeks to recapture a naive "reality." This is a much longer argument which I hope to develop elsewhere.) "Roberta Williams didn't know what she wanted to do with her life until she designed her first microcomputer adventure game three years ago. Today, she is one of the leading designers of home computer games and part owner . . . of a $20 million business. . . . There is something exciting about the continuous motion in arcade games and to use 'real time' (industry lingo for the continuous action that is programmed into the game) within adventure games." Later in the same issue, speaking of "the search business" for women executives, the magazine uses some symptomatic metaphors. "The process is essentially matchmaking. . . . You don't have to have that Dolly [*Hello Dolly!*] Levi commonsense instinct [read ideology at its strongest] of who-goes-with-whom, and also the diplomacy of Kissinger" [*Ms* 12:2 (August 1983): 20, 73]. The relationship between feminist individualism and the military-industrial complex on the one hand, and the problem of anti-sexism within the capitalist enclosure being understood as feminism on the other, is too overdetermined for me to deal with it in more than a footnote. The emergence of an unexamined genitalist axiology of women's suffering and universal sisterhood is also at issue here. What complicates the situation is the overarching presence of hegemonic masculism.

[16] I am grateful to Todd Snyder for suggesting this line of thought to me.

[17] A representative essay would be Fredric Jameson, "Postmodernism and Consumer Society," Hal Foster, ed., *The Anti-Aesthetic*. As is demonstrated in

the revised version of this essay, to be found in *New Left Review* as "Postmodernism, or the Cultural Logic of Late Capitalism," Jameson is ambivalent about these possibilities.

[18] The Marx that is useful here is not the philosopher of history, but rather the theoretician of crisis. It is in the sketched theory of crisis that Marx most anticipates the international division of labor, least imposing the normative narrative of modes of production in the world outside Western Europe. Concise accounts of crisis theory, and crisis theory and contemporary imperialism, are to be found in Robert I. Rhodes, ed., *Imperialism and Underdevelopment: A Reader* (New York: Monthly Review Press, 1970). A systematic development of Marx's theory of production, distribution, and circulation into the regulation of crises is to be found in Michel Aglietta, *A Theory of Capitalist Regulation*. Peter F. Bell and Harry Cleaver give an account of the development of Marx's own theory of crisis in "Marx's Crisis Theory as a Theory of Class Struggle," *Research in Political Economy* 5 (1982).

[19] "Marx's Transformation Problem," p. 576. This, incidentally, also reveals the mistake of the layperson who "refutes" the labor theory of value because "you cannot deduce prices from it." Marx's theory is one where politics, economics, and ideology are relatively autonomous in the determination of class relations in the broadest sense. The point, therefore, is not to reduce value to a calculus of price, especially within models of general equilibrium. Wolff, et al. do produce equations that take this into account. They are, however, aware that the more important issue is that the practical moment in Marx questions abstract economic rigor; even as I argue in the body of this essay that the axiological moment in Marx questions mere philosophical justice.

[20] The most powerful development of this conception is the mysterious *Spurs: Nietzsche's Styles*, trans. Barbara Harlow (Chicago: University of Chicago Press, 1978). Part of the mystery lies, I think, in that Derrida is here trying to make "woman his subject" (his "interest"?) and hint enigmatically at "affirmative deconstruction." As I will soon explain, my notion of interest must take the risk of being related to the deliberative consciousness. Over a year after the writing of this essay, at the point of implementing the final editorial suggestions, I begin to realize how astutely Paul de Man had predicted this move from "false" metaphor to "literalization" in the field of political practice. It would take a careful elaboration of de Man's entire complex argument in *Allegories of Reading* to establish the parallel between my move here and grammar and "figure" in the following definition of textuality: "We call text any entity that can be considered from . . . a double perspective: as a generative, open-ended, non-referential grammatical system and as a figural system closed off by a transcendental signification that subverts the grammatical code to which the text owes its existence" [Paul de Man, *Allegories of Reading* 270; italics mine]. Suffice it here to consolidate the parallel by pointing out that, towards the bottom of the same page, de Man aphoristically describes the necessity of this subversion, this closing off, in the following way: " . . . and if a text does not *act*, it cannot state what it knows" (italics mine).

[21] "On An Apocalyptic Tone Recently Adopted in Philosophy," trans. John P. Leavey, Jr., *Semeia* 23 (1982). I believe it is possible to read in this obscure text a practical politics of the open end. I hope to write in detail of it in my forthcoming book on Derrida. I will content myself with quoting a relatively less aphoristic sentence: "To raise or set the tone higher . . . is to . . . make the inner voice delirious, the inner voice that is the voice of the other in us" [71].

11. *"Draupadi"* by Mahasweta Devi

[1] For elaborations upon such a suggestion, see Jean-François Lyotard, *La Condition post-moderne: Rapport sur le savoir* (Paris, 1979).

[2] See my "Three Feminist Readings: McCullers, Drabble, Habermas," *Union Seminary Quarterly Review* 1–2 (Fall–Winter 1979–80), and "French Feminism in an International Frame" [see above pp. 134–53].

[3] I develop this argument in my review of Jacques Derrida's *Memoires* in *boundary 2* forthcoming.

[4] This list represents a distillation of suggestions to be found in the work of Jacques Derrida: see, e.g., "The Exorbitant. Question of Method," *Of Grammatology*, trans. Spivak (Baltimore: Johns Hopkins University Press, 1976); "Limited Inc," trans. Samuel Weber, *Glyph* 2 (1977); "Ou commence et comment finit un corps enseignant," in *Politiques de la philosophie*, ed. Dominique Grisoni (Paris: B. Grasset, 1976); and my "Revolutions That as Yet Have No Model: Derrida's 'Limited Inc,'" *Diacritics* 10 (Dec. 1980), and "Sex and History in Wordsworth's *The Prelude* (1805) IX–XIII" [see pp. 46–76 above].

[5] It is a sign of E. M. Forster's acute perception of India that *A Passage to India* contains a glimpse of such an ex-orbitant tribal in the figure of the punkha puller in the courtroom.

[6] Mahasweta, *Agnigarbha* (Calcutta, 1978), p. 8.

[7] For a discussion of the relationship between academic degrees in English and the production of revolutionary literature, see my "A Vulgar Inquiry into the Relationship between Academic Criticism and Literary Production in West Bengal" (paper delivered at the Annual Convention of the Modern Language Association, Houston, 1980).

[8] These figures are an average of the 1971 census in West Bengal and the projected figure for the 1974 census in Bangladesh.

[9] See Dinesh Chandra Sen, *History of Bengali Language and Literature* (Calcutta, 1911). A sense of Bengali literary nationalism can be gained from the (doubtless apocryphal) report that, upon returning from his first investigative tour of India, Macaulay remarked: "The British Crown presides over two great literatures: the English and the Bengali."

[10] See Gautam Chattopadhyay, *Communism and the Freedom Movement in Bengal* (New Delhi, 1970).

[11] Marcus F. Franda, *Radical Politics in West Bengal* (Cambridge: MIT Press, 1971), p. 153. I am grateful to Michael Ryan for having located this accessible account of the Naxalbari movement. There now exists an excellent study by Sumanta Banerjee, *India's Simmering Revolution: The Naxalite Uprising* (London: Zed Press, 1984).

[12] See Samar Sen, et al., eds., *Naxalbari and After: A Frontier Anthology*, 2 vols. (Calcutta, 1978).

[13] See Bernard-Henri Lévy, *Bangla Desh: Nationalisme dans la révolution* (Paris, 1973).

[14] Franda, *Radical Politics*, pp. 163–64. See also p. 164, n.22.

[15] Lawrence Lifschultz, *Bangladesh: The Unfinished Revolution* (London: Zed Press, 1979), pp. 25, 26.

[16] For my understanding of this aspect of the *Mahabharata*, I am indebted to Romila Thapar of Jawaharlal Nehru University, New Delhi.

[17] I borrow this sense of singularity from Jacques Lacan, "Seminar on 'The Purloined Letter'," trans. Jeffrey Mehlman, *Yale French Studies* 48 (1972): 53, 59.

[18] As a result of the imposition of the capitalist mode of production and the Imperial Civil Service, and massive conversions of the lowest castes to Christianity, the invariable identity of caste and trade no longer holds. Here, too, there is the possibility of a taxonomy micrologically deconstructive of the caste-class opposition, functioning heterogeneously in terms of the social hierarchy.

[19] If indeed the model for this character is Ranjit Gupta, the notorious inspector general of police of West Bengal, the delicate textuality, in the interest of a political position, of Senanayak's delineation in the story takes us far beyond the limits of a reference *à clef*. I am grateful to Michael Ryan for suggesting the possibility of such a reference.

[20] The relationship between phallocentrism, the patriarchy, and clean binary oppositions is a pervasive theme in Derrida's critique of the metaphysics of presence. See my "Unmaking and Making in *To the Lighthouse*" [see pp. 30–45 above].

[21] "My dearest Sati, through the walls and the miles that separate us I can hear you saying, 'In Sawan it will be two years since Comrade left us.' The other women will nod. It is you who have taught them the meaning of Comrade" (Mary Tyler, "Letter to a Former Cell-Mate," in *Naxalbari and After*, 1:307; see also Tyler, *My Years in an Indian Prison* [Harmondsworth: Penguin, 1977]).

[22] I am grateful to Soumya Chakravarti for his help in solving occasional problems of English synonyms and archival research.

12. Subaltern Studies: Deconstructing Historiography

[1] Ranajit Guha, ed., *Subaltern Studies III: Writings on South Asian History and Society* (Delhi: Oxford University Press, 1984), p. 351. The three volumes of *Subaltern Studies* are hereafter cited in my text as 1, 2, and 3, with page references following.

[2] Paul de Man, *Blindness and Insight: Essays in the Rhetoric of Contemporary Criticism* (Minneapolis: Univ. of Minnesota Press, 1983), p. 8.

[3] Jacques Derrida, *Writing and Difference*, trans. Alan Bass (Chicago: University of Chicago Press, 1982), p. 289. All translations modified when deemed necessary.

[4] 1.83, 86, 186; 2.65, 115; 3.21, 71. Also Ranajit Guha, *Elementary Aspects of Peasant Insurgency in Colonial India* (Delhi: Oxford University Press, 1983), pp. 88, 226, 30, 318; hereafter cited in my text as *EAP*, with page references following.

[5] See Edward W. Said, *The World, the Text, and the Critic* (Cambridge: Harvard University Press, 1983), pp. 170–2 for a discussion of "elaboration" in Gramsci.

[6] Friedrich Nietzsche, *On the Genealogy of Morals and Ecce Homo*, trans. Walter J. Kaufmann (New York: Vintage Books, 1969), pp. 77, 80.

[7] I am using the word "Imaginary" loosely in the sense given to it by Jacques Lacan. For a short definition, see Jean Laplanche and J. B. Pontalis, *The Language of Psycho-Analysis*, trans. David Nicholson-Smith (New York: Norton, 1973), p. 210.

[8] As always my preferred example of a theoretical fiction remains the primary process in Freud. *The Complete Psychological Works*, trans. James Strachey et al. (London: Hogarth Press, 1961), vol. 5, p. 598f.

[9] For an excellent discussion of this, see Judith Butler, "Geist ist Zeit: French Interpretations of Hegel's Absolute," *Berkshire Review* (Summer, 1985; forthcoming).

[10] Antonio Gramsci, cited in *EAP* 28.

[11] Derrida, *Of Grammatology*, trans. Spivak (Baltimore: the Johns Hopkins University Press, 1976), p. 24.

[12] Since the historian is gender-specific in the work of the collective (see pp. 33–43), I have consistently used "he."

[13] The most important example of this is Dominick LaCapra, *Rethinking Intellectual History* (Ithaca: Cornell University Press, 1983), and *History and Criticism* (Ithaca: Cornell University Press, 1984).

[14] Derrida, *Of Grammatology*, p. 93. Since my intention here is simply to offer a moment of transcoding, I have not undertaken to "explain" the Derridean passage.

[15] Spivak, "Can the Subaltern Speak?" in Larry Grossberg and Cary Nelson, eds., *Marxist Interpretations of Literature and Culture: Limits, Frontiers, Boundaries* (Urbana: University of Illinois Press, forthcoming).

[16] The most, perhaps too, spectacular deployment of the argument is in Gilles Deleuze and Félix Guattari, *Anti-Oedipus: Capitalism and Schizophrenia*, trans. Robert Hurley, et al. (New York: Viking Press, 1977).

[17] Gramsci, *Prison Notebooks*, trans. Quintin Hoare and Geoffrey Nowell-Smith (New York: International Publishers, 1971), p. 421.

[18] Karl Marx and Friedrich Engels, "The Manifesto of the Communist Party," in *Selected Works* (Moscow: Foreign Languages Publishing House, 1951), p. 51.

[19] Georg Friedrich Wilhelm Hegel, *The Science of Logic*, trans. A. V. Miller (New York: Humanities Press, 1976), p. 107.

[20] This concept-metaphor of "interest" is orchestrated by Derrida in *Spurs*, trans. Barbara Harlow (Chicago: University of Chicago Press, 1978) with notions of "affirmative deconstructions," which would acknowledge that no example of deconstruction can match its discourse.

[21] Michel Foucault, *Language, Counter-Memory, Practice*, trans. Donald F. Bouchard and Sherry Simon (Ithaca: Cornell University Press, 1977), pp. 156, 154.

[22] Louis Althusser, *Lenin and Philosophy and Other Essays*, trans. Ben Fowkes (New York: Monthly Review Press, 1971), p. 68.

[23] I discuss the mechanics of Thompson's critique briefly in "Explanation and Culture: Marginalia" [see pp. 103–17 above].

[24] An exemplary statement is to be found in "Intellectuals and Power," in *Language, Counter-Memory, Practice*.

[25] Jean Baudrillard, *In the Shadow of the Silent Majorities or the End of the Social and Other Essays*, trans. Paul Foss, et al. (New York: Semiotext(e), 1983), p. 26; and Deleuze and Guattari, *On the Line*, trans. John Johnston (New York: Semiotext(e), 1983), p. 1.

[26] Spivak, "Can the Subaltern Speak?"

[27] Althusser, "Sur le rapport de Marx à Hegel," in *Hegel et la pensée moderne*, ed. Jacques d'Hondt (Paris: Presses universitaires, 1970), pp. 108–9.

[28] Karl Marx, "The Eighteenth Brumaire of Louis Bonaparte," in *Surveys from Exile*, ed. David Fernbach (New York: Vintage Books, 1974), p. 147.

[29] For historical work that would relate to the contemporary struggle, see John Womack, *Zapata and the Mexican Revolution* (New York: Knopf, 1969).

[30] Steven Ungar, *Roland Barthes: the Professor of Desire* (Lincoln: The University of Nebraska Press, 1983).

[31] Derrida, "Signature Event Context," in *Margins of Philosophy*, trans. Alan Bass (Chicago: University of Chicago Press, 1982), pp. 318–18.

[32] For another contemporary transformation of this notion see Antonio Negri, *Marx Beyond Marx: Lessons on the Grundrisse*, trans. Harry Cleaver, et al. (South Hadley: Begin and Garvey, 1984), pp. 41–58.

[33] Derrida, "Plato's Pharmacy," in *Dissemination*, trans. Barbara Johnson (Chicago: University of Chicago Press, 1981), p. 146.

[34] Hobbes's discussion of authority in the *Leviathan* and Kant's discussion of the genius in *The Critique of Judgment* are two of the many *loci classici*. There are lengthy discussions of this thematic,—as found in the Platonic Socrates, in Rousseau, and in J. L. Austin,—in Derrida's "Plato's Pharmacy," *Of Grammatology*, and "Signature Event Context," respectively.

[35] Terry Eagleton, *Walter Benjamin: or Towards A Revolutionary Criticism* (London: Verso Press, 1981), p. 140.

[36] See Hardiman, "Adivasi Assertion in South Gujarat: the Devi Movement of 1922–3," in 3.

[37] June Nash and Maria Patricia Fernandez Kelley, eds., *Women, Men, and the International Division of Labor* (Albany: SUNY Press, 1983), p. viii.

[38] I discuss this issue in "The Politics of 'Feminist Culture,'" in progress.

[39] Claude Lévi-Strauss, *Structural Anthropology*, trans. Claire Jacobson and Brooke Grundfest Schoepf (Garden City: Anchor Books, 1967), p. 60.

[40] Derrida, *Spurs*, pp. 109–11.

14. *A Literary Representation of the Subaltern: A Woman's Text from the Third World*

[1] I am grateful to Jill Matthews for a critical reading of this paper.

[2] Mahasweta Devi, "Stanadayini," *Ekshan* (Autumn, Bengali year 1384). My translation, "Breast-Giver," appears as Chapter Thirteen of this volume. Page references to it are parenthetically included in my text.

[3] Ernesto Laclau and Chantal Mouffe, *Hegemony and Socialist Strategy: Towards a Radical Democratic Politics*, trans. Winston Moore and Paul Cammack (London: Verso, 1985), p. 108.

[4] The two are nicely if somewhat metaphysically combined in Ilya Prigogine and Isabelle Stengers, *Order Out of Chaos: Man's New Dialogue with Nature* (Boulder: Shambhala Publishers, 1984).

[5] Michel Foucault, *The Archaeology of Knowledge and the Discourse on Language*,

trans. A. M. Sheridan Smith (London: Tavistock, 1972), p. 86. Translations from all texts modified wherever necessary.

[6] Foucault, *Archaeology,* pp. 95–96. Emphasis mine.

[7] Foucault, "Discursive Formations," *Archaeology,* pp. 31–39.

[8] See especially Foucault, "The Confession of the Flesh," *Power/Knowledge: Selected Interviews and Other Writings 1972–1977,* trans. Colin Gordon, et. al. (New York: Pantheon, 1980), pp. 196–198.

[9] Jacques Derrida, "Limited Inc," *Glyph* 2 (1977), especially p. 239.

[10] Roland Barthes, "The Reality-Effect," in *The Rustle of Language,* trans. Richard Howard (New York: Hill and Wang, 1984).

[11] The relationship between the two words that relate through this approximate differential is, of course, not "the same" in all languages. There is, however, always a differential. In modern French and German, for example, the words for "history" and "story" being roughly the same, the maneuverings would be somewhat different from what we, writing in English, would argue. Ultimately the distinction is between the true and the sanctioned non-true.

[12] Samik Bandyopadhyay, "Introduction," in Mahasweta Devi, *Five Plays: Mother of 1084/Aajir/Bayen/Urvashi and Johnny/Water* (Calcutta: Seagull Press, 1986), p. xi.

[13] Unpublished intervention, Subaltern Studies Conference, Calcutta, January 9, 1986.

[14] "The tenor is the gist of the thought concerning the subject [here India as Slave/Mother] . . . and the vehicle is that which embodies the tenor—the analogy [here the specificity of Jashoda as subaltern] . . . by which the tenor is conveyed" (Sylvan Barnet, et al., *A Dictionary of Literary, Dramatic, and Cinematic Terms* (second edition, Boston: Little, Brown, 1971), p. 51.

[15] This is the implicit grounding presupposition of Benedict Anderson, *Imagined Communities: Reflections on the Origin and Spread of Nationalism* (London: New Left Books, 1983). For a review expressing the criticism that I here echo, see Ranajit Guha, "Nationalism Reduced to 'Official Nationalism'," *ASAA Review* 9, 1 (July 1985).

[16] See Edward W. Said, "Culture and Imperialism" (the Clark Lectures, University of Kent, December 1985: forthcoming).

[17] See Partha Chatterjee, *Nationalist Thought and the Colonial World: A Derivative Discourse* (London: Zed Press, 1986). Uday Mehta, Assistant Professor of Government at Cornell University, is engaged in similar work on Lockean liberalism.

[18] David Hardiman has examined some of the received wisdom on this issue in "Bureaucratic Recruitment and Subordination in Colonial India: The Madras Constabulary, 1859–1947," *Subaltern Studies,* vol. 4.

[19] Hardiman, "'Subaltern Studies' at Crossroads," *Economic and Political Weekly* (Feb 15, 1986).

[20] *Mutatis mutandis*. Louis Althusser, "Ideology and Ideological State Apparatuses (Notes Towards An Investigation)," *Lenin and Philosophy and Other Essays*, trans. Ben Brewster (New York: Monthly Review Press, 1971), still seems the most authoritative account of this phenomenon. Disciplinary productions such as historiography and literary pedagogy would probably fall between "the educational" and "the cultural ISA"-s (p. 143).

[21] See Terry Eagleton, "The Rise of English," *Literary Theory: An Introduction* (Minneapolis: University of Minnesota Press, 1983).

[22] The most spirited discussion of the historicity of affects is to be found in the debate on pornography in the United States. For a discussion of the phenomenality of affects see Robert C. Solomon, *The Passions* (Notre Dame: University of Notre Dame Press, 1976). For a provocative suggestion about Freud's contribution to the latter issue, see Derrida, *Of Grammatology*, trans. Spivak (Baltimore, 1976). p. 88.

[23] I am, of course, describing deconstructive literary criticism when I cite these special themes. I take this position in spite of Derrida's cautionary words regarding the too positivistic use of "themes" in an assessment of his own work ("The Double Session," *Dissemination*, trans. Barbara Johnson [Chicago: University of Chicago Press, 1981], p. 245). In fact, in "Varieties of Deconstructive Practice," a widely publicized paper which will eventually be forthcoming, I have distinguished Derrida's reading of literature from his reading of philosophical texts in terms of the issue of "themes." I mention this because that argument is also an issue of disciplinary production: of philosophy and literature, as here of history and literary pedagogy. For one of the most astute formulaic reductions of deconstruction to thematic reading, see Barbara Johnson, "Teaching Deconstructively," in G. Douglas Atkins and Michael L. Johnson, eds., *Writing and Reading Differently: Deconstruction and the Teaching of Composition and Literature* (Lawrence: University of Kansas Press, 1985). For an example of my own excursion into thematizing "affirmative deconstruction," see note 81 of this essay.

[24] Quoted in Abiola Irele, *The African Experience in Literature and Ideology* (London: Heinemann, 1981), p. 1.

[25] In the U.S., anti-economistic "cultural" Marxism, feminist or androcentric, faults Althusser's work because it apparently underplays the class struggle by structuralizing the mode of production narrative. In Britain, the general impact of E. P. Thompson's critique, as reflected in *The Poverty of Theory and Other Essays* (London: Merlin, 1978) diagnosed Althusser as using Hegel as a code word for Stalin and betraying the spirit of Marxism by structuralizing the mode of production of narrative. On and around the issue of essentialism, a certain alliance between British post-Althusserianism and British Marxist feminism may be found. The work of Toril Moi in *Sexual/Textual Politics: Feminist Literary Theory* (New York: Methuen, 1985) would be a good example.

[26] Lise Vogel, *Marxism and the Oppression of Women: Toward a Unitary Theory* (New Brunswick: Rutgers University Press, 1983), p. 147.

[27] Perry Anderson, *Passages from Antiquity to Feudalism* (London: New Left Books, 1974), pp. 24–25.

[28] Some well-known examples among many would be Mary O'Brien, *The Politics of Reproduction* (Boston: Routledge & Kegan Paul, 1981), Annette Kuhn and AnnMarie Wolpe, "Feminism and Materialism," in Kuhn and Wolpe, eds., *Feminism and Materialism: Women and Modes of Production* (London, 1978), and Rosalind Coward, *Patriarchal Precedents: Sexuality and Social Relations* (London: Methuen, 1983). See also Lydia Sargent, ed., *Women and Revolution* (Boston: South End Press, 1981).

[29] Vogel, *Marxism and the Oppression of Women*, pp. 141–142. For a sound critique of the Engelsian-feminist position, see Coward, "The Concept of the Family in Marxist Theory," *Patriarchal Precedents*. It seems to me unfortunate that Coward's critique should be used to lead us back into Freud.

[30] Karl Marx, *Capital*, trans. David Fernbach (New York: Vintage Books, 1978), vol. 2, pp. 469–471.

[31] Marx, *Capital*, vol. 2, pp. 180 and 180f. in general.

[32] (Paris, 1980.)

[33] V. N. Volosinov, *Marxism and the Philosophy of Language*, trans. Ladislav Matejka and I. R. Titunik (Cambridge: Harvard University Press, 1973), p. 68.

[34] I am not arguing here for individual differences. On the social character of "solitary self-experience," see Volosinov, *Marxism and the Philosophy of Language*, pp. 89–94. In a more essentialist form, assuming that there is such a thing as "life in its immediacy," one might say, with Adorno: "He [sic] who wishes to know the truth about life in its immediacy must scrutinise its estranged form, the objective powers that determine individual existence even in its most hidden recesses" (Theodor Adorno, *Minima Moralia: Reflections from a Damaged Life*, trans. E. F. N. Jephcott, London: New Left Books, 1974, p. 15). Institutional subject-positions are social vacancies that are of course not filled in the same way by different individuals. All generalizations made from subject-positions are untotalizable.

[35] See note 28 and, for the best-known examples, see Ann Oakley, *The Sociology of Housework* (New York: Pantheon, 1975), and the excellent documentation in Anne Ferguson, "On Conceiving Motherhood and Sexuality: A Feminist Materialist Approach," in Joyce Trebilcot, ed., *Mothering: Essays in Feminist Theory* (Totowa: Rowman & Allenheld, 1984), an essay I discuss below. Extended considerations might take their lead from the papers of the International Wages for Housework Campaign and check such sources as Gary S. Becker, *Human Capital: A Theoretical and Empirical Analysis with Special Reference to Education* (Chicago: University of Chicago Press, 1983).

[36] For a discussion of feminist knowledge within existing paradigms, I have profited from listening to Susan Magarey, "Transgressing Barriers, Centralising Margins, and Transcending Boundaries: Feminism as Politicised Knowledge," unpublished paper, conference on "Feminist Enquiry As A Transdisciplinary Enterprise," University of Adelaide, August 21, 1986.

[37] Here I am invoking one of the earliest deconstructive positions: that reversals of positions legitimize each other and therefore a persistent effort at displacement is in order. For the later suggestion of a distancing from the project of reason, see Derrida, "The Principle of Reason: the University in the Eyes of its Pupils," *Diacritics* 13, 3 (Fall 1983).

[38] Ferguson, "Conceiving Motherhood," p. 176.

[39] In fact, Ferguson sees foster-mothering as one among many types of "social mothering (adoptive mothers, step and foster mothers, older sisters, other mother surrogates) [which] involves a second or different kind of mother-daughter bond" (p. 177). I discuss "Stanadayini"'s treatment of varieties of mother-child relationships later in the essay.

[40] Ferguson, "Conceiving Motherhood," p. 156.

[41] This is to be distinguished from uninformed anti-Marxist positions. I have in mind generalizations in such powerful essays as Catharine A. McKinnon, "Feminism, Marxism, Method, and the State: An Agenda for Theory," in Nannerl O. Keohane, ed., *Feminist Theory: A Critique of Ideology* (Chicago: University of Chicago Press, 1982), Luce Irigaray, "The Power of Discourse" and "Commodities Among Themselves," *This Sex Which Is Not One*, trans. Catherine Porter (Ithaca: Cornell University Press, 1985), pp. 82–85, 192–197, and Rosalind Coward, "The Concept of the Family in Marxist Theory," *Patriarchal Precedents*. It should be mentioned here that, in spite of her over-simplification of Marx's positions on value and ideology, Ferguson is generally politically astute in her assessment of the relationships between various domination systems in Euramerica.

[42] Ferguson, "Conceiving Motherhood," p. 155.

[43] Hannelore Mabry, "The Feminist Theory of Surplus Value," in Edith Hoshino Altbach et al. eds., *German Feminism: Readings in Politics and Literature* (Albany: State University of New York Press, 1986), tries interestingly to bridge the two spheres.

[44] Anna Davin, "Imperialism and Motherhood," *History Workshop* 5 (1978).

[45] See Jennifer Sharpe, "The Double Discourse of Colonialism and Nationalism: the Production of A Colonial Subject in British India," *Dissertation Abstracts* (University of Texas-Austin, forthcoming).

[46] Ferguson, "Conceiving Motherhood," p. 175.

[47] See Chandra Talpade Mohanty, "Under Western Eyes: Feminist Scholarship and Colonial Discourses," *boundary* 2 12,3/13,1 (Spring–Fall 1984) and "Fem-

inist Theory and the Production of Universal Sisterhood," unpublished paper, conference on "Race, Culture, Class: Challenges to Feminism," Hampshire College, December 1985, and Spivak, "Imperialism and Sexual Difference," *Oxford Literary Review* 8, 1–2, 1986.

[48] The discontinuities between the three domination systems are quietly revealed by the asymmetry in the articulation of the three pairs.

[49] Antonio Gramsci, "Some Aspects of the Southern Question," *Selections from Political Writing: 1921–1926*, trans. Quintin Hoare (New York, 1978): Marx, *Capital*, trans. David Fernbach (New York, 1981), vol. 3, p. 1016.

[50] Georg Wilhelm Friedrich Hegel, *Lectures on the Philosophy of History*, trans. J. Sibree (New York: Dover, 1956), p. 105, Adorno, *Minima Moralia*, p. 53, Jürgen Habermas, "A Philosophico-Political Profile," *New Left Review* 151, Julia Kristeva, "Mémoires," *L'infini* 1.

[51] Meaghan Morris, "Identity Anecdotes," *Camera Obscura* 12 (1984), p. 43.

[52] Davin, "Imperialism," p. 54.

[53] Bharati Mukherjee, *Wife* (Boston: Houghton Mifflin, 1975) and *Darkness* (Markham, Ontario: Penguin, 1985).

[54] Parvathy Hadley, "The Betrayal of Superwoman," *Committee on South Asian Women Bulletin* 4,1 (1986), p. 18.

[55] One of the pioneering statements, Zillah Eisenstein's "Developing A Theory of Capitalist Patriarchy and Socialist Feminism," in Eisenstein, ed., *Capitalist Patriarchy and the Case for Socialist Feminism* (New York, 1979), shows both the strengths and the weaknesses of this approach.

[56] This is not in disagreement with the identification of rape with violence, as in Catherine A. McKinnon, *Sexual Harassment of Working Women: A Case of Sex Discrimination* (New Haven: Yale University Press, 1979).

[57] See Mahmoud Mamdani, *The Myth of Population Control: Family, Caste and Class in An Indian Village* (New York: Monthly Review Press, 1973). For an unfortunate articulation of this contradiction, see Germaine Greer, *Sex and Destiny: the Politics of Human Fertility* (New York: Harper & Row, 1984).

[58] For a use of the phrase in a single-issue class-context see "Right to Life, but . . ." *Economic and Political Weekly* 20.29 (July 20, 1985), editorial.

[59] This is a general feeling that is too pervasive to document satisfactorily. But notice the interesting undertone emerging in "French Texts/American Contexts," *Yale French Studies* 62 (1981).

[60] For representative pieces see Irigaray, "When Our Lips Speak Together," *This Sex*, Monique Wittig, *The Lesbian Body*, trans. David Le Vay (New York: Avon, 1975), Alice Schwarzer, "The Function of Sexuality in the Oppression of Women," in *German Feminism*, and Spivak, "French Feminism in An Interna-

tional Frame." I have not yet seen no. 26 of *Les Cahiers du grif* (Paris/Brussels), entitled *Jouir*.

[61] In *Feminine Sexuality: Jacques Lacan and the école freudienne*, trans. Juliet Mitchell and Jacqueline Rose (London: Routledge & Kegan Paul, 1982).

[62] Lacan, "Love Letter," p. 159.

[63] See, for examples, Hegel, *Aesthetics: Lectures on Fine Art*, trans. T. M. Knox (Oxford: Oxford University Press, 1975), Georg Lukács, *Theory of the Novel*, trans. Anna Bostock (Cambridge: MIT Press, 1971), and Roland Barthes, *S/Z*, trans. Richard Miller (New York: Hill and Wang, 1974).

[64] Jameson, *The Political Unconscious: Narrative As a Socially Symbolic Act* (Ithaca: Cornell University Press, 1981).

[65] It is possible to deduce Althusser's reading of Lacan in this way. See Althusser, "Freud and Lacan," in *Lenin and Philosophy*.

[66] Lacan, "God and the Jouissance of the Woman," in *Feminine Sexuality*, p. 142.

[67] Derrida at once participates in and criticizes this gender-positioned definition of the object that cannot be known as the feminine thing when, in *Glas* (Paris: Galilée, 1981), he abbreviates the Hegelian Absolute Knowledge (*savoir absolu*), beyond the grasp of the individual subject, as *Sa*. In French this is a possessive pronominal article which merely indicates that its object is feminine.

[68] For a discussion of use-value as theoretical fiction see Spivak, "Speculation on Reading Marx: After Reading Derrida," in Derek Attridge et al., eds., *Post-Structuralism and the Question of History* (Cambridge Univ. Press, forthcoming), pp. 39–40.

[69] "Guiding Remarks for A Congress," in *Feminine Sexuality*, p. 89.

[70] For discussions of giving a face to the wholly other, see Derrida, "Violence and Metaphysics: An Essay on the Thought of Emmanuel Lévinas," in *Writing and Difference*, trans. Alan Bass (Chicago, 1978), and Paul de Man, "Autobiography As De-facement," *The Rhetoric of Romanticism* (New York: Columbia University Press, 1984).

[71] Subhas Bhattacharya, *Adhunik Banglar Prayog Abhidhan* (Calcutta: D.M. Library, 1984), p. 222.

[72] Susan Sontag, *Illness As Metaphor* (New York: Random House, 1979).

[73] Sontag, *Illness*, p. 43.

[74] Lacan, "Love Letter," p. 159.

[75] In "Can the Subaltern Speak? Speculations on Widow-Sacrifice," *Wedge* 7/8 (Winter/Spring 1985).

[76] Franz Fanon's comments on "Colonial War and Mental Disorders" are par-

ticularly pertinent here (*The Wretched of the Earth*, tr. Constance Farrington, New York: Grove Press, 1963).

[77] Lacan, "Love Letter," p. 160.

[78] Spivak, "Can the Subaltern," p. 123.

[79] "For the wish to sleep is the indeterminably significative tendency that is marking or repetition, and also the wish to forget about it, and to go on with the hypothesis that one is perceiving a meaningful form," Cynthia Chase, "The Witty Butcher's Wife: Freud, Lacan, and the Conversion of Resistance to Theory," revised version, unpublished paper, conference on "Psychoanalysis and Feminism," State University of Illinois, May 1–4, 1986.

[80] Suggestion made at Subaltern Studies Conference, Calcutta, January, 1986. I believe it is a comparable impulse that prompts Derrida to place, in the right hand column of *Glas*, the torrential production of an unsystematizable slang in Jean Genet over against the definitive establishment of philosophical vocabulary in Hegel's work, treated in the left-hand column of the book. See also my treatment of "rumor" in "Subaltern Studies."

[81] Most rhetorical questions, such as the cook's "What's there to tell?" imply a negative answer: "Nothing." Jashoda's story tells itself by (mis)understanding the question as literal and answering: "this." Such would be the morphology of "affirmative deconstruction," which says "yes" to everything, not as a proper negation which leads to a strategically exclusive synthesis, but by way of an irreducible and originary "mistake" that will not allow it to totalize its practice. This affirmation is not the "yes" of pluralism or repressive tolerance, which is given from a position of power. "Stanadayini" as *énonciation* might thus be an example of an ever-compromised affirmative deconstruction.

[82] Kristeva, "Ne dis rien," *Tel Quel* 90 (1981). I am grateful to Cynthia Chase for having brought this essay to my attention.

[83] Incidentally, her method here is conservative, in that she annuls what was most radical in Freud's hypothesis, namely infantile sexuality. ("In the hands of post-Freudians, helped no doubt by hesitations in Freud's own account, orthodox assumptions reasserted themselves," Jeffrey Weeks, "Masculinity and the Science of Desire," *Oxford Literary Review* 8.1–2 (1986), p. 32.) She positivizes and naturalizes into a psychic scenario the pre-originary space that is no more than an unavoidable methodological presupposition.

[84] Kristeva is openly anti-Marxist. By aligning her work with Althusser's— "interpellation" is his notion of the subject's being "hailed" in ideology ("Ideology and the State," *Lenin and Philosophy*. pp. 170–77)—I am giving her the benefit of the doubt.

[85] See Kristeva, "Stabat mater," in Susan Rubin Suleiman, ed., *The Female Body in Western Culture: Contemporary Perspectives* (Cambridge: Harvard University Press, 1986). Generalizing about femininity on the avowed basis of monotheism, and dismissing "progressive activism" as versions of "feminine psy-

chosis," this celebrated essay is a paean to motherhood sustained by thinly veiled autobiographical "evidence" in the left-hand column and sweeping historico-psychoanalytic conclusions in the right about the "virgin maternal" as coping with female paranoia" (pp. 116, 117, 114). With reference to Anne Ferguson's excellent essay, I had mentioned the sudden appearance of a "cross-cultural referent" (see pages 16–17). These quick and often misleading definitive moments invoking an imaginary "Third World" influence feminist thinking. In Eisenstein for example, the description of "pre-capitalist society" where "men, women, and children worked together in the home, the farm, or on the land to produce the goods necessary for their lives," [and] women were procreators and child-rearers, but the organization of work limited the impact of this sexual role distinction" (*Capitalist Patriarchy*, p. 30), would be instantly corrected by the account of gendering within the heterogeneity of decolonized space offered by "Stanadayini." In Kristeva, the Blessed Virgin appropriates reincarnation in a flash: "Mary does not die but rather—echoing Taoist and other oriental beliefs in which human bodies pass from one place to another in a never-ending flow [*flux*] which is in itself an imprint [*calque*] of the maternal receptacle [*réceptacle maternal*]—she passes over [*transite*]" (Suleiman, *Female Body*, p. 105).

[86] The question of the gaze has been most fully discussed in film theory. See for example, Laura Mulvey, "Visual Pleasure and Narrative Cinema," *Screen* 16.3 (1975), E. Ann Kaplan, *Women and Film: Both Sides of the Camera* (London: Methuen, 1983), Teresa de Lauretis, *Alice Doesn't: Feminism, Semiotics, Cinema* (Bloomington: Indiana University Press, 1984). See also Norman Bryson, *Vision and Painting: the Logic of the Gaze* (New Haven: Yale University Press, 1983). I am grateful to Frances Bartkowski for suggesting this book to me.

[87] See Spivak, "Displacement and the Discourse of Woman."

[88] In this connection, see Temma Kaplan's interesting notion of "female consciousness" in "Female Consciousness and Collective Action: the Case of Barcelona, 1910–1918," in Keohane ed., *Feminist Theory*.

[89] For two examples among many, consider Rabindranath Tagore, *Bhanusingher Padabali* (1291, Bengali year) and Bankimchandra Chattyopadhyaya, *Krishnacharitra* (1886).

[90] I am grateful to Sudipto Kaviraj for having suggested to me that English is a medium of defilement in "Stanadayini."

[91] It is immaterial to my point that there is an actual place by this name in Bengal.

[92] Hardiman, "Subaltern Studies," p. 290.

[93] Spivak, "Subaltern Studies," pp. 356–363.